Globalizing the Caribbean

Jeb Sprague

Globalizing the Caribbean

Political Economy, Social Change, and the
Transnational Capitalist Class

TEMPLE UNIVERSITY PRESS
Philadelphia • *Rome* • *Tokyo*

TEMPLE UNIVERSITY PRESS
Philadelphia, Pennsylvania 19122
tupress.temple.edu

Paperback edition published 2020
Cloth edition published 2019

Library of Congress Cataloging-in-Publication Data

Names: Sprague, Jeb, author.
Title: Globalizing the Caribbean : political economy, social change, and the
   transnational capitalist class / Jeb Sprague.
Other titles: Globalising the Caribbean
Description: Philadelphia : Temple University Press, 2019. | Includes
   bibliographical references and index. |
Identifiers: LCCN 2018047830 (print) | LCCN 2019000057 (ebook) | ISBN
   9781439916568 (E-book) | ISBN 9781439916544 (hardback)
Subjects: LCSH: International business enterprises—Caribbean Area. |
   Caribbean Area—Economic conditions—1945- | Caribbean Area—Social
   conditions—1945- | Elite (Social science)—Caribbean Area. |
   Capitalism—Caribbean Area. | Globalization—Caribbean Area. | BISAC:
   SOCIAL SCIENCE / Sociology / General. | POLITICAL SCIENCE / Globalization. |
   BUSINESS & ECONOMICS / Economic History.
Classification: LCC HD2820 (ebook) | LCC HD2820 .S67 2019 (print) | DDC
   337.729—dc23
LC record available at https://lccn.loc.gov/2018047830

ISBN 9781439916551 (paperback : alk. paper)

Printed in the United States of America

071020P

For Jersson

Contents

Figure 0.1 Map of Western Caribbean.

Figure 0.2 Map of Eastern Caribbean.

Figures and Tables

Figures

Tables

Acknowledgments

All intellectual labor is collective, as my work here builds on the intellectual labor of many others, some of whom I have had the opportunity to know. First I must acknowledge the support, feedback, and inspiration from Dr. William I. Robinson and Dr. Hilbourne Watson. In addition, I thank for their help during different stages of completing this manuscript (in alphabetical order): Dr. Kevin B. Anderson, Jamie Armstrong, Dr. Jennifer Lynn Bair, Dr. Yousef Baker, Kristin Bricker, Dr. Christopher Chase-Dunn, Emilio David Colon Rivera, Lloyd D'Aguilar, Roberto Danipour, Monica Dryer, Joe Emersberger, Dr. Paul Farmer, David Feldman, Vahan Ghazaryan, Jamella Gow, Dr. Jerry Harris, Sterling Harris, Elisa Herrera, Dr. Phillip Andrew Hough, Dr. Jasmin Hristov, Jade Hunter, Laura Huxley, Dr. Athena Kolbe, Khusdeep Malhotra, Dr. Christopher McAuley, Dr. Sreerekha Mullassery Sathiamma, Ryan Mulligan, Dr. Humberto Garcia Muniz, Dr. Georgina Murray, Dr. Daniel Olmos, Dr. Steven Osuna, Dr. Vladimir Douglas Pacheco Cueva, Eli Portella, Salvador Rangel, Tim Shenk, Dr. Robert Sierakowski, Rosio Silgado Batista, Dr. Leslie Sklair, Dr. Jackie Smith, Henry and Jane Sprague, Dr. Jason Struna, Dr. Luis Suárez, Dr. Alicia Swords, and Dr. Howard Winant. This manuscript would not have been possible without the encouragement from my close friends and loved ones. Also, I wish to thank the editors and anonymous reviewers at Temple University Press, *Caribbean Studies*, the *Journal of World-Systems Research*, *Latin American Perspectives*, and NACLA, as well as those who attended talks that I have given on chapters in this book at scholarly conferences and invited presentations in North America and the Caribbean. For any mistakes or errors herein, I take sole responsibility.

Selected Abbreviations

ACILS	American Center for International Labor Solidarity
ACP	The African, Caribbean and Pacific group of states
AIFLD	American Institute for Free Labor Development
ALBA	Bolivarian Alliance for the Peoples of Our America
BBC	British Broadcasting Channel
BRICS	The grouping of Brazil, Russia, India, China, and South Africa
BWI	British West Indies
CAFTA-DR	Central America Free Trade Agreement-Dominican Republic
CARICOM	Caribbean Community
CARIFORUM	The group that comprises Caribbean ACP states
CARIFTA	Caribbean Free Trade Area
CBI	Caribbean Basin Initiative
CDR	Comités de Defensa de la Revolución
CIA	Central Intelligence Agency
CLC	Caribbean Labor Congress
DEA	Drug Enforcement Administration
ECLAC	Economic Commission for Latin America and the Caribbean
EEC	European Economic Community
EPZ	Export-processing zone
EU	European Union

FDI	Foreign direct investment
FTAA	Free Trade Area of the Americas
FTZ	Free trade zone
GDP	Gross domestic product
GKRS-WU	Grace Kennedy-Western Union alliance
HAL	Holland America
IACHR	Inter-American Commission on Human Rights
ICFTU	International Confederation of Free Trade Unions
IDB	Inter-American Development Bank
IFIs	International financial institutions
ILO	International Labour Organization
IMF	International Monetary Fund
IOM	International Organization of Migration
IPO	Initial public offering
ISI	Import substitution industrialization
IT	Information technology
ITF	International Transport Workers' Federation
M&A	Merger and acquisition
MINUSTAH	United Nations Stabilization Mission in Haiti
MNCs	Multinational corporations
NAFTA	North American Free Trade Agreement
NAM	Non-Aligned Movement
NATO	North Atlantic Treaty Organization
NCL	Norwegian Cruise Line
NED	National Endowment for Democracy
NGO	Nongovernmental organization
NYSE	New York Stock Exchange
OAS	Organization of American States
OECD	Organization for Economic Co-operation and Development
PAHO	Pan American Health Organization
PMC	Private military contractor
PRM	Puerto Rican Model
PVDC	Pueblo Viejo Dominicana Corporation
R&D	Research and development
RCL	Royal Caribbean
SAP	Structural adjustment program
SEZ	Special economic zone
SOMINE	Society Minière du Nord-Est S.A.
SWIFT	Society for Worldwide Interbank Financial Telecommunication

TCC	Transnational capitalist class
TNCs	Transnational corporations
U.K.	United Kingdom
UN	United Nations
UNASUR	Union of South American Nations
UNCTAD	United Nations Conference on Trade and Development
UNWTO	United Nations World Tourism Organization
U.S.	United States of America
USAID	United States Agency for International Development
USSR	Union of Soviet Socialist Republics
WFTU	World Federation of Trade Unions
WHO	World Health Organization
WTO	World Trade Organization

Globalizing the Caribbean

1

The Caribbean and Global Capitalism

Imagine being on a beach on the island of Saint Barts where some of the world's wealthiest vacation—or taking a stroll down a privatized beach in the Dominican Republic's Punta Cana where locals cannot set foot as planeloads of travelers mostly from Europe and North America party late into the night. This is the Caribbean as it is often known to well-off foreign tourists. But what of Tivoli Gardens in Jamaica; or the seaside community of La Saline in Port-au-Prince, Haiti; or the Laventville slum in Trinidad's Port of Spain—the Caribbean experience where much of the region's people survive on the bare minimum.

Those areas of the Caribbean are not dreamed about by wealthy foreigners, or even by the middle class of the First World who can splurge on an occasional trip to a well-guarded resort. The beautiful Caribbean basin that seduces tourists is actually disfigured by inequality: it is home to the most profitable tax havens in history combined with worker exploitation backed by governments (most important, the United States) that increasingly are using militarized policing among other tactics. This book offers an account of the Caribbean's experience of economic globalization, while taking into account the marginalized and the exploitation of racialized and gendered working people.

The Caribbean was the place of the first colonial expeditions and colonial institutions. It was at the center of the brutal slave-plantation complex, where world capitalism's racialized class relations were initially forged and took shape by the mid-seventeenth century. But, significantly, it was also one of the first places to win independence from Europe and abolish slavery. In reaction, the United States, as a nascent empire, cut its teeth in the region, in the shape of repeated military interventions.

There have been revolts against four centuries of slavery and colonialism and a fifth century of economic dependency. It is a history that has left indelible marks on the people, land, languages, and cultures of the region—most of all in the ongoing daily life struggles of people facing grinding inequality and injustice. In the late twentieth and early twenty-first centuries, the Caribbean has increasingly become a place for transnational companies and their local affiliates to get their way at the expense of the majority. So-called "vulture" companies have profited extraordinarily off governments in the region facing debt and high-risk "troubled assets" near default or bankruptcy—the starkest example being Puerto Rico, where of its $74.8 billion debt, $33.5 billion is interest and another $1.6 billion is from the fees paid to Citigroup and Goldman Sachs (Arbasetti et al., 2017).

Meanwhile, some of the wealthiest people in the world stash vast fortunes in the region's banks to avoid paying taxes or to avoid their home countries' jurisdiction. The Caribbean has become home to some of the most successful tax havens in world history: In 2013, $92 billion flowed into the British Virgin Islands alone. It is estimated that tax evasion in the Caribbean costs the U.S. government upwards of $100 billion each year (Jilani, 2015). From the "panama papers" to the "paradise papers," news reports in recent years expose a global web of financial holdings that intersect with the region.

The role and emergence of a transnational capitalist class (Harris, 2016; Phillips, 2018; Sklair, 2002), with its different fractions and allies, can be seen across the Caribbean region. The Cayman Islands is now the chosen headquarters for over 40 percent of the companies listed on the Hong Kong Stock Exchange. Richard Branson, founder of the transnational Virgin Group, owns a 30-hectare island in the British Virgin Islands, where he hosted President Barack Obama shortly after he left office. In the Bahamas, the Walt Disney Corporation owns a private island, "Castaway Cay," which its cruise line uses. Also in the Bahamas, China's Export-Import Bank recently provided a $2.5 billion loan to develop the Baha Mar resort. An Iranian-born businessperson Ali Pascal Mahvi, head of the Switzerland-based M Group Corporation, helped develop the Sugar Beach resort in Saint Lucia. A transnational company, Rusal, based out of Moscow (and in part owned by both a Chinese and an American tycoon, with its major owner being Russian transnational capitalist Oleg Deripaska), now owns some of the largest mines in Jamaica and Guyana (A Qatari sovereign wealth fund in turn is partial owner of one of the major investors in Rusal). In Jamaica and smaller islands, such as Saint Martin and Dominica, hubs of Chinese businesspeople have formed (Grell-Brisk, 2018)). Meanwhile, in Cuba, Brazilian-based companies have largely financed a massive new cargo and manufacturing hub, managed by a Singaporean firm. Numerous transnationally-oriented U.S. capitalists use accounting strategies to "shift" profits to Puerto Rico to avoid mainland taxes, while blockchain billionaires taking up residency on the island are looking to remake it into a "crypto currency utopia." In another example of the new globally competitive market relations subsuming the region, just shortly prior to the 2010 earthquake, Haiti privatized the majority of its public telephone company, selling it to a Vietnamese company. The region has become engulfed in a whirlpool of global capitalist accumulation.

In addition, a growing array of transnational capitalists hail from the Caribbean. For example, Trinidad and Tobago is home to numerous transnational capitalists, such as the Sabga family, who originally migrated from Syria in the early twentieth century. Gustavo A. Cisneros, a Venezuelan Dominican national of Cuban descent, of the Florida-headquartered Cisneros Group, has a fortune estimated at over $1 billion. With financial holdings spanning the globe, he is a major shareholder in prominent Spanish-language media and entertainment outlets such as Univision and Venevisión. One of the wealthiest Jamaican businesspersons, Michael Lee-Chin, is an investor and philanthropist with dual Jamaican and Canadian citizenship, with an estimated worth of $1.1 billion. Among numerous other holdings, he was the executive chairman of AIC Limited, a Canadian mutual fund, and the chairman of the National Commercial Bank of Jamaica since December 2014. Haiti, often described as the poorest country in the Western Hemisphere—and the most unequal—is home to a growing number of transnational capitalists. Dumas Siméus, originally from Haiti but now living in the United States, is a former CEO and founder of Siméus Foods International. He holds investments in many other companies, and has powerful political connections, including within the Republican Party establishment in Florida.

In short, the Caribbean is fertile ground for a study of capitalism past and present.

Global capitalist accumulation has meant immense gains for many dominant groups, and as some segments of the population have become deeply entwined with consumerism—with new air-conditioned malls, high-priced real estate, and gated communities. Yet the vast majority of the region's population face thoroughly exploitative or marginalized conditions. Even with improved access to health care and cheap goods, the majority of Caribbean people face numerous crises. Facing some of the toughest conditions in the region, of Haiti's 10 million people, 6.3 million are unable to meet their basic needs and 2.5 million cannot meet food needs, with just 2 percent of the population consuming the equivalent of $10 a day or more, according to data from the World Bank.[1] Meanwhile, a fifth of the population in Jamaica lives in poverty, according to the World Bank, yet the structural reality is clearly much starker with so many people facing underemployment or low wages alongside a lack of public infrastructure and rising costs of living. According to local Jamaican activists I spoke with, unemployment can reach between 40 and 50 percent in Kingston's lowest-income neighborhood, Tivoli Gardens. As the world globalizes around them, impoverished people across the region struggle to scrape by.

Over recent decades, as state and transnational capitalist forces have recalibrated and facilitated new accumulation networks, many in the popular classes have been compelled to participate in globalizing value chains. By value chains I refer to the value that is determined by production for the ends of private accumulation via concrete social relations mediated by power interactions between unequal class forces at the point of production. Yet, even alongside capitalist globalization and the exploitation of labor, significant portions of the Caribbean's population face structural marginalization and labor market exclusion and are, in turn, the main targets of state security forces. Many are in turn compelled to seek out new means of survival, such as migration. With shrinking options, if they seek employment that violates legal codes, the poor can expect the worst, suffering humiliation and repression. The struggle of the subaltern in a globalizing world remains an open-ended challenge.

As a historic crossroads, as an entrepôt or crucible throughout the modern era, the region has passed through all the phases of world capitalism—from mercantilism to national formation and international monopoly capitalism to today's transnational/global capitalism. Throughout the latter decades of the twentieth century, the Caribbean has functioned as a laboratory for transnational capitalism and the neoliberal Washington Consensus, promulgating austerity policies alongside expanding tourism, nontraditional agricultural exports, and export-processing zones (EPZs) that serve as platforms for integrating local productive relations with the global economy. Periods of economic stagnation, political tumult, and renewed U.S. intervention (Grandin, 2007) have simultaneously affected the region. Acts of aggression, which include six decades of a U.S. led financial and trade embargo on Cuba, cost the country's economy over $130 billion according to the United Nations (Acosta and Marsh, 2018). The larger backdrop to this turbulence has been the integration of the region into the new global capitalism, with novel rearrangements taking place among its social groups and classes (Regalado, 2007; Robinson, 2003). The region has been swept up in global crises of social polarization, the legitimacy failure of governmental officials, and capitalist overaccumulation with risky investments in cryptocurrencies and derivatives markets. Over the closing decades of the twentieth century and into the twenty-first century, with the intensification of the global climate crisis, more than half of the region's coral reefs have been lost and the damage done by hurricanes continues to grow.

This book focuses on the social and material nature of this new era of world capitalism, examining the sweeping transformations and contradictions it has ushered in. It investigates the changing political economy of the global era in the context of the Caribbean. A reconfiguration of social, economic, and political relations is taking place, rooted in the dynamic and ruthless competitive processes of globalizing capitalism. Instead of viewing the world as populations bundled into core and peripheral nation-states, the core and periphery can also denote social groups and classes through a *transnational* context (Hoogvelt, 2001; Sklair, 2002; H. Watson, 2015). This helps us consider how social polarization rooted in the rising transnationalization of material (economic) relations reflects on regions and nations. Pools of the "first world" (such as high-consuming strata) now also exist in the "third world," and vice versa—large migrant and marginalized populations live in the global north. These groups are linked in diverse ways to new transnational networks of production, finance, and consumption.[2]

Global Capitalism: A New Phase in the History of World Capitalism

What accounts for the massive changes washing over the shores of the Caribbean and the world as a whole? Around us are advances unique in our species' history: revolutionizing technologies, bursting flows of information, and global economic integration. Yet these occur alongside unprecedented inequality (Holt-Giménez and Patel, 2012; Kloby, 2004), shifting means for achieving hegemonic consent and coercive domination (Bieler and Morton, 2006; Robinson, 1994; Sprague-Silgado, 2018a), and a climate crisis that imperils life across our planet (Chew, 2006; N. Klein, 2014; Kolbert, 2014; World Bank, 2012).

While Caribbean societies have throughout their history exhibited differences and continuities, how are new dynamics taking shape in the Caribbean under the capitalist globalization of the late twentieth century and into the twenty-first century?

Analytical tools help make sense of the changes taking place. One such way to analyze the changes taking place is through the "transnational processes" that describe a diverse array of structural, institutional, and organizational phenomena that link regions and nations more organically with global society and economy.

Here it is useful to emphasize the differences between national, international, and transnational processes. Whereas national processes occur within the frontiers of the national state, international processes occur across borders. A transnational process, while occurring across borders, takes place through functional integration. Functional integration refers to how amalgamations of different components (or agents) are constituted through their joint operation.

The *nature of this integration* is something completely new in the history of human civilization and regions around the world (including the Caribbean). Processes that take place across frontiers in this functionally integrated manner alter the very ways in which space and geography are implicated in material and social production.[3] A new kind of immediacy has come into existence—through communications, finance, social media, information flows, and so on.

With these shifting political economic dynamics in mind, below I propose a periodization of the Caribbean's relationship to the larger world system, arguing that what has taken place in recent decades is the region's insertion into world capitalism under an entirely new (globalizing) model of economy and society.

Different methodological approaches have been used to make sense of the ways in which human social formation has occurred historically. The methodological approach deployed here looks at how the development of (and changes to) human society is rooted in how people together produce the necessities of life (Marx, 1867/1992). Fundamental to this is the conflict that occurs between social classes. "Social classes" are relationships generated and reproduced through the productive processes and economic life of a society. Social classes do not appear in isolation or as something permanent; rather they are a product of social relations in which human beings seek (or are compelled) to produce and reproduce the material requirements of life (Wright, 1998). These classes thus contain individuals who are carriers of productive relationships. Producing their existence in fundamentally different ways an antagonism occurs between different classes, such as between waged laborers and the owners of large companies (Szymanski, 1983). Furthermore, the very consciousness of individuals occurs through the life process, so how people perceive their situation (and their own class interests) undergoes change.[4]

In considering how history is rooted in class conflict, the classical concept of "modes of production" helps us conceptualize the varied ways in which human societies have changed over time (Marx, 1867/1992). A mode of production refers to the combination of (1) productive forces: all of those forces that are applied by people in the production process (body and brain, tools and techniques, materials, resources, and equipment); and (2) relations of production: the sum total of social relationships that people *must* enter into in order to survive, to produce, and to reproduce their means of life

(Marx, 1867/1992). The totality of these relationships constitutes a relatively stable and long-lasting structure.

The capitalist mode of production is qualitatively and structurally divergent from modes of production that had dominated the precapitalist world. Unlike the ancient, tributary, feudal, and other modes of production, capitalism is based on systems of production and distribution organized around private ownership and wage labor (De Ste. Croix, 1981; Donaldson, 2012). Though a market of trade and commodity production already existed, the capitalist mode of production came about through a new social relation: a monetized system based on land rents, wages, and (in the Caribbean) chattel slavery, used to create surplus value appropriated by a dominant class owning the means of production (Galeano, 1997; Wood, 1998). Even as the capitalist mode of production came to dominate, Eric Wolf (1997) observes: other modes of production have often existed alongside it, such as unwaged sharecropping or trade and barter systems during different historical periods in the Caribbean. More generally, though, capitalism as a system, has historically gone through different phases rooted in novel changes to productive forces and social relationships (Hobsbawm, 1996a, 1996b, 1996c, 1996d).[5]

Human history is bound up with interconnections and movement, but it was under capitalism that a common system came to envelop a world society (Stavrianos, 1998). Capital is expansionary by nature, with an unending drive toward constant growth and the conquest of new markets (Marx, 1993a). The Cuban scholar Roberto Regalado describes how in recent decades this drive for capitalist expansion has caused a "merger of the national cycles into a single transnational cycle of capital flow and accumulation" (2007, p. 19). In examining history, four major phases of world capitalism can be identified here as: (1) the emergence of capitalism through Western Europe's countryside, towns, and early manufacturing, alongside colonial mercantilism and chattel slave production that occurred from the 1400s through the 1800s; (2) the industrial capitalism phase that emerged in the late 1700s with the first industrial revolution and continued until the latter part of the 1800s; (3) the international capitalism (or international monopoly capitalism) phase that developed in the mid- to late 1800s and continued up through the decades following World War II[6] and the late 1900s; and (4), most recently, the global capitalism (or globalization) phase that emerged in the later decades of the twentieth century and has intensified in the twenty-first century.[7]

A key turning point in the emerging shift from the "international" phase to the "global/transnational" phase occurred during the 1970s, when a crisis of economic stagnation evolved in connection with inflation caused by high wages in developed countries for unionized (mostly white male) workers, alongside the disbandment of the Bretton Woods system and the energy crisis of that decade. These occurred also as major new technological innovations were coming about, which business leaders sought to use to increase profits. Elites in the United States greatly intensified a push for the dismantling of welfare, statist, and domestically geared policies at home and abroad, bringing many governmental practices in-line with the logic of the market (Harvey, 1997; Panitch and Gindin, 2013; Robinson, 1996). Overtime these neoliberal policies were carried out not just in the United States but also (to different degrees) within other metropole and developing states, eventually spreading across much of the planet.

Capital needed to break free from the national constraints of the Fordist-Keynesian "new deal" era. This earlier era had been marked by protections and programs developed after significant popular struggles, not only in the United States but in other countries as well. Policy makers in many postcolonial and developing states, though with far fewer resources and faced with uneven exchange and legacies of colonialism, had attempted their own Keynesian-influenced policies: promoting forms of state-induced industrialization. Known as import substitution industrialization (ISI), this had sought to replace particular foreign imports with domestic production. Among the constraints that capital faced by the 1970s was the responsibility of ensuring the social reproduction of particular national labor forces (within the more highly developed "core" states), as well as the mounting barriers of ISI in many postcolonial and developing countries.

"Going global" thus allowed capitalists to do away with this concern, as they now could tap into an ever-growing worldwide pool of marginalized workers. Technological advances further allowed elites to expand capitalist modes of production in the semiperiphery and the periphery, while forcing indebted governments to serve foreign investors and sever many social and national commitments to their populations. In core states, many of the labor-capital compromises that had come about earlier in the century were replaced by "flexible" practices imposed on workforces (Harvey, 1991). Defining the "flexibilization" of capitalist accumulation, David Harvey writes:

> Flexible accumulation . . . is marked by a direct confrontation with the rigidities of Fordism. It rests on flexibility with respect to labour processes, labour markets, products, and patterns of consumption . . . It has entrained rapid shifts in the patterning of uneven development, both between sectors and between geographical regions, giving rise, for example, to a vast surge in so-called "service sector" employment as well as to entirely new industrial ensembles in hitherto underdevel-

oped regions . . . It has also entailed a new round of . . . "time-space compression" . . . in the capitalist world—the time horizons of both private and public decision-making have shrunk, while satellite communication and declining transport costs have made it increasingly possible to spread those decisions immediately over an ever wider and variegated space. (1991, p. 147)

Capital also needed to break apart those areas of the world system that it had limited access to, such as with the socialist and postcolonial statist projects (such as in the Warsaw Pact nations and their allies in the Third World and many of the states participating at one time or another in the nonaligned movement [NAM]). Big steps toward achieving this goal occurred between the late 1970s and the early 1990s. Leo Panitch and Sam Gindin (2013) observe the role of the informal "American empire" and U.S. capital in the formation of the contemporary global system, pressuring the lifting of capital controls around the world in the wake of the economic crisis of the 1970s. Alongside this, an emergent transnationalization of capital began through ramped up foreign direct investment (FDI), cross-border mergers and acquisitions (M&As), a host of new financial cross-border interlinkages, and the rise of nontraditional exports worldwide.

By 1991, the United States (aided by its NATO allies) had succeeded in wearing down the Soviet Union. The USSR, in the context of the Cold War, also had developed many of its own internal contradictions, such as a structurally militarized economy, alongside numerous other economic, political, and social strains and a weakening of its ideological foundation (Lebowitz, 2012; Lewin, 2016; Sakwa, 2013).[8] Meanwhile, "capitalist-roaders" had taken power in China in the late 1970s and 1980s (Harvey, 1997).[9] This allowed for the *extensive* spread of capitalism across the planet.

These events furthermore opened the door to the *intensive* expansion of capitalism, drilling down into the socioeconomic fabric of nearly every country, with the imposition of neoliberal economic policies and the emergent transnationalization of capital. Consumer culture, meanwhile, reached mesmerizing new heights. In the 1990s and early twenty-first century many remnants of the reforms and protections for working people (achieved through earlier struggles and class compromises) continued to be rolled back. Organized labor came under new attacks worldwide, and as new labor-eliminating technologies were developed through the digital age. A new round of U.S.-led interventions and regime change campaigns were launched from Yugoslavia to Iraq and Libya, to covert operations in Syria, to new strategies of soft power in Latin America, and the gruesome economic war targeting Bolivarian Venezuela.[10] A "restoration of class power," as Harvey

(1997) has described it, came about. Power was consolidated, this time, in the hands of an emerging transnational bourgeoisie. Though, as I discuss in Chapters 2 and 3, many divisions, tensions, and conflicts have emerged.

Transnational processes and practices have thus emerged operating across an uneven global system, interconnected with regional, national, and local constituencies in the economic, political, cultural, and ideological arenas. As global networks of production and finance promulgated by transnational corporations (TNCs) and other institutions redefine the scale of the world economy (Castells, 2009; Dicken, 2007), transnational social relations have formed within and between many classes and class fractions. Financial interests involved in the remittance industry, for example, spread through global networks of accumulation and became functionally entwined with local banks across the Caribbean basin. Growing diaspora communities, in sending home remittances, became integrated with their homelands in a new, more immediate way, with their money circulating through globalizing chains of accumulation. The role of transnational integration can thus be seen through the rise of many new social and class relations (Harris, 2006; McMichael, 1996; Robinson, 2004, 2014a; Rodriguez, 2010; Sassen, 1991; Sklair, 2001, 2002; Van der Pijl, 1998).[11] Leslie Sklair argues, in fact, that operating outside of the global system "is becoming increasingly more difficult as capitalist globalization penetrates ever more widely and deeply" (2009, p. 528).

"Globalization," a term often bandied about, is in fact the latest epoch in the development of the heterogeneous capitalist system—an uneven and diverse system of accumulation and exploitation. Theorists (starting in the early twentieth century) argued that a "law of uneven and combined development" existed, through which separate national capitals and power blocs conflicted and connected with one another. This led to varied histories of development in the interstate system, between nations and other geographic units, and the role of imperialism (Hilferding, 1910/2006; Lenin, 1917/1969; Sweezy, 1942). Uneven and combined development has been inherent in the fundamental capitalist process, stemming from the law of value/production for private capitalist accumulation (as theorized by political economists starting in the early twentieth century). Yet, combined and uneven development does not mean that capitalism is inherently organized to produce *national* economic development. Rather, capitalism is organized to produce private capital accumulation as an end in itself, a fact made all the more clear through the rise of transnational forms of accumulation (Robinson and Sprague, 2018). With the rise of globalization (or what is better described as "global capitalism"), I argue, along with others (Harris, 2016;

Liodakis, 2010; Robinson, 2003; Sklair, 2002; H. Watson, 1994a, 2015), that we need to understand how new and uneven *transnational* practices and processes are playing out through a heterogeneous world context.

Among the most important of these, I argue, is the rise of a transnational capitalist class (TCC), a hegemonic class oriented toward transnational accumulation. Within this class exist various fractions oriented toward different institutions and forms of accumulation. A deeper understanding of this class (and other social classes active in the region) can be gained by looking at the Caribbean in relation to the changing political economic and social dynamics: a study that gets at the shifting structural patterns and combinations of various circumstances (the conjunctural dynamics) that have occurred through the region but within a world framework and up to the contemporary period.

Capitalism has flowed and congealed through Caribbean societies (as structures) but through the complexity of unique human beings (as agents of production or carriers of productive relations) who do "make their own history" (Marx, 1869/1994). This means that even in the face of exploitative relations, humans create and construct new (and possibly emancipatory) endeavors yet are also constrained by the social structures through which they live. Their restraints are the restraints on humans everywhere because they operate under circumstances not of their own choosing but under the nature of their social system (with its class-related activities) and the many circumstances coiled back to the lives of lost generations.

The Caribbean, the first region of the "new world" to be conquered by the late-feudal absolutist states of Western Europe (P. Anderson, 1974; Wolf, 1997), has passed through all of the different phases of capitalism. The region was a major site of wealth accumulation that helped jump-start capitalism (Galeano, 1997, p. 28; Williams, 1944). Caribbean societies were inserted into *international* chains of accumulation, with social and material relations moving back and forth slowly across frontiers and over long distances. These international processes developed through particular systems, such as British, French, and Spanish mercantilism, where international trade with the colonies was funneled in large part back into the empire's internal metropole market.[12] Most notable among these international processes were the triangles of Atlantic trade,[13] which resulted in the forced mass movement and enslavement of millions of Africans. During the oceanic passage from Africa to the Americas, regularly more than 20 percent of the enslaved would die. The accumulation of the vast new wealth was thus steeped in extreme violence.

International relationships intensified into the nineteenth and twentieth centuries and under the new nation-states that formed. Major developments

occurred that impacted the Caribbean region, such as the collapse of mercantilism, the overthrow and abolition of slavery, the completion of the Panama
Canal, and the rising role of U.S. imperialism and international corporations.

The nature of these *international* processes, and the social formation
therein, was qualitatively distinct from the transnational processes emerging
in the late twentieth century and into the twenty-first century. This is because in the earlier phases of capitalism the mode of production was largely
articulated within the production relations of various nation-states and colonies and through the interstate framework that existed. What has changed
is that with the rise of global capitalism the prior processes of material and
social production within these territorially confined units is breaking down.

As *national* and *international* circuits of accumulation fragment, they are
becoming enveloped by newly emerging *transnational* circuits of accumulation.
As William I. Robinson (2003, p. 16) writes: "There has been a progressive dismantling of autonomous or 'autocentric' national production systems and their
reactivation as constituent elements of an integral world production system."

Key to this process is what Harvey (1991) describes as "time-space compression" where many forms of transportation, communication, and economic processes overcome long-standing spatial limitations and barriers. The
very qualities and relationship between space and time are altered. The ongoing transformation of the time-space dynamics of accumulation and the
apparatuses and arrangements through which they take place is fundamental
to the new global epoch. A central feature of this is the spatial reconfiguration
of *social relations* and *place*, as a growing array of processes are becoming
transnationally oriented (see also Robinson, 2003, pp. 106–110). This book
notes particular examples of how this is playing out in the Caribbean, such
as: the exploitation of flexibilized labor through the export-processing model
and in the tourism industry and the manner in which the labor power of
migrant communities is inserted into transnational remittance networks and
new transnational chains of accumulation.

Authors such as Michael Hardt and Antonio Negri (2001), Jerry Harris
(2006, 2016), Ankie Hoogvelt (2001), George Liodakis (2010), Philip McMichael
(1996), Roberto Regalado (2007), William I. Robinson (2004, 2014a), Leslie
Sklair (2001, 2002), Bastiaan van Apeldoorn (2003), and Hilbourne Watson
(2015) and others, take the view that "globalization represents a new stage in
the evolving world capitalist system that came into being some five centuries
ago," thus advancing a "global capitalism thesis or school" (Robinson, 2004,
p. 2). Although there are many differences between the approaches of these
authors, all of them suggest that (1) global capitalism represents a qualitatively
new epoch in the history of capitalism, and (2) the fundamental structure of
our global system is not only driven by U.S. imperialism but rather is increas-

ingly propelled by a much wider array of interconnected material and social relations (Sprague, 2011a). Thus, together these approaches are described well as the "global capitalism school."

In addition to the studies of the "global capitalism school" and many other past works on political economy, this book takes inspiration from critical approaches to Caribbean and Latin American studies (to just list a small number: Beckford, 1999; Itzigsohn, 2000; Mintz, 1974; Regalado, 2007; Trouillot, 2000; H. Watson, 2015; Williams, 1944; Valdez and Miranda, 1999). During the mid- to late twentieth century, prior to the end of the Cold War and before the flood of literature on globalization, many other scholars published class analyses, Third Worldist and historical materialist-influenced studies that focused on the Caribbean region or on specific countries in the area.

While there have been numerous studies on the political economy of the region and many of its nations under globalization (G. Baker, 2007; Bishop, 2013; H. Dunn, 1995; Klak, 1997; L. Lewis, 2012a; Palmer, 2009; Sansavior and Scholar, 2015; Sheller, 2003; Werner, 2016), there has yet to be a major study of the Caribbean from the perspective of the "global capitalism school," emphasizing the novel and contradictory nature of the transnational processes that have developed over the last decades of the twentieth century and into the twenty-first century.[14] While understanding capitalist globalization as part of a longer process of world capitalism, this book also emphasizes the uniqueness of what has come about in the most recent epoch.

This book thus focuses on (1) the underlying socioeconomic structure of the Caribbean, (2) its political dynamics, and (3) in general, how, through capitalist globalization, many nationally and internationally oriented processes in the region are becoming transnationalized. Prior to going more in depth about the novel relations occurring through the globalizing Caribbean, let us first lay some groundwork by clarifying this book's class analysis approach with its gendered and racialized dynamics.

Class and Inequality

How has humanity reached the extreme inequality that characterizes our present era? Furthermore, what are the structural features of the globalizing social order in a region such as the Caribbean? How is this social order being reproduced?

While many theorists (going all the way back to the Enlightenment) have suggested that capitalism is a naturally evolved "system" that reflects natural human urges and striving, nothing could be further from the truth based on a concrete observation of how it emerged out of qualitatively new and exploitative relations.

It was the development of capitalism that introduced the capital-labor relation, in which a part of society came to own the means of production while another was compelled to sell its labor "on pain of extinction."[15] Vital also during this period was the development of new technologies and methods—the "productive forces" as Marx described them—that allowed for higher levels of surplus output in farming and manufacturing. Communal small farmer and familial landholdings gave way to monetized property and production relations, and a new capitalist class arose. This represented a qualitatively new distinction between possessors and nonpossessors (Wood, 1998).

Interconnected to the transformations in Europe were the extermination of many indigenous peoples and the brutal mass exploitation of chattel slaves that began in the colonial Caribbean, appropriating vast wealth and producing significant surplus for European planters and merchant capitalists (Galeano, 1997; McAuley, 2001). Elites, while competing among themselves (with some succeeding and others failing), gained tremendous wealth through the expansion of international trade and colonialism (Brenner, 2003), their power solidifying further through the modern nation-state and the rise of industrialization and international business monopolies. Meanwhile, among the popular classes (the working, marginalized, and poor populations) divisions formed along various lines, including economic differences, racialization, nationalism, culture, religion, and other dynamics. While a splintering among subaltern strata is often generated, there also exists a constant relation of mutual aid, solidarity, and struggles from below. The divisions though (also fomented by the upper classes) can make it more difficult for different fractions of the popular classes to cooperate in a common class struggle.

For the purposes of this book, which focuses on political economy, it is important to elaborate on the structural features of the class systems that emerged. A class system refers to the division of society into social classes made of people related in different ways to the production and distribution of wealth. Szymanski (1983, pp. 84–119) describes, for example, the capitalist class (who owns the means of production), the working and popular classes (who have nothing but their labor to sell), and the intermediate or middle strata ("middle-class positions") in class structures.

Within the broader working population there are certain privileged strata, often composed of individuals with professional and skilled jobs that allow them to obtain better wages and positions. Going back to the early twentieth century some theorized the existence of a "labor aristocracy," or those well-paid and better-off members of the working class (often within comfortable and nonmilitant labor unions, or those working in professional and often high-status careers). One class fraction often associated with the "middle strata" is described as the "petit bourgeoisie," who are the small-scale merchants, shop owners, and semiautonomous farmers who often identify with and seek to imitate the owning class but, who, for the most part, do not own the means of production themselves and instead are compelled to work alongside their employees. Over recent decades in many parts of the Caribbean, and, for that matter, throughout the Third World, there has evolved a vast expanse of gated community enclaves, where the middle and upper strata live spatially apart from the popular classes (Atkinson and Blandy, 2005).

A variety of other class fractions exist, such as the unemployed (or what we might describe as the "reserve army of labor," whose very existence ensures a downward wage-pressure on working people) and the structurally excluded (or marginalized). The structurally excluded or marginalized are those sectors of the population whose labor power is not required by capital. The international system that spread through colonialism and world capitalism developed in a manner where some were employed in new forms of wage labor, while others were unemployed and yet others became structurally locked out (among them vast pools of people marginalized and forced into desperate conditions). Today, this continues to occur but in the context of a globalized system. As discussed in Chapter 2, many dominant groups and states operating in the Caribbean alongside powerful supranational institutions have sought to contain these structurally excluded populations through various mechanisms.

Another dimension of the labor-capital relation is "superexploitation." This refers to the practice of paying workers less than what would be required for them to remain on even the fringes of mainstream society (paying them less than what they require to socially reproduce themselves). The "superexploited" thus form another part of the popular classes. In the contemporary period, we can see how many such workers serve as cogs in a negatively racialized market with its bureaucratized institutionalism. These workers often face situations of "illegality" without official citizenship status or the papers needed to obtain certain rights and protections, or they have been stripped by the state of protections that benefit those with full citizenship. This is especially relevant when considering the condition of superexploited *migrant* labor and how many such people are struggling daily to get by and at the same time have become inserted into transnational chains of just accumulation, such as through their jobs, the money sent through remittance companies, or the markets where they can purchase a variety of goods.

Another intensifying phenomenon over recent years has been the exploitation of precarious workers, a layer of the workforce that some describe as a "precariate" (Standing, 2013). This refers to those workers who often hold multiple part-time jobs and labor without contract, workers who are often constantly in search of jobs and alienated from other workers through the new more mobile and flexible workplaces of the twenty-first century, giving them shrinking bargaining power with capital.[16] Individual workers may even be treated as subcontractors, competing with one another (such as with Uber or Lyft drivers); atomized conditions under which labor organizing is made extremely difficult.

Historically many other classes have existed as well, such as chattel slaves, who through the initial phase of world capitalism made up a large portion of the Caribbean population. In many parts of the Caribbean, slaves far outnumbered European planters and colonialists, sometimes by a proportion of up to twenty to one (Horne, 2014a).[17] The term "chattel" emphasizes that these slaves were considered valuable property and were exploited through despotic labor regimes. This emergent capitalist process developed over long periods of time, through what Sidney Mintz (1986) described as a synthesis of field and factory.

At first this occurred through a "formal subsumption," under which capitalists took command of labor processes (or slave labor processes) that originated prior to *or* outside of capital's imposition of wage labor. It was only over a longer time that a "real subsumption" occurred, where labor processes were internally reorganized to meet the dictates of capital. Capitalist slavery in the Caribbean functioned then as a vital but also emergent and anomalous process in the new social order.[18]

In regions such as the Caribbean, colonial expansion lugged with it these early social relations of the capitalist mode of production. Yet these new exploitative social relations also carried seeds of resistance and liberation, as human beings by their nature will seek out freedom (C. James, 1980, 1989). For this reason, the new plantation and extractive industries of the Caribbean became cauldrons of class struggle and slave rebellion (C. James, 1989; Linebaugh and Rediker, 2013; Shepherd and Beckles, 1999).

Ultimately, how a class is formed depends on a variety of subjective and objective factors. Here it is useful to differentiate between a "class for itself" and a "class in itself." A "class for itself" is class conscious: its individuals are aware of their shared interests and consider themselves as a unit that acts upon the basis of a common feeling in pursuing their general class interests. This has often been used to refer to, for example, a proletarian working class whose workers are mobilized to fight for their class interests against capital. By contrast, a "class in itself," while sharing a common position in relation to production, is not class conscious as it neither understands its group interests nor thinks of itself as a collective or a class.

As E. P. Thompson (1963/2002) further elaborates in regard to social formation, the individuals of the working class are not just victims but also proactive agents of history, developing their own culture that leaves a legacy through the stories, art, and songs passed down over the generations. Class has become central, then, to the actions, dispositions, and ideologies of poor and working people, impacting the role of institutions and political struggles (Katznelson and Zolberg, 1987).

The class systems of the Caribbean have of course involved many subjective and objective dynamics. Ken Post, examining Jamaica's social formation, points out how the "process of the determination of forms of class consciousness and action" occur on two levels: (1) "the generation of social actions (most importantly, but not exclusively, that of classes), necessarily involving some level of consciousness," and (2) "the shaping of such action into particular forms of certain points in time, what have been termed . . . instances of practices" (1978, p. 51). Class subjectivity can become more pronounced at certain times and at others recede. This is interesting to think about in regard to how Guyanese scholar Clive Thomas argued that class structure in the periphery is more fluid and fragile, with social changes occurring at times very rapidly and sometimes out of desperation (Thomas, 1984, pp. 62–63).[19] What is clear is that particular subjective and objective dynamics develop through the experiences of colonial and slave societies, as individuals' lives are in part shaped as colonial subjects or as the human property of a planter elite, but also through their own agency in society. Contradictory sets of ideas thus develop through the consciousness of people experiencing specific historical circumstances (Bakan, 1990, pp. 15–17). Objectively structured and experienced, the lived experience of social class (with its racialized and gendered dynamics) involves different perceptions and responses, for instance, to work, family, community, culture, religion, and politics.

Furthermore, within a social class there are "class fractions," which are segments or portions of the whole class—who are "grouped around different forms of economic activity or around the place occupied within these activities" (Wright, 1980, p. 335, quoting Francesca Freedman).[20] There also exists the "social group," a group of people who come together based on some common interest but may or may not be made up of individuals from the same social class. Another term, "strata," often used by sociologists and political economists, refers to a layer of society with internally consistent characteristics that distinguish it from other layers.[21]

Racialized Class Relations

In considering the social cartography of capitalism in the Caribbean, racialized dimensions are particularly salient. While earlier xenophobic and religious hatreds existed, the social construction of "race" emerged through the new capitalist slavery that arose, where what were viewed previously as amorphous ethnic groupings were placed into concretized racialized structures and hierarchies (Callinicos, 1995; Reed, 2000; Snowden, 1983). Through the early period of capitalism and in response to the crisis of feudalism in the late Middle Ages, various populations became socially constructed so as to appear to be members of distinct and biologically configured "races" (eventually depicted by the 1860s through the racist "social Darwinism" of Herbert Spencer [1863/2018]). Ideological justifications were constructed after a material relation of domination in order to justify the subjugation of colonized and enslaved peoples in the capitalist order (Allen, 2012; Callinicos, 1995).

Racism, as a new mechanism to differentiate labor and exploited classes, would later take on its own ideological and cultural dimensions. What we need to escape is the separation of racism from its origins, the disconnection of racism from its genesis. Social hierarchy within Europe itself (during the formation of capitalism) was also described through biology, for example, with poor white people sometimes described as biologically inferior to elite white people. When white elites in colonies began to require a differentiation between workers in order to socially control them, they began to construct biological differentiations between Europeans, Africans, indigenous, mulattos, and so on. It is vital then to see how a racist ideology was formed after actual material relations of exploitation and repression came about.

Practices of "limpia sangre" had begun in late-feudal Iberia (Fredrickson, 2002), where those whose ancestors were not traced to Jewish or Moorish communities could be considered to have a higher status, or "clean blood." Yet during periods of pogrom and violent inquisition, religious converts could often escape what could otherwise be a death sentence. A new inescapable racial construct soon evolved through the capitalist relations of production that spread through the Caribbean plantation system and the new capitalist world system that formed. This is where socially constructed racial hierarchies had their most important roots, especially early on in the relations of reproduction that involved chattel slavery—as a historically contingent colonial project emanating from powerful capitalistic groups from Europe it was built up through the objectification and subjugation of African labor.

Initial attempts to coerce the labor of the Caribbean's indigenous failed. Susceptible to diseases from the other side of the Atlantic and violently repressed after rebelling, their populations declined rapidly. Under the encomienda system (where colonialists and crown officials were rewarded with the labor of groups from the conquered "heathen" indigenous populations), the Spanish had attempted to force indigenous labor to work under "trusteeships." Rather than justify this exploitation through a racial construct, it was reproduced through a religious construct, where the slavery of "heathens" was deemed acceptable. This labor regime was developed specifically to suit late-feudal royal financial interests, rather than private ownership (Seed, 2015, pp. 68–73).[22] Reflecting the inability to effectively exploit indigenous labor under the encomienda system in the Caribbean basin, by the latter half of the six-teenth century, the Catholic clergy began to move away from the coerced labor of the indigenous and toward promoting the chattel enslavement of Africans.

Slave labor (in its new brutal form of monetized plantation production) was necessary for the new colonial system in the West Indies to operate profitably (Williams, 1944). European elites found that the nearest replenishable source of slave labor was in sub-Saharan Africa. Chiefs and slave-raiders would bring captured peoples from Africa's interior to European coastal forts (where their superior military technology could be wielded)—a dynamic that devastated social formation in Africa and set the stage for centuries of European colonialism (Rodney, 1981; Wolf, 1997). The Trinidadian political economist Eric Williams observed: without the exploitation of African chattel slave labor between 1650 and 1850, the rapid expansion and output of plantations throughout much of the [Caribbean] region would not have been possible (1944, p. 29).

Up through the seventeenth century, some African slaves worked along-side or nearby Irish prisoners and indentured servants who had been forcibly relocated across the Atlantic[23] after English forces under Oliver Cromwell con-quered Ireland.[24] Particular turning points occurred in the mid- to late seven-teenth century when African slaves working alongside white people (such as Irish and convict labor) rebelled together, as in Barbados in 1649 and later in Virginia (Linebaugh and Rediker, 2013). Following the suppression of these and other uprisings, the dominant colonial orders through their apparatuses began to systematically differentiate between "blacks" and "whites," privileg-ing white labor ideologically (and to an extent materially) through an evolving social construct (and class system) that placed them concretely above nonwhite workers, especially black chattel labor. As Linebaugh and Rediker explain:

> To stabilize their regime, the rulers of Barbados separated the servants, slaves, and religious radicals from each other. This they accomplished in the 1650s and 1660s . . . The division between servant and slave was codified in the comprehensive slave and servant code of 1661, which became the model for similar codes in Jamaica, South Carolina, Anti-gua, and Saint Christopher. The planters legally and socially differenti-ated slave from servant, defining the former as absolute private property and offering the latter new protections against violence and exploitation. The effort to recompose the class by giving servants and slaves different material positions within the plantation system con-tinued as planters transformed the remaining servants into a labor

elite, as artisans, overseers, and members of the militia, who, bearing arms, would be used to put down slave revolts (2013, pp. 126–127).[25]

Slavery for black people was made hereditary, while by the mid-eighteenth century nearly all of the Irish (who were far fewer in number) were released from their harshest forms of servitude. In order to solidify racialized inequality and the new social construct, marriage between white people and black people was made illegal. New slave codes were stiffened, depriving the negatively racialized of many of the most basic of human dignities. In order to effectively exploit and repress African slave labor in the new regimented chattel system, European planter elites and the colonial apparatus needed to distinguish Africans (and their enslaved descendants) from other laborers. They needed to create the illusion of Africans as subhuman (Federici, 2004; Horne, 2014a; also see, Szymanski, 1983, pp. 355–432).

Racialization as a process thus formed as a material relation prior to an ideological justification: whereas, prior to racialized social relations, African slaves were described as "non-Christian" heathen, it took some years for racism as a sociocultural practice to develop (Callinicos, 1995; Fredrickson, 2002). It was only *after* an objective relationship of domination existed that new ideological justifications of race were created. Consensus formation among the European settler and planter population in the colonial Caribbean (alongside various forms of coercion) around these ideological constructs solidified the rule of the dominant class within the dominant ethnic group and over enslaved laborers brought from another part of the world. This took on the form of dominant white planter classes ruling over a much larger enslaved black population and various intermediary strata, including the creole (or mestizo) populations that expanded over time, as well as some groups of lower-income white people. The racialized orders thus often appeared largely as one and the same within the class system.

Yet, as Kenan Malik (1996) observes: contrary to classical enlightenment (or bourgeois liberal) assertions, *race* is not the cause of inequality. Rather, it is the economic (capitalist) organization of society that informs the racial classification of humanity. Of course, when race is appreciated as an ideological social construction and racism as a form of sociocultural practice, it becomes clear that the very ideological construct of race is an "unattainable thing."[26] It is the *practice* of racism that then reproduces the illusion of race (Fields and Fields, 2014). These notions provide insights for thinking about waging antiracist struggles within the larger context of class struggle (C. Johnson, 2017; Michaels, 2016).

The racialized forms of the class structures that came about through capitalism by way of European colonialism, and, later, through the formation of many new nation-states, have had long-lasting effects but also have been reconfigured over the years. Colonial capitalism, with its chattel slavery of Africans, and the continued capitalist organization of society, with its large repressed and marginalized populations, exist structurally through racialized class relations that have been reproduced through the generations (A. Thompson, 1997). This is not a static condition, however, but rather a relation in flux, one that entails many particularities for how racialized class relations are reproduced in today's global era.

Notable present-day examples of racialized class relations include the globalizing export-processing model that specifically targets negatively racialized and feminized workforces (H. Watson, 1994b, pp. 227–228) living in parts of the world with low levels of development after centuries of colonialism, imperialism, and world capitalism. The aid and donor apparatuses set up to operate in much of the Third World also have functioned in a racialized and gendered manner, in part through pervasive discourses of superiority and inferiority: perpetuating a "civilizing" mission for the global era (Goudge, 2003).[27] Occurring in the post–World War II and postcolonial period, these new apparatuses dovetailed with racialized rhetoric on "cultures of poverty," the newest iteration in the racialized logic of the dominant order. Today's exploitative projects have been revamped. They do not occur through the old systems of chattel slavery and colonial conquest nor through the old, sharply defined legal frameworks of racial apartheid or formal segregation. Whereas "capitalist colonialism and imperialism" set many of the early terms under which "different social classes and their racialized ethnic and gendered components" came to produce their existence, capitalist society has undergone major changes over time and in how it reproduces inequality and repression (H. Watson, 2015, p. 9). Such relations are now being shaped through a system of *globalized* capitalism, with its restructured mechanisms for achieving hegemony and domination (as discussed in Chapter 2).[28]

Racialization has occurred unevenly and under different circumstances (O. Cox, 1948; Dikotter, 1997; Solomos, 1986). Whereas the indigenous peoples of the Caribbean islands were almost completely eliminated during the initial period of colonialism, racialized colonial hierarchies between "black," "white," and "mestizo" populations were constructed and reproduced over time (M. G. Smith, 1965, p. 9). In parts of the colonial Caribbean, such as in Cuba, dozens and dozens of different racial categories were invented to describe people with different phenotypic traits (Morales Dominguez, 2012). "Coolie labor" from China, India, and other areas made these racialized structures more complex, since they, like others, were compelled to act under the socially constructed lenses of race. Racialized class formations have taken on different shapes in various parts of the world, with such dynamics in the Caribbean context having been heavily studied and debated (to cite just a small number of these, see, e.g., de la Fuente, 2001; Dupuy, 1996; Meeks, 2007; Mills, C. 2010; Reyes-Santos, 2015; Linebaugh and Rediker, 2013).

While the Caribbean has become one of the most ethnically diverse regions worldwide, there is still a strong correlation between race and class. For instance, many of those within local dominant groups are the descendants of European colonial strata, ex-pat North Americans, or migrant business families from the Levant and other areas. On some islands, such as in Dominica, Chinese migrant businesspeople own many of the local markets. Simultaneously, lower-income and marginalized populations across much of the Caribbean more often have a larger part of their ancestry traced to the African-born slave population.

Even still, racialization is a relation that has constantly been in flux throughout the history of the Caribbean and other regions. The radical Trinidadian scholar C.L.R. James (1989), for example, examines the class struggle that occurred in revolutionary Haiti between black slaves, freed mulatto groups, planter elites, French officials, émigré, and poor white people. This struggle led to a new situation, in which the racist white ruling classes on the island were overthrown. More recently, scholars have looked, for example, at the shifting particularities of racialization in Cuban society in the wake of the 1959 revolution (Morales Dominguez, 2012).

Plenty of examples of social relations in flux in today's globalizing Caribbean can be seen, such as with the growing number of economic and political elites and new middle strata of Caribbean society who come from historically repressed and negatively racialized communities. Stepping foot into the tourist hotspots in the region (such as at a hotel in Cartagena, or at a high-priced tourist restaurant in Havana), the racialized logic and "standards of beauty" of global capitalist society become quickly apparent. Populations across the spectrum at some level are incorporated into the global system. Some are able to improve upon their economic situation. Among these are strata that have become drawn into transnational markets of consumption. At the same time, perceptions of colorism have shaped class relations and many racialized differences are continually reproduced *because of* the class system. As the radical Barbadian political economist Hilbourne Watson (2015) observes: racialization has been inherent to and constituted through capitalism.

These objective conditions can also be seen through cultural socialization—where for instance "marrying up" can subconsciously (or consciously) be equated with marrying into whiteness (part of the internalized negative legacies of capitalist slavery and colonialism [Fanon, 1967]). How people are acculturated is impacted then by various subjectivities, such as discourse around what is considered "exotic," what is seen to be or viewed as "normal" or "upwardly mobile," or what is thought of as "dangerous." Gerald Horne (2014b) explains how as slaves resisted and fought back against their masters (by escaping, lashing out, cutting throats in the middle of the night, or the common practice of poisoning slaveholders, for instance), dominant white society began to portray all slaves as potentially dangerous, a menace for which various brutal precautions were required to maintain control. Horne argues that echoes of this can be seen in the modern-day "black scare," where people are socialized to be afraid of and view as dangerous those with the phenotypic traits of sub-Saharan Africans. A whole array of cultural production with a variety of elements around race thus takes place.

Illuminating this contradiction of "Western thought" flowing out from the enlightenment, the poet, author, and politician from Martinique, Aimé Césaire (2010), observed in the mid-twentieth century how white society had become acculturated to regularly view violence against black people as normalized, whereas violence when it occurred against white people was unacceptable. Violence external to Europe, such as war and genocide conducted in the Third World, were part of the "civilizing mission." By contrast, war and genocide *inside* Europe was a tragedy and failure of the interstate system. What Césaire understood is that centuries of colonial and capitalist violence had far surpassed the violence of the Nazi behemoth.[29] It can even be said that precursors of the genocidal policies undertaken by the Hitlerian regime were present within the policies of the European colonizers as they slaughtered and oppressed people around the world for centuries (see, e.g., Galeano, 1997; Prashad, 2008; Ribbe, 2005). Césaire wrote starkly of European society:

> Before they were its victims, they were its accomplices; that they tolerated that Nazism before it was inflicted on them, that they absolved it, shut their eyes to it, legitimized it, because, until then, it had been applied only to non-European peoples; that they have cultivated that Nazism, that they are responsible for it, and that before engulfing the whole edifice of Western, Christian civilization in its reddened waters, it oozes, seeps, and trickles from every crack. (Césaire, 2010, p. 36)

Another famed Martiniquais, author and revolutionary Franz Fanon (1967, p. 53), points to the social construction of race with its historical particularities, arguing: "What is called the black soul is a construction by white folk." The condition of *lu noir* (black persons), he argued, had been not just physically manacled but also subliminally twisted through the dominant order, the colonial capitalism of Europe, and later, the United States superpower.[30]

Blackness, as Fanon argued, was the creation of white people. Yet by this Fanon was not characterizing all as white-versus-black but rather he recognized the racialized class structure and the historical role of world capitalism. That is, the problem was not "white people" in general but the power structure of class society that had emanated from Europe and then deployed "whiteness" to its advantage, successfully subsuming so many of the positively racialized from across the classes into its logic and the new sociocultural practices of racism.[31] It was through such processes, as Fanon argued (1967), that white supremacy became embedded formally and informally within the institutions of capitalism.

W.E.B. Du Bois (1935/1998), in his study of the postbellum Reconstruction era U.S. South, described a new subjective dynamic that he called a "public and psychological wage," where white workers held a subjective feeling of superiority over African Americans. This phenomenon drove a wedge between white and black workers, creating fear and mistrust, where white workers (even if heavily exploited and paid little by capital) subconsciously came to see themselves as better because of their "whiteness," which was positively racialized in bourgeois society. Historically in different Caribbean nations a version of Du Bois's idea played out, as racialized ideological wedges between black, mulatto, white, and migrant populations were socially constructed, along with a lived material reality. Many particular examples of this exist in today's Caribbean such as the racialized politics in Guyana (Bulkan, 2014; Mars and Young, 2004), the treatment of Guyanese laborers in Barbados (B. Niles, 2006), and the repression faced by Haitian migrant communities in the Dominican Republic (Wucker, 2000), among others.

Whereas, in the past, processes of racialization occurred through the earlier mercantile, industrial, and international eras, shifting iterations of this dynamic are also reproduced under global capitalism. A racialized global division of labor is on clear display in today's Caribbean, with negatively racialized groups often concentrated in the lowest rungs of the economy, while positively racialized groups often dominate local professional and high-status positions or visit as tourists (sometimes buying beachfront condos, glamorized through TV shows such as *House Hunters International*).

In this now global iteration of racialization, formerly colonized peoples worldwide make up vast pools of those exploited and marginalized by transnational capital, even as their working and consumer lives are increasingly entwined with transnational capitalist chains of accumulation. Racialized labor regimes exist across the region, for example within the hotel tourism industry and onboard cruise ships. As Robinson writes: "The racialized nature of tourism in the Caribbean is overlaid with class and is reflected, beyond mostly light-skinned tourists served by Afro-Caribbeans, in a distribution of benefits from the industry that go disproportionately to lighter-skinned elites and industry workers and professionals" (2003, p. 147).

Racialized structures are thus part and parcel of capitalism's class relations (R. Patterson, 2013), continuing to have a real and deleterious impact on so many in the globalizing Caribbean (H. Watson, 2015; Allahar, 2005). Furthermore, it is a condition constructed through many societal dynamics and institutions, and coercively reproduced through a variety of policing and repressive apparatuses (Gilmore, 2007; Hall et al., 1978/2013). This is the everyday reality for the urban and rural popular classes that dot the Caribbean basin's landscape as well as for those individuals and families from the region who move abroad in search of work and opportunity.

The rise of capitalism, its spread into the Caribbean, and the formation of a racialized class system also exist as a *gendered* social process.

Gendered Social Relations

A gendered hierarchy appears to have been the earliest social division among humans, though this gendered hierarchy is different from a gendered division of labor (Edgell, 2012; Harman, 2008, p. 8). Patriarchy and different kinds of gendered hierarchies clearly flourished in societies of the precapitalist Old World. Yet, the rise of capitalism resulted in a qualitatively new type of patriarchy and gendered social relation, one rooted in new forms of labor, social reproduction, and property relations (Delphy, 2015; Leacock and Safa, 1986). Capitalism constructed new relations of exploitation and inequality initially through primitive accumulation, a process through which people were propelled away from rural subsistence living and into the lives of waged workers. The structural features of this phenomenon initially congealed during the crisis of the late feudal formations of Western Europe during the sixteenth and seventeenth centuries. Processes of primitive accumulation "divorc[ed] the producer from the means of production" by removing small noncapitalist producers from their lands and inserting them into relations of waged labor (Marx, 1867/1992, p. 875). What did this mean for women?

Primitive accumulation brought with it many upheavals and among the most significant were the destruction of many old customs, a criminalization of contraception, an attack on communal living, and an erosion of peasant assemblies and of folkloric spiritualities. At its core this process entailed what Silvia Federici calls a "historic defeat" for women; where childbearing and -rearing were reframed as nonprofitable activities. This occurred even as the exploitation of unwaged reproductive labor became more important than ever (as it produced the workers to be exploited in factories, to serve in armies, or to work the fields). As Federici states: "In the new monetary regime, only production-for-market was defined as a value-creating activity, whereas the reproduction of the worker began to be considered as valueless

from an economic viewpoint and even ceased to be considered as work"
(2004, p. 75).

The state would come to play a key role in enforcing this new system and
in securing a divided and coerced workforce. New gendered wedges formed
within communities and families. Finding themselves in new exploitative
waged relations, many workingmen began to support displacing women
from paid labor, removing a potential competitor who could undermine
their own wages (Murray and Peetz, 2010). Capitalists and the state supported this process as it was profitable for them, and it helped to mold the
institution of the family.

All of this enabled the state and employers to use the men's wages as a
way to command women's labor. The family itself evolved into a microunit
for disciplining women (Engels, 1884/1972; Federici, 2004). The very meaning of labor changed. If a waged working man wove a piece of fabric it was
considered "production" and a special product, but if a woman produced the
same item it was seen as a kind of "natural resource" of low value (Federici,
2004). A new sexual division of labor thus formed, fixing women to unwaged
reproductive work and making them more dependent on men (whose labor
became waged). The entire edifice then, down to the day-to-day subsistence
and upbringing of working people and their communities (in turn exploited
by capital), came to rest upon unwaged surplus and the devalued social reproduction carried out in large part by women (Bhattacharya, 2017).

An array of sociocultural practices came about functioning to reproduce
capitalist patriarchy, one of the worst being heterosexism. While some of
these had already begun to form in the Old World, through organized religion and other institutions, capitalist society enforced more rigid and systematic practices, such as through what Nancy Fraser calls a "compulsory
heterosexuality" (1997). Meanwhile the "traditional" nuclear family came
about, premised on the high degree of exclusion of women from the sphere
of socially recognized work and monetary relations, with women's labor
concealed. Capitalism evolved then through changing cultural processes
that targeted certain groups and benefited others.

So how did these new relations translate to the Caribbean? What were
the particularities of this process, with its gendered and racialized class dynamics (i.e., planter elite women versus enslaved women)?

As world capitalism spread through colonialism, enslaved African
women and indigenous women were subjected to all manner of violence—
from murder to torture and rape. The brutally exploitative relations placed
upon proletarian European women under capitalism were even more widely
heaped upon slave and indigenous women (Federici, 2004, pp. 103–115). This
class division among women was even more pronounced in the Caribbean

through the process of racialization. Women within the planter elite, for instance, benefited from not only being positively racialized but also part of the upper class. By contrast, the structural features of slavery led to new stratifications that further negatively impacted enslaved women (Morrissey, 1989), such as the sale of an enslaved woman's child on auction blocks. As the value of slaves increased, European planters attempted to expand their slave workforces through "natural reproduction," but this often failed due either to resistance or to the harsh conditions causing the physical debilitation of enslaved women. As slaves forged relations of mutual aid and resistance, slaveholders responded with more disciplined regimes of forced labor. This consumed one's time and energy, requiring slaves to survive in conditions of heavy scarcity.

In the Caribbean, enslaved women were among the staunchest defenders of the culture brought from Africa, and they consequently suffered extreme punishment (Federici, 2004; Mair, 2006). In order to preserve their cultures, and because slaves were brought together onto Caribbean plantations from different geographic areas and societies in sub-Saharan Africa, slaves forged their own hybrid languages and cultures. Communicating and engaging in forms of cultural production that planters could not decipher became important for maintaining resistance (Scott, 2018). Differences among these subaltern communities occurred across the region, between coastal and hinterland, over ritual representations, or the secret histories that emerged (Apter and Derby, 2010). The role of enslaved women was especially vital to the struggles for liberation that took place and the eventual end of chattel slavery (Finch, 2015).

Slavery, though, had also carried with it many gendered and sexual dynamics. Makeda Silvera has examined how heterosexual patriarchy was produced and reproduced through the dehumanizing processes of capitalist slavery, where "to be male was to be the stud, the procreator; to be female was to be fecund, and one's femininity was measured by the ability to attract and hold a man and to bear children" (1992, pp. 529–530).

The end of slavery during the nineteenth century and the rise of the postcolonial era brought about many new social dynamics for Caribbean women, while still remaining under the umbrella of world capitalism (Scully and Paton, 2005). It was under a heightened internationalization of capitalism that women would face waged and unwaged (but free) labor, impacting so many lived situations. One study has looked at how Afro-Caribbean and South Asian women serving as line workers in a Trinidadian factory fit within a "new international division of labor" (Yelvington, 1995). Throughout the region, and worldwide, the under- and unpaid labor of women domestic workers serves as a hidden subsidy for the global capitalist economy (Chang, 2000; Flynn, 2011).

The role (and exploitation) of women historically and contemporarily has been fundamental to the evolving nature of world society.[32] A more intensive subphase of the internationalization of capitalism occurred after World War II, as the labor of women was increasingly inserted into circuits of capital accumulation (Mies, 1986). It was during the post–World War II period that international capitalist groups increasingly began to exploit women workers in the developing world, whose unwaged condition served as a readily exploitable situation. EPZs were formed in this period based largely upon the waged labor exploitation of large groups of (mostly young) women workers. While subjugated under an international division of labor, the opportunity of waged work for women could allow a degree of independence from men and bring them into closer contact with other women sharing similar experiences. The documentary *Global Assembly Line*, for example, shows how the first EPZ labor strike in the Americas, at a maquiladora factory in northern Mexico, was led by militant women workers (Gray, 1986).

Through globalization, the labor power of many women workers has become inserted into transnational chains of accumulation (Abbassi and Lutjens, 2002; Desai, 2009), even among agricultural workers, such as with the women laborers in the region's banana industry (Frank, 2016). Over recent decades many Caribbean women have worked in EPZs—exploited as low-cost laborers to produce garments, plastic goods, shoes, and other goods (Gammage, 2004, p. 751; Ho, 1999, p. 40; Klak, 1999). Different parts of manufacturing processes have come to depend on feminized labor, such as the high-tech informatics production that has taken place in Barbados, where particular cultural and identity formations occur (Freeman, 2000).

Sex work in the contemporary Caribbean has consistently been linked to global tourism (Brennan, 2004; Kempadoo, 1999, 2004). Across the Caribbean, for instance, payment in exchange for sexual services has become common in tourism zones. Yet, this also plays out with many local particularities, as sex workers in Cuba undergo more medical tests as compared with other parts of the region (Hamilton, 2012). Some sex workers in the region have become part of a mobile fraction of the globalizing proletariat with, for example, the traveling or trafficking of women from parts of the region for sexual exploitation abroad (IOM, 1996). A growing trend of regional-mobility of sex work can be seen on display in Costa Rica, a country frequented by many well-off foreign tourists. Mobile sex workers face a contradiction of barriers to care and rising risks of violence or contracting AIDS, HIV, and other sexually transmitted diseases alongside socioeconomic opportunities not otherwise available (Goldenberg et al., 2014; Johnson and Kerrigan, 2013; Maher et al., 2014).

Gendered labor, in both productive and reproductive processes, has thus been at the core of devalued labor in capitalist society—seeping into ideology and many cultural practices. Ultimately, great flows of today's transnational capitalist accumulation are secured on the backs of women's under- and unwaged labor, especially among the lower-income and negatively racialized and those lacking institutional protections.

Conclusion: A Brief Overview

The aim of this book is to understand how the latest transition, toward *globalization*, is taking place in the Caribbean—from the international to the global/transnational phase of world capitalism—from the latter half of the twentieth century into the twenty-first century, and how, while new, it is rooted in a system, capitalism, that has been at least five hundred years in the making. It combines a historical overview of capitalism in the region with theoretical analysis backed by case studies.

Chapter 2 elaborates on the role of class formation in regard to capitalist globalization and the Caribbean and then looks at the shifting dynamics of the state and the hegemonic tensions occurring throughout the region.

Chapter 3 provides a brief look at the Caribbean's history in light of the different phases of world capitalism and its mode of production. Subsequent chapters will look at different socioeconomic sectors in the region, emphasizing their particularities in the global restructuring taking place and the state's role.

Chapter 4 examines the globalization of the cruise ship business in the region, bearing in mind who accumulates capital and under what conditions. It looks at how transnational capitalists have come to control the business and the labor force and at the material changes wrought by this social process.

Chapter 5 looks at the exportation of Caribbean labor, the reverse flow of remittances, and the formation of a global remittance industry. By exploiting migrant labor, transnational capitalists have come to profit tremendously by appropriating not only the surplus value of superexploitable workers but also portions of the redistributed value (in the form of remittances) that migrant workers send back to family members in their country of origin.

Chapter 6 looks at the formation and evolving role of EPZs and so-called export-processing development from the closing decades of the twentieth century and into the twenty-first century, showcasing the increasing integration of Caribbean manufacturing with transnational capital as well as the great lengths to which state policy makers have gone to promote export processing even as it faces many difficulties.

Chapter 7 looks at mining in the Caribbean, specifically in regard to the transition from an international mining industry geared toward the interests of national capitalist power blocs alongside heavy state involvement toward a globally competitive and privatized mining industry benefiting transnational capital.

The comparative historical studies in this book have been structured largely around looking at five strategic traits. All of these traits hinge upon a new era of transnational *accumulation*, *integration*, and *inequality*. The traits are as follows:

1. The emergence of a transnational financial system, within which the Caribbean is becoming integrated.
2. The formation of transnational production networks that are enveloping and forming through the region.
3. The precarization and flexibilization of labor in the Caribbean, as the labor power of racialized and gendered workforces is inserted into transnational chains of accumulation and as large parts of the region's population are structurally marginalized—their social reproduction not required by transnational capital.
4. A move away, by state policy makers, from indicative development planning (with an eye to national goals), as they shift toward a transnational orientation and promote global competitiveness. While local state strata are vital for this process, policy makers operating through apparatuses of the U.S. state and supranational agencies play a particularly vital role.
5. The new subcontractor networks evolving in the region, which function to integrate many local and regional businesses into transnational chains. This point illustrates how the globalization process draws in local contingents in diverse ways.

Throughout these chapters, it is recognized how capitalist globalization in the region occurs alongside shifting political, institutional, and organizational dynamics. Furthermore, this book comments on how labor, political, and social movements are clashing with dominant groups and adapting to or facing difficulties with the changes taking place. It considers as well how revamped hegemonic strategies and institutional apparatuses have developed to further market integration, the exploitation of labor, and the policing (or disciplining) of the region's marginalized and resistant communities. The integration of a new global capitalism into the region has foregrounded this turbulence, which has led to significant social and class transformations.

Paralleling these recent developments have been some gains for those workers in the upwardly mobile and professional strata of Caribbean society. Also, it must be said, that the overproduction and advancements of global capitalism have allowed for certain material benefits, such as the wide-scale access to cellular phone technology and many cheap products. The region has also begun to have wider access to generic medicines. Yet, alongside increased access to consumer goods and medicines, the region has experienced rising inequality and high levels of joblessness and underemployment. As these new commoditized relations (and what Sklair [2002, pp. 164–207] describes as the "culture-ideology of consumerism") have swept across the planet and the region, they have also occurred alongside mounting global social polarization and a global environmental crisis (Oxfam, 2017; Piketty, 2014). Lower-income communities in the Caribbean are especially vulnerable to the ravages of climate change (Elie, 2017).

Because the Caribbean basin is located on the imperial frontier with such a long history of U.S. imperial intervention, challenging the dominant conditions is, of course, easier said than done. For many people in the region it is now difficult to imagine an alternative political project such that now even minor progressive reforms are portrayed as radical. The many economic and political victories of dominant social forces, as well as the many cultural and psychological dimensions in which social oppression sustains itself (Jeffries, 2016), can understandably lead to confusion, cynicism, individualism, and a mentality of "everyone for themselves" among the working and popular classes. Yet, as we know from history, what appears as stable on the surface is in fact rife with contradictions and can undergo rapid and unforeseen changes. Even while the TCC is much more advanced in its integration and holds tremendous power (Phillips, 2018), subaltern social and political struggles do and will continue to exist across the region. It is my contention that grassroots social justice and political movements from below, while continuing their domestic struggles, must work to build regional and transnational coordination and infrastructure. Progressives, leftists, socialists, and social movement forces in the global north need to build linkages and networks with their counterparts among the subaltern forces in the global south, and on the subjective level move toward a global consciousness from below; from *internacionalismo* to *transnacionalismo*. This entails a direct clash with the national chauvinism that remains so widely present, and is useful for dominant groups.

Before jumping into this book's concrete examination of the shift from international to transnational capitalism in the region, let us first recall the important findings of previous studies' regarding political economy and the particularities of the region's class societies. Let us also first look in more depth at the global capitalism school of thought and as it relates to understanding the region's political economy.

This book closes with some theoretical reflections on the broader implications of economic restructuring and the transformation of class relations in the region and with suggestions for future research on the Caribbean and global capitalism.

2

The Challenge of Understanding Social Formation in the Global Era

In order to demystify capitalist accumulation and the racialized and gendered exploitation of labor, we need a theoretical understanding that illuminates their structural features. Although global markets seem to have a life of their own with flows of finance, production, and trade, we must move beyond this view of capitalism as just an "immense collection of commodities" (Marx, 1867/1992, p. 125). We need to engage in an analysis of its intrinsic characteristics, such as how its services and commodities are produced and utilized. However, rather than seeing these as the normal function of a faceless market, we need to comprehend how human beings with particular interests operate through and behind these economic structures.

We need then to understand how social forces operate and how they reproduce their existence through today's globalizing form of capitalism. We need to understand the social cartography of global capitalism with all of its unevenness and particularities, as it "integrates the various polities, cultures, and institutions of national societies into an emergent transnational or global society" (Robinson, 2003, p. 13). In this book, we consider how social and political economic dynamics undergo change through the rise of transnational processes.

Theorizing Social Cartography and Global Capitalism

Understanding social formation is made all the more difficult because social forces under capitalism, and in relation to the world market, have traditionally operated through the institutional framework of the interstate system (for instance, through national social classes, a homeland's business community or capitalist class, or a nation-state's working class). Yet, with its tendency toward expansion, capitalism created a world market. As part of this process, an array of colonial apparatuses, international monopolies, and various forms of labor exploitation were constructed. Resisting this process, popular and radical movements struggled within their nations, and at times formed international bonds.

This understanding is present in the classical theories of political economy (Marx, 1867/1992; A. Smith, 2003), the historical materialist understanding of international monopoly capitalism (Hilferding, 1910/2006; Lenin, 1917/1969; Sweezy, 1942), and the more recent "new imperialism" approaches (Harvey, 2005; Wood, 2005).[1] A class system, as commonly understood from these perspectives, is made up of capitalists, laborers, and various other strata bunched within nations or empires. As the key structural feature of the class orders of the interstate system there exists different class *fractions* (e.g., a "lumpenproletariat" fraction of a country's working class or the financial, merchant, and industrial fractions of a country's capitalist class, some of which might be engaged in international activities). These fractions have reflected historic circumstances and the alignment of social forces but within specific geographic areas. Expanding on classical political economy and the "international monopoly capitalism" approach, it has been argued since the 1970s (Hymer, 1971, 1972, 1976, 1979) that fractions of (or the entirety of) some capitalist classes of different nations have become internationally oriented alongside the internationalization of the division of labor in the mid-twentieth century (Barnet and Muller, 1974; Panitch and Gindin, 2013).[2]

When examining our present era's world society, much of the discourse takes up surface-layer views of geopolitical and national competition occurring through the interstate system—reflecting the stale language of Westphalian state-centrism. Populations are viewed as domestically rooted and engaged essentially in class struggles within their states, where from time to time some groups are involved in international activities. Domestic capitalist power blocs may engage in international alliances and rivalries, where "national" business groups and conglomerates must deal with foreign competitors. This is a conflict between "homelands," between competing states, with their spheres of elites and policy makers pursuing "national" interests. While such state-centric perspectives can and do shed light on important dynamics, they ignore the emerging social (and material) reality.

My argument is that we need inventive approaches to understand the changes taking place. During the closing decades of the twentieth century and into the twenty-first century, we have seen a shift from *international* processes toward *transnational* processes and the rise of transnational class relations. A problem in understanding the changes taking place is that social relations have long been reduced to "technical" relations between or within states. The unfortunate result is that everything is forced to fit into the ideological construct of the state (and the back-and-forth relations between states) without attention as to how the state is produced and reproduced and how it inevitably, inescapably, and necessarily expresses contradictory social relations. The central point here is that the state is not reducible to a place or a thing. The very state one might see as an irreducible unit (e.g., through the analysis of international relations scholars) is in fact an apparatus through which social forces operate, which play a role in shaping political economic dynamics nationally, internationally, and transnationally. As systems of production were organized on a national and international basis during earlier phases of capitalism, this made an analytical focus through the scope of the nation-state and interstate system easier to sustain. The unit of analyses has thus long been the nation-state.

This has then led often to a development (West) versus underdevelopment (Third World) discourse that is discerned in place-bound terms and place-bound notions of geography. I contend that we need to avoid false inside-outside dichotomies, such as a state-centric logic that takes as a priority a dichotomy of place (each country) versus spatial analysis (the dialectic of an interconnected world). For transnational capitalists, the real economy is not a mass of independent national economies but an interconnected (global) space in which place and space form a heterogeneous unity that never reaches a simple whole: an open-ended, heterogeneous, "nontotalizable" totality. Put in more simple terms, capital accumulation is a worldwide process.

An examination of how class systems are rooted primarily in the framework of the interstate system and nation-state competition was taken up by scholars of "dependency theory," and thinkers of the similar "plantation school" who are well known in the anglophone Caribbean (Beckford, 1999; Best, 1968; Best et al., 2009; Thomas, 1968). These scholars essentially have sought to look at the problems of "underdevelopment" within colonial and postcolonial states, as wealthy nations sustained themselves through the subjugation of a peripheral group of poorer nations. Emphasizing how this process played out over the history of world capitalism (and a world system), important works were produced by scholars such as Andre Gunder Frank (1967), Samir Amin (1978), Immanuel Wallerstein (1979), Walter Rodney (1981), and Giovanni Arrighi (1983). These scholars broke with the earlier Marxian focus on development among the core states of the capitalist system by instead focusing on underdevelopment in the periphery (Brewer, 1980/1990, p. 161).[3] They argued that resources from countries of the "periphery" and colonial or postcolonial areas flow to the "core" and to the dominant groups of the metropole states—specifically to the nations of Western Europe, North America, and Japan—enriching the latter at the expense of the former (Arrighi, 1994; Wallerstein, 1979). Many political economists studying the Caribbean in recent years have taken up a similar approach (see, e.g., Fatton, 2013; Karagiannis and Polychroniou, 2015).

While I recognize the importance of these in helping us understand social formation and political economy in the postcolonial world, it is my view that in today's era of global/transnational capitalism that the nation-state scope can also blind us to many of the fundamental ways in which we exist. These approaches can blur our understanding of many deep changes that are occurring. While critically appropriating ideas from such important perspectives, the argument here is that to best understand the deep structural features of our society and the novel dynamics of recent decades, we need to recalibrate our understanding of social formation.

Many other contemporary studies on the Caribbean focus on cultural criticism, or what was previously called "literary criticism." Also, as I see it, many journalists and scholars, when examining conflicts and struggles in the region, often take up a double standard that simplifies the nature of political economic processes in the global south, ignoring many important dynamics and historical contingencies. This can, in my view, lead problematically to a judgment of events in the global south through different standards than would be used to look at the global north (Koerner, 2019; Macdonald, 2008). Another problematic approach can be seen in the reports of many human rights groups that regularly treat human rights as if it is the sole responsibility of domestic authorities, without recognizing the role of capitalism, or the actions of powerful interventionist state apparatuses and institutions (i.e., the imposition of debt, or the role of sanctions and other aggressive acts). Ultimately, in this way, mainstream (liberal) analysis fragments, seeks to dissolve, and externalizes social relations and contradictions, reducing everything that is substantive to technical reflections (Layne, 2006, pp. 118–132). The outcome is that nothing remains but fragments that cannot be properly restored to their place in a complex and heterogeneous totality.

In recent years, there has been a turn among many critical scholars of development toward a post-structuralist approach, seeking to deconstruct assumptions and knowledge systems, rejecting notions of precise interpretation and singular meanings.[4] This approach is apparent in the work of Marion Werner, with her critique of the "assumptions, discourses, and spatial imaginaries" of narratives on development in the region (2016, p. 5), and in Mimi Sheller's historical examination of the commoditized image of the Caribbean (2003). While these studies provide us many important granular observations and understandings of the contradictory narratives that form, they also allow for bits and pieces of rhetoric to take precedence over social reality. Their focus becomes centered on questions such as on how discourse constructs reality. In my view, this post-structuralist approach can detract from our understanding of the overall substance. An idealist understanding (where ideas are the motive force of world development) is just short of saying in traditional Cartesian terms that thinking it makes it so. From this perspective, discourse and narratives on development seem to be privileged at the expense of concrete processes of global accumulation. Development is feudal, or capitalist, or socialist (i.e., for some purpose or end). We must ask: where are the social relations of production? Where are the factors and forces that propel the postwar deepening of the internationalization of capital that shaped the dialectic of globalization?

So let us look at the shifting concrete conditions. It is during the latter decades of the twentieth century and into the twenty-first century that numerous production networks and financial systems have become functionally integrated across multiple frontiers. Propelling this restructuring of the world economy is the emerging TCC. This class, composed of different fractions, has emerged as the segment of the world bourgeoisie that owns the leading worldwide means of production embodied in TNCs and the most powerful financial institutions. As global networks of production and finance, along with TNCs and other institutions, redefine the scale of the world economy through new functionally integrated circuits of accumulation (Dicken, 2007), transnational relations form within and between various class fractions and social groups.[5] Transnational capitalists now seek out profits globally and hail from around the world not just from the "global north" (del Castillo-Mussot et al., 2013; Harris 2009b, 2016; Murray and Scott, 2012).

Working and popular class fractions around the world have also undergone major changes associated with globalization, as labor power itself has been reconfigured and incorporated into transnational value chains (Struna, 2009). Many studies and documentaries have shown well the common struggle that women workers face in the globalizing economy. The documentary *Global Assembly Lines*, for instance, examines how women workers in the United States, Mexico, and the Philippines have faced exploitation through the rise of a new global circuit of capitalist production, which benefited from microprocessors and other new technological and organizational advancements (Gray, 1986). Meanwhile new pools of middle strata, with rising patterns of consumption linked deeply into the globalizing economy, while more numerous in the "global north" have appeared in regions around the world including the Caribbean (Harris, 2006; Liodakis, 2010; Robinson, 2003; Sklair, 2001; Sprague, 2016a; Sprague-Silgado, 2017b).

Here it is key to recognize the shift from an *international* to a *global* division of labor, with its various regional and local/national dynamics. By the latter half of the twentieth century, the heightening *international* division of labor, or what scholars dubbed the "new international division of labor" (Liodakis, 1990; Mies, 1986/2014), described how different countries had become specialized in the production of various types of products, so that labor across the interstate system was concentrated within nations and geared toward specific export-oriented productive forces. Through globalization, by contrast, we can now also identify "peripheral" pools of labor in the "core" and "core" pools of labor in the "periphery" (Robert Cox, 1987), meaning that we see a *global* division of labor, "which implies differential participation in global production according to social standing and not necessarily geographic location" (Robinson, 2003, p. 59). A flexibilization in production has occurred, with increasingly rapid shifts in production lines and the rise of labor's insertion into *transnational* chains of accumulation.

For instance, in downtown Los Angeles, low-wage migrant workers (often without legal status) are busy producing garments for TNCs and their subcontractors. Meanwhile, we see new pockets of middle strata growing in the periphery, with consumers who identify more with global cultural products than they do with locally grounded cultural production, hooked in to new communication and information flows through satellites and high-speed internet. At the same time, many higher-paid, professional workers—including from the Caribbean—increasingly compete in globalized industries, searching out jobs wherever and whenever they can find them. Many poor working-class Caribbeans, by contrast, have sought to improve their situation by working abroad: as nannies, cooks, Uber drivers, and janitorial workers in airports and in construction. They also work some of the most difficult and low-wage jobs. For decades, Caribbean migrants have worked harvesting sugar cane in Florida (NACLA, 1977). In recent years a growing number of slaughterhouse and meatpacking workers in the southeast United States are from the Caribbean diaspora (Salvador Rangel, personal communication, 2017).

Labor exploitation (and, concomitant with this, the movement of populations) is being restructured as earlier international accumulation networks are fragmenting and becoming inserted intro transnational chains of accumulation (Lin, 2016; Struna, 2009). Developmental models (aiming to foment national economic development) or relations glued to the interstate system continue to erode, as state planners seek to promote transnational capitalist interests and global competitiveness, even if this includes national rhetoric and some policies that are in apparent contradiction. There is a need then to refocus our attention on social groups and not just nation-states as units of analysis.

This does not mean, however, that national dynamics have disappeared or are no longer relevant. What it suggests is that new transnationally oriented social relations are beginning to entwine with and, in many circumstances, absorb earlier forms of class structure. New social dynamics and integrative processes associated with the global economy are bound up with contradictions. Many differences remain, as new, uneven transnational processes intersect and clash with regional, international, national, and local processes—and as transnational social forces must deal with the local alignment of forces in different locations. It is also important to recognize how many transnational groups in the late twentieth and early twenty-first century emerged out of places of intense activity, arising "in 'hothouse' fashion" from earlier internationally oriented groups "such as from state-supported and family-based trading groups in the 1960s and 1970s" (Chacko and Jayasuriya, 2017, p. 8). During the last quarter of the twentieth century, transnational fractions began to emerge within the bourgeoisie of numerous countries including within the Third World (Robinson, 2003).

This gets at how global capitalism plays out through a heterogeneous context. Uneven and combined development thus continues to remain integral to capitalism's spatial motion, with a "tendency for capital to concentrate in particular built environments" (Robinson, 2009, p. 74). At the same time, these built environments are not necessarily nation-state spaces, and "in fact a great deal of empirical evidence indicates an ongoing erosion of the correspondence of national space with such economies and the accumulation circuits and levels of social development that adhere to them" (Robinson, 2009, p. 74). Even as transnational processes intensify, local and regional particularities and the influence of geography and history play a vital role in how societies develop (Richardson, 1993). We can thus see important instances of transnational material and social formation occurring throughout the Caribbean but in a heterogeneous manner, bound up with tension.

Digicel: An Example of a Major TNC Operating in the Caribbean

Look, for instance, at the ways TNCs have come to operate in this environment. For example, take a TNC with a wide presence in the Caribbean region, the mobile telephone network provider Digicel. Cellular technology has radically transformed consumption for large populations across the planet, including in the Caribbean.

Founded in 2001, Digicel is headquartered in Jamaica but incorporated in Bermuda (an island with a long history as a tax haven). The company has institutional investors from a growing array of companies ranging from private equity houses, such as the London-based CDC Capital Partners, to government firms. Facilitating its operations in Haiti, the World Bank has also

Figure 2.1 Digicel billboard in Haiti. (Source: Wikimedia Commons.)

invested in Digicel operations. A number of Caribbean-based capitalists have also provided launching costs for new Digicel operations in the region, such as in Barbados (Telecompaper, 2003). Deepening the company's integration into global finance, in 2007, Digicel sold $1.4 billion of high-yielding junk bonds to its worldwide investors (Beesley, 2007). In 2012 authorities in Jamaica accused the company of engaging in massive tax evasion (Hall, 2012).

While not yet publicly traded on Wall Street, Digicel is majority-owned by a transnational capitalist, Denis O'Brien. O'Brien, who is Irish by birth, officially resides in Malta (a country that charges no tax on worldwide assets or income brought in by permanent residents and only requires a "permanent resident" to visit Malta once a year). With investments in a variety of businesses and stocks in companies active around the world, O'Brien is said to be worth close to $5 billion.[6] After initially entering the telecom business by promoting its liberalization in the early 1990s in Ireland, his company Digicel now focuses on marketing mobile services in small countries in developing regions such as in the Caribbean, Central America, and Oceania. Digicel has expanded rapidly by purchasing mobile licensing contracts from governments, liberalizing their communications sector. The company's growth strategy has relied on the ramping up of neoliberal austerity and privatization policies undertaken by state elites in recent decades (mainly, through the sales of formerly state-owned telecommunications enterprises, similar to the strategy undertaken by the transnational capitalist Carlos Slims with his purchase of Mexico's privatized telecommunication enterprise TELMEX). Powerful state apparatuses, such as those of the United States, the EU, and supranational agencies such as the International Monetary Fund (IMF) and World Bank, have been some of the strongest proponents of privatization of public telephone companies, which have benefited TNCs like Digicel and Carlos Slims's company Grupo Carso.

Digicel's board of directors (including Denis O'Brien) currently comprises individuals from Irish and British backgrounds. Through the lens of earlier "nation-state centric" theoretical scopes, O'Brien and the other executives of Digicel would therein be viewed as part of an Irish or British Isles capitalist class, possibly part of an internationally active fraction. However, under the new regime of transnational capitalism, these businesspeople increasingly have no overriding incentive to develop their European home nations, nor interest in repatriating profits to them. Rather, his businesses and investments are based on the functional integration of capital across borders and taking advantage of an uneven and globally competitive environment by exercising his company's economy of scale and harnessing the technological and organizational advancements of recent decades. Investors have sought to free themselves from national constraints, a goal shared by many political allies.

The cellular and mobile systems industry through which O'Brien profits so handsomely is just one example of the rapid changes that have occurred through globalization. The company has benefited from technology that only emerged during the latter part of the twentieth century (technology that was also developed in part through government funding). Furthermore, Digicel's growth has been tied to the formation of a global consumer base of cell phone users. In the early 1990s, there were only a few hundred thousand subscribers to mobile systems worldwide, yet little more than a decade later there were approximately 1.5 billion (Dicken, 2007, p. 89).[7] While O'Brien and other Digicel board members might well maintain activities in their nations of birth, it is clear that their orientation is toward transnational accumulation.

Importantly for our story, while capital accumulation (at the most general level) is often misrepresented as national economic development, it is now increasingly clear that capital is not motivated to make the economic development of any single country its priority. Rather it is focused on enriching a handful of individuals and private institutions at its core. Transnational processes are used as a more efficient means by which capital can extract even more wealth from every corner of the globe while being less accountable to populations.

TNCs and Chains of Accumulation

Political economists since the 1970s have studied the role of the multination-al corporation (MNC), and, more recently, the TNC. Barnet and Muller (1974) observed that internationally footloose MNCs had come to touch every aspect of daily life, establishing through their activities a new international corporate economy. Stephen Hymer (1978), in a series of articles in the 1970s, pointed to the importance of FDI and theorized that an internationalization of the division of labor was being reproduced through the expanding activ-ities of MNCs. Following this analysis, others, such as Grazia Ietto-Gillies, suggested that expanding MNCs have taken on a "transnationality of oper-ations and globality of decisions" (Grazia Ietto-Gillies, 1992, p. 181).[8] In re-cent decades, political economists have differentiated between MNCs and TNCs: whereas MNCs have extensive international operations, they are clearly identified with a home base (Hirst and Thompson, 1999); the TNC business model, by contrast, is based on functional cross-border diversity in market capitalization, ownership, administration, production, and so on. It is also seen as far less identifiable with one home country. In recent decades, the TNC model has emerged as the standard form of top corporate organiz-ations (from Microsoft to Digicel). In looking at specific companies and cap-italists, we can observe broad traits associated with capitalist globalization.

New cross-border financial flows constitute part of the process of global-ization under way since the late twentieth century. We can trace parts of the history of this phenomenon to the creation of the Society for Worldwide Interbank Financial Telecommunications Network (SWIFT), established in the 1970s to standardize cross-border banking transactions, as well as to the interlinking of national stock markets that started in the 1980s, and the mas-sive growth of FDI. Another important indicator is the growing number of cross-border M&A deals over recent decades. This is when companies domi-ciled in different countries agree to form one company together, or they make a deal in which the company domiciled in one country purchases the company domiciled in another country. Around the world the relaxing of capital controls and other barriers has allowed for rapid financial liberaliza-tion, evidenced by rising FDI and the huge increases in cross-border M&A deals, as shown in Figure 2.2. This and other factors have occurred as part of the formation of vast new transnational circuits of accumulation.

Worldwide cross-border M&As increased from around 98 billion USD in 1990 to over one trillion USD in 2007 (and then following their decline during the 2007–2008 global economic crisis rebounded to 822 billion USD by 2018).[9] We also see rising cross-border flows of shares issued by companies and traded over multiple different national stock exchanges, impacting businesspeople worldwide, including within the Caribbean. As Mohan and Watson observe:

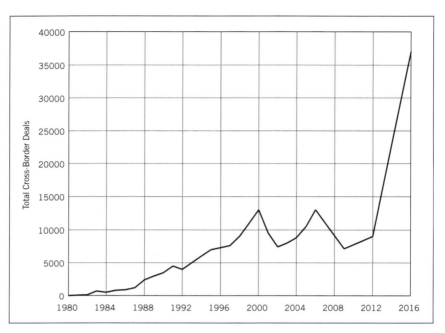

Figure 2.2 Worldwide cross-border M&A deals. (Source: UNCTAD, 2017; Kim, 2010.)

"Globalization and financial integration have caused a phenomenal growth in cross-border equity flows both internationally and regionally among Caribbean Community (CARICOM) member states. All CARICOM countries have open financial markets and have been subject to worldwide equity flows" (Mohan and Watson, 2010, p. 2). As a sign of an emerging intraregional transnationalization, more and more Caribbean-domiciled companies are taking part in stock exchanges in the region and becoming inserted into global circuits of finance. Transnational economic relations are coming to exist between businesses, investors, and global banking interests across the region (Mohan and Watson, 2010). New supranational forums, such as the Central American Free Trade Association-Dominican Republic (CAFTA-DR), further help ease this process.

The rising flows of FDI are another indicator of growing capitalist transnational embeddedness. While a majority of the FDI stocks and flows in the Caribbean come from companies based in the United States and Europe (Mohan and Watson, 2010), companies and state firms from other areas of the world are also increasingly active in the region (Nienaber, 2017).[10] However, as Dicken's (2007) work suggests, even measurements such as FDI have their limitations, for example, as the domicile of a company (as compared to decades ago) bears less significance in regard to the objective and subjective orientation of its executives and investors. While the state-centric way in which such data is collected and most-often understood can mask the transnational processes taking place, we have no choice but to make use of the available data.

For instance, TNCs domiciled in Europe, the United States, and China and seeking out profits globally are caught up in business activities entwined with a rising number of investors from around the world and local businesspeople seeking global profitability. While a TNC may enjoy a special relationship with certain governments, they are increasingly oriented toward global competitiveness and profits. While local Caribbean capitalists mostly seek out inputs into the global economy through foreign-domiciled TNCs, the intraregional FDI of Caribbean transnational capitalists has begun to grow over recent decades. For example, Trinidad and Tobago (with its tremendous oil wealth) is a key player for FDI in the CARICOM states (Mohan and Watson, 2010).

The data in Table 2.1 show the intensifying inflows and outflows of FDI through the "developing" Caribbean. Not included in this graph are the gigantic FDI flows for Puerto Rico or the archipelago tax havens, such as the Bahamas, British Virgin Islands, and Cayman Islands. As tax haven nodes of global finance, the FDI flows through banks domiciled in these havens now *dwarf* FDI into most of the world's nations.

In 2013, more than \$92 billion flowed into the British Virgin Islands. The tiny island territory pulled in more foreign investment than every nation except China, Russia, and the United States (Miles, 2014). At around the same time, FDI flows into the Cayman Islands reached \$15 billion. Puerto Rico, as a tax haven, is home to many TNC affiliates that produce little relative to their (reported) FDI stocks. As Bridgman (2012, p. 38) observes, many large U.S.-domiciled TNCs actively engage in "accounting gimmicks, to 'shift' profits to Puerto Rico" where a firm can pretend its production took place in a subsidiary based in Puerto Rico to avoid mainland U.S. taxes. This relates to how the portfolios of many TNCs have become heavily financialized. For instance, in 1999, it was reported that those companies active in tax havens obtained 30 percent of their profits through their affiliates, whereas these tax haven–based affiliates account for less than 4 percent of the companies' employment (Bridgman, 2012, pp. 38–39). Many large TNCs have

TABLE 2.1. FDI FLOWS FOR DEVELOPING COUNTRIES OF THE CARIBBEAN*					
	1970	1980	1990	2000	2012
Inflows	320	277	425	2,114	6,164
Outflows	1	0	29	161	1,761
Source: UNCTAD, 2017.					
*Based on US\$ millions; excludes tax havens, Cuba, and Puerto Rico.					

moved their headquarters into the Caribbean region. Grand Cayman (the largest of the three islands that make up the Cayman Islands) is already the chosen domicile for over 40 percent of Hong Kong–listed companies. Heavily representative of the transnationalization process are the banking interests that have become inseparable from the global financial system (see, especially, the work of Anthony van Fossen, 2012).

There are a rising number of Caribbean-based contractors and capitalists who now work with TCC fractions. In fact over recent decades we see across the region transnational fractions arising among many local capitalists and elites (Robinson, 2003). A growing number of top Caribbean capitalists with companies based in the region and abroad are becoming active globally, some with subsidiaries and business operations in the Americas, Asia, Europe, and Africa, entwined with investments moving functionally through the region. Many small and midlevel businesses and subcontractors are constantly seeking to link into global chains of accumulation, to connect into the markets of TNCs—from real estate to import sales, banking, and the economic sectors examined in this study. Many businesses, though, have gone under, having become unsuccessful over the transition of recent decades.

Global capitalist flows appear as a capillary system, with large arteries and organs entwined with other smaller bodies—where, rather than just pulsing back and forth, they become linked together in a new immediate manner operating together across great distances (Castillo-Mussot et al., 2013). This is nowhere more apparent than in global finance, such as in algorithmic trading where automated and long-distance trades take place at a speed and frequency impossible for any human to match. A variety of accumulation processes are functioning through new technologies and organizational advancements—productive forces that allow for new kinds of linkages. Helping us consider the growing transnationality of economic relations, Dicken points out the need for understanding the economy through "multiple scales," describing as problematic the aggregation into "national boxes" of most "statistical data on production, trade, investment and the like." To escape these boxes, we can think "in terms of production circuits and networks" that "cut through, and across, all geographical scales, including the bounded territory of the state" (Dicken, 2007, p. 13). This is not to say that built environments within national and regional settings are unimportant, as discussed further below.

Transnational Class Formation

Central for global capitalism remains the role of *social classes*. Capitalist relations are still dominant, having been reconstituted in the global era. One of the new classes, the TCC, is tied together as a self-conscious class, a class in and for itself whose material basis is in TNCs and the accumulation of global capital (Carroll, 2013; Phillips, 2018; Robinson and Sprague, 2018; Sklair, 2001). Unlike earlier epochs in the history of world capitalism, the concentration and centralization of capital does not involve the amassing and growing power of national, but rather of *transnational*, capitalist groups. For instance, a 2011 analysis of the share ownerships of 43,000 transnational corporations undertaken by scholars at the Swiss Federal Institute of Technology identified a core of 1,318 TNCs with interlocking ownerships (Vitali, Glattfelder, and Battiston, 2011). Each of these core TNCs had ties to two or more other companies and on average they were connected to twenty. Although they represented only 20 percent of global operating revenues, these 1,318 TNCs appeared to collectively own through their shares the majority of the world's largest blue chip and manufacturing firms, representing a further 60 percent of global revenues—for a total of 80 percent of the world's revenue (Robinson and Sprague, 2018).

Theoretical approaches for understanding the TCC have differed. For Robinson (2004, 2014a), global capitalism represents a qualitatively new stage in ongoing and open-ended crisis-prone evolution of world capitalism. The TCC is the dominant social class in the newest era, an age of global capitalism. Conceptually, Robinson, and other theorists (such as, Harris, 2006; Liodakis, 2010; H. Watson, 2013), use a historical materialist understanding of the division of labor into social classes. They understand individual members of the TCC as those directly involved in global capital accumulation, while others involved in its promotion but not accumulation are described as transnationally oriented elites, functionaries, or other professional and managerial strata. In addition, these scholars do not see the TCC as monolithic. As Harris (2016) has pointed out, for instance, different fractions exist within this class—such as statist-TCC fractions in Russia, China, and the Persian Gulf where sovereign wealth funds and state enterprises are used for global accumulation. With various geopolitical (or geoeconomic) conflicts now playing out on the world stage, beneath the surface we can see how these are often in part rooted in the competition and tension between different fractions of transnational capital, with the need for transnational capitalists to constantly expand their profits.

By comparison, Leslie Sklair constructs a TCC model that not only includes people directly involved in global capital accumulation but also those who promote it as well, such as media and state functionaries. He presents a TCC structure that includes four fractions: those who (1) own and/or control the major TNCs and their local affiliates (corporate fraction), (2) globalizing bureaucrats and politicians (state fraction), (3) globalizing professionals (technical fraction), and (4) globalizing merchants and media (consumerist fraction). While, in my view, this approach fails to identify the fundamental differences in the relations of production and power that some of these groups wield, his idea of a "global system" lays out well how globalizing forces around the world are conflicting and engaging in contradictory relations with more domestically rooted groups. Sklair furthermore outlines four major propositions in regard to the TCC. First, it is a class that benefits from its relation to TNCs, emerging "more or less in control of the processes of globalization" (Sklair, 2001, p. 5). Second, it acts as a "transnational dominant class in some spheres." Third, a "profit-driven culture-ideology of consumerism" exists as a mechanism of persuasion, solidifying the participation of populations in global capitalist chains of consumption. And, finally, he argues convincingly, the TCC is faced with two global crises: class polarization and ecological crisis (Sklair, 2001, p. 6).

Much debate and research in political sociology, political economy, and political science have also centered on the study of "power elites" (as pioneered by C. Wright Mills [1956/2000] through a Weberian-influenced analysis of status and power, and continued in the work of Domhoff [1967/2013]). Some more recent studies have examined the rise of global power elites. One of the more notable studies in this regard is David Rothkopf's (2009) *Superclass*. Rothkopf, a former high-level U.S. government official and associate of Henry Kissinger, interviewed several hundred of the top global elite and found considerable evidence for increasing social and cultural integration of global elites.

The existence of a TCC and transnational elite does not mean that these groups are internally consistent and free of conflict. There are still warring elements within a brotherhood divided by the endemically competitive nature of capitalism. For instance, specific fractions of capital hold closer ties with some state strata compared to others. As Ietto-Gillies explains, transnationally oriented capitalists with interests across various countries "use their economic position and clout to strengthen their ties and claims . . . [with] specific countr[ies] and exercise influence to secure special treatment" (Sprague and Ietto Gillies, 2014, p. 44). We can see many examples of intense rivalry and competition among transnational capitalist conglomerates. Whereas the policies of many state apparatuses may benefit transnational capital over more locally or nationally oriented capitalists, this does not mean that these policies benefit *all* transnational capitalist fractions equally. Rather, state policies may most benefit certain TCC fractions and TNC groupings over others (i.e., loopholes in regulatory systems that benefit finance firms, or auto companies that are in part subsidized by a strong state, or tax holidays and other policies benefiting mining companies so as to ensure their con-

Figure 2.3 A small shopping center in Kingston, Jamaica. (Photo by author.)

tinued profitability—these are policies first and foremost that benefit transnational capitalists).

Transnational class relations are also emerging among the working and popular classes, with, for instance, different static, diaspora, and dynamic global social relations forming (Lin, 2016; Robinson, 2014a; Struna, 2009). In their consumption and production, popular classes around the world are becoming tied into transnational accumulation. In the Caribbean, for example, a vast array of new minimalls and air-conditioned shopping centers have been set up in recent decades, where many go to buy imported products or to eat in restaurant chains. (See Figure 2.3.)

As considered below, a broad array of middle-strata groups are also becoming entwined with global capitalism. Key among these in the Caribbean are contractors and business networks that, as local contingents, are becoming incorporated in diverse ways into transnational chains of accumulation. Here it is useful to recall Manuel Castells's concept of a network society, wherein novel "business networks, under different forms, in different contexts, and from different cultural expressions" have come about during the era of global capitalism (2009, p. 211).

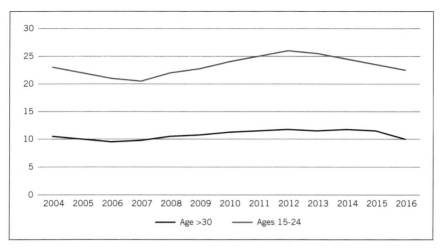

Figure 2.4 Youth and adult unemployment in the Caribbean. (IMF, 2018.)

Also under this globalized phase of capitalism, large groups of "surplus humanity" have been rendered useless, as a structurally marginalized part of the popular classes (M. Davis, 2007). Some workers, meanwhile, who in the past had more protected statuses, have been propelled into the newly dispossessed or precarious urban life. In many Caribbean nations this is a hard-felt reality, with one of the world's highest levels of youth unemployment and many others struggling just to get by (Ball et al., 2011; M. Forbes, 2015). (See Figure 2.4.)

The popular classes have a difficult challenge in organizing in the face of transnational capital and unresponsive political authorities (Lin, 2016; Scipes, 2011). With the rolling back of the state's responsibilities and large parts of the region's population existing as marginalized surplus, their political struggle is made more difficult as leftist political parties and infrastructure have been historically undermined. In recent years, many inspired youth and grassroots efforts have been channeled into NGO (nongovernmental organization) work and nonprofit charities, rather than political mobilization from below. Arundhati Roy (2014) describes an "NGO-ization of resistance" as having a pernicious impact on movements from below. In places such as Haiti, a donor and NGO complex has been a key plank for stabilizing the country while at the same time providing a bare amount of aid for people living in desperate conditions (though riddled with inefficiencies and moneymaking schemes). This gets at the structural limitations and contradictions of global capitalism in the most impoverished zones of the Third World (Edmonds, 2012a).

Even those who are unemployed, or structurally marginalized, may consume (even if only at low levels) in markets that link them into transnational chains. Furthermore many cultural and commoditized relations (from entertainment to social media) can function in part to bind the oppressed and marginalized into the system (Rowling, 1987). We also see concerted efforts in this regard. World Bank projects, for example, are seeking to propel a process under which marginalized and lower-income populations become engaged in more commoditized relations. World Bank programs to support microfinancing in rural communities in Haiti, for instance, are aiming to get marginalized rural communities more involved in monetized social relations, by funding small rural stores with imported products. While this can have the positive benefits of heightened consumption and access to goods for locals, it also needs to be seen as a mechanism through which poor rural people are entered into global capitalist relations—even if this occurs at a very minimal level—their social reproduction slowly becomes reconfigured, reflecting a process of "social and political reengineering" and deepening inequality. As a contradictory process it entails a reconstruction of hegemonic consent in the countryside (see, e.g., Haiti Grassroots Watch, 2012e).

In Jamaica, some of the lowest income urban populations have long had no access to property deeds. Projects by local state and transnational institutions are working to extend housing deeds even to families who dwell in the most dilapidated of slum housing. This can provide people access to credit and helps integrate them at a very low level into local banking structures. These are banks that in turn are entwined with larger global financial institutions. So, we can see how various institutional mechanisms have worked to integrate some of the region's poorest and most marginalized communities into marketized relations that are in fact entwined with the transnational capitalist economy. New linkages into the global capitalist system thus can create opportunities but also intensify inequality and precarity and bring on new rounds of primitive accumulation (Gafar, 1998). These transformative processes faced by the popular classes also include an array of gendered and racialized dynamics. While potentially allowing more investment and disposable income, it serves also to produce inequality and threaten some of the country's social compacts—as states seek to roll back their social spending.

Across many parts of the region, working and popular classes (even those without formal employment in major industries) are becoming integrated (to various degrees) into the global capitalist economy. Global capitalism seeps into the crevices of the fragmenting national economies, where even people living on very low levels of consumption, the structurally marginalized, what Mike Davis describes as the inhabitants of a "planet of slums," are becoming objectively connected with today's global society (even if it is through sparse consumption, relying on one another, hustling to survive, or dependence on aid groups or the crumb's left behind by the upper and middle strata). All of this said, the structural features of one's society, and one's very existence in it, can be difficult to ascertain. Yet the proactive organization of the marginalized, the poor, and working people of the region, those exploited by or shut out from the global capitalist economy (with many examples in the contemporary Caribbean), gives voice to the tenuous nature of global capitalism.

Transnationally Oriented Policy Makers and the State Apparatus

How can we conceptualize the role of the state—and those operating through the state—in the era of global capitalism? Rather than looking at the state as a monolithic or a static edifice, I emphasize here that the state is a social relation of domination (a social power relation), wherein different social groups operate through its apparatuses. In capitalist society, the state takes on a vital managerial role for stabilizing and reproducing capitalist social relations especially when dominant groups are unable to coordinate successfully among themselves (Poulantzas, 1978; Resch, 1992).

The reproduction of state apparatuses (as a social power relation) are constantly being determined through socio-political conflict, which is shaped by many structural constraints and contingencies. The state, as Gramsci understood it, is "the entire complex of practical and theoretical activities with which the ruling class not only justifies and maintains its dominance, but manages to win the active consent of those over whom it rules" (Gramsci, 1971, p. 244). As Robinson adds "the state becomes the 'integral' or 'extended' state, in Gramsci's formula, encompassing political plus civil society, a conception aimed at overcoming the illusory dualism of the political and the economic" (2005, p. 4). Rather than a cold lifeless state institution we need to consider the state as a social power relation. Consider, for example, the struggles occurring between contending forces within a resource-starved state or a city municipality, the manner in which officials use coercive force against the poor, the historical and spatial dynamics that institutional agents operate from, or the role of wealthy and powerful interests that seek to influence public opinion and the policymakers of a state. From this perspective, the "state is a social power relation, expressing the agency, interests, and ideologies of specific socio-political forces, particularly classes and class fractions, in given historical contexts. Political outcomes, including governance outcomes, are thus understood as the contingent products of struggles between contending forces" (Hameiri and Jones, 2015, p. 52).

Hilbourne Watson explains the historical importance of the development of the state for capitalism. Institutionalizing the right to exploit (Watson,

2015, p. 32) is indispensable for "providing the infrastructure of capitalism by levying and collecting taxes; funding or subsidizing research and development activities; building or financing the construction of public projects like ports, roads, highways, and defense and military security programmes; providing education and supporting the arts and other cultural activities" (p. 11).

Liberal universalized rights that emerged with the rise of the nation-state were supposed to promote a new fraternalism. Yet these rights evolved concomitant with systems of exploitation and repression, engulfed by political systems designed by sectors of the bourgeoisie. These new rights were never · meant to extend relative equality to the masses, as is often believed. Hannah Arendt (1966, pp. 267, 298–301) famously made a similar point in her critique of the nation-state and in the context of the "rights of man."

State apparatuses thus serve as structures through which the powers of class relations congeal and operate, and they serve to stabilize and help produce (and reproduce) the social order. As Nicos Poulantzas observes, rather than members of the capitalist class serving directly in the state (though this does occur sometimes as a revolving door), governing political groups normally carry out this task. As "relatively autonomous," these political groups and state elites seek to maintain legitimacy in the eyes of the citizenry or electorate, even as they overwhelmingly operate in the "collective" interests of capital (Poulantzas, 1978). To stabilize and reproduce themselves in power, state policy makers must gain the consent of the exploited (Gramsci, 1971) and cement cross-class alliances. In order to do this they must make compromises, all in the name of solidifying the greater good, or, rather, the dominant order.

Alongside the changes occurring through globalization in recent decades, our common argument (Harris, 2006; Jayasuriya, 2005; Robinson, 2004, 2014a) has become that many state elites and policy makers have become transnationally oriented. While many political conflicts and competitions (such as through elections) take on heated nationalistic rhetoric and play out through local frameworks, groups have arisen that are transnationally oriented. This can be confusing to watch play out, especially as what elites and those in power say in public and what they say behind closed doors can be two drastically different things. While praising the nation, many state elites and policy makers in fact have increasingly come to depend on *transnational* capital for their own social reproduction—from their own financial and property assets to campaign funding, from the income brought in from taxes to the role of the media, to policy planning, and to the securing of jobs for friends or family and themselves when out of office.

State elites though must still appeal to their constituencies at home. They must often interact with a variety of less mobile and less privileged social groups and classes, from the middle strata and working class to the unemployed, marginalized, and working poor. Because of this, even as ties between state policy makers and the TCC deepen, national rhetoric and state policies at times are in *apparent contradiction* with TCC interests. In this way, political leaders attempt to maintain political legitimacy at home even while deepening practices of a transnational nature. Here they must navigate a crisis of legitimacy as they abandon earlier indicative development planning with a view to foment national economic development. As these state elites become entangled with—and dependent on—processes of global capital accumulation, they have helped spur on the transition from national or international processes to transnational processes. The state itself is not disappearing, rather it is transforming into a proactive instrument for promoting the interests of transnational capital (and often, particular fractions within it).

Some governments, such as in Saint Kitts and Dominica, have resorted to selling citizenship. This allows wealthy individuals abroad, often from China or the Middle East, to obtain passports, allowing them to travel to more than a hundred countries (Edmonds, 2012b; Grell-Brisk, 2018). Many states in the Caribbean also have placed new fees and taxes on remittances. Such measures are highly unpopular, as so many depend on these remittances for their livelihoods. In other instances, Caribbean governments have failed to collect significant revenue, for example, from the visitors on cruise ships—such tourists pay an average of just $15 to the countries where their boats land. Caribbean policy makers attempted but failed to cooperate in agreeing on a common head tax for cruise ship passengers in the 1990s and early 2000s, when cruise company lobbyists defeated the effort, playing the various island governments against each other. In navigating a globally competitive arena state elites face tensions and pressures but also find avenues for their own enrichment and advancement.

Regarding the role of the state, my approach in this book is influenced by (1) Robinson's "transnationally oriented elite" argument regarding how groups of state functionaries are promoting a parallel political project connected to the TCC's class power (2010b),[11] and (2) Sklair's "global system" approach (2002), which argues that contemporary states can face ongoing struggles between locally and transnationally oriented class fractions. However, whereas Sklair describes a transnationally oriented elite fraction of globalizing bureaucrats and politicians as part of the TCC, I do not concur (Sprague, 2009). Rather, I describe them as transnationally oriented policy makers, functionaries, and state elites who are not necessarily a part of the TCC. I argue, echoing Harris (2016) and Robinson (2014a), that many of these state elites (as social groups operating as managerial and technocratic cadre through state apparatuses) have shifted away from being oriented toward national and international accumulation and instead are becoming oriented toward an interest in transnational accumulation. This does not mean that transnationally oriented elites operate in the interests of all transnational capitalists. As Robinson (2016, p. 264) explains, "There is intense competition and rivalry among transnational capitalist conglomerates so that state policies may benefit some conglomerates over others." It suggests, though, that many state policies have come to benefit transnational capital over older forms of capital.

Here, similar to other scholars of the "global capitalism school" (Harris, 2016; Robinson, 2004; Sklair, 2002), I posit a break from the "New Imperialism" schools of thought that focus on the U.S. nation-state and its corporations as the sole force behind capitalist globalization while its elites pursue their own imperial interests (Harvey, 2005; Panitch and Gindin, 2013; Wood, 2005).[12] Instead, I aim to emphasize the integrative, expansive, and unequal nature of global capitalism, the endemic competitive nature of the circuits of capital, and how diverse social and political forces have come to entwine with these changes in contradictory and crisis-prone ways. Clearly the U.S. state apparatus is the dominant world and regional power (Maingot and Lozano, 2005), but we need to consider this in light of the changes and shifting structural features occurring through globalization (Sprague, 2014b). In addressing the role of governments in facilitating the Caribbean's heightened integration with the global economy, this work emphasizes not just the role of the most influential state apparatus in the region, the United States, but also acknowledges the role of transnationally oriented state strata in countries across the region and abroad (as well as the role of other local and regional groups). While policy makers operating through the U.S. state and its various apparatuses play a central role in the region, they also increasingly have come to promote conditions beneficial for circuits of *global capital accumulation* and in the interests of the TCC, not domestically oriented capitalists.

Examining the new linkages that are formed among state, business, and elite forces, we can ask: What does this mean for notions of national democracy and sovereignty, as certain key areas of national decision-making are being shifted upward and outward via the capitalist transnationalization process? When national state policy makers and managers participate in that shifting process and implement those decisions while claiming that they have no alternative in a globalizing world, they often seem to imply that they are being forced by others to act against the "national interest." This requires us to probe more critically into the future of the nation-state form and the limits of bourgeois democracy on a domestic plane. What role does the national state play in the relationships of power in the global era? How is hegemony and domination being restructured in the global/transnational era and in the Caribbean in particular?

I suggest that, rather than the old nation-state imperialism promoted by national elites and solidified through their international alliances and monopolies, we are now seeing power dynamics under which a wider variety of state managers, most important among these, those operating out of Washington, DC, are promoting conditions beneficial for fractions of the TCC. Even more stark than the tensions that sometimes occur between different TCC fractions are the conflicts that TCC fractions (aligned with the United States and NATO) have had with other more nationally oriented groups or policymakers promoting leftist projects. These include groups and policymakers facilitating more endogenous developmental goals, often promoting alternative political models or sources of national legitimacy, and multipolarity on the world stage. Robinson observes that "a new class fractionation, or axis, has been occurring between national and transnational fractions of classes" where many "states have been captured by transnationally oriented dominant groups who use them to integrate their countries into emergent global capitalist structures" (Robinson, 2005, p. 5). This contestation occurs in different ways—for instance, from a nation's political scene to more forceful integration and through culture-ideology.

Let us consider the example of Iraq: rather than construct a new imperialist domain, the illegal U.S. invasion and occupation of Iraq in the early twenty-first century was first and foremost a project to bring Iraq *into* global capitalism under the U.S. umbrella, where particular fractions of the TCC most benefit. While many of these TCC fractions are aligned with elites in the U.S. government and its allies, Yousef Baker (2014) points out how a variety of fractions of the TCC have benefited under that nation's postwar economic restructuring (such as with the transnationally oriented capitalists from Australia, and statist fractions of the TCC from China, as well as top elites from many other parts of the world).

Officials operating through U.S. state apparatuses then have at times taken on the role of a cudgel, smashing barriers to TCC power. At the same time many of these officials hold some subjective framings tied to ideas of the old international order, and are nestled within bloated military and security budgets that need reasons to exist (Harris, 2013, p. 739). Even as new transnational relations emerge this occurs in a heterogeneous system where unilateral policy initiatives exist, especially in regard to the major powers connected with military-industrial-intelligence apparatuses. The U.S. strategy has proven effective in promoting globalization that moved beyond classical imperialism. U.S. leaders have sought an elusive, absolute global hegemony that is compromised by the need to form alliances with many, bearing in mind that hegemony is never absolute. This kind of relationship, though, is different than a so-called global empire. Often we don't consider that ruling classes around the world are clear that they benefit immensely from having the United States help to direct and facilitate the global economy, while being compelled to subordinate itself to many global norms and institutions and never ceding its dominant role in the process. Dialectically, transformation always entails degrees of preservation.

Different strategic visions are pursued within the halls of power. New soft power strategies, for example, are being honed. In the Caribbean in recent years certain TCC fractions with close ties to the U.S. establishment lobbied to drop the more than fifty-year embargo on Cuba, especially as transnational capitalist interests in Brazil, Russia, China, and other countries have increased their business in Cuba (Klapper, 2015). Over time, some U.S. officials have come into alignment with this position. Rather than an embargo, many top U.S. strategic thinkers now see a policy of gradually opening Cuba to global investors as more advantageous, as it can help reestablish a proper-tied class that they believe could help break apart the country's socialist project from within. Still, more militarist wings within the U.S. establishment seek to renew hard-line policies, especially those reactionary elements aligned with the right wing of the Cuban diaspora in south Florida.

Transnationally oriented dominant groups have nuanced strategies and various mechanisms to construct their hegemony and coercive domination. Throughout the history of capitalism, dominant groups have developed means of maintaining and protecting their class rule. Through the era of global capitalism, we can see how restructured means for reproducing hegemony and domination are emerging, including within the Caribbean basin. Even still, these groups often vie with one another and utilize diverse "enlightened" and "unenlightened" strategies for managing their various interests.

In theorizing global political economy, many scholars have chosen to emphasize a mechanical basis of change, where parts of society are externally related: whereas the capitalist economy globalizes, states as political entities pursue a self-interested territorial logic. Yet this is an approach that ignores real-world policy-making processes, in which "the state extends backward, is grounded in the forces of civil society, and is fused in a myriad of ways with capital itself." (Robinson, 2014a, p. 105). State-centrism thus ignores the emergent transnational orientation of many state actors whose activities cannot be separated from broader civil society and capitalist relations. Robinson explains how we need to see the diverse segments of our changing society in their dialectical totality:

> The hallmark of a dialectical approach is recognition that relations between different parts—processes, phenomena—are *internal* relationships. An *internal relation* is one in which each part is constituted

in its relation to the other, so that one cannot exist without the other and has meaning only when seen within the relation, whereas an *external relation* is one in which each part has an existence independent of its relation to the other. The different dimensions of social reality in the dialectical approach do not have an "independent" status insofar as each aspect of reality is constituted by, and is constitutive of, a larger whole of which it is an internal element. Distinct dimensions of social reality may be *analytically distinct* yet are *internally interpenetrated* and *mutually constitutive* of each other as internal elements of a more encompassing process, so that, for example, the economic/capital and the political/state are *internal* to capitalist relations. (Robinson, 2014a, p. 104)

Emphasizing the role of social production and how processes such as uneven geographic development are rooted in it helps us best understand our world. Understanding globalization in this way presents a challenge for social scientists who have long grouped institutions and social classes into separate national boxes according to the frontiers in which their orientations were apparently largely affixed. Media analyses as well as many scholarly approaches regularly echo nation-state centrism (see, e.g., Padget, 2008), where many processes are reduced to conflict and cooperation between nations and nation-state based groups. By focusing on our world through its social contours, we are forced to reconsider how social forces congeal and operate through institutions in the global era—processes that are not solely rooted in the national. Here we are forced to think about how the deep changes that have occurred over the closing decades of the twentieth century and into the twenty-first century hold unique implications for our world society.

National and Regional Particularities

This book's theorization of a TCC and the rise of transnationally oriented technocrats and other elites should not be seen as discounting national and regional particularities and the role of phenomena such as nationalism. Nationalism has been instrumental in the integration of the region into global capitalism. While some argue that nationalism serves as a countertrend to globalization, let us consider here how nationalism has been used by transnationally oriented elites and capitalist forces. As the contradictory nature of capitalist globalization becomes more and more explosive and unstable, nationalist rhetoric and discourse becomes very much a reaction to the instability but one that is usually absent of a class-based analysis. However, some political projects and movements from below have sought to recast patriotism and national myths, even incorporating them into regional and internationalist narratives of resistance. Through the lens of nationalism, sovereignty, geopolitics, and historical memory, we can see how diverse particularities coexist with the rising transnational forces that I identify.

Nationalism is regularly described as the feeling of one's country having traits superior to other countries or the advocating for political independence and sovereignty for one's country. Hilbourne Watson describes nationalism as a "bourgeois ideology that privileges and fetishizes territoriality, equates bourgeois class interests with the universal interests of the nation, blunts the class struggle, and works against the working class becoming a class for itself" (2013, p. 42). During the period in which capitalist nation-states arose, there came about the "imagined community" of the so-called national society (B. Anderson, 1991), where each nation-state was seen as existing as a separate social system. As an ideological mechanism, nationalism is important for the legitimization of those in power, as is the construction of historical narratives where the nation's polity holds a shared identity and joins together against so-called common enemies.

Yet, nationalism has been an important factor in many Third World struggles against colonial and elite rule. Once national liberation was won, nationalism was vital for reproducing the ideological bedrock of the emergent postcolonial states. Linden Lewis explains that this took place in the region through the combination of multiple factors: "History, culture, imperial coercion, monetary pressures, and geopolitics combine to configure received notions of sovereignty, development, and democracy in the Caribbean" (2013, p. 9). Franz Fanon (1968) looking at the contradictions of national formation in the periphery, and in regard to class, warned that new elite groups were forming within the postcolonial world, even while relying for their legitimacy on a discourse of national liberation. Yet, during the closing decades of the twentieth century and into the twenty-first century, especially, the nationalist discourses linked to states with leftist and national liberation origins became more and more tenuous, and as "without the alternative Soviet bloc, virtually the whole world has been obliged to conform to anti-social neoliberal policies" (D. Johnson, 2018). Here we can point to many examples around the world, from the Middle East and Southeast Asia to Africa, Latin America, and the Caribbean. The realities of the globalizing capitalist market alongside extreme pressures exerted by powerful political interests have forced even socialist Cuba into making major compromises (such as with the growing privatization of parts of the island's economy) (Bell Lara, 2008).

In recent years, right-wing nationalism has been on the ascent in many parts of the western hemisphere, in both the global north and the global south, often seeming to embrace protectionist and isolationist stances, in apparent contradiction with globalization.[13] Confronted with the political realities of populist frustration with rising inequality, crime, and disappearing opportunities, some reactionary groups strike tones that frame their actions as championing working people's ideals even while strengthening neoliberal, antiunion, and ultimately racist policies and structures. This has entailed reproducing the dominant order but under a refurbished conservative ideology (Rangel and Sprague-Silgado, 2017). In the name of protecting the "middle class," blue-collar jobs, and even the illusion of defying the establishment, right-wing groups marshal antimigrant policies and specifically target those that organize for worker rights and gender equality.

A case in point is Trumpism. Some observers see Trump's nationalist rhetoric and his call for renegotiating the North American Free Trade Agreement (NAFTA) as a move toward protectionism. However, the Trumpian right functions as "a highly contradictory and unstable far-right response to the crisis of global capitalism," rather than "a trenchant policy of protectionism and populism" (Robinson, 2017). Trump's so-called nationalist backlash against NAFTA is better seen as a need by elites to "update the treaty alongside the transformation of the US and the global economy in the years since NAFTA went into effect in 1994" (Robinson, 2017). Since NAFTA and the World Trade Organization (WTO) went into effect in the mid-1990s, "the global economy has continued to experience development and transformation. In particular, the transnationalization of services and the rise of the so-called digital/data economy—including communications, informatics, digital and platform technology, e-commerce, financial services, professional and technical work, and a host of other intangible products, such as film and music, that require intellectual property protections—have moved to the center of the global capitalist agenda" (Robinson, 2017). For top elites there is a need then to update NAFTA with provisions related to the digital trade, as well as to help Mexican elites gain new tools for bringing about the privatization of the country's public assets and revise the country's labor code by lifting regulations on the hiring and firing of workers (Salas Porras, 2017). By promoting nationalist rhetoric, arguing that Mexican leaders have outsmarted U.S. leaders, and so on, the Trumpian right helps distract from and obscure the actual goals of renegotiating NAFTA, which are to promote the advancing interests of transnational business elites. As Robinson (2017) concludes: "Beyond public discourse, there is nothing populist in the policies that the Trump government has so far put forth. Trumponomics involves deregulation, slashing social spending, dismantling of what remains of the welfare state, privatization, tax breaks to corporations and the rich, and an expansion of state subsidies to capital—in short, neoliberalism on steroids." Supranational treaties such as NAFTA not only are planned out in an undemocratic manner but are clearly meant to benefit big business.[14]

With mounting crises, we see then the rise of rightist populism and some neo-fascistic contingents where certain elites have ridden waves of discontent through nationalist rhetoric and by channeling popular discontent against marginalized groups and migrants, or against neoliberal bureaucrats aloof and disconnected from local sentiments. It should not escape our attention that the main reason for the comeback of the right and the rise of some fascistic tendencies and their increasing contemporary psychosocial appeal does not lie in their own mobilization or recruitment drives but rather in the reign of neoliberalism and the failure of liberal democracy to offer any real hope to large segments of the population facing increasing inequality and a downward spiral of social and economic mobility. To be clear, any form that Fascism takes in the twenty-first century will be very different from its earlier manifestations.

Rightist currents, some within the TCC, have at times challenged the plans of "enlightened" liberal segments of the TCC, with different parts of the ruling class engaged in varying ideological strategies to renew its legitimacy. Key among these are ideological mechanisms of splitting and disorganizing the working classes, including the old tried-and-true racism, jingoism, and xenophobia. In the Caribbean so too elites face legitimacy crises, where right-wing groups in the region have peddled nationalist discourses while unleashing xenophobic campaigns and assaults on marginalized and exploited populations—seeking to reproduce the dominant order but under a refurbished ideology. A vital part of this has been the constant demonization of the left and grassroots movements, and the manipulation of historical memory so as to suit elite interests, as is on constant display in the region's media monopolies.

Sivakumar Velayutham (2016) points out how national symbols and rhetoric have become a mechanism through which a wide variety of policy makers facilitate competitive engagement with the global economy. He emphasizes how, through the era of global capitalism, state elites promote "national champions," even as government regulation and labor protections have been undermined through neoliberal reforms that have strengthened transnational capital. This is on clear display with regards to sports. Nationalism and national identity is repackaged as a discursive tool for competition in the global arena. Audiences celebrate "national champions" on media outlets that are owned by transnational capitalists, cheering for their local sports heroes wearing jerseys made in subcontracted sweatshops linked into global supply chains.

The capitalist state has always functioned to institutionalize unequal power relations. Yet in the global phase of world capitalism, state elites increasingly come to see their interests neither in national development nor in finding strategies that develop the capacities of local popular classes or meet the desires of national capitalists. Many policy makers have abandoned or are being forced to abandon policies of domestic development and "national goals," and instead are moving toward policies of elite-oriented transnational engagement, which might be shrouded in packages of "national heroes," but where in fact the emphasis is on constructing a climate conducive to global investors. National states as political organs, with all of their repressive and ideological forces, are (to different degrees and through particular conditions and forms) being tasked for "reconfiguring sovereignty to meet challenges and demands that stem from relentless global market integration to strengthen and broaden global capital accumulation" (H. Watson, 2015, p. 10).

Patriotic calls are taken up by various political currents, with divergent narratives and goals. Leftist, popular, and socialistic groups have sought, for instance, to illuminate the international and national histories of struggles from below against the powers that be. Venezuela's populist left-wing project, for example, has promoted Bolivarianism in seeking to counter regional domination by the U.S. state, western transnational oil companies, and many other powerful capitalist interests. While facing its own internal problems, Venezuela's Bolivarian Chavista movement has linked the local struggle of the popular classes with a national and regional anti-imperialist narrative and headed up the creation of new regional bodies such as ALBA (as will be discussed further in Chapter 3).

At the same time, the United States and its NATO allies, with their tremendous resources, have ceaselessly targeted Venezuela for regime change and are currently carrying out an economic war against the country; this has combined with local speculation and a disastrous exchange rate system, alongside the dropping of world oil prices, leading to a severe crisis in the country. Caught in this unforgiving and contradictory arena, Venezuela's Bolivarian project has relied on making financial and trade deals with Chinese and Russian government enterprises and statist-fractions of the TCC (Harris, 2009b; OilVoice, 2018). By 2018, the Venezuelan state was working with a transnationally oriented Russian bank to launch the first state-backed cryptocurrency ("the Petro"), in order to get around an expanding U.S. financial blockade. Even as the socialistic-oriented project faces an intense economic war (i.e., with its ability to refinance loans cut off by the U.S. state) (Weisbrot, 2017), Venezuela remains enwrapped in the global market, where a number of businesses from around the world continue to be active in the country, and with the cryptocurrency BitCoin now commonly used by the population. The "soft power" strategies by Washington and its allies look set only to intensify, targeting opponents with destabilization and alternative political projects with regime change (especially within those third world countries that are wealthy in natural resources). Venezuelans in particular have every reason to fear a foreign sponsored proxy war.

A number of states in the Caribbean and the Americas have over the years cooperated with Bolivarian Venezuela and taken part in the antineoliberal Bolivarian Alliance for the Peoples of Our America (ALBA) bloc. The experiences of these nations have reflected the extremely contradictory and tenuous path for alternative attempts at development in the region, with resource-starved states facing pressures to boost social spending alongside market pressures and the always present potential for corruption (Cusack, 2019; Edmonds, 2012b; Robinson, 2018). For small, resource-starved Caribbean states a progressive path forward is marked by innumerable hazards and pitfalls.

With all of this in mind, geopolitical conflicts clearly exist. I argue, though, that we need to see this in the context of global capitalism. Across the region, national states are being restructured within the globalization process that many state officials have helped advance, partly through neoliberal initiatives. Even those political projects resisting neoliberal policies (or, at least, rejecting some such policies) are required to make numerous compromises and interactions with global market forces. U.S. state elites and their apparatuses have been key for enforcing and promoting neoliberal policies and transnational capitalism in the region and have come to work alongside an emergent network of transnationally oriented state elites and a variety of supranational and national state apparatuses. While we can point to many dominant trends, this remains an open-ended and conflict-ridden process, especially as state officials must still deal with domestic issues and many other particularities.

When considering local, national, and regional particularities it is useful to consider what Hilbourne Watson (2015) describes as sovereignty existing in "soft" and "advanced" forms. As a powerful state exhibiting "advanced" sovereignty, the United States intervenes militarily, diplomatically, and so on. U.S. nationalism is entwined then with justifying these incursions, where U.S. citizens who challenge their country's ad infinitum wars are deemed unpatriotic. Nationalism then cloaks the actual role of corporate and state elites, portraying them as part of a national polity rather than as part of an oppressive ruling group promoting exploitation and repression. "Soft" sovereignty, by contrast, describes how many other state elites (often in the global south) operate with capabilities that are much more limited. So too, though, these state elites often use nationalist rhetoric to shore up their legitimacy, even while regularly pursuing policies beneficial to fractions of the TCC. There is a vast unevenness, though, between the capacities and resources that the policy makers of different states can bring to bear, especially when contrasting post-colonial states to major powers. While many postcolonial and developmental states "have found their margin for manoeuvre reduced by debt and the demands of global integration," more powerful states (many of them in the West) more "generally retain considerable resources to shape global outcomes and global ideas" (Grugel, 2004, p. 31).

Let us consider some concrete examples of these dynamics at play in the region, especially with regard to the "advanced" sovereignty of the United States in the region. In one example, officials of Caribbean states have agreed to a "ship-rider agreement," where U.S. law enforcement officials can board a vessel sailing under a Caribbean nation's flag. These U.S. officials operate as unaccountable to local laws and have the right to board and search any vessel suspected of involvement in drug trafficking—reflecting the wide-scale "authorization" that the U.S. Coast Guard operates under in the basin (L. Lewis, 2012b, pp. 73–74). U.S. diplomatic officials in the Caribbean have important influence and often advise or lobby local officials in regard to se-curity matters. It is common even for security officials of local states, such as with Colombian police in the Caribbean port city of Cartagena, to, at the same time, receive a paycheck from the United States DEA (Drug Enforce-ment Administration) (Colombian police official interviewed by the author requested anonymity, personal communication, 2015).

In other examples, we can see how Caribbean state officials, whose very social reproduction has come to be dependent on their nation's integration with transnational capital, have agreed to subject their national institutions to financial supervision by supranational institutions. Jamaican officials, for instance, are required to report on a daily basis to IMF staff residing in the country (Girvan, 2011, p. 20). In Barbados, an IMF representative sits within the country's Central Bank, where, as Linden Lewis explains (2012b, p. 77), "placing an IMF representative in this central financial institution was in-tended to ensure compliance with structural requirements of the neoliberal agenda." In fact, for state officials in the Caribbean, the most important strategies for development are largely not left up to their administrations to choose. When it comes, for instance, to currency and financialization mat-ters in the Caribbean, the key decisions are not made by the central banks of states in the region, but rather at the counters of the transnational banks and TNCs. Neoliberal strategies and policies adopted by local state elites (mostly transnationally oriented themselves) have been designed by and large to ac-celerate the pace of global market integration where the real strength of transnational capitalists' forces is grounded. Important for propelling this process, the Caribbean has long been a target of IMF loans, World Bank programs, USAID financed projects, and Inter-American Development Bank operations. (See Figure 2.5 and Table 2.2.)

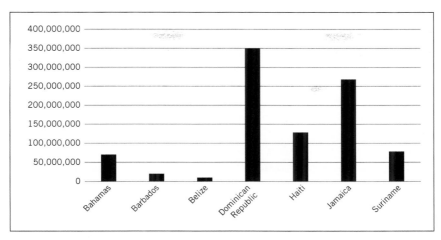

Figure 2.5 Inter-American Development Bank approved operations for 2017 in the Caribbean in US$. (Source: IDB, 2017, pp. 19–20).

TABLE 2.2. USAID SPENDING IN THE CARIBBEAN BY COUNTRY (IN USD, CONSTANT DOLLARS), 1970–2017*

	1970	1980	1990	2000	2010	2017
Bahamas	5,338	49,179	2,667,084	8,401,885	12,504,041	2,013,935
Barbados	2,892,747	774,362	1,379,585	1,545,271	1,436,514	1,132,700
Cuba	N/A	N/A	306,954	6,019,919	19,952,213	6,303,750
Dom. Rep.	110,659,635	153,832,882	47,987,045	33,382,385	77,775,020	69,701,758
Guyana	8,109,771	12,808,145	14,899,176	12,166,822	29,655,136	6,422,639
Haiti	18,747,198	70,607,213	104,149,280	117,199,518	1,123,585,651	449,376,935
Jamaica	10,637,427	37,925,522	133,204,123	30,006,533	25,819,816	33,579,138
Suriname	5,065	38,978	34,106	1,500,881	3,390,424	269,010
Trinidad and Tobago	482,125	660,026	1,594,452	2,236,064	2,545,151	1,896,879

Source: USAID, 2019.
*1970–2000 are obligations, and 2010 and 2017 are disbursements, which began being tracked in 2001.

Fundamental for a nation-state's integration into global capitalism has been the construction and manipulation of historical memory, which has occurred in an uneven way. Michel-Rolph Trouillot describes how, in many ways, "the production of historical narratives involves uneven contribution of competing groups and individuals who have unequal access to the means for such production" (Trouillot, 1997, p. xix).

Even while rhetoric of national liberation and the anticolonial struggles is recycled, this occurs at a time where the political economic structure has become fundamentally altered. While development is no longer geared toward "national goals" and "national development," many play upon the historical memory of earlier periods, a narrative that is now so important for establishing and reproducing the legitimacy of leading local political and economic interests, many who are now seeking to integrate with the global system. However, as a discursive response to the disruptions of globalization, nationalist rhetoric provides no real alternative.

Throughout the late twentieth century, manufacturing and extractive industries, as well as consumer markets, became increasingly integrated into transnational accumulation networks. This is shifting the very structural features of how capitalism functions in the Caribbean. The establishment of a host of supranational agreements, such as the Caribbean Basin Initiative (CBI), Dominican Republic-Central American Free Trade Agreement (DR-CAFTA), various European Union and Caribbean Community (CARICOM) forums, as well as bilateral accords, have helped facilitate this process. A more conducive climate for big business in the region has been fostered through financial liberalization, the standardization of regulations, and creation of new supply chain infrastructure such as with the advent of container shipping and the ongoing construction of deep-water ports. While the region has been entwined with international processes for centuries, so many linkages are now playing out through new and more immediate transnational systems. Even the environmental effects of this can be clearly seen, with fishing stocks exhausted and high levels of plastics circulating in the sea (World Bank, 2016).

Here we must distinguish between surface level appearances and the deeper trends that are occurring. If, as Hilbourne Watson, John Agnew, Ankie Hoogvelt, and others insist, the process of globalization mirrors the unevenness that characterizes the capitalist process, then globalization is not an absolute outcome but a moment. In other words, it is not an irreversible march through history but a complex movement with starts and reversals in which our human destiny remains to be made. Chaos and anarchy are inevitable under capitalism, and while emphasis on what we see in nations and regions (such as with Obama's "Pivot to Asia," Trumpism, Brexit, China's new silk road, and so on) needs consideration, I argue that the whole (heterogeneous and open-ended as it is) is always greater than the sum of its parts. These particularities in many ways reflect the chaos in global processes and draw attention to the symptoms of these processes, even as they escalate. These symptoms, the various strategies, and the stops and starts do not negate or reverse the core trends. In other words, the world is not going back to the late nineteenth century or to the economic world order of the World War II era, or even the early 1970s; however, many reversals that might occur are part of the nodal line of history, a nonlinear but forward historical motion. We need to see national and regional particularities, I argue, in the context of the moment, a moment marked by the profound rise of transnational/global capitalism.

Hegemony and Domination in the Caribbean under Global Capitalism

By hegemony, I refer to the classical Gramscian idea that in different historical periods and societies there has arisen a historic bloc, an alliance of different class forces politically organized around a set of dominant ideas that provide coherence and a planned direction. Moreover, this "historic bloc" operates under one dominant social class that has established its intellectual and moral leadership (Gramsci, 1971, p. 215). Hegemony is developed through the construction of consent (through culture, ideology, the political scene, and other dynamics). Yet, at the same time, depending upon the shifting balance of forces, the ruling class (and its historic bloc) relies heavily on the domination achieved through direct coercion (Budd, 2007). Gramsci observed (writing in the early twentieth century) that powerful groups in capitalist nation-states, particularly in the "west" (as opposed to the "east" [that is Russia]), where civil society was much more entrenched and articulated—increasingly relied on an array of means for constructing consent, but this was always "protected by the armour of coercion" (1971, p. 263).

To promote its hegemony over a crisis-prone global system, the TCC has required a new broad alliance of social forces, a *global historic bloc*. This new historic bloc (with the TCC as its hegemonic class) is made up of TNCs and transnational financial institutions, elites that manage the supranational economic planning agencies, major forces in the dominant political parties, media conglomerates and technocratic elites, and state managers in both North and South (Robinson and Sprague, 2018). Over recent decades, many powerful dominant national groups have transitioned (or begun to transition) toward a transnational orientation, undergoing an insertion into this new global historic bloc. Yet, this new bloc also includes within it many fractures and tensions.

The need by the historic bloc to establish hegemonic consent and coercive control comes in direct response to resistance and struggles for change. While occurring in some periods as isolated or uncoordinated challenges, emancipatory movements (and their ideas) from below can well up, take power, and culminate in their own historic bloc. It is because of peoples' varying views, our striving for freedom and autonomy, our organizing, and the unending threat of a historic bloc being upturned that consent is never fully secured. Consent must constantly be gained—whether through compromise or ideological mystification.

Importantly, the establishment of hegemonic consent must be on an ideological and cultural level with various institutions established to reinforce the norms that then form the basis of a society's "common worldview" or "common sense" (Gramsci, 2000). This refers to peoples' way of thinking and feeling, our conception of the world, and the standards of moral conduct that help us to make sense of our lives. Gramsci argued that the way in which many people in capitalist society perceive the world is often confused and contradictory, containing ideas absorbed from a variety of elite-oriented sources from the present and past, which, for instance, can allow them to accept inequality and oppression as natural. This "common worldview," vital for solidifying the historic bloc of the dominant classes, is thus "created" and "molded" by the hegemonic class and its consensual subalterns (a strata of "organizers of culture" and functionaries who exercise professional and technical activities) (Resch, 1992). Cultural and ideological attacks emanating from the organs of power often are aimed at those not conforming to dominant narratives and agendas.

At the same time, the use of force is always present through legal mechanisms, police, and military or paramilitary apparatuses. The use of force directly impacts the objective material situation of different types of physical and juridical enforcement corporeally cracking down on those competing against established ideological, economic, cultural, and political norms, especially nonconforming social groups and subalterns looking to transform the system.

Here the state plays a vital role through its monopoly on legitimate force, as does the class system with the resources dominant groups can bring to bear. We see numerous examples of this, not just within "metropole" nations but also within the so-called developing world, where coercive force has been promoted as more "acceptable" having been used for centuries to integrate populations into competitively vying markets and imperial systems.

Importantly, as Poulantzas (1978) elaborates, the state cannot be reduced to just the couplet of ideology and repression. Pushed by struggles from below (and sometimes, being from and/or sympathizing with the popular classes), some capitalist state policy makers at times can institute positive material reforms that can provide real benefits for working and popular classes (pp. 28–34). While representing hard-earned victories, such reforms can also be used by enlightened elites to justify their own legitimacy. This flexibility of many advanced capitalist states, for instance, expresses policy makers' ability to head off more radical change by way of enhancing the state's legitimacy among the aggrieved masses—practices that might also be backed by "enlightened groups" within the upper strata. Yet in many parts of the world, especially the Third World, where much larger parts of the population are structurally marginalized, what would appear as progressive reforms in more advanced capitalist states take on a more radical tone. Leftist and popular movements have a long history in the greater Caribbean of successfully pushing political projects that challenge the limits of the bourgeoisie state (Ciccariello-Maher, 2016; Hallward, 2008).

In reaction, U.S. state apparatuses and its allies have launched ceaseless attempts at undermining and overthrowing these projects and others that are not sufficiently acquiescent. The United States has shown time and again that it is the most belligerent actor in the world, continuously creating conditions for ongoing instability, coercion, and violence. Whereas decades ago it was often required to sell Western audiences on particular wars and interventions before they could actually be launched, post–September 11, 2001, warfare and varying forms of western intervention have become more generalized and widely unreported.[15] The internet long used as a tool for surveillance, by 2016 was being increasingly refined for influence operations over social media (Levine, 2018; Blumenthal and Sprague, 2018).

In less developed capitalist states, where the local power blocs are not as stable and where, for instance, the local fraction of the TCC often is weak, states are typically less flexible to popular demands. In this environment, achieving and maintaining reforms benefiting lower-income populations can be violently overridden by less-enlightened dominant groups, a "morally repugnant elite" (Freed, 1994). While reforms in these settings might appear weak and minor from the outside, within a society where vast pools of the population are marginalized (such as in Haiti), even just basic steps of enforcing the rule of law—such as putting on trial wealthy businesspeople who finance paramilitaries—is intensely opposed by powerful interests (Hallward, 2008; Sprague, 2012a).

We can see many instances of contradictory developments. Across many parts of the contemporary Caribbean, for example, state policy makers have facilitated low-cost programs for generic medicines, the availability of which have had a positive impact for many (Pinto Pereira et al., 1998). Important new health care initiatives and coalitions have worked with local states to improve local capabilities. Even in the Dominican Republic, for example, while new laws and policing strategies target migrants and popular movements, at the same time generic antibiotics and other medicines are extremely cheap, and hospital wards in the country have done much to help Haitian migrants crossing over into the country—especially Haitians arriving from small towns and rural areas far away from the capital with a lack of health care infrastructure.

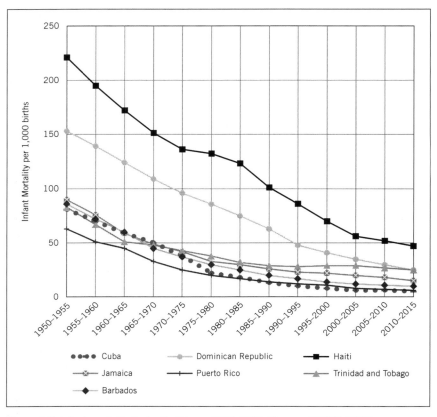

Figure 2.6 Infant mortality in the Caribbean, 1950–2015. (Source: UNICEF, 2017.)

Among the most important of the supranational groups active in the region is the Pan American Health Organization (PAHO), which has helped make great strides in fighting infectious diseases and expanding access, working alongside local health ministries and other supranational groups such as the World Health Organization (WHO), and some smaller UN agencies. Some other groups, such as Partners in Health (PIH), while depending primarily on Western donors, foundations, and trusts, have developed major life-saving infrastructure in helping improve access to health care in Haiti and a number of other countries (see, e.g., Farmer and Sen, 2004). These factors and improving technologies and accessible low-cost medicines have helped contribute to important improvements in health care, as Figure 2.6 reflects.

Yet, at the same time, it is important for the reproduction of dominant groups that those measures—bringing about positive material gains for the popular classes—be undertaken under the umbrella of the common worldview, under the aegis of accepted political practices. Aid and medical efforts thus are framed in a certain way and presented as such to the populace. Socialist Cuba is the starkest example of when this does not take place. Cuba's health care system based on preventive medicine has achieved some of the best results of any lower-income country worldwide and with low expenditures. However, these outstanding results are widely ignored in the global corporate media. Take for instance the Cuban medical brigades operating abroad under the umbrella of a state socialist project, which promotes medical internationalism (Brouwer, 2011; Maxwell, 2008a). In just one of its many international missions, the Cuban medical brigades were among the most decisive initial responders to the earthquake in Port-au-Prince on January 12, 2010. Cuban doctors and medical workers went on to treat over thirty thousand cholera patients in Haiti in the final months of that year (as a cholera outbreak had been introduced through the human waste from outhouses of the Nepalese soldiers serving in the UN occupation force at the time). Cuban efforts received little coverage in the global media, in contrast to the much more expensive (yet often more ineffectual) efforts by Western states and donor-backed efforts (Fawthrop, 2010).

The successes, contradictions, and limitations of such progressive initiatives in the region can be seen through the "dialectic of transformation/ preservation" (Schavelzon and Webber, 2017, p. 178): where under repressive conditions, important gains can be both achieved and ultimately co-opted back into the system (Gramsci, 2000, p. 247). Such contradictory gains, though, which can be used to stabilize the dominant order, also need to be seen within the variety of structural limitations that exist, as well as in connection with the political struggles that take place in these states, and in the context of a global system and the immediate needs of living people. Here we can see how when subaltern forces begin to move from small steps toward fundamentally altering some of the relations of domination, the reaction from dominant groups takes on fanatical form.[16]

Those political projects that seek to go beyond the common worldview, and the normal state of affairs, are always seen as dangerous—especially considering the revolutionary and radical upheavals against many ruling elites and big business monopolies that occurred in the twentieth century. The alternative projects that came about did exhibit many of their own internal contradictions and failures but also accomplished major advances all the while under intense pressure and attack. In order to prevent *major* progressive reforms or revolutionary alternatives, the hegemonic class and its allied social forces (in its historic bloc) rely on a variety of means for achieving domination (Morton, 2007) as they did in undermining earlier alternatives.

Initially, these historic blocs arose out of different capitalist nation-states, so that their means for constructing hegemony and direct domination were oriented toward international, national, regional, or local power—through their militaries, colonial gendarmerie, courts, churches and missionary schools, media, and various civil society institutions that depended on and upheld the social order. Next we see how new and restructured means for constructing hegemony and enforcing the social order are coming about in the global system, even transforming from within some of these earlier institutions. This revamping of hegemony and coercive domination occurs, I argue, in order to uphold the restructuring taking place in the interest of transnational capital and its global historic bloc.

Hilbourne Watson (2015, p. 10) argues that under global capitalism, the state as a political organ, with all of its repressive and ideological forces, is being tasked with "reconfiguring sovereignty to meet challenges and demands that stem from relentless global market integration to strengthen and broaden global capital accumulation." The means for developing hegemony and domination then, many of which the state plays a vital role in deploying, are increasingly geared toward the interests of the new global historic bloc and its hegemonic class, the TCC.

While coercive force remains the "armor" of the dominant order, as discussed further below, increasingly important in a world of rapid and dispersed information flows are the means for achieving hegemonic consent: an array of ideological, cultural, and political mechanisms. This consists of the variety of means through which thoughts, perceptions, and societal activities are reproduced. For capitalism to expand, it is necessary for cultural, moral, and social processes to be brought under its umbrella, remolded, and altered according to its requirements (Gramsci, 1971).

The construction of consent also occurs through the political scene, where people identify many of their official and civic interests with the national state and the confines of party politics that they are allowed to engage with. Stuart Hall and his coauthors observed the leadership role of the state apparatus in developing hegemonic consent and coercive domination, soaking into a general self-disciplining among the working class:

> In a system based on capitalist reproduction, labor has, if necessary, to be *disciplined* to labor; in bourgeois society, the propertyless have to be disciplined to the respect for private property; in a society of "free individuals," men and women have to be disciplined to respect and obey the overarching framework of the nation-state itself. Coercion is one necessary face or aspect of "the order of the state." The law and the legal institutions are the clearest institutional expression of this "reserve army" of enforced social discipline. But society clearly works better when men learn to discipline themselves; or when dis-

cipline appears to be the result of the spontaneous consent of each to a common and necessary social and political order: or where, at least, the reserve exercise of coercion is put into effect with everyone's consent. (Hall et al., 1978/2013, p. 202)

Next, we will look in more detail at how processes of hegemonic consent formation and coercive domination play out with regard to the region and the changes occurring under capitalist globalization.

Constructing Consent under the Region's Integration into the Global Order

Here, I want to identify some key features of hegemonic consent, as these are crucial to understanding the Caribbean region's insertion into the global order. Among the most important characteristics are: the role of the "political scene," cultural production, and ideological formation. In explaining these, some particular instances unique to the Caribbean emerge.

The Role of the "Political Scene"

Throughout the history of world capitalism, a wide variety of state forms have existed, often authoritarian or "Bonapartist," in which the hegemonic balance leans toward coercion (Thomas, 1984). This has often led to legitimacy crises for state leaders as the advancement and role of civil society is held back. As new information flows and emphases on democracy and human rights spread around the world in the latter decades of the twentieth century (Frezzo, 2015), U.S. policy makers and elites operating through other advanced capitalist states sought to solidify allied regimes around the world by shifting the hegemonic balance toward more legitimizing (consent-based) means of domination. They sought to transition away from overt support for authoritarian regimes and move toward systems of "polyarchy" (Robinson, 1996).

Polyarchy refers to a system under which the electoral process is restricted to choosing among a small group of elites, so that political leadership operates on behalf of capital. In some ways this mirrored political processes that had been developed in the United States. Political power thus was concentrated through elections and political scenes through which top elites sought to construct consensual domination around its interests (Robinson, 1996).

In contrast to the cumbersome and embarrassing regimes of the Cold War, the new polyarchic democracies would serve as more responsive to elites than actual demands of popular classes. Transnationally oriented groups, with contingents operating in and outside of developing nations, have worked to facilitate these favorable transitions (Domínguez, 1996; Robinson, 1996). "Promoting democracy" and "democratic transitions" have become subterfuges for sponsoring local transnationally oriented elite and technocratic rule through the political scene, rather than grassroots democracy (Herman and Brodhead, 1984). Scholars have shown the role of polyarchy in Haiti in remaking the electoral landscape (Hallward, 2008) and the foreign financing of general elections in the Commonwealth Caribbean, such as in the Bahamas, Barbados, Guyana, Jamaica, and Trinidad and Tobago, as well as foreign funding of targeted labor union activities and programs, which has been going on for many years as part of the antileftist policies during and after the Cold War (Barrow-Giles and Thomas, 2010; Scipes, 2011; Sprague, 2008).

Polyarchic practices have thus been solidified in many countries in the region, such as within the CARICOM countries, and in Hispanophone countries such as the Dominican Republic. In other nations, major pushbacks have occurred against the polyarchic strategies of elites, such as with the constant mobilization of grassroots movements in Haiti or the leftist and center-left political forces in the ALBA-bloc countries (such as in Cuba, Venezuela, Ecuador, and Bolivia).

In Jamaica and the Dominican Republic, the political scenes, made up of the major political parties and governing officials, now contain few ideologically driven differences. Political actors across Jamaica's mainstream political spectrum agree on core economic policies (Sprague, 2014c; Sprague-Silgado, 2016). This has occurred after decades of postcolonial independence, the opening and expansion of new markets, as well as U.S. and European Union (EU) civil society training and funding programs. It also occurred after years of efforts by transnationally oriented elites (within and outside these nations) to shape the local political scenes, with the surrounding institutions also playing an important role.

Those countries where major political forces have resisted the polyarchic model have become targets of Washington, its allies, and aligned fractions of the TCC. Scholars have documented, for instance, the largescale USAID (United States Agency for International Development) and NED (National Endowment for Democracy) support and funding for pro-Washington forces in Venezuela (Golinger, 2005). Agencies from Spain and the European Union have taken part, as well as powerful right-wing forces from South America. Meanwhile, for the Western media establishment, any news is fit to print on Venezuela, as long as it is negative coverage (A. Johnson, 2017; Podur, 2017).

One of the most long-targeted countries in the history of U.S. foreign policy has been Cuba (Lamrani, 2013). Yet, as we can see in the global era, Washington's regime change policies targeting Cuba have increasingly included not just coercive strategies aimed at economic destabilization (Pérez, 2016) and sabotage campaigns by intelligence agencies (Agee, 1975) but also civil society strategies meant to promote deeper and longer-term societal transformation (Bigwood, 2014). Consent is never fully solidified or achieved but rather functions as an ongoing process, always under construction, always under contestation.

Cultural Production

Another key means for building hegemonic consent has been through cultural production, which arises out of particular historical conditions and is linked to certain socioeconomic interests and thus carries out important social functions. If we define culture broadly in terms of the material expressions, discourses, and practices we engage in while reproducing ourselves, then a range of social activities qualify as cultural production. By extension, the activities of capitalist forces in their various specializations bear on and affect cultural life as part of social reproduction (Mintz, 1989; Szymanski, 1983). How do *they* define progress, democracy, the role of "free markets," limited government, and good governance? Or, how do they argue that state regulation of the labor process should be in their interest, why globalization is a "win-win" situation for the world, or why reducing taxes benefits all, and so on? In this sense, global capitalist culture plays a role in reproducing the cultural framework via which consent is manufactured as part of waging class struggle from above.

Our immersion, under capitalism, in a fantasy world of material well-being and consumerist pursuits ensures that we lose sight of deeper societal processes and struggles, a reality for not only many in the global north but also for many in the global south, with an expanding consumerist strata in many countries including in the Caribbean. As Jeffries (2016, p. 87) writes, describing the thinking of Frankfurt scholar Walter Benjamin in understanding how we become captivated by material wealth and its cultural expressions, losing sight of the reality under which we exist: "It is as though capitalism, having rubbed out the true nature of class struggle and airbrushed historical contingency, had covered up the tracks of its murder and diverted us from our detective work with the captivating allure of commodities . . . a ring of hell in which the consumerist faithful endlessly buy and sell, eternally deluded in believing that this activity will bring fulfillment."

The social form that culture takes on thus corresponds to the way in which people reproduce their existence. Throughout history, different cultural forms have reflected the experiences and interests of different groups in society. For example, the lengthy and ornate symphonies like the work of

Wolfgang Amadeus Mozart (1756–1791) in the Hapsburg dominions reflect in many ways ruling class cultural logic and the resources its Viennese elites would bring to bear on cultural production. By contrast, the rise of salsa music emerging from low-income Afro-Cuban communities reflects a very different social reality (Robinson, 2014b).

What of today's glitzy Caribbean pop music and its glamorous entertainment stars? Here we see how the social forms of a highly marketized consumer society bleed into cultural production. Cultural forms can be co-opted and used in different ways depending on the circumstances. Calypso music was once considered poor people's sounds, and then, as a result of global tourism, elite groups claimed it as part of "national culture." In the era of global capitalism, we see a commodification of music, for example, with reggae and salsa (also, initially coming out of low-income communities) now "reinvented" as global commodities, a massive moneymaking venture, with its most well-known acts becoming far removed from the social content and character from which the music emerged. Ultimately, the culture-ideology of consumerism is vital for legitimizing today's dominant order.

Caribbeans and their diaspora are not just consumers of hybrid culture in the global era, but also are major producers of it (Ho and Nurse, 2005). Reggaetón, at first called "underground," spread through bootlegs in the barrios of Puerto Rico but has now become a global phenomenon, with reggaetón artists often topping billboard charts. High-status musicians with Caribbean roots are now some of the most well-known and highest-paid entertainers worldwide. Autotuned tracks produced in glitzy Miami high-rises replace the organic rhythm of barrio struggle. Different cultural forms have always been vital for upholding a dominant order. In the global era, a new "global hybridity" and homogenization associated with corporatized cultural forms has come about, mirroring to a certain extent the new and flexibilized form of production (Harvey, 1991). Consumer-oriented cultural forms are promoted through media, civil society, entertainment, and the arts and in general through the common worldview. At the same time, cultural forms from below exist but are often demonized, less accessible through major platforms, and seen as valueless or grotesque in the dominant racialized and gendered class narratives. These play key roles in consent formation, impacting people's perceptions and even their imaginations.

The challenge then is in how to subvert the lie-dream of capitalism and to push for emancipatory and progressive futures. Many have tried—through art, music, plays, subculture, novels, various radical struggles, critical theory, or, as the Frankfurt school scholars suggested meditating on past disappointments (to free ourselves from future disappointments) (Jeffries, 2016). Reflecting our species' constant efforts for emancipation, the most powerful and inspirational cultural expressions start as protest or expressions of lived struggle. In Jamaica, for instance, this is reflected in the class consciousness of local reggae and dancehall music with lyrics about poor urban youths, the sufferers, the haves and the have nots, and politicians taking advantage. New more progressive reggae groups, for instance, are replacing homophobic "battyman" lyrics with "capitalist" as the target of derision. In another unique example, Sujatha Fernandes (2006) has looked at the artistic endeavors of filmmakers, hip-hop artists, and visual artists in Cuba, showing the complex and contradictory ways in which popular culture intersects with Cuba's socialist project and the creeping role of market forces on Cuban society. Cultural production thus plays out with a multitude of particularities and influences, as a key part of society's top-down integration with the dominant order but also as a way of struggle from below.

Ideological Formation

Possibly above all other means for achieving hegemonic consent is through ideological and subjective formation (Ramos, 1982). These develop in unique ways as people integrate into vast systems of consumption and production, through mass media, intensifying forms of advertising, industrial management, and contemporary modes of thought. By ideological and subjective formation, I refer to the formation and reproduction of systems of conscious and unconscious ideas and ideals that make up one's beliefs, goals, expectations, and motivations. Marcuse (1964) argued that in the modern consumerist society, individuals pursue false needs, where people live in a state of "unfreedom" acting out irrationally by working long hours to purchase things they do not need, by ignoring psychologically destructive effects upon the individual, the family, and broader society, by ignoring the damage and waste of consumerism, and, ultimately, by searching for social connection through material items (Jeffries, 2016).

This formation process does not occur in a vacuum but rather takes place through a structured world of power and inequality. In some areas of the world, such as in many parts of the Caribbean, there are larger parts of the population that are structurally marginalized. The marginalized can be explosive politically, and for that reason we see growing attempts by elites to entwine them more concretely within the system, through various forms of consent and coercion. This reflects also capital's search to find every last crevice through which it can accumulate, down to the dispossessed.

Many public matters are framed through ideological systems and the abstract meanings are constructed and consumed by their audiences. Take, for example, the large number of underemployed, unemployed, and informal workers in the Caribbean. These sectors are virtually forgotten by the state, ignored by the business media, and disparaged by elite society as lazy and uneducated targets for social control and fear. The idea of economic sectors being organized in connection to social need, rather than profit, is not taken seriously. Bob Marley once sang that, "In the abundance of water, the fool is thirsty." The fool is a metaphor for a socially alienated person. There is water all around but people don't have access because society is not organized around meeting social needs.

Similarly, the idea of mass media being run democratically, rather than owned by a handful of transnational oligarchs, is not taken seriously. A solution to this problem, suggested by John Nichols and Robert McChesney, is to allow each voting age person control over an equal amount of government money (or vouchers) that he or she can direct to any nonadvertising, nonprofit media outlet of their choice (Wu, 2010).

Yet no alternative such as this is ever allowed to be seriously considered in capitalist society; nor any real substitute for the grinding repression many endure; nor structural alternative to the way that systems of power are organized. The media, churches, schools, and a variety of civil society institutions thus play vital roles in facilitating ideological production. While these institutions form part of the complex mosaic of human society, and many such organizations and people in such institutions obviously engage in positive and necessary work, we all operate through contradictory structural conditions and are impacted in different ways by ideologies that defy reality.

In the global era, many ideological apparatuses and institutions in society have become interconnected with TNCs and new transnational chains of accumulation. For instance, the media's role in ideological formation: television, radio, and print outlets linked to massive TNCs now dominate the Caribbean's media landscape, from the New York City–based Univision, to CNN's different language channels, or regionally based corporate outlets such as Haiti's Télé Caraïbes. Peoples' views on worldly events regularly become shaped by corporate media. Mass marketed organized religions meanwhile are heavily present across the region, following in the footsteps of a long history of missionaries and "civilizing missions." Traveling in taxis and setting foot in Jamaica's Kingston airport, for example, one can often hear televangelist shows being broadcast from radios or flat screen TVs.

Some scholars have begun to look at the internal dynamics of the Caribbean media landscape, for instance, at how elite-oriented images and visions of Caribbean society dominate media narratives (Pertierra and Horst, 2009). This cultural production occurs through media outlets that are linked to major transnational capitalist conglomerates. At the same time, public media, just like public education, is increasingly on the chopping block of

Figure 2.7 Graffiti adjacent to the Universidad Autónoma de Santo Domingo in the Dominican Republic, where students were mobilizing against the privatization of education in May 2015. (Photo by author.)

neoliberal privatization, not just in the global north but also in the Caribbean and other regions of the global south. Defending and expanding these public spaces and infrastructure is vital for popular struggle and movements from below. Across the Caribbean we see marginalized youths as well as student movements often taking a lead in the struggles against neoliberalism, for example, opposing the privatization of education and organizing against police brutality and the so-called war on drugs (Edmonds, 2014c; Kerrigan, 2015, 2016; Kerrigan et al., 2017; Sanatan, 2017). (See Figure 2.7.)

It is also important to recognize the nuances of ideological formation. There is, for example, a tension between conservative ideologies that preach chauvinism, homophobia, and xenophobia (in which dominant reactionary bourgeois have partaken and most benefit), and multicultural liberalism, in which subjects can be treated rhetorically as a kind of homogeneous labor to be integrated into global commodity chains. We see support for the latter from some transnational capitalists, including the heads of Digicel, promoting antihomophobia campaigns in Jamaica to improve the country's image as a location for investment and tourism. Some corporate leaders have also criticized the new laws put in place by the Dominican government that target Haitian migrants. These "enlightened" transnational capitalists understandably see such laws as leading to an international ostracization of these Caribbean nations, having negative implications for their economic interests. Yet still, other capitalists, and powerful individuals within global capital's historic bloc (such as many religious leaders), have taken on more conservative agendas, while others have tried to remain uninvolved in these local concerns. Lesbian, gay, bisexual, and transgender individuals whose very form of intimacy has been historically criminalized in parts of the Caribbean, face many pressures and dangers especially in countries such as the Bahamas, Jamaica, and Trinidad and Tobago (Gaskins, 2013).

While not acting in one unified manner, the general interests of capital and its historic bloc do remain unified in their jointly agreed-upon need to exploit waged labor within the highly competitive processes involved in the accumulation of profit.[17] Ideological, cultural, and political formation in global capitalist society subject us all to mystified understandings of our world and the conditions under which we exist (H. Watson, 1994b). Understanding and challenging power and the exploitative relations that undergird our reality while taking into account the objective conditions on the ground remain the unending challenge for emancipatory and grassroots struggle.

The Changing Face of Coercive Rule in the Caribbean

Throughout the history of capitalism, particular dominant groups have developed means of achieving both hegemonic consent and direct domination to maintain and project their class rule. Among the most important of these has been the coercive apparatus. While the new global historic bloc has depended on novel and restructured means for achieving hegemonic consent, as discussed previously, repression has long been used in the Caribbean and other regions worldwide to maintain the class and colonial systems that arose out of capitalism.

The changing face of coercion is coming about through the restructuring of society and its institutions, for instance, through the mechanisms needed to contain populations whose social reproduction is not required by transnational capital. We see this crystallized through many capitalist states, where policy makers, seek to facilitate policies in the interests of transnational capital. By contrast, the popular classes, their political vehicles and social movements from below, the marginalized, those pools of reserve labor, and superexploited (often migrant) populations, in turn, are targets for repression.

These processes evolve through a built architecture, where the U.S. state apparatus is the world and regional power, and with a network of allies. Across the Caribbean, U.S. military and security apparatuses have consist-

Figure 2.8 Emblem of the United States Southern Command, which is one of ten Unified Combatant Commands. Its zone of operation is in the Caribbean as well as Central and South America. (Source: Wikimedia Commons.)

ently intervened, most notably in the blockade of socialist Cuba since 1959. Washington's bases now dot the basin—from the U.S. Southern Command and Fourth Fleet's home in south Florida; to U.S. military deployments and presence in Colombia, Curaçao and Aruba, and Antigua and Barbuda; to the installations in Guantánamo Bay in Cuba; to Andros Island in the Bahamas; and to activities in Panama, Honduras, and El Salvador (COHA, 2009; García Muñiz and Vega Rodríguez, 2002). The U.S. Southern Command's destructive capabilities are clearly unparalleled in the region. (See Figure 2.8.)

In recent years Colombia, with its sizable Caribbean coast, has become a part of NATO (Feldman, 2013). Some states in the region, such as the Dominican Republic, even supported the illegal invasion and occupation of Iraq, with Santo Domingo sending a military contingent of several hundred troops under the command of Spanish foreign legion officers (though the Dominican government briskly withdrew its military contingent when it started incurring casualties). Whereas some of the U.S. bases in the region are permanent sites, others serve as smaller flexible "lily pad" bases, where local authorities (such as in Costa Rica) have tried to deny their existence. In the wake of September 11, 2001, U.S. state authorities carried out a new "state of exception," with vast new security initiatives and interventionist policies abroad alongside new rounds of militarized accumulation (Agamben, 2005).

There have also been large-scale protests against the U.S. military presence, especially in Puerto Rico, where in recent decades activists successfully pressured the U.S. military to shut down many of its activities. In the United

States, groups such as the School of the Americas Watch (SOA) have for many decades now protested and organized against the role of the U.S. military in Latin America and the Caribbean, in particular its training at Fort Benning in Georgia of foreign military officers who have been complicit in state violence against poor and negatively racialized populations. Leftwing movements in many other parts of the Americas, such as in Venezuela, have rallied for years against U.S. imperialism. Relaunching an antiwar movement *inside* the United States, on March 16, 2019, thousands of people marched in Washington DC, in front of the White House, demanding that the Trump administration end its economic war and campaign of terror against Venezuela.

Yet the alignment of forces in the region clearly favors transnational capital and transnationally oriented elites. While playing out through an uneven institutional landscape (with the U.S. state apparatus as the major world power), these elites are helping restructure and facilitate new types of coordination, hegemonic relations, and coercive actions across the region. We can see how among many Caribbean state apparatuses there are growing coordinative relations with powerful interests and agencies. This includes apparatuses of the United States as well as the EU, the UN, and the Organization of American States (OAS), who have helped develop the institutional capacity for local security forces in the region (Muggah et al., 2013). Alongside this, new supranational forums and juridical frameworks have been created to help foster legal frameworks beneficial for transnational capital and its allies in state power (Ronald Cox, 2008).

A variety of coercive mechanisms, many undergoing restructuring processes, are now used to maintain and reproduce the social order. While this includes some important policing functions, repressive operations are constantly aimed at lower-income populations.[18] Police agencies in the region increasingly cooperate with supranational agencies, such as those supported by the EU and the United States. "Peacekeeping" troops in Haiti have included contingents from countries around the world, such as from Argentina, Bangladesh, Brazil, Canada, Chile, China, Jordan, and Nepal. These forces also operate alongside strata of UN officials and NGO workers operating within the intervened country. These new "sanitized" operations and governance structures, unlike the old colonial, imperial, and postcolonial authoritarian regimes, seek to operate in a flexible manner seen as legitimate by the "global community" (Sprague-Silgado, 2018a). This leads to concrete conditions under which political authorities aligned with transnational capital favor certain groups and strategies over others (Schuller, 2007; Sprague-Silgado, 2018).

Many examples exist of this new face of coercive force, where state forces act out in brief and decisive operations against elements within poor neighborhoods. On June 22, 2010, in Jamaica, security forces carried out an extremely violent raid into the urban community of Tivoli Gardens in West Kingston. The Jamaican police and army raid (called for by the U.S. embassy and supported by a U.S. reconnaissance drone) occurred under the administration of JLP (Jamaican Labor Party) prime minister Bruce Golding. Ostensibly targeting a gang leader for extradition to the United States for drug trafficking, the official death toll was seventy-three people, whereas locals claim the number was two hundred (Lloyd D'Aguilar, personal communication, 2014; Schwartz, 2011).[19] Violent confrontations with criminal elements or those labeled criminal elements have been used as justifications for major acts of state sanctioned violence, where the lives of people in surrounding low-income communities are taken largely for granted (Hallward, 2008; Kerrigan, 2016; Sprague, 2014c, 2018; Sprague and Pierre, 2007).

Criminality itself is part of a disoriented social melee, where many perceive themselves to be totally disconnected. Many factors exist, for example: the economy is not working for many, one's family life may be in shambles, and many suffer from a lack of social moorings. Sociologists describe a "breakdown of institutional norms," for instance, where some police engage in corruption or kidnapping rings, or where at certain points the criminality of gangs can become accelerated (as in recent years in Trinidad's Port of Spain). However, this also has broader social consequences, where people lock doors and windows (so much so that houses look like mini-fortresses), where luxury suburbs are targeted heavily, and where poor attack poor. In this situation some fall back on religion as an anchor, or look to hide behind the boundaries of the state through nationalism. One is kept away from connecting to a sense of the other.

Over the latter decades of the twentieth century and into the twenty-first century, the Caribbean has also experienced a growth in transnational narco-trafficking—such as the transportation of cocaine—creating a new set of contradictions for communities and state officials in the region (Griffith, 2000). In Jamaica's "garrison" communities, for example, a mix of high unemployment and other pressures creates desperate conditions exploited by transnational criminal syndicates who are capitalists themselves, though engage in nonlegal chains of accumulation (Munroe, 2013). In this situation, making money from criminalized activities can be one of the options for some young people, and a lifeline to communities existing on the edge. Criminal networks thus have become "embedded within specific localities" yet often "require cooperation from corruptible elements of the state" while they seek "to take advantage of global Markets" (Munroe, 2013, p. 250). State apparatuses in the region (especially those with few resources) run up against structural limitations, such as with the low pay of many state and security workers in the region, which can incentivize some to engage in corruption. Furthermore, this creates a situation under which powerful agencies, such as the DEA and U.S.

Figure 2.9 UN troops outside the National Palace in Port-au-Prince, Haiti, in August 2007. (Photo by author.)

Figure 2.10 Haitian national police in Port-au-Prince targeting youth protesters in 2017. (Source: Haiti Liberté.)

intelligence apparatuses, can more readily penetrate local state institutions and police within the region. For many working and lower-income people in the region, the security conditions rightly feel out of their control, with security forces regularly unaccountable to local communities and often manipulated by powerful and well-heeled interests.

Among the most painful results of this can be seen in the state violence targeting marginalized communities in the region. Human rights investigators in Haiti, for instance, following the 2004 coup d'état, documented heavy-handed raids targeting anticoup neighborhoods in the country's capital.[20] As a University of Miami Haiti Human Rights Investigation in late 2004 documented: under the watchful eye of the UN, local paramilitary and police forces carried out mass murder, complete with cramped prisons, mass graves, no-medicine hospitals, corpse-strewn streets, and maggot-infested morgues—a means of dealing with the supporters of an elected government ousted by a U.S. regime-change operation (Griffin, 2004).[21] As Sprague and Pierre observe: "Buildings throughout Cité Soleil were pockmarked by bullets; many showing huge holes made by heavy calibre UN weapons, as residents attest. Often pipes that once brought in water to the slum community now lay shattered" (2007). Numerous residents in Cité Soleil were murdered by the high-caliber weaponry of UN troops, including Stephanie, seven, and Alexandra Lubin, four (Sprague and Pierre, 2007). The popular neighborhoods of Cité Soleil are home to hundreds of thousands of people. It is considered the lowest income urban area in the Western Hemisphere.

One declassified document from the U.S. embassy in Port-au-Prince revealed that during an operation carried out in July 2005, MINUSTAH (United Nations Stabilization Mission in Haiti) expended twenty-two thousand bullets over several hours. In the report, an official from MINUSTAH acknowledged, "Given the flimsy construction of homes in Cité Soleil and the large quantity of ammunition expended, it is likely that rounds penetrated many buildings, striking unintended targets" (Sprague and Pierre, 2007).

Haitian author Edwidge Danticat wrote of her family's experience during this period:

> I spent the first twelve years of my life in an impoverished neighborhood in Port-au-Prince called Bel Air, where many Aristide supporters live [referring to the president overthrown by the United States in 2004]. My eighty-one-year-old uncle, a minister, had called this neighborhood home since the nineteen-fifties, and was there on September 30, 2004, when protests began on the thirteenth anniversary of the first coup d'état. In response, the Haitian national police and *minustah* soldiers conducted joint raids in Bel Air that led to dozens of mostly unreported injuries and deaths. The following month, UN soldiers and Haitian riot police climbed up to the roof of my uncle's church and killed some of his neighbors below. My uncle was forced to flee to Miami, where he died in the custody of U.S. immigration officials after being denied asylum. (2017)

State operations targeting marginalized populations are part of today's globalized world order and have far-reaching effects, devastating families and communities. While means for strengthening domination have long been used by ruling groups against low-income and supernumerary people, this now occurs increasingly through a web of governmental, police, military, intelligence, and private security groups linked with transnational agencies. Across the region, an array of supranational agencies train and coordinate between states in matters of "securitization." Jamaican security forces, for instance, receive training and funding from U.S. and EU groups, as have other military and police apparatuses and contractors active in the region, such as in Trinidad and Tobago. Joint initiatives also exist within CARICOM and other institutions in the hemisphere (Muggah et al., 2013). Private military contractors (PMCs), businesses that specialize in security and combat operations around the world, are also increasingly being used in the region. As I documented in 2018, Haitian state and state-sponsored groups carried out a massacre in the Port-au-Prince seaside neighborhood of La Saline (a site of constant antigovernment demonstrations), in which PMC mercenaries and a new, local, fast-reaction force were utilized, reflecting a restructured and more flexible form of coercion (Sprague, 2018).

In the Dominican Republic, the country's military and border forces, financially supported by U.S. and EU agencies, are now mainly used as a mechanism for labor discipline and patrolling Haitian migrant communities (Miller, 2014, pp. 177–208). While obviously different from the wide-scale massacres targeting Haitian border communities under the Trujillo dictatorship in the mid-twentieth century, the new "sanitized" repression not only seeks to suppress marginalized groups in a more stable manner but more fundamentally to maintain the reproduction of a reserve army of agrarian laborers at a time when the Dominican Republic is becoming deeply integrated into transnational chains of accumulation. Here we can distinguish between but also see the intermingling between the marginalized, who are structurally excluded and unrequired by capital, and the "reserve army of labor," who are unemployed but essentially kept in reserve to replace potentially unruly laborers, placing a downward pressure on wages by their very existence.

Meanwhile, U.S. immigration agencies, the DEA, and those forces engaged in the counternarcotics "war on drugs" have had an extensive role in the region over the closing decades of the twentieth century and into the twenty-first century (Miller, 2014; Paley, 2014). What are the human costs of this unending war? How else could these resources be used? Large parts of the Caribbean's population are underemployed or unemployed, and if one's search for work or survival violates the legal codes, he or she can expect the worst (Edmonds, 2014b; Hall et al., 1978). Among the marginalized and reserve pools of labor, the youths and the negatively racialized suffer some of the worst humiliation and repression; caught with shrinking options in impoverished districts or stopped, frisked, and racially profiled as they make their way through life abroad (Golash-Boz, 2016; Robinson and Santos, 2014).

Racialized scapegoating of migrants has become a dog whistle for resurgent rightist groups in the twenty-first century. Dominant groups and their allies, not just in the global north but also in the global south, seek to mystify the socioeconomic forces that compel migration. As capital moves unrestricted, human beings are compartmentalized and privileged according to their citizenship status and wealth. In Barbados, antimigrant campaigns have targeted undocumented migrants from Guyana, especially targeting those of Indo-Guyanese descent (Stabroek News, 2009). In Aruba, migrants from Venezuela feel a growing xenophobia (Venezuelan migrant family interviewed by the author requested anonymity, personal communication, 2018). Having left their home country, which is in crisis with falling oil prices and targeted in an economic war launched by Washington and various powerful sectors (Ellner, 2017b), Venezuelan migrants have sought valuable job opportunities in nearby states including within the Caribbean.

The most concrete antimigrant campaign has been launched in recent years in the Dominican Republic, targeting Haitians and Dominicans of Haitian descent, which seeks to reproduce the exploitation (and often, superexploitation) of migrant workers who have been negatively racialized (Blake, 2014; Ferguson, 2003; Sprague-Silgado, 2016). In 2013, a Dominican Supreme Constitutional Tribunal stripped over two hundred thousand Dominicans of Haitian descent of their citizenship. This author has witnessed a web of policing authorities stretch inland across the Dominican side of the border, reflecting the state's function in regulating and repressing migrant labor.

The ability to physically stage an outcome, achieved through force, remains the decisive factor for securing the rule of the global historic bloc and its dominant class, the TCC. For more than a century, the United States has dominated the region with its naval armadas and military forces. With most state apparatuses across the region having long ago "bent the knee" to U.S. state power, increasingly it is the repression of the supernumeraries—those whose social reproduction is not required by the transnational capitalist order—that is a top priority for governing groups in the region. New militarized state and private platforms with an array of high-tech advancements are being used to monitor and contain the subaltern, a trend that looks set to intensify. New systems of mass incarceration, including within the Caribbean, have come about in order to jail (and profit from the condition of parts of) the marginalized population (Sassen, 2014).

Other coercive mechanisms exist such as the various private security and military, and paramilitary, apparatuses. Tori Aarseth (2012) has looked at the relationship of private military companies to the TCC, with new globally oriented contractors (such as Blackwater) directly linked to TNCs and powerful states. Paramilitary groups, meanwhile, are made up of local armed groups operating outside of the jurisdiction of the official police or military but sometimes acting in coordination with them. They regularly hold relationships with powerful political and economic interests (D. Davis, 2009). I have argued elsewhere that these coercive mechanisms used to preserve elite domination are being remolded in the global era, allowing for their reproduction under the changing circumstances associated with the rise of global capitalism (Sprague-Silgado, 2018a).

Many studies have shown the role of right-wing paramilitaries in enforcing the interests of national power blocs and U.S. imperialism during the Cold War and over recent years. Yet, as I have argued, paramilitarism has been altered through the global epoch, and this has occurred as a part of the changing strategies of elites (most important, transnationally oriented elites). This is reflected by the emergence of smaller, temporary paramilitary groups that can be called on at a moment's notice but no longer mobilize so openly or in such a large scale as in Colombia, El Salvador, or Haiti in earlier decades (Hristov, 2009). Under capitalist globalization, top elites, facing off against struggles from below have sought flexible and legitimizing mechanisms for which to maintain the global order (Sprague-Silgado, 2018a). These elites, especially those heavily invested in global accumulation, have sought to downplay and transition away from the crude and flagrant means of constructing the nationally and internationally oriented hegemony of the past. In Haiti, for example, instead of a U.S. occupation there exists a UN occupation; instead of an openly Duvalierist military, OAS and Haitian officials claim to be building a new sanitized army; instead of tens of thousands of paramilitaries (with stations in every community), leaner covert paramilitaries and parapolice operate alongside foreign PMCs (Sprague, 2012c; Sprague-Silgado, 2018a).

The earlier power blocs of countries across the region are transforming in significant ways, reflecting a broadening of the mode of accumulation of local elites as they seek to integrate with transnational capital. Under this situation, some forms of coercion have been more effective than others as complements to capitalist accumulation. We might argue that there is a certain learning curve or evolution in the effectiveness of local elites in employing coercive force to supplement their economic and political interests. The agenda of many transnational elites has been to stabilize countries only to the extent to which they can function as secure platforms through which global capital can flow and where lower-income populations become a node in a process that strengthens the revenue base and profitability of TNCs. This has also meant, at times, taking advantage of or softening attempts by antiquated ultraright groups seeking to reinstitutionalize aspects of the "old order."

An unavoidable problem is that transnational capital does not require the social reproduction of a large part of the planet's population. This means that a significant portion of the world's population, such as with many in the region, are structurally marginalized. For this reason, we see different attempts by elites to manage the problems associated with using coercive force, apparatuses that they have sometimes required to repress marginalized and exploited populations.

The TCC and their allied strata in the new historic bloc regularly downplay the rough edges of hegemonic coercion, seeking to deploy force in sanitized, covert, or brief decisive operations. Here it is important to note how violence against the poor is regularly misreported, decontextualized, or not covered at all by private media monopolies. Yet some critical reports do make it through the news "filters," which regularly dilute the raw news into a content that suits the dominant capitalist and state entities (Chomsky and Herman, 2002). In breaking through this conspiracy of silence, grassroots journalists and progressive and leftist media outlets have done exceptional work illuminating the contradictions of global capitalism, the injustices and impunity, the various forms of repression, and foreign interventions.[22]

Crises, Alternatives, and Struggles from Below

We are living through a time of global crises. In addition to global social polarization (with the creation of increasing poverty and increasing wealth within and between communities and societies), which is discussed throughout this book, we are also seeing: (1) an ecological crisis with the unsustainability of the global system, (2) a crisis of overaccumulation, and (3) a crisis of legitimacy for state actors in many parts of the world. Without the space here to delve into other crises, the threat of nuclear warfare still remains, and there are now constant warnings about the future role of artificial intelligence.

The ecological crisis plays out on an epic scale. Geologists are pointing to the rise of the "Anthropocene," the first geological epoch that is a direct consequence of human impact, by our influence on land use, ecosystems, and massive species extinction leading to a large decline in the earth's biodiversity (Waters, et al., 2016). Unlike any period in the planet's history—one species is qualitatively altering the very geological makeup of the planet, and in a drastically negative manner—a true earth crisis. While industrialization and high-consumption patterns, mostly in the global north are responsible for this human-made crisis, worldwide (even in areas of the Third World) we see growing energy use, pools of new consumerist strata, and rising carbon emissions. (See Figure 2.11.)

The economic, social, and political disruption caused by climate change is just starting to be understood. The science, however, has become clear.[23] As shown below, through earlier eras of world capitalism and especially into the epoch of globalization, there has been a catastrophic rise of global carbon

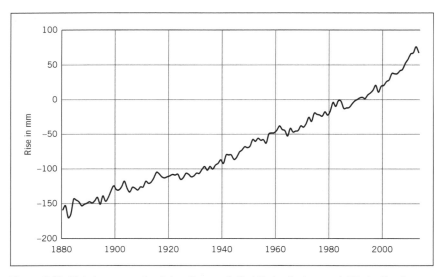

Figure 2.11 Global mean sea level rise. (Source: United States Environmental Protection Agency, 2017.)

dioxide emissions and a growing acidification of the oceans. The peoples of the Caribbean are at ground zero of this global crisis (see, e.g., Beckford and Rhiney, 2016; NASA, 2010; Taylor et al., 2012). As a recent study published from Tufts University (Bueno et al., 2008, p. 2) observes:

> The two dozen island nations of the Caribbean, and the 40 million people who live there, are in the front lines of vulnerability to climate change. Hotter temperatures, sea-level rise and increased hurricane intensity threaten lives, property and livelihoods throughout the Caribbean. As ocean levels rise, the smallest, low-lying islands may disappear under the waves. As temperatures rise and storms become more severe, tourism—the life-blood of many Caribbean economies—will shrink and with it both private incomes and the public tax revenues that support education, social services, and infrastructure. And these devastating impacts will occur regardless of the fact that Caribbean nations have contributed little to the release of the greenhouse gases that drive climate change.

Another fundamental problem for our global system is that capitalist crisis is immanent, in that it is "normal." Continual crises are generated by the many interrelated contradictions internal to capitalism. At the heart of this in globalization is capitalist overaccumulation. This refers to the situation in which capitalists cannot obtain a profit if the workers who produce wealth are paid for the value of what they produce, meaning that working people around the world produce more goods and services than they are actually able to buy. As Robinson writes:

> Capitalists would have no incentive to invest their money if the price fetched for the goods and services produced were exactly equal to wages, that is, if they were not assured a profit by appropriating a portion of the value produced by labor in the form of profits . . . At a certain point, more goods and services are produced than can be purchased by that mass of laborers, and the economy enters a recession or a depression because capitalists cannot "unload" the surplus. This situation of "overproduction" or "underconsumption,". . . means that in order for capitalists to make ("realize") a profit they must actually sell the goods and services produced; otherwise, it simply accumulates and the capitalist loses the money invested in the production process. (2014a, p. 130)

In recent years we see this playing out through a global economic crisis in 2008 (McNally, 2011; Sprague, 2009), initially described as the subprime mortgage crisis in the United States. Transnationally oriented policy makers operating through a host of national and supranational state apparatuses, while seeking ways to stave off immediate collapse, have worked to find new ways to promote investor confidence in the global economy and set up mechanisms and institutions for responding to economic crises that threaten the stability of global markets, such as the 2008 crisis. Yet this relies on finding new avenues through which the TCC can accumulate wealth, and reproduce its logic. A central factor for easing the most recent crisis, was the TCC's drive to intensify militarized accumulation, with, for instance, U.S. military spending of $325 billion in 1997 growing to $1.1 trillion in 2017 (Hartung, 2017; Robinson, 2014a, pp. 147–154). From regime change and occupation to strategies of social control and the targeting of activist and left-wing movements, to vast new "homeland security" and intelligence complexes, and through the war on terror and war on drugs, vast sums of wealth are being poured into destructive capabilities.

Yet the TCC and transnationally oriented state managers in the United States and in many other countries (including within the Caribbean) also face growing legitimacy crises, with rising cynicism after years of anti–working class policies. This plays out through new conflicts within the political scenes of many nation-states. For example, as I have argued rightist forces in the United States and in other parts of the world are now seeking out a newfangled ideological wedge into the popular classes that benefits the TCC while singing the song of nationalism and protectionism in order to confuse and recruit (Rangel and Sprague-Silgado, 2017). While this might result in some limited, targeted, and politically expedient strategies, it is only a temporary way out of the legitimacy crisis that top elites face. As capitalist globalization continues to intensively expand into the social fabric of societies worldwide, such crises will continue to flare up.

No matter what advantage capital has achieved in the current historical juncture of transnational capitalist integration it has not won any absolute war over the working class—clearly it wins skirmishes and battles but the war continues; the subsuming of labor under capital gives capital a certain leverage in extracting surplus value in a variety of forms. This is part of the larger process in which the adoption of policies (often neoliberal policies) to speed up capitalist globalization and advance the rolling back of the state's social borders is tied up with various means of achieving hegemony.

Concomitant with these crises, advancing forms of exploitation and integration are creating a dialectical foundation for transcending the relations and processes it has created (H. Watson, 2015). It is my view that working and popular classes in the Caribbean and worldwide, while continuing local and national struggles, must move toward new transnational forms of organizing and in the direction of coordinative relations that build and greatly expand on the old models of international solidarity. The struggle of subaltern forces in a globalizing world remains the open-ended challenge for this century.

In spite of every effort to achieve hegemonic consent on the part of the ruling class, political and social movements from below continue to percolate in the region. So how can an alternative globalization from below occur? How can popular and leftist movements push not just for progressive reforms, but also in the direction of a liberatory structural alternative? Hilbourne Watson (2015) describes the revolutionary Cuban project as showing the "contingent nature of state sovereignty and of hegemony," illuminating an alternative (though contradictory) path for development, and, as he also observes, one that has elicited constant attacks by the U.S. superpower. Furthermore, Cuban state socialism and its viability came out of a distinct and historically contingent *international* phase of world capitalism. Adapting and facing new contradictions as it becomes more integrated with the global capitalist economy, Cuba's socialist project faces many new challenges (Carmona Baez, 2004; Lara Jose, 2008;).

Watson argues the long-term goal is "to look beyond the sovereign state for solutions to problems and challenges humans face, with a view to pursuing human emancipation" (H. Watson, 2015, p. 30).[24] Yet, this does not mean we can abandon ongoing battles over the state and other institutions. Emancipatory struggles from below are not exclusive of progressive reform campaigns or struggles over the state. It is useful here to recall how Marx supported struggles during his life: he not only advocated for emancipatory structural alternatives such as the revolutionary project of the Paris Communards and the cause of radical abolitionism in the United States but also supported reforms that moved in a progressive direction, ranging from campaigns for a shorter working day to support for migrant workers and for the Northern cause in the U.S. Civil War (K. Anderson, 2010). Here we can recognize the importance of examining not only concrete historical developments but also a constant reevaluation of conditions on the ground, with a vision toward considering *what is possible* in the struggle for human emancipation and progress. This includes a critical examination of objective conditions (that requires one to search for the truth) rather than always attributing authenticity to elite and corporate media portrayals. Beneath the surface of mainstream approaches, there is always the liberal tendency to believe that the popular classes cannot politically mobilize and organize of their own accord.[25]

Through the labyrinth of capitalist restructuring are renewed efforts to transcend and resist (H. Watson, 2015). Labor protests and ongoing grassroots and union organizing continue in the region, for instance within EPZs and mining communities in the Dominican Republic. Student movements and anticorruption campaigns have gained steam, pushing back against persistent neoliberal and oligarchic political models. There have also been large-scale protests against the U.S. military presence, especially in Puerto Rico, where, in recent decades, activists successfully pressured the military to shut down many of its activities, such as U.S. navy training and bombing activities in Vieques. In Haiti, grassroots pressure is growing against the rebuilding of the country's brutal military apparatus. The antineoliberal state alliance, ALBA, has been an important development of the twenty-first century. But, in recent years the Venezuelan-led project has suffered from its own internal contradictions, declining oil prices, a currency crisis, and intensified U.S. and elite aggression.[26] Socialist Cuba faces its own difficulties as it seeks to further integrate with the global economy, a peculiar case in the region, as novel social and political economic dynamics unleash contradictory transformations. While leftist and popular political currents exist across the region, they face considerable challenges.

Throughout this book, the role of different social and political forces engaging with the challenges and conditions faced under capitalist globalization are noted and related to what is occurring regionally and nationally. Next, we look at a short historical overview of the region's insertion into the capitalist world economy: how this has reverberated through class struggle and different political orders. I want especially to emphasize the shifting manner in which peoples in or operating through the region have produced (and come to understand) their existence under the changing dynamics of world capitalism.

3

History of the Modern Caribbean

For many millennia prior to the European conquest, indigenous peoples inhabited the islands and surrounding lands of the Caribbean, building a variety of societies (Mann, 2011). The Crown of Castile's conquest of the Caribbean, begun by Cristóbal Colón and his conquistadores in 1492, subjected the indigenous inhabitants—initially the Arawak and then others—to large-scale massacres, slavery, and infectious diseases (Farmer, 2005, p. 53). Instead of a synthesis with the earlier indigenous societies, colonialism imposed a violent rupture. The conquerors erased and rewrote the history of the region's indigenous inhabitants. Various ideological and cultural mechanisms functioned to reproduce the new dominant order (Horne, 2018; Wolf, 1997). Whereas non-European societies would come to be portrayed as premodern and static, the Western world would be promoted as the birthplace of modernity from which new capitalist societies would eventually spring forth.

Prior to the solidification of mercantilism and plantation slavery in the region, Spain's early conquests and initial colonial system profited through the forced labor of indigenous people in gathering gold and rare metals (Diaz del Castillo, 2003). Through Spain's empire that stretched across the region and deep into the Americas, an initial flow of goods and capital developed, reflecting the early international nature of capitalism. Initially, in many respects, the Caribbean islands served as way stations for the merchants and galleons of the Castilian empire, with most of its island holdings remaining lightly populated by Spanish colonialists. Importantly, though, they provided a link in the chain to the larger wealth that was being brutally acquired on the continent, such as in Mexico, where Mexico City became the capital of the first viceroyalty of the Americas.

By the seventeenth century, other European powers—England, France, and the Netherlands—had inserted themselves into the Caribbean, annexing and gaining through wars and treaties lightly populated areas of Spain's immense holdings. Planter elites from these states put into place in the region a new labor regime for the exploitation of chattel slave–based production. The region's entry into world capitalism thus came to function through a new form of slavery—capitalist slavery (Curtin, 1990; Williams, 1944). With the genocide of the original inhabitants of the Caribbean island chains and the high cost and low number of European laborers willing to work in the harsh and humid environment, elites required another source of labor. This occurred through the exploitation of African slave labor. It is believed that the Caribbean received approximately 47 percent of the approximately 10 million African slaves that were brought to the Americas.

Over time, planter classes came to dominate many of the new colonial societies, with their wealth built upon the blood and labor of the growing slave population. While planter elites owned and benefited the most from the plantation complex, some middle-strata European colonial groups also became wrapped up in and profited from slavery (BBC, 2015). As part of this process, local institutions came into being. For example, colonial assemblies often formed to represent the interests of local elites and privileged middle strata. Europeans and Africans produced new generations together (sometimes through the rape of enslaved women by men of the planter class), which through social constructs of race came to be known as new "creole" populations. Over time, complex racially constructed class hierarchies would form across the region.

Slave-plantation production came to be a major structural feature of early capitalism. Slave production altered the very development of the emergent world capitalism, becoming part of its lifeblood. Into the eighteenth century the production of sugarcane was taken to new heights, as it was exported to Europe where it permanently altered Europeans' diets (Mintz, 1986). The high sugarcane yields, from Saint-Domingue in particular, coincided with France's rising wealth. Eric Williams explains, "Between 1715 and 1789 French imports from the colonies multiplied eleven times, French colonial products re-exported abroad ten times" (Williams, 1944, p. 145). Meanwhile, slaves themselves resisted their brutal conditions, launching uprisings and often escaping, obliging a slew of colonial militia and security apparatuses to respond—creating conflict that became more and more violent and costly to maintain. Groups of escaped and freed slaves existed in parts of the region, forming Maroon communities (Price, 1996; A. Thompson, 2006).

The new colonial markets developed as appendages of the European market where the vast amount of wealth was centered (Galeano, 1997, p. 29). This set into motion major inequalities between regions of the planet and among the people living in those regions. As industrial and merchant capital concentrated in Europe, populations in the Caribbean were primarily exploited through the labor-intensive extraction of raw resources. These historical processes have had a long-term impact on, what Walter Rodney (1981) and Andre Gunder Frank (1967) described as "underdevelopment," as only a small part of the surplus capital from these economic interactions remained in the colonies (Galeano, 1997). In addition to this, within the Caribbean the accumulation of capital was concentrated into the hands of a small colonial elite strata, which spent much of its wealth on maintaining their enterprises or on foreign luxury goods and building up their own landed estates.

Spain exhausted a portion of its treasury building up fortified centers in the region, as its rulers sought to protect themselves from the strong naval fleets of their enemies. Major fortified settlements were constructed with slave labor: the fortification system in Havana, the Castillo San Felipe del Morro in San Juan, and the massive walled city and its overlooking fortress in Cartagena.

As a large portion of colonial profits from the foodstuffs and metals exported to Europe stayed in Europe, this provided an impetus to capitalist development in the metropole. For instance, the huge profits made in Saint-Domingue and other French colonies were an important factor in the development of the French bourgeoisie, the class that then backed the overthrow of the French monarchy and helped usher in major changes across Europe. The colonial enterprises also resulted in massive profits for the English merchant class and the new planter classes—those capitalizing on the slave trade and monoculture farming. Yet, it must be pointed out that in the wake of the French Revolution and with the rising abolitionist movement in England, a growing number of voices in Europe began challenging the institution of slavery (C. James, 1989). Movements grew, as Mimi Sheller (2003) describes, around boycotting goods produced through slavery, such as with sugar. It must also be noted that across the Atlantic World there grew a variety of economic interactions, often contradicting the policies set out by the "Old World" empires (Leonard and Pretel, 2015).

Yet the massive new wealth produced in the region continued to serve as a valuable prize over which elites and the emergent European capitalist nation-states would deploy massive armies and fleets to battle. At some points, white planter assemblies in the Caribbean broke with state, or crown, or church officials, spawning complex struggles. Slaves and peasants, for instance, sometimes came to view the crown as a benevolent despot in comparison to the planters' harsh immediacy. Moreover, as European powers fought one another, at times these rivalries occurred alongside or helped facilitate slave uprisings. C.L.R. James (1989) explains how different classes and strata of society existed within the French colony of Saint-Domingue (what became Haiti) at the close of the eighteenth century. He examines the geopolitical conflict between the Spanish, British, and French empires, as they often engaged in wars and competition with one another, and explains how the revolutionaries in Haiti, for instance, skillfully used this to their advantage. The success of the Haitian slave revolution in 1804 was scarred into the minds of European and North American planters (Horne, 2015).

Differing political economic dynamics evolved across the region. Whereas many of the region's British, French, and Dutch colonies excelled at agricultural expansion and trade, the Spanish colonies were unable to sustain their own efforts at sugar-and-slave plantations in the Caribbean. In part, this was because of Spain's long-standing mercantilist policies and lack of early trade liberalization. In contrast, the formerly enslaved population that had risen up to form the region's first independent nation, Haiti, engaged mostly in small-scale peasant farming throughout the nineteenth century. Some larger plantation farms controlled by a new black landowning class also formed.

Eventually, industrial and metropolitan capital in Europe turned against the expensive subsidizing of the remaining Caribbean colonies and their outdated systems of slavery. Sidney Mintz explains that "the increasing tempo of slave revolts, high interest rates, and the wastefulness of their own productive arrangements" all led to a deepening of the colonial plantation system's contradictions, where a tiny segment of society benefited from the extreme misery and suffering of the great majority (1989, p. 86). With the economic status of the Caribbean in decline, the very bedrock of its social structure, built on slavery, came into question, and the old mercantile order soon collapsed. Reflecting the Caribbean plantations' decreasing importance, Britain formally abolished slavery across most of its empire in 1833. The shift away from mercantilism and slavery also echoed the rise of major liberal philosophies at the time. Liberal ideology, as present in Adam Smith's strong critique of mercantilism, helped spark opposition to the monopolizing sugar merchants (Williams, 1984, p. 235). The second nail in the coffin of the power of the slaveholding planter class came with the rise of the sugar trade with the British colony of India (Williams, 1984, pp. 235–236). In addition to the sugar trade, commercial power in Britain had strengthened among cotton manufacturers.

Despite the abolition of slavery in some Caribbean colonies and nations, other parts of the region remained more backward. Slavery continued in

Cuba, for example, until the end of the nineteenth century, even as it had been abolished throughout the region during the middle and early parts of the century. Over time, local slaveholding elites in Cuba had become "mindful of the constraints their social reality imposed on their ambitions," and so stayed heavily dependent on support from Spain to maintain the brutal plantation system (Pérez, 2003, p. 30). The dependence of the island's local elite on the long-standing slave system kept them away from advocating independence. "The specter of slave rebellion in Cuba dampened planters' enthusiasm for an independent nation, especially one without adequate resources to suppress the dreaded slave uprising" (Pérez, 2003, p. 30).[1]

By contrast, in Haiti, where slaves first won their freedom before 1800, cliques of military leaders, a new bourgeoisie in the cities, and a powerful rural landowning class solidified during the nineteenth century, whereas the vast majority of Haitians remained involved in small-scale familial farm production. In the early 1800s, faced with constant external threats, Haitian forces liberated their slave brethren on the Spanish-speaking eastern side of Hispaniola and attempted to unite the island as a single nation. At that time, the population of the eastern side of Hispaniola was much smaller in comparison to the western side.

Following emancipation, former slaves known as Maroons or *cimarrones* often tried to support themselves through private land cultivation. They often did this rather than accept coercive, but nominally free, wage labor on plantations. Their private land cultivation was mostly familial farming, which included those who squatted previously uncultivated or abandoned land—with landownership itself becoming a site of class conflict. Over time, racialized class relations developed in these former slave societies. For instance, as Bakan (1990, p. 6) observes, the "slave origins of the modern Jamaican working class led to the development of a general correlation between class and race in the society as a whole: the fairer the skin colour, the higher the individual's social status was likely to be." This correlation, which was maintained and institutionalized through plantation slavery, continued in the postslavery era, though always in flux, moderated to a degree by the advance of small segments of society.

Meanwhile there were many divisions within the ruling classes of Europe and its colonial counterparts in the Caribbean, with shortsightedness among many dominant groups often occurring and eventually creating major problems for them (Williams, 1944, p. 210). The orientation of different bourgeoisie and other classes varied across the region, and over time. While independence movements (often led by sectors of the local bourgeois) raged in parts the hemisphere, up until the late 1800s Cuba's local bourgeoisie, rather than forming into a nationalistic bourgeoisie, advocated for continued Spanish rule or even U.S. annexation (Pérez, 2003). A similar phenomenon occurred in the mid-nineteenth century in what would become the Dominican Republic (Horne, 2015). Many such historically distinct scenarios played out in the region.

Eventually by the mid-nineteenth century a section of the local Hispanophone elite on the western side of Hispaniola (some of whom had gone into exile when the island had been joined together under the Haitian flag) successfully backed an insurrection, with military strongmen taking hold of the eastern part of the island, which would form the Dominican Republic (Franco Pichardo, 2009). Historian Gerald Horne (2015) has shown how this was also one of the first conflicts in which U.S. intelligence forces operated abroad, playing a role in facilitating the groups that rebelled against Haitian forces on the eastern side of the island.

With the Dominican Republic an independent country and with new nation-states rising across the mainland, by the mid-nineteenth century, Cuba and Puerto Rico were the only remaining Spanish holdings in the Western Hemisphere. Britain, France, and Holland maintained a presence through their various small colonial outposts. And in 1823 the so-called Monroe Doctrine was declared, which meant that U.S. officials would henceforth view Latin America and the Caribbean islands as the United States' "backyard," imperial hubris used to justify future interventions.

During the latter half of the nineteenth century, a new phase in world capitalism emerged, described as "industrial capitalism." Changing class dynamics occurred alongside advancements in technology and organizational forms, quickly impacting regions across the world, including the Caribbean (Girvan, 1978, p. 13), for instance, with the spread of steamships. Yet, at the same time, Caribbean planters had become less important to the international markets that they had once held a monopoly over.

The abolition of slavery, the role of new sites of production (such as in India), new technologies, and the dropping of mercantile protections meant that local elites no longer had many of the earlier market advantages that they required. Many of the descendants of the formerly enslaved populations took to small-scale farming, choosing not to work for the exploitative large farming estates.

With the abolition and decline of slavery across the region, many of the owners of latifundia (the estates worked by slaves) required new pools of labor whose desperation and instability they could exploit. It was under this new situation that European elites (especially from the UK) facilitated the exportation of semi-slave labor through what has been described as "coolie labor" exported from India and China to far-flung areas of the British Empire. As Eric Williams described, "The Caribbean planter, Africa denied to him, was encouraged to turn to India and China" (1984, p. 346). Laborers from India were brought into many parts of the Caribbean, such as Trinidad, British Guiana, Guadeloupe, Suriname, Saint Lucia, Saint Vincent, Grenada, and Jamaica (Williams, 1984, pp. 347–360). Guyana, in particular, with its large landmass, became a destination for Indian sugar workers. Chinese immigration also was encouraged, and many Chinese migrants ended up in Cuba. The same tactics of playing impoverished communities against one another continued as with the conflicts between migrant workers, people of African descent, and the "infinite gradations, shadings and mixtures produced by miscegenation" (p. 350).[2]

The alignment of class forces in the region varied. Historically across many parts of Caribbean society, class relations could not always be concretely demarcated, as so many social relations overlapped (Thomas, 1984, p. 58).[3] Yet, capital fashioned various ways to pump surplus labor out of the toiling population, as class formation in different parts of the region began to differ markedly from earlier periods.

Political scenes evolved differently across the region. Whereas universal suffrage was achieved in the 1870s in the Dominican Republic, by contrast, in the Anglophone Caribbean, only limited voting franchises were created. In Barbados, for example, only those with a sizable annual income and nominal amount of property were allowed to vote (Watson, 2019). This of course excluded the island's black majority and upheld the capitalist interests of the island's small "lily white" establishment. Furthermore, due to primogeniture (where property was transfered through the male line), women were restricted from inheritances and did not have property in their names.

Different parts of the region took on distinctive profiles, with the blossoming of unique and hybrid cultures (Martinez-Vergne and Knight, 2005). In certain instances peasant and rural populations in the region served as protagonists of social conflict, but during other periods they were heavily beaten down or marginalized (G. Lewis, 2004; Mintz, 1974).

When France's early attempts to construct the Panama Canal failed in the 1880s, the U.S. state and capital oversaw a relaunching of the project in the early 1900s, exploiting the labor of a great number of Caribbean workers, many from Jamaica and Barbados (Ives, 2012; Senior, 2014). With its construction, with new large flows of oceanic traffic passing through, the Caribbean once again became a key geostrategic zone of the world economy. Meanwhile, many canal workers stayed in Panama, and others returned to their islands; having saved money, they bought small land plots and started businesses, becoming materially better off than others in their communities.

Toward the end of the eighteenth century, rural capitalistic agricultural production in the Caribbean gained another new impetus with increasing

American capital investment. U.S. capital and state projects invested heavily in upgrading and solidifying rural latifundia production in Cuba, Haiti, and the Dominican Republic.

This also reflected a new international monopoly era of world capitalism, under which the real subsumption of Caribbean agrarian production under capitalism intensified, with agricultural labor internally reorganized to meet the dictates of capital. As the involvement of traditional European powers in the Caribbean basin stagnated during parts of the nineteenth and early twentieth centuries, U.S. capitalists assumed a growing role, and rising levels of U.S. trade and interventionist policies targeted Caribbean nations.

So came the rise of Pax Americana. By the turn of the century, the United States had begun regularly to intervene in the Caribbean and Central America, in large part to protect and expand U.S. capitalist interests (Butler, 1935/2003). This new era of Pax Americana was made clear through the Spanish-American War (April–August 1898), when the U.S. military seized Puerto Rico and the Philippines and invaded Cuba. By 1915, the United States was in control of Haiti, and a year later, the Dominican Republic (Schmidt, 1995). As part of this, as Hudson (2017) observes, U.S. bankers and wall street financiers took an active role in U.S. imperialism and the racism it promoted in the region. They influenced the region's financial architecture, trampled over local sovereignty, and laid the groundwork for future tax havens. Criticizing his country's militarism and reflecting on his own role in it, U.S. Marine Corps major general Smedley Butler would later write:

> I spent 33 years and four months in active military service and during that period I spent most of my time as a high class muscle man for Big Business, for Wall Street and the bankers. In short, I was a racketeer, a gangster for capitalism. I helped make Mexico and especially Tampico safe for American oil interests in 1914. I helped make Haiti and Cuba a decent place for the National City Bank boys to collect revenues in. I helped in the raping of half a dozen Central American republics for the benefit of Wall Street. I helped purify Nicaragua for the International Banking House of Brown Brothers in 1902–1912. I brought light to the Dominican Republic for the American sugar interests in 1916. I helped make Honduras right for the American fruit companies in 1903. In China in 1927 I helped see to it that Standard Oil went on its way unmolested. Looking back on it, I might have given Al Capone a few hints. The best he could do was to operate his racket in three districts. I operated on three continents. (Butler, 1935/2003)

Finding the new colonial operations in the Philippines and the Caribbean expensive, and with a racist outlook toward the local populations, rather than lay down permanent colonist populations (such as with the centuries of colonialism carried out by the European powers), U.S. policy makers would choose to work through decisive interventions and then ostensibly independent or proxy forces, though sometimes setting these into motion through decades of occupation. "The period between 1897 and 1930 saw the enormous concentration of latifundia in the Caribbean under the stimulus of American capital investment," observes Williams (1984, p. 429). Yet even with the heavy investment, class relations in many of these nations, such as in Hispaniola, were slow to change—with petty commodity relations dominating through the early decades of the twentieth century (Crouch, 1981, p. 18). Over time, agricultural output began to increase, but occurred largely through traditional monoculture exports (such as coffee and sugar). New property rights, road systems, and monetary systems were set in motion as some Caribbean states fell under U.S. occupation or became more tightly connected with U.S. capital, and others were influenced by policies under the tutelage of European colonial administrators (Kiernan, 1969).

The formation of local industrial working classes and productive capital was constrained by a number of factors. These included the uneven international context in which Caribbean economies existed under centuries of colonial rule and imperial intervention, as well as often the local authoritarian and neo-patrimonial structures built up within the emergent nation-states and late or post-colonial societies (Itzigsohn, 2000, p. 40; Thomas, 1984). Caribbean societies, of course, were also hindered by geographic restrictions.

Just as slave uprisings had fought the plantation elites, major resistance movements also opposed the late colonial regimes and U.S. occupations. Major social and political struggles ensued. In Haiti, the new landed elites faced constant rural revolts, this struggle taking on an anticolonial logic when the U.S. occupied the country from 1915 to 1934. The rebels, wearing red patches and headbands, were known as the Caco, the name of a red-plumed bird that was found on the island. In Jamaica, large-scale rebellions by the laboring classes took place in 1831, 1865, and 1938. Bolland (2001) has written on the labor struggles of people in the Anglophone Caribbean, explaining how such struggles helped push forward democratic reforms, self-government, and eventually independence.

In the aftermath of the 1937 labor rebellion in Jamaica—which to this day many observers still refer wrongly to as "riots"—there was an attempt via the creation of the Caribbean Labor Congress (CLC) to build a pan–British West Indies (BWI) labor movement, to address working class concerns in extremely agriculture-dependent semi-industrial capitalist environments. Within a decade the CLC was destroyed by regional and metropolitan politicians and liberal trade union leaders, with a good deal of Washington's involvement through the American Institute for Free Labor Development (AIFLD) and the Alliance for Progress (Horne, 2007). London also was of course involved. By the 1940s, the British Labor Party and the Trade Union Congress were dispatching delegations to the English-speaking Caribbean beseeching the political parties, labor, and trade union movements to avoid any connection with socialists and communists in the region and internationally in return for ample financial support. The strategy succeeded. The lack of any sound institutional base for promoting the popular classes' interests within a historical context has been fundamental to the reproduction of capitalist hegemony in the region.

Pressured from below and devastated from the Second World War, the British did begin, though, to grant concessions to their Caribbean colonies. The colonial societies were not similarly situated, and they had not experienced constitutional developments at the same pace (Watson, 2019). The scope and intensity of reforms thus varied from colony to colony. Full universal suffrage was slowly rolled out; Jamaica in 1944, Trinidad and Tobago in 1945, Grenada and Barbados in 1951, and Guyana in 1953.

The large-scale labor struggles that had occurred in the Anglophone Caribbean never became as deeply associated with Marxist and socialist movements as in the Hispanosphere. In the Spanish-speaking Caribbean, the historical record shows early development of socialist, Marxist, and communist formations with varying tendencies (Franco Pichardo, 2009). Out of these formations emerged tendencies within and around the working-class trade union movement to do battle at the point of production, in the streets, through party politics, and in other spaces, while providing leadership and guidance for working-class activities. The British Caribbean did not have any equivalent.

For instance, it is worth noting that with the working-class eruption that took place during the 1930s across the BWI there was no core leadership of a Marxist-Leninist type. The progressive tendencies often prefaced their utterances with phrases like "we loyal colonial subjects of the British Empire." This was very different from the revolutionary political currents growing in other parts of the region, especially in comparison with the Marxist-Leninist groups. As an outgrowth of Marxism, Leninism (with its roots in the Russian Revolution) was a political theory for the organization of a revolutionary vanguard party that could lead and organize toward socialism but had to organize in a disciplined and often covert manner to avoid being detected by the authorities. This was the path that Che Guevara and others eventually took in Cuba—after witnessing less regimented political projects of the left, which had come to power through bourgeois elections, and were then either co-opted or violently crushed by capital and U.S. power. The starkest example of this at that time was Guatemala in 1954 when a CIA-led terror campaign overthrew the country's elected progressive president Jacobo Árbenz (Schlesinger and Kinzer, 2005).

By contrast, in the postwar mid-twentieth century, the capitalist metropole states had advanced so much so that their societies had grown increasingly capable of containing social change. Herbert Marcuse observed at the time:

> Contemporary society seems capable of containing social change— qualitative change which would establish essentially different institutions, a new direction of the productive process, new modes of human existence . . . This containment of social change is perhaps the most singular achievement of advanced industrial society the general acceptance of the National Purpose, bipartisan policy . . . the collusion of Business and Labor within the strong State testify to the integration of opposites which is the result as well as the prerequisite of this achievement . . . The fact that the vast majority of the population accepts, and is made to accept, this society does not render it less irrational and less reprehensible. (1964, p. 42)

By contrast a variety of radical political projects spread through the colonial world, especially in the years following World War II, and soon ruling elites began to crack down on these fledgling groups. Policymakers of the United States, the major power in the hemisphere, reacted sharply. George Kennan, the leading architect of U.S. Cold War strategy, declared in 1948 that the effectiveness of the American national security strategy would depend on devising "a pattern of relationships" to maintain and increase the "position of disparity" in which the United States had "about 50 percent of the world's wealth but only 3.6 percent of its population." Kennan insisted it was idealistic to "talk about vague and unreal objectives such as human rights, the raising of living standards and democratization," and he expressed that America preferred to have "a strong regime in power than a liberal government if it is indulgent and relaxed and penetrated by Communists" (quoted in Landau 1988, p. 33). Colonial apparatuses and U.S. occupations in the region thus relied heavily on coercive means to solidify elite rule.

In parts of the Francophone and Hispanophone Caribbean, movements for radical reform and militant labor struggles continued to percolate, even under severe repression and the state violence of U.S.-allied regimes (Mathew J. Smith, 2009). A kind of pattern emerged: in Cuba with the revolution of the 1930s, in Haiti with student unrest and the 1946 Noir revolution, and in the Dominican Republic with the Great Sugar Strike of 1946 alongside the resistance against the pro-U.S. dictator Rafael Trujillo (Derby, 2009). This reached its zenith in Cuba in 1959 when a small guerrilla army with grass-roots support overcame the U.S.-backed regime of Fulgencio Batista (Cushion, 2016). Events that followed would lead to the particularity of Cuba's state-socialist model.

In Puerto Rico, a massive level of U.S. investment entered into the island and increasing migration flows to the U.S. mainland functioned to meld Puerto Rico with the United States. During the first half of the twentieth century on the island, many of the powerful local families had managed to maintain dominant positions locally even throughout the major political and economic changes in the country (G. Lewis, 2004). During the mid-twentieth century, Puerto Rico (along with Ireland) would become an early laboratory for the export-processing model, which restructured the local economy to produce nontraditional exports for the international market (Ayala and Bernabe, 2007).

It is important to note the international context. In the years following World War II, the metropole capitalist states came into increasing conflict with anticolonial struggles and the socialist bloc states. Washington, working with its allies in the hemisphere, attempted to create mechanisms to solidify upper-class rule, with regional bodies such as the Organization of the American States (OAS), which was founded in 1948. It was in this climate that in 1949 the International Confederation of Free Trade Unions (ICFTU) was formed, and its task (with CIA direction) was to destroy the World Federation of Trade Unions (WFTU), the main international labor federation of socialists, communists, and their allies. The U.K. demanded that all trade union and labor organizations in the BWI withdraw from the WFTU and join the ICFTU. They all did, except for the leftist politician Cheddi Jagan's group in British Guiana, at a very steep price. Only days after Jagan was elected by a large majority of the Guyanese population as chief minister of British Guiana, British military forces under Winston Churchill intervened, ousting Jagan from office (Palmer, 2014).

In May of 1960 the United States began a trade and financial embargo on socialist Cuba, which would intensify over the coming years and continue on into the present day. Think of the social costs to such a small country and its people of such a deliberate, brutal, and criminal act. Among the things that helped Cuba survive, apart from the USSR and China, were a number of European countries that violated the blockade in defiance of Washington, signaling that hegemony is never absolute. It speaks to the pragmatism of many of those European capitalists that benefited from trading with Cuba and made it clear to their governments that Washington's punishing of Cuba was not necessarily consistent with their capital accumulation priorities.

Meanwhile, the OAS (headquartered in Washington) took on an increasingly interventionist role, excluding Cuba from the body in 1962. The OAS meeting to expel Cuba took place at a beach resort known as Punta del Este in Uruguay. It was at that meeting that the foreign minister of Cuba, Dr. Raúl Roa García, baptized that organization as "The Ministry of Yankee Colonies." As longtime participants in the OAS, many bourgeoisie democracies in the region have a checkered history of aiding and abetting, or ignoring, Washington's crimes.

Yet, in the wake of the Cuban revolution in 1959, leftist movements across the region began to grow. In response, the United States sought to shore up allied regimes while ousting potential threats. This included propping up the Duvalier dynasty and its paramilitary apparatus in Haiti and supporting a rightist military insurrection against constitutionalist forces in the Dominican Republic (Moya Pons, 1986). When the United States invaded the Dominican Republic and supported the removal of the country's elected government from power, the geopolitics of capital accumulation and its priorities worked to marginalize and fragment the working class and weaken its resistance. The 1965 Dominican Revolution cracked open the old National Guard built by the United States, but with its defeat, U.S. policy makers turned their attention toward funding a new Dominican army in an attempt to reconstruct a local proxy force.

A consolidation of the postcolonial states in the region occurred in the wake of occupations, interventions, and programs of tutelage following World War II, as the region increasingly became a site for foreign investment. Following World War II, all of the major capitalist development projects in the British Caribbean, for instance, depended heavily on inflows of international capital, most often from the United States. The British Empire, greatly weakened by the war and under pressure around the world (such as in India and Egypt), began new programs to better train and educate local pools of technocrats in their colonies, including in the Caribbean basin, practices that were meant to lead to independence (Mawby, 2012). Parts of the Caribbean, like Barbados, Trinidad and Tobago, Jamaica, and Guyana, were closely managed and monitored in their political transition toward independence.

During the initial stage of independence, matters like joint ventures, attracting FDI, nationalization, taxation, and other measures associated with so-called modernization (nation-building) were compromised from the outset. Of course, the fledgling working classes in the post–World War II Caribbean nations were promised that they would see a qualitative social and economic transformation in their lives in return for supporting and electing labor parties. Yet it did not materialize, and signs of discontent appeared in the first decade of independence. Examples of discontent include the so-called Rodney riots in Jamaica in 1968, the offensive against Trinidad and Tobago's first prime minister Eric Williams in 1970 (when elements of the army were in a state of near rebellion, albeit guided by nationalist sentimentalism), and the "Black Power Movement" that began to assert itself in the region in the early 1970s.

Meanwhile, the question and problem of the small size of Caribbean states dominated much of the discussion on economic growth and development in the English-speaking Caribbean throughout the postwar period (Potter, 1989). Development plans prepared by officials in the individual territories consistently referred to the constraints of their small size, with reference to scale and scope, routinely drawing attention to the need for regional cooperation (Best, 1966; Brewster and Thomas, 1967). With emphasis on resources such as bauxite and oil, they argued in favor of pooling raw materials to promote regional integration. Everything was being viewed via the prism of regional integration to overcome constraints of smallness.[4] These thinkers, for instance, argued that Jamaica, Guyana, and Trinidad should integrate on the basis of their raw materials. U.S. policy makers and powerful MNCs active in the region, though, worked against the idea of federation. Ultimately, with divisions in the region stoked and with any hope of a federation dimmed, there was the 1967 formation of the U.S.-approved Caribbean Free Trade Area (CARIFTA), and then the creation of CARICOM in 1973.

As the institutional mechanisms[5] for anchoring decolonization were set in place, the decision had already been made that progressive forces in the working class would not be allowed to manage the process leading to independence (Parker, 2002). Labor leaders were encouraged not to look beyond the immediate sectoral interests of their members, what could be described as "business unionism." Labor militancy hardly departed from workplace issues. It began to have more nationalist undercurrents and close ties to certain bourgeois political parties, with most workers preoccupied with bread-and-butter issues. There was much pragmatism and complicity with capital across the board, with unions, party leaders, and technocrats having various motivations—and often with heated competition over scarce resources. Labor movements predictably sided with their nation-states.

In other parts of the Caribbean more militant forms of labor did exist. In Trinidad, for example, the oil workers' union took up a "social movement unionism." Its organizers recognized how various factors had been used to divide the working class, and they took strong positions against U.S. intervention in the region (Kiely, 1996). However, it was in Hispaniola through the struggle against the authoritarian regimes of Batista, Trujillo, and François and Jean-Claude Duvalier that labor took on one of its most militant forms in the region—as the United States sought to prop up its local political allies and support business unionism or yellow unions in hopes of sidelining worker militancy and the left's influence. The popular movements in both countries came to include within them important labor contingents.

Throughout this period, though, many of the socialist and Marxist tendencies within and outside the political parties, and also within some labor organizations, were undermined or destroyed—often at the instigation of Washington and London. In Haiti, this occurred violently under the regimes of François Duvalier and, his son, Jean-Claude, where Communists and leftists were tortured and murdered, and many fled the country. Even the death penalty was reinstated in 1969 to deter left-wing activity. The governing elites' goal here was for the working class to not have strong foundations for the development of any revolutionary organizations.

These coercive actions (as well as the ideological and cultural factors that were set into motion) have had a long-term impact, having far-reaching consequences and implications for the historical development of institutions across the region. For any major progressive reform or structural alterations, there has to be a political movement with revolutionary or radical potential, which offers possibilities for people to be nurtured and skilled in struggle and for building and reproducing cooperative and community-oriented structures. Furthermore, the social and political soil must be conducive to this process developing. Through the latter half of the twentieth century, various elite groups and policy makers, especially in Washington and London, sought consistently to undermine this potential in the Third World.

It was also over these decades that anti-IMF and anti–foreign debt movements first emerged, with socialist Cuba at the forefront of the campaign. Cuba's revolutionary project early on had fostered projects of *internacionalismo*, supporting armed liberation struggles as well as educational brigades that were overtly political. It played a central role in bringing about the Tricontinental conference (Portella, 2017). At the conference in Havana in 1966, delegates from socialist and national liberation parties and movements from thirty-five nations (in Africa, Asia, the Middle East, and the Americas) met together, improving ties and communicating over the common struggles they faced. Yet the contradictions and differences between and within these projects remained manifold.

Throughout the 1960s and 1970s, U.S. policy makers were reacting strongly, working to isolate and undermine socialist and anticolonial movements in particular but also even moderate left-of-center "non-aligned" governments and movements that had sprouted up. It was during this time that Washington intensified its efforts at undermining Puerto Rico's independence movement, using various intelligence apparatuses, as it had against the civil rights and antiwar movements in the United States. In the wake of U.S. military aggression against the people of Southeast Asia, U.S. policy makers sought also to prop up their apartheid allies in southern Africa.

In 1975, in a rare event in history, revolutionary Cuba carried out a large-scale military operation halfway around the globe in southern Africa. It sent tens of thousands of soldiers, backed up by equipment (much of it from the USSR and eastern bloc countries), to support local leftist forces in Angola. The Cuban forces faced off in combat against invading U.S.-backed apartheid South African forces (Villegas, 2017). It was a rare moment in modern history when an independent country in the Third World had sent a large number of revolutionary forces across an ocean to another continent; even more extraordinary it was the continent where hundreds of years prior the ancestors of many Caribbeans had been captured, removed from, and forced into slavery. Socialist Cuba would continue in its internationalist endeavors, coming to the aid of many postcolonial peoples. The late Jamaican journalist John Maxwell (2008a) writes:

> May 26th . . . in 1963 Cuba dispatched a medical brigade to Algeria, then still bleeding from a successful but incredibly bloody war of independence against France. Fortuitously on the same date in 2008, a consignment of 4.5 tons of serum, medicines and sanitary materials donated by Cuba arrived in the earthquake ravaged capital of the Chinese province of Sichuan to help some of those injured in the May 12 earthquake. In the 45 years between those events the Cuban people have sent abroad as many health workers as US troops in Iraq—140,000 of them—to more than a hundred foreign countries, some considerably richer than Cuba but all in need of help. They range from Nicaragua to Pakistan, Venezuela to Vietnam, Haiti and Jamaica to Angola and Bolivia.

Through the 1960s, 1970s, and 1980s, as Cuba developed its particular form of state socialism, its economy became in part dependent on trade and material support from the Soviet Union; however, these new trade relations were unique in being based on fixing prices in large part to the quantity of labor that had been required (J. Smith, 2016, p. 210; Tablada, 1998). Cuba under Fidel Castro took a leading role in forming the Non-Aligned Movement (NAM), which came to include two-thirds of the United Nations' members, promoting the sovereignty and independence of many postcolonial societies and at time of constant imperial aggression.

Meanwhile, in other parts of the Caribbean, some economic sectors within the newly independent Caribbean states had begun to develop but in a manner that always privileged capital, of course. New mixed-state-capitalistic developmental projects had begun in some parts of the region, with some Caribbean policy makers influenced by Keynesian ideas and seeing the developments occurring in Cuba. By the 1970s, some Caribbean states, such as the Dominican Republic and Jamaica, were engaged in limited forms of ISI.

This occurred at a time in which new mining and tourism industries had already begun to expand in the region, which, of course, were built off the exploitation of local labor (Girvan, 1978; Gmelch, 2003; Merrill, 2009; Pattullo, 2005; Stephens and Stephens, 1986). Postcolonial states did in some instances engage in indicative (development) planning seeking to foment national economic development; however, indicative planning for national development bore limited fruit because where the state or worker associations do not own or control the means of production they cannot really plan the economy. Indicative planning is not central planning; of course, state managers can set targets that the capitalists can ignore, unless they are determining how those targets are to be pursued with profitability in mind. Yet, through the growth of the postcolonial governments in the region, and their various economic relationships, there was arising a new state bourgeoisie who used the state apparatus to accumulate power and wealth.[6]

Into the 1970s and especially by the 1980s, international capitalist investors (or what we could describe as incipient transnational capitalists) had begun to expand manufacturing industries in the region, taking advantage of low labor costs and the region's geographic proximity to North America and Europe. Apparatuses of the U.S. state and the Washington Consensus institutions increasingly sought to break apart any statist projects in the Third World, bringing down tariff restrictions and other barriers to capital, and further integrating region's such as the Caribbean with globalizing capital through neoliberal policies (Panitch and Gindin, 2013). Washington Consensus institutions—the IMF, World Bank, and the U.S. Treasury Department—came to play a key role in influencing the financial decisions of state officials across the Caribbean and Latin America (Layne, 2006).

Over these decades, grassroots movements' struggles continued in the face of a changing economic climate. Limited democratic openings did occur at different moments in the region. The expansion of new communication mediums, new media, and the rise of human rights networks brought additional pressure and a spotlight on the violent activities of the United States and the regimes it supported. In response, the strategies of U.S. policy makers began to shift. New emergent "soft power" strategies were developed in more depth. In those nations where right-wing dictatorships reigned, pressure built for democratic transitions and transparency. These transitions, though, were messy and often fraught with political violence, such as with the assassination of Walter Rodney in Guyana (Edmonds, 2014a).

Again forces from below reconstituted themselves, achieving briefly a counterhegemonic moment in the region, from around 1979 to 1983, with socialist Cuba remaining a radical beacon of revolutionary upheaval, then joined by the left-wing Sandinista and New Jewel revolutions, in Nicaragua and Grenada, respectively. This was also at a time when revolutionary forces in El Salvador gained momentum, along with Manley's social democratic government in Jamaica. It is important to remember that this was a period in which these political projects in the Caribbean could engage in trade and foreign relations with the Soviet Union and the eastern bloc, though by this time the United States and its allies had far surpassed their Cold War foes in military and economic capacity.

With its new "soft power" policies only beginning to become well-honed, U.S. policy makers and their allies reacted violently to the setbacks, supporting from bases in Honduras a paramilitary insurgency against the Nicaraguan people and openly invading Grenada. In Jamaica, U.S. intelligence agencies helped prop up paramilitary groups that would be used to target communities supportive of Manley's administration. Across the region, U.S. intelligence apparatuses played a leading role in undermining the new leftist and progressive initiatives, working with local sectors of the elite and the local right-wing political strata (Gane-McCalla, 2016; Ridgeway, 1994).

With the collapse of the Soviet Union in the late 1980s and early 1990s— many top elites and U.S. policy makers increasingly sought to broaden and solidify their new strategies of "soft power," while continuing to support targeted regime change operations, most notably in the Middle East. A new array of civil society groups and funding outlets were developed to promote U.S. policies abroad, most important, the new "democracy promotion" groups, alongside strategies for influencing media coverage, seeking to erase the violence caused by the United States and its allies and proxies. While in some cases, when the United States and its allies were unable to control a political transition, elections of more populist-progressive governments succeeded (as in Haiti in 1990 and 2000), but a new moment of regional upheaval and progressive possibility would not again emerge until the early part of the new century with the formation of an antineoliberal coalition backed by Venezuela.

With the Caribbean and Latin America as a laboratory, U.S. state managers worked to promote conditions under which tightly managed electoral systems would be allowed with citizens confined to choosing between competing elites (Robinson, 1996). This sought to allow for the illusory role of democracy, but as a policy of containment, reproducing conditions palatable to investors and with the goal of engendering less resistance as compared to the previous pro-Western authoritarian regimes. Reflective of this was the Caribbean Basin Initiative (CBI), developed under the Reagan administration, to help strengthen U.S. political influence as well as facilitate the growth of capitalist interests in the region.

The Reagan administration even promoted the exportation of Christian Pentecostal missionaries from the U.S. Bible Belt into Latin America and the Caribbean as a form of counterinsurgency (Melander, 1999; Preston, 2012). Evangelical communities, through their conservative ideology and connections with wealthy churches in the global north, serve as useful bulwarks against subaltern movements. Also, over the closing decades of the twentieth century, and posing a problem for Washington (and for the Vatican), there was the rise of Liberation Theology—a leftwing form of Catholicism. It preached liberation from social, political, and economic oppression as an anticipation of ultimate salvation. The theology would serve as an inspiration for many popular movements in the region, such as in Haiti and El Salvador.

Shifting political economic conditions were reflected in the changing lived circumstances and situations that many found themselves propelled into. Working class people became essentially trained to create sets of false dichotomies in their minds. Local practices and cultures became viewed as backwards, while the world of modernity, formed through a rupture with the past, represented progress. In one concrete example of this, by the 1970s and 1980s pregnant women increasingly began to give birth to their children in hospitals, with midwifery becoming less common. Being modern then became seen as having to separate oneself from the old ways, having to separate from nature, from community. In this new all-encompassing capitalist world the only way to relate to the world around oneself is through dichotomizing phenomena that are contradictory and dialectically interconnected, so that we are set against ourselves, breaking apart things that are fundamentally interconnected.

Into the latter part of the twentieth century, neoliberal practices intensified, imposed by emerging transnationally oriented elites: from devalued local currencies to downsized government apparatuses that freed up state assets for privatization, and further opened the region to globalizing chains of production and finance. Political struggles played out between different emergent transnational and more nationally oriented factions of the elites (Robinson, 2003). This occurred alongside what I describe as an incipient transformation of capitalist accumulation, from international to transnational process, as financial flows and stock exchanges expanded and began to become decoupled from the nation-state and increasingly functionally linked across borders. Yet at the same time many state policy makers and business groups in the region have at times struggled to gain global invest-

Figure 3.1 A variety of mass-produced trinkets sold to tourists at a store in Puerto Rico. Some of these goods were produced in China. (Photo by author.)

ment in certain sectors (such as in textile manufacturing), facing off against those economic interests exploiting labor in other parts of the world and operating often through more advanced built environments.

During the last decades of the twentieth century and into the new century, U.S. policy makers and leading dominant forces increasingly began to rely on more advanced means for constructing hegemonic consent (as discussed in the previous chapter). This occurred in part through polyarchy but also through the culture-ideology of consumerism that swept the planet and a variety of other dynamics of hegemony and domination. It was at this time that American political scientist Samuel Huntington updated George Kennan's formula of rule by force by insisting on "strong post-colonial states" that could mold "social agents . . . in order to establish stability and political control that" influence the "politics of development and the promotion of democratization throughout the 1980s and 1990s" instead of the old colonial or authoritarian regimes (Bilgin and Morton, 2002, p. 62). This revamping of political scenes occurred importantly at a time of intensifying capitalist cultural production and the increased availability of cheap consumer products. (See Figure 3.1.)

Populations and institutions across the region became more entwined with global finance and new global networks of production and trade. Large

Figure 3.2 Workers and passengers onboard a Carnival cruise ship active in the Caribbean basin. (Photo by author.)

swaths of the region were restructured as centers of tourism, where wealthy and middle-income tourists relax on beautiful beaches and buy exotic products reflecting or thought to reflect local culture. The destinations range from the ultimate in high-priced luxury to budget travel for the middle strata mostly from the global north, as well as ecotourism and various types of sporting holidays. New real estate developments have expanded across the region, servicing Western retirees and the region's new consumerist strata or those from the diaspora returning home for vacation or to live. Across the region this is reflected in high-cost gentrifying housing markets, new air-conditioned minimalls, and the massive spread of privatized beaches—so much so that in many areas it is impossible for locals to find affordable housing or even outlets to the coast. Airports in Miami, Fort Lauderdale, and Panama City meanwhile serve as nodes in the region's interconnectivity, with air travel (for those with the requisite papers) between many parts of the region only possible by way of these axes. The region has thus become enmeshed within an uneven but highly advanced web of capitalist relations.

New trade agreements and structural adjustment policies were set into motion, especially into the 1980s, during the late Cold War when a new financial architecture was laid out (Werner, 2016, p. 39). By 1983, the government of the Dominican Republic, for example, facing major fiscal and current accounts deficits, agreed to an IMF plan that reduced public spending, cut food subsidies, restrained the money supply, implemented a sales tax, and liberalized the local currency. Other countries followed suit:

> competition within the region intensified ... As a given state devalued its currency, neighboring states competing for the same investment faced extraordinary pressure to do the same, pushing wage rates down across the region and eroding the purchasing power of workers. Over the decade, the effective devaluation of circum-Caribbean currencies was more than 20 percent relative to their exchange rate with the US dollar in 1980. The cost of not following the trend of competitive devaluation was disinvestment. In Barbados, for example, a government commitment to a stable currency "priced" Barbadian labor out of this type of investment, leading to the swift exit of garment and other assembly jobs by the end of the decade. (Werner, 2016, p. 38)

The advancement of hegemonic consent has occurred with sweeping but also uneven and ruthless success, having a deep impact on populations across the region. Poor and working people have dealt in different ways with their changing life conditions under capitalist globalization. I have attempted in this book to be attentive to grassroots and radical aspirations and popular movements in the region, and the local life conditions, while recognizing the reproduction of the class system and the relations of power in the global arena. As I note in Chapters 4–7, across the Caribbean there are labor, social, and political movements that continue to conflict and engage in different ways with neoliberalism and the other practices of transnational elites. Dominant groups and state managers must also contend with struggles from below, with some popularly elected officials and at times some enlightened or pressured elites backing or allowing certain beneficial programs. Thus alongside rising social polarization and overaccumulation, the legitimacy crises of state actors, and global ecological disaster, we also see achievements and compromises in the Caribbean and other parts of the world—such as with the major improvements in education and health care, as well as expanded access to basic goods and high technology.

Cuba has stood out as an isolated example of a structural alternative to the bourgeoisie state in the region (Chailloux et al., 1999). But for its part, the Cuban state by the late twentieth century found itself up against the limits of socialism in one small country, an issue that is bound to come to the fore much more dramatically on the shifting terrain of the struggle over the state. The expression of these limitations has taken the form of increasing marketization and what has, more recently, been understood as a near-unmanageable amount of foreign investment toward tourism and the housing market. Cuba has undergone a shift: away from supporting armed struggles and leftist educational brigades abroad and toward medical internationalism, almost exclusively since the Special Period (this refers to the 1990s, the years immediately following the collapse of the Soviet Union, during which Cuba's economy suffered greatly). These can be read as concessions or limitations imposed by the capitalist global order, yet, at the same time, Cuba's medical internationalism has brought about major improvements in the quality of health care for millions (Brouwer, 2011). Cuba came to serve as a leading model of environmental sustainability and local organizing in the face of disastrous hurricanes, but throughout the 1990s, with the end of Soviet aid, the country faced a major crisis, the so-called "special period."

Meanwhile, the United States had become the sole world power. Ultimately though, as Mark Weisbrot (2015) points out: after decades of neoliberal Washington Consensus policies, by the late 1990s, many across Latin America and the Caribbean had benefited little or largely lost out. U.S. officials and their neoliberal allies went so far as to promote a Free Trade Area of the Americas (FTAA), meant first and foremost to further solidify and expand the huge profits of the TCC and its various emerging groups across the hemisphere. President Hugo Chavez of Venezuela, the sole leader to refuse the FTAA, quickly became the victim of a brief U.S.-sponsored coup on April 11, 2002, which ultimately failed (Wilpert, 2006).

The negative consequences of neoliberal policies in the Americas, though, was a key factor in the resurgence of leftist and progressive forces across many parts of the Americas in the early twenty-first century (Dangl, 2010). Such leaders came to office through elections in capitalist states, in Argentina, Bolivia, Ecuador, Honduras, Venezuela, and in other countries. This came to be known as the "pink tide." Important new regional bodies were formed, with the intention of promoting regional integration and less dependency on Washington and the U.S. dollar, what some described as "endogenous development" where they sought for capital accumulation to become tied to these local sites and populations in the global south. A key developmental trend, though, among these projects was the growing state revenues obtained through the global commodity boom of the early part of the century (due in part to rising demand of the BRICS). "Pink tide" states would rely heavily upon the distribution of proceeds from the sale of extracted natural resources.

While rentier models existed in previous decades (during which state income was in part derived from the rent of local resources to external clients), it was the aim of these "pink tide" projects to develop this model through regional and progressive initiatives (where revenues could finance vital infrastructure, education, health care, and so on). Though facing different conditions and particularities, the linkages of these states with the globalizing world economy continued to grow, with new mining, oil, and agricultural ventures linked into various transnational corporations.

While much remains to be seen, states within the alternative regional bloc known as ALBA (Alianza Bolivariana para los Pueblos de Nuestra América) have promoted an important antineoliberal developmental model, an alternative to that of the Washington Consensus. Yet, policymakers of the ALBA states, while attempting to forge new regionally geared integration, consistently found it impossible to break with rules set up under the World Trade Organization (WTO) (Cusack, 2019). Their attempts at indicative or regionally geared "endogenous" developmental strategies also exist with their own contradictions, such as the constant (though, sometimes necessary) compromises with the global market and TCC forces, as well as innumerable national and regional struggles, and major failures. Examples of this, as Joe Emersberger (2017) elaborates, include many macroeconomic policy errors under Venezuela's Bolivarian government and the failure of Ecuador's Citizen's Revolution to develop a strong grassroots structure, or to help build up an independent and combative grassroots media.

A number of Caribbean states in the Lesser Antilles entered ALBA (such as Antigua and Barbuda, Grenada, Dominica, Saint Kitts and Nevis, Saint Lucia, and Saint Vincent and the Grenadines) or, as in the case of Haiti, held an observer status with the bloc. These states, and others, such as Jamaica and the Dominican Republic, benefited greatly through Venezuela's Petro-Caribe oil agreement, which allowed for governments to pay only 60 percent of the oil shipments they purchase from Venezuela. The remaining 40 percent could be financed over twenty-five years at 1 percent interest, as long as oil prices stayed above $40 per barrel.

Furthermore, the ALBA bloc (which included Venezuela, Bolivia, Cuba, Nicaragua, and Ecuador) promoted regionalized social missions, state-oriented enterprises, a development bank, the so-called People's Trade Agreement, SUCRE virtual currency, the PetroCaribe soft-loan scheme, and the teleSUR media outlet. Unsurprisingly, the outcome of these ALBA initatives differed from country to country. The various national dynamics of the participating states, and deficiencies in control, administrative culture, and accountability have, as Asa Cusack (2019) argues, existed alongside shared commitments between many ALBA officials to a postneoliberal model and important new infrastructure and social investment projects. With the support of ALBA, officials of many of these countries sought out ways to avoid IMF loans and expand south-south economic cooperation, and, through a patchwork of sources, invest in needed social programs (Cusack, 2019, p. 167). This occurred in some of the microstates of the eastern Caribbean, for example:

> Dominica's "Yes, We Care" program was backed by Libya and Petro-Caribe; low-income mortgages relied on Venezuelan development bank BANDES . . . and numerous infrastructural projects were funded by a Chinese government grateful to Dominica for its sudden rethink on Taiwanese sovereignty. In Antigua, the Senior Citizens' Subsidy and the People's Benefit were funded by PetroCaribe; affordable housing schemes were made possible by cheap credit from Venezuela; a large solar-powered desalination project was backed by the United Arab Emirates (UAE), and as in Dominica, fishing infrastructure was revitalized by Japanese aid. . . . In St. Vincent, laptops provided to schoolchildren via the Education Revolution were donated by Portugal and assembled in Venezuela; Cuban equipment and expertise enabled the state-of-art Georgetown medical centre; expansion into geothermal electricity generation was funded by the UAE; and, crucially, construction of Argyle airport was supported by Mexico, Trinidad and Tobago, the Caribbean Community (CARICOM), Venezuela, Cuba, ALBA, PetroCaribe, Iran, Libya, and Austria, with every dollar of public money matched by from international partners. This common aid-seeking behavior was a conscious strategy to bring in capital and create employment without lightening the meager state purse or asking the taxpayer to refill it. (Cusak, 2019, pp. 81–82)

Meanwhile, some in the region clearly took advantage of ALBA's largess. Corrupt officials and elite-oriented political groups (such as the right-wing governments of Presidents Michel Martelly and Jovenel Moïse in Haiti and Danilo Medina in the Dominican Republic) siphoned off funds from Venezuela's subsidized oil aid program PetroCaribe (Danticat, 2018).

In recent years the ALBA initiative has faced a structural crisis. For nearly a decade, starting in 2008, commodity prices went into steep decline, creating significant problems for these leftist and progressive political projects that had relied upon the revenues gained through resource extraction. This crisis would mount especially for the main financier of ALBA, Bolivarian Venezuela, post-2013. The "pink tide" projects, with many internal contradictions of their own, came under tremendous pressure and destabilization campaigns by powerful elite-oriented groups and especially from officials operating through U.S. state apparatuses and its regional and international allies. In bringing about political transitions, U.S. policy makers and the transnationally oriented bourgeoisie use the most sophisticated forms of soft power (and, at times, backed up by force), as exemplified by the coups in Haiti, Honduras, Paraguay, and, more recently, Brazil, and the manipulated political transition in Ecuador. They can rely on "international peacekeepers" (such as MINUSTAH, the UN occupation force in Haiti), organizations such as the NED, philanthropists and NGOs, missionary groups, the corporate media, and covert, complex financial and political sabotage campaigns (see, e.g., Beeton, 2006).

It remains to be seen if this postneoliberal regional alternative will be able to survive, or how long it may last with Venezuela facing compounded crises and limitations, a disastrous currency system and falling commodity prices leading to a deep economic depression, and under constant attacks by the U.S. state apparatus and its allies. What is clear, though, is that Venezuelan support has provided a major boost to the ability of many regional states to expand their social investment projects and find alternative forms of financing. Also, while not included in Figure 3.3, Venezuela has provided vital aid for socialist Cuba, and vice versa.

In a particularly difficult and contradictory scenario, Nicaragua's officials, while participating in ALBA and thereby gaining important resources for in-

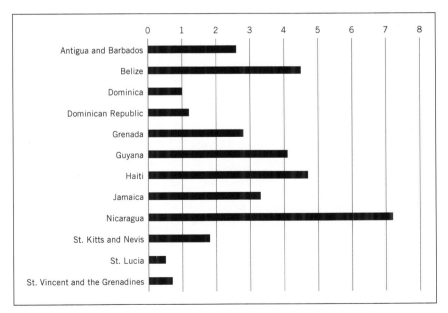

Figure 3.3 External financing from Venezuela as a percent of national GDP, 2012. (Source: National authorities, Petroleos de Venezuela S.A. (PDV SA), and IMF staff calculations, cited in Goldwyn and Gill, 2014, p. 9.)

vesting in social infrastructure, have also bent over backward in cutting deals with the United States, transnational capital, and local dominant groups. Down this contradictory path, while achieving economic growth and more investment in education and health care, inequality has grown. This balancing act has proven difficult, and it is a scenario that reflects both the contradictory and tenuous nature of attempting to construct an alternative political project with so few resources and with so many limitations and tensions.

In mid-2018, with ALBA weakened due to mounting crises in Venezuela and a right-wing counteroffensive across South America, Nicaragua's government faced unrest as it sought to reform its pension system in a manner conflicting with the neoliberal plans promoted by the IMF and its local business allies (Blumenthal, 2018). Soon some within the Nicaraguan police and groups supporting the government carried out a violent response against antigovernment demonstrators (Robinson, 2018), while at the same time (though receiving much less coverage in the media) some U.S.-backed antigovernment groups lashed out violently against supporters of the elected government (Blumenthal, 2018). This has led to an even more tenuous and escalated fight over political power, especially once the United States in late 2018 targeted Managua with economic sanctions through the bipartisan NICA Act (The Nicaragua Investment Conditionally Act of 2018).

Venezuela, with the largest oil reserves worldwide, will continue to be a primary target for U.S. governing elites and their right-wing and neoliberal allies in the region and in Western Europe. They see the country's ruination as a way to spark internal revolt and regime change. Trump's national security advisor John Bolton has spoken openly of how U.S. and regional businesspeople will benefit financially from a toppling of Bolivarian Venezuela and a privatization of the state's petroleum enterprise (Limitone, 2019). According to former FBI director Andrew McCabe, starting in 2017, U.S. President Donald Trump was talking behind closed doors about war on Venezuela (Elmaazi, 2019). This is further evidence that peace is never a defining feature of U.S. security strategy. Violence, oppression, and insecurity stamp the character of global capitalism with distinct fascistic undertones that the U.S. state helps to cultivate to protect this brutal, exploitative order.

In early 2019, the governments of the Dominican Republic, Haiti, and Jamaica folded to U.S. pressure, and sided with the Trump administration and other right-wing and neoliberal administrations in the hemisphere against Venezuela. This occurs after years of Venezuelan solidarity with these countries; 90 percent of Haiti's social investment budget long depended on Venezuelan aid (Cusack, 2019, p. 176); Jamaica benefited tremendously from PetroCaribe funds that softened its debt repayment obligations to the IMF, and Venezuela in part financed the country's only petroleum refinery PETROJAM; and, the Venezuelan government had financed the building up of Santo Domingo's oil refining capacity as well. By 2018, though, Venezuelan solidarity had dried up with the country facing an economic depression.

However, immediately following an OAS vote to go along with Washington in isolating Venezuela, huge protests broke out in Haiti demanding the resignation of the country's corrupt pro-U.S. president. A revolutionary moment in the country, huge protests have criticized his carrying out of IMF austerity measures and siding with Trump against Venezuela (Fornari, 2019). Socialist groups meanwhile protested in Santo Domingo and Santiago against their own government's siding with Trump.

The vast majority of the CARICOM states, like the states of Africa, Asia, and the Middle East, refused to go along with the U.S.-backed OAS vote against Venezuela. This illustrated a long-standing commitment by Caribbeans for the the region to remain a "zone of peace," and where the history of colonialism and imperialism is well remembered. Once again, the reaction of U.S. policymakers and their allies has been to work toward splintering the region geopolitically. This was on display when leaders of the Bahamas, the Dominican Republic, Haiti, Jamaica, and St. Lucia all met with Trump at his affluent Mar-a-Lago club in late March of 2019, discussing U.S. plans for the further isolation of Venezuela's constitutional government.

It is important also to recognize the restructuring processes that have occurred in the wake of hurricanes and natural disasters to hit the region. From New Orleans to the small islands of the southern Caribbean, large investors have sought to buy up real estate in the wake of hurricanes, as Naomi Klein (2018) has so comprehensively demonstrated in her work. The U.S. government's indifferent and inhumane response to the devastation wrought by Hurricane Maria in Puerto Rico is sure to have profound social, economic, and political consequences for the island and perhaps the region as a whole. Major components of postearthquake development strategy in Haiti, meanwhile, have centered on drawing in global investors, as the United States and World Bank facilitate export-processing ventures, new mining developments, and a host of undemocratic investment laws. According to major policy makers and investors, the solution to the emergencies that the region faces is to further deepen integration into the global capitalist economy and develop mechanisms to contain marginalized populations (Pyles, et al., 2017).

Local conflicts as well as shifting political scenes play out alongside persistent campaigns of elite political, economic, and media aggression, targeting working people as well as any alternatives in the region (Ellner, 2014). Such campaigns have a long history in the Americas, from U.S. imperialism in the late nineteenth century to the Cold War and post–Cold War interventions and containment strategies. Importantly, and in regard to the Caribbean context, Cuba has been one of the few countries in history that has been able to withstand such an onslaught and maintain a decent quality of life for its people. Yet, can Cuba float alone in a sea of capitalism? Faced with its own internal contradictions (such as a level of social control its socialist state maintains,[7] especially as it is under constant attack by the world superpower and rightist subversion), the future is unclear. While the island has pioneered efforts at surviving catastrophic hurricanes and U.S. state terrorism, socialism in one country cannot exist indefinitely.

Many, living in the Caribbean, have moved from one emergency to the next: in the midst of a global climate crisis and struggling under difficult economic conditions and the political realities of living on the imperial frontier and under systems that have entrenched elite power. The historical knowledge of Caribbean peoples, though, shapes a shared sense of struggle, so much so that it is not rare to find praise among broad swaths of Caribbean society for socialist Cuba's standing up against U.S. imperialism, or popular rage against the IMF, and the popularity of the CARICOM reparations campaign. Yet, across the region, leading dominant groups and their allied strata see capitalistic development and further integration into the global economy as the main solution. Working to link into the emerging global historic bloc, all is premised upon the exploitation of labor, whereas the social reproduction of large pools of populations are treated as supernumerary and not required. Global capitalist institutions and elites as well as their local allies are thus mobilizing an array of mechanisms to reproduce their hegemony and rule over those restive, marginalized, and surplus populations in the region. Entangled with all of this, of course, is a complex array of beliefs, cultural practices, and struggles to survive (Martinez-Vergne and Knight, 2005; Roorda et al., 2014). While developing through their own local particularities, it would be a mistake to posit an internal/external dichotomy where colonialism and imperialism have represented a purely external imposition. As Hilbourne Watson (2018) points out: after religious, economic, military, and other structures have been built up in the Caribbean for centuries, these became the basis of how much of everyday life was constructed. In this way many dominant practices and beliefs become internalized, a fact that is ignored through nationalist and nation-state centered discourse.

These are societies that have developed along different paths but also down common routes, whose populations are now becoming inserted into networks of transnational capitalist accumulation. Caribbean peoples exist through their complex life situations, but also largely under conditions of exploitation and marginalization. Even under all this a variety of forms of mutual aid and popular struggles do exist, a shining light into the future.

Conclusion: The Caribbean in a Transnational World

Moving into the new century, policies of global competitiveness and transnational integration manifest themselves in contradictory ways across the region. Transnational capital, rooted in the exploitation of labor, competes and flows across the globe. Many transnationally oriented elites and powerful state officials (most importantly, those operating through U.S. state apparatuses) have sought to disrupt possibilities of indicative planning or so-called endogenous development in the region. By contrast, some fractions of the TCC, such as statist groups operating out of China and Russia, at times do engage in policies that go against Washington's diktat (as with their current economic activities in Cuba, Nicaragua, and Venezuela). However, as many state and corporate elites seek out ways to promote chains of transnational accumulation, both businesspeople and officials and managers of many state institutions operating in the Caribbean are moving in a similar direction (Dayen, 2015; Robinson, 2014a). In this globally integrated yet conflict ridden world the threats to the popular classes are manifold, with crises converging on the horizon.

Through the Cold War, a variety of apparatuses and strategies were developed, usually through the United States and its allies, in order to react to the "internationalist" threats from below.[8] In recent decades we see how many of these mechanisms for achieving national and international hegemony have been restructured and reproduced. Rather than simply promoting a metropolitan elite or a nation-state's geopolitical "interests," these mechanisms increasingly function to promote a global system in the interest of the TCC.

The popular classes need to seek out routes for coordinating and integrating their struggle across borders, and toward a "global working class consciousness"—the open-ended challenge for this century. Given all the above, it is my contention that movements from below, while continuing to struggle through their national and regional institutions, must also seek out new forms of transnational coordination. Subaltern forces need infrastructure and organizational capabilities that work within but also beyond the national level.

The changes brought about through globalization have occurred unevenly and have deeply impacted populations across the region. What are the particularities of this political economic restructuring and the associated social changes that undergird this unfolding historical process?

To understand this, let us now focus our attention on the shift from the international phase of world capitalism to the transnational phase of world capitalism, examining comparative examples of how this has played out in the Caribbean basin. Let us think about how social production has become wrapped up in this transnationalization process, where we see many state managerial elite, labor leaders, technocrats, and others flocking to support and even defend the TCC's interests. The human costs fall on the direct producers, the working and popular classes, the negatively racialized, the impoverished women workers (waged and unwaged), the marginalized, and the superexploited.

Below I look at some of the major socio-economic dynamics in the region, such as labor export/migration, the reverse flows of remittances, export processing, mining, and cruise ship tourism. All these activities have undergone major transformations in the era of globalization, as have the distinct social groups tied to them. Caribbean society thus is deeply linked to these ongoing developments, a new epoch but part of processes going back centuries. These structural changes, manifested through the social conflicts and rearrangements taking place, need to be understood in their totality. This globalization era is novel in many ways, but it is also rooted in a system that has been at least five hundred years in the making.

4

The Caribbean Cruise Ship Business and the Emergence of a Transnational Capitalist Class

L ooking at the cruise business in the Caribbean, we can see one example of how the emergence of a TCC has led to restructuring processes that have been geared toward global accumulation, alongside an insertion of labor and consumer activities into transnational chains of accumulation. Processes of restructuring are taking place through circuits of transnational capitalist accumulation, connected most notably to the flexibilized exploitation of labor—with its gendered and racialized components—as well as changing corporate relations with the state.[1] Examining the political economy and historical development of the cruise ship business in the context of the Caribbean, this chapter asks: What are the fundamental ways in which it has been transformed during the globalization phase of world capitalism?

The cruise ship business is not motivated by the national economic development of any single country. Rather, it is capitalism's antisocial character at the local, national, regional, international, and, most important, in recent decades, the transnational level, that propels this business. When the ecological impact of mass cruise ship tourism is factored in, the costs to humanity become increasingly unbearable. This analysis of the expansion of capitalism in the Caribbean via leisure travel reinforces the point that capital accumulation is substantively a contradictory and unsustainable global process in which those exercising state power play a very important role. Policy makers from a variety of states (most important, from the United States) have become complicit in the reworking of capital-labor relations to benefit the TCC. It shows us that sovereignty, states, and power are not so tightly tethered to a self-interested territorial logic, but, rather, exhibit what John Agnew (2009) calls "certain migratory propensities." The number and range of incentives provided to cruise companies deepen processes of global market integration to the advantage of the TCC. Dramatically expanded cruise travel also draws growing numbers of the middle strata and working class into its circuits of consumption.

Global tourism—and, most notably, the cruise ship sector—stands out as a leading yet underexplored example of the growing transnationalization (the functional integration across borders) of many material and social relations.[2] Vacationers from among a growing number of affluent places worldwide partake in tourism, experiencing new commoditized and hypermobilized social relations. The Caribbean subregion accounts for 34.4 percent of cruise ship deployments worldwide. Whereas around 3.7 million passengers traveled worldwide on cruise ships in 1990, this number grew to 23 million in 2015 (Cruise Market Watch website, 2016). With the Caribbean the most popular subregion for the cruise business, the most highly visited destinations have included Cozumel on Mexico's Caribbean coast, the Cayman Islands, the U.S. Virgin Islands, Puerto Rico, Saint Martin, and Jamaica (Pattullo, 2005, p. 195). Tourism, the cruise business, and associated commercial and financial activity have grown as a dynamic core of the Caribbean's service sector (Daye et al., 2011) and a major spigot through which the region's population has been thrust into the globalized economy.

One of the largest and fastest-growing sectors within global tourism has been the cruise ship business (Pattuloo, 2005). While a number of studies have examined cruise ships (most notably, R. Klein, 2005, 2009) and other globalizing tourism businesses (Theobald, 2004), few have looked at these changing industries in relation to the formation of transnational capital and its dialectical relation with labor (Robinson, 2003). How are the shifting capital-labor relations of the globalizing cruise business occurring through the context of the Caribbean? Next, I look more broadly at contradictions underlying global tourism, focusing on the unequal social relations that undergird the business and how these connect with the rise of a TCC. After that I look at the history of the cruise business in the Caribbean, attending to the importance of shifting forms of capitalist accumulation. Last, I consider the changing contours of the business in the Dominican Republic, Haiti, and Jamaica, elaborating on its uneven and transnational structural features.

A growing body of work (going back through the last quarter of the twentieth century) on the sociology of global tourism has looked at tourist motivations, roles, and relationships, as well as institutions and their impact on tourists and tourist-receiving communities (Gmelch, 2003; MacCannell, 1976; Urry, 1990). Such studies force us to consider the nature of consumerism and cultural commoditization in the global era. Scholars have also looked at the role of tourism in regard to sex work, illuminating gendered and racialized aspects of class and productive relations in regions such as the Caribbean (Cabezas, 2009; Kempadoo, 2004; Pattullo, 2005; Wonders and Michalowski, 2001; Yelvington, 1995).

Chin (2008) has written on the gendered labor patterns onboard cruise ships. Not only are there few women ship captains but unequal gendered dynamics permeate labor relations across the business. Women workers from lower-income backgrounds are usually "performing the 'frontline' work of interacting with passengers, and/or the 'backstage' work of cleaning cabins" (Chin, 2008, p. 13). While it is common for the "white" Eastern European women workers to greet passengers, negatively racialized women workers from the global south are most often tasked with cleaning cabins.

The racialization of labor in the cruise ship sector, as so many other parts of the global economy, has been built up through social constructs and material relations that reproduce ethnic divisions and racialized exploitation. To provide just two examples, Terry (2013) has written specifically on the discursive makings of Filipinos through the global division of labor present in the cruise business, while Oyogoa (2016a, 2016b) has pointed out how racialized class relations of the world system have been reproduced onboard today's cruise ships. Negatively racialized populations, recruited mostly from former colonial countries, have been idealized as the perfect crew members to perform menial, low-wage services. Some scholars have described the situation developing in the Caribbean region as "plantation tourism," with labor-intensive hotels and cruises evolving from the old plantation agriculture and other labor intensive exploitive models, where low-wage jobs are reserved for Caribbean, Central American, East Asian, Pacific Islander, and other former colonial peoples (Boyce, 2003; Weaver, 2001, p. 166).

Traditionally, scholars have looked at different nation-state-based elites as dominating the resort and cruise ship destinations. Dotting the Caribbean's new array of privatized beaches, these businesses are under the control of a coalition of foreign, expatriate, and local elites (R. Klein, 2005, 2009). In fact, it is clear that the world system that came about through earlier phases of capitalism has played a key role in shaping many terms and conditions of today's capitalist globalization (H. Watson, 2015).

World systems scholars have looked at the cruise ship business and tourism industry in the developing world based on the flow of resources from periphery nations to wealthy core nations (Boyce, 2003; Weaver, 2001). Through this perspective, we would then see the U.S. state as facilitating the profiteering activities of U.S. national capitalists (with a fraction being internationally oriented) (Sprague, 2014b). This is in fact also a perspective underlying nationalist sentiments that many scholars and activists have embraced, including within the

Caribbean: that poorer nations and their business communities must compete with influential foreign national power blocs. Yet as capitalist accumulation has undergone fundamental changes over recent decades, we need to recalibrate how we understand political economy in the global era. Developmental models and relations tied to the interstate system continue to erode, as many state leaders and local elites promote transnational capitalist interests and global competitiveness—even if this does include national rhetoric.

State apparatuses and power blocs in society cannot be understood outside of changing processes of production, labor struggles, and class and ideology formation (Poulantzas, 1978, p. 27). With this in mind, we must understand capitalism and the state in its historical *and* contemporary relations. Over the closing decades of the twentieth century and into the twenty-first century, international chains of accumulation and the previous indicative development planning (with an eye to national goals) of state managers has largely fragmented and become subsumed within processes of global competiveness and transnational accumulation. The social reproduction of corporate and state elites is less and less tied to competing national interests but, rather, is geared toward profiting through the functionally integrated cross-border networks of capitalist accumulation that have formed.

With the Caribbean as an example, my central argument here is that the restructuring of the cruise ship business is tied up with the emergence of a TCC and the globally exploitative relations that it promotes. At the heart of this are altered labor relations, the restructuring of state-capital relations, and a reorganization of financial and productive processes within the business.

Global Tourism and Cruise Ships

The rise of a global tourist industry, and a TCC, has been a consequence not only of major technological and organizational transformations associated with global capitalism (Lumsdon and Page, 2003; Rodrigue, et al., 2013; Theobald, 2004) but also, and most important, changing social and class relations. Tourism is estimated to account for approximately 9 percent of global GDP, or more than $6 trillion (World Travel and Tourism Council, 2013). TNCs involved in transportation, hotels, and various tourism-related activities have proliferated worldwide (Dowling, 2006). This has been aided by well-organized lobbies of industry representatives and allies, as well as transnationally oriented elites and technocrats operating through state apparatuses. Alongside the increasing transnational integration among dominant groups, lower- and middle-income populations (including those from the global south) have become inserted into these transnational chains of accumulation. As Robinson explains, "The globalization of the tourist industry draws in local contingents around the world in diverse ways" (2003, p. 198).

TABLE 4.1. OVERALL TOURISM ARRIVALS*					
	1970	1980	1990	2000	2010
World	165.8	278.2	441	680	940
To Developed Countries	—	194	296	417	498
To Developing Countries	—	83	139	257	442
Caribbean	4.2	6.9	12.8	20.3	23.1
Over Surface	—	0.7	0.4	1	1.4
By Air	—	6	10.9	16.1	18.6
Source: UNWTO, 2011. *Millions.					

TABLE 4.2. OVERALL EXPENDITURES BY TOURISTS*				
	1980	1990	2000	2010
World	106.5	269.5	495.6	960
Caribbean	3.5	9.8	19.9	—
Source: UNWTO, 2011. *US$ billions.				

Another key factor in the global tourism industry's phenomenal expansion has been the reconfiguration and growth of social strata worldwide that have disposable income for leisure activities (Liechty, 2003; Rohde, 2012). While inseparably linked to rising global income inequality and social polarization, a growing portion of the global population takes part in mass tourism, and hundreds of millions of jobs are tied to the industry (Mowforth and Munt, 2008). According to the United Nations World Tourism Organization, more than one billion people now take part annually in tourism outside of their home country (UNWTO, 2012).

The Caribbean has been a major site for global tourism. In 1996, for example, $7 billion was spent on tourism in the Caribbean annually (Uebersax, 1996), and, by 2013, this had risen to $28.1 billion. Meanwhile, with a growth rate above 7 percent annually since 1990, the global market for cruising had approximately 18.3 million customers in 2010 (Rodrigue, et al., 2013). Various segmented and niche markets have come into being, where wealthy and privileged working-class clients of global society are channeled into different lifestyles, featuring a variety of entertainment to fulfill their desires and experiences. Cruise costs for passengers, at one point, ranged from US$100 per night to more than US$1,000 per night (Tortello, 2006). Tourists are increasingly incorporated into chains of global accumulations and what Sklair (2002) describes as a globalized consumerist culture. (See Tables 4.1 and 4.2.)

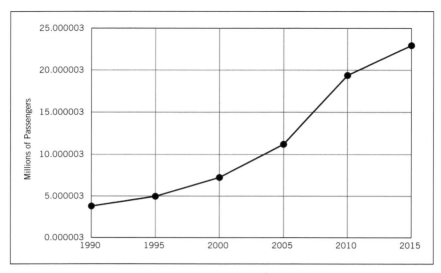

Figure 4.1 Number of cruise ship passengers carried worldwide. (Source: Business Research & Economic Advisors, 2015.)

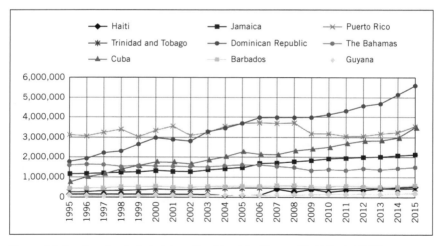

Figure 4.2 Number of arrivals by international tourists. (Source: World Bank, 2017.)

While all regions have experienced growth in tourism arrivals over recent decades, the share of overall arrivals to "peripheral" countries has grown faster relative to the share of arrivals to "core" countries. As Table 4.1 shows, while only 83 million people visited developing economies in 1980, this reached 442 million by 2010. By 2030, it is believed that annually more than 1 billion tourists will visit "emerging economies" (UNWTO, 2011, p. 15). Also, whereas 8 percent of tourists in the mid-1970s were from core countries visiting periphery countries, by the mid-1980s, this figure had grown to 17 percent, reaching 20 percent by the mid-1990s, and then 25 percent by the new century (Robinson, 2003, p. 131). The total number of tourists traveling aboard cruise ships has grown tremendously over recent decades, with the total number of tourists visiting different countries, such as in the Caribbean, also varying greatly but growing over recent decades. (See Figures 4.1 and 4.2.)

In turn, the development of the global cruise ship business has occurred in the context of the rise of transnational production and financial systems in the world economy. The business underwent a transformation during the late twentieth and early twenty-first centuries, as the maximization of profits and streamlining of the passenger experience occurred alongside a centralization of capitalist interests. The cruise ship business has become oligopolized by two companies, Royal Caribbean and Carnival Cruise Lines, which together control around 70 percent of the cruise sector. Both companies have become involved in a large number of corporate synergies, interacting with a broad range of businesses (Rodrigue, et al., 2013). According to Bloomberg, as of January 2018, Carnival Corporation has a market capitalization of US$47.98 billion while Royal Caribbean has a market capitalization of US$26.2 billion. The two companies also own numerous subsidiaries and have purchased or eliminated many of their former competitors. A magnet for investor confidence, a number of transnational capitalists and large global investment firms have increased their stakes in these companies.

Meanwhile, the cruise business has increasingly sought to squeeze labor, limit regulatory oversight, and micromanage the passenger experience. In regard to the impact on local populations in regions such as the Caribbean only a very small strata of the Caribbean population gains long-term benefits from the business, and local tax revenues are small, whereas the industry's environmental damage has been significant and well documented (R. Klein, 2009).

The major cruise companies and their owners have come to embody "transnational capital"—that part of capital that traverses borders through transnational circuits of accumulation. By influencing and benefiting from the new transnational orientation of many state policy makers, circumventing regulatory regimes, and penetrating local economies, cruise companies sell "exotic" experiences to high-consuming sectors while simultaneously exploiting workers and locals. Through the expansion of the cruise ship and other global businesses, nations in the Caribbean and other regions have become more organically linked into the global economy. Local elites and officials compete to entice global investment, which they rely on more and more for their own social reproduction.

TABLE 4.3. NUMBER OF CRUISE SHIP PASSENGER VISITS BY COUNTRY, 2015			
Antigua & Barbuda	576,000	Haiti	600,000
Aruba	546,600	Jamaica	1,349,100
Bahamas	2,940,000	Martinique	263,700
Barbados	554,400	Puerto Rico	1,393,900
Belize	876,600	St. Kitts & Nevis	676,500
Cayman Islands	1,446,300	St. Lucia	603,200
Cozumel (Mexico)	2,538,100	St. Martin	1,854,400
Dominica	226,000	Tobago	30,900
Dominican Republic	480,600	Trinidad	10,800
Grenada	201,500	U.S. Virgin Islands	1,839,700
Source: Business Research and Economic Advisors, 2015.			

TABLE 4.4. NUMBER OF CRUISE SHIP PASSENGER VISITS BY SUBREGION, 2015	
Eastern Caribbean	11,208,000
Western Caribbean	5,012,000
Southern Caribbean	3,060,000
Mexico	4,345,000
Source: Business Research and Economic Advisors, 2015.	

The data in Tables 4.3 and 4.4 show the large number of cruise ship passengers that visited Caribbean destinations in 2015. This data does not include Cuba, which went from a negligible amount earlier in the century up to 184,000 cruise ship passenger visits in 2016, and in 2017 witnessed a massive growth to 541,000 passenger visits (Associated Press, 2018). Even under Trump's rolling back of some of the "enlightened" Obama era policies toward Cuba, cruise ship visits to the island have continued to expand.

Shifting social relations are at the core of the restructuring process. For example, while wealthy and middle-strata passengers experience pleasurable vacations, they are subsumed within a highly advanced and segmented capitalist society that socially alienates them through the reality they experience and the inability to conceive of or determine the true character of what they temporarily interact with and inhabit (Marx, 1867/1992, pp. 163–177). Even while enjoying pleasurable experiences, passengers are disconnected from understanding the social, economic, political, and ecological nature of the regions in which they travel. We can consider, for example, recent changes in the business that guarantee passengers are channeled into cruise company-controlled or connected service sector zones. In the past, cruise ship passengers could more easily interact with locals, independent merchants, and the informal market. In recent decades, passengers have increasingly been channeled into company-controlled markets. This reflects an intensified social alienation, where passengers believe they are shopping or taking part in local markets, when in fact they are operating through chains of accumulation controlled by a transnational cruise ship company. As scholars have begun to examine, the commodity relations and consumerist culture of tourism and travel, with their new "hypermobilities," have helped shape modern social life, including many imaginations and aspirations (Cwerner, Kesselring, and Urry, 2009; Sheller, 2003).

The Historical Formation of the Cruise Ship Business

With the European imperialistic conquest of the Caribbean region and the ethnic cleansing of its indigenous inhabitants, African chattel slaves and a smaller number of impoverished European migrants composed the initial labor imported into the region (Linebaugh and Rediker, 2013; Williams, 1944; Wolf, 1997). Beginning in the 1830s, the use of steamships significantly reduced the time of the journey from Europe, eliminating the reliance on sailing vessels. By the latter part of the century, a handful of tourists from privileged strata in North America and Europe began to visit Caribbean destinations. Where they visited usually reflected their nationality, as English tourists predominantly visited the British colonies of Nevis, Barbados, and Jamaica, while French tourists went to Martinique, the Dutch to Curaçao, and North Americans mostly to Cuba and the Bahamas, islands in close proximity to south Florida (Gmelch, 2003).

By the early twentieth century, modern oceanic liner designs debuted, which immediately introduced a rigid class system onboard the vessels. As the luxurious first-class experience above decks improved, the cramped unventilated spaces below deck housed the rest of the ship's passengers and crew. The 1997 Hollywood film *Titanic* illustrates this dichotomy quite vividly. Yet, as migration slowed, shipping liners sought to provide cheap tickets to people in the United States who wanted to return to visit Europe. "If the westbound traffic had dried up, the thinking went, perhaps the new prosperity in the U.S. might give rise to a new flow in the other direction" (Garin, 2006, p. 17).

Transatlantic merchant shipping operations went through tough times, especially as luxury travel and mass migration came to a halt during World War I. As they tried to salvage their investments following the war and during the pre-Depression economic boom of the 1920s, some companies began to seek out new customers among the U.S. middle and upper strata by offering improved accommodations, or "affordable luxury."

During the winter months of this period, early cruises to the Caribbean became essential to the viability and profitability of many ship companies. These early visitors, for instance, from Europe and North America visited Jamaica aboard steamers of the United Fruit Company or onboard the Hamburg-American West Indian cruises (Tortello, 2006). Yet many factors continued to impede a full-scale cruise ship business, including the fact that the passenger ships at the time were ill-suited to the Caribbean climate with their limited deck space, small windows, lack of air-conditioning, and recreational facilities deep in the hulls of ships (Garin, 2006, p. 19).

Transatlantic passenger shipping slowly declined during the first half of the twentieth century and, by the 1950s, had collapsed. This decline was linked to the advent of large passenger jet aircraft in the decades following World War II, when intercontinental travel largely shifted from oceanic liners to planes. The antiquated and uncomfortable liners had been designed to maximize passenger numbers, with stifling cabins that often lacked windows. In addition, the ships suffered from high fuel consumption and had deep hulls that prevented them from entering shallow ports.

Into this scene entered a capitalist entrepreneur, Frank Fraser, who sought to build the first year-round cruise-only business that would operate out of south Florida. Miami's proximity to the warm climate and islands of the Caribbean made it an ideal choice. It also signaled the shift in the role of the maritime passenger ship from transatlantic transportation to cruise tourism. During the 1960s, a handful of cruise businesses formed in Miami, most often operating excursions into the Bahamas using prewar U.S. coastal passenger ships. In fact, the rise of an international cruise ship tourist business in the region was facilitated in part due to the United States. After World War II, new U.S. government policies seeking to open international markets helped instigate the flow of U.S. capital and tourists into the Caribbean. Some Caribbean elites profited from new construction projects, marketing, and the management of modern resorts.

Similarly, with the transition away from British colonial rule, many Caribbean governments and businesses adjusted their practices, seeking out foreign investment. U.S.-domiciled international cruise ship companies became an important new source of foreign capital for the region. Caribbean states began to reduce tariffs and other barriers to travelers entering Caribbean countries, eliminating taxes on arriving and departing tourists, and providing waivers for visa requirements. The growth of tourism, as Chase (2002) argues, also helped shift a more significant segment of West Indian labor into the service sector. Scholars have also argued that the expansion of the tourism industry impacted the social structure of the Caribbean, where the rising hegemony of the United States and new interactions associated with tourism impacted locals by "reinforcing or rearticulating conceptions of national, historical, racial, and economic difference" (Hogue, 2013).

The first major international cruise corporation was Royal Caribbean Cruise Lines, which was owned in large part by wealthy Scandinavian shipping families, the Skaugens and Wilhelmsens, and operated by experienced businesspeople in Miami. One of these capitalists, Ted Arison, founded Carnival Cruise Lines in 1972. From a long-established Jewish shipping family, Arison had invested in *Nili*, one of the Fraser family's cruise ships in the mid-1960s. While a number of cruise lines began during the 1960s and 1970s, by the latter decades of the twentieth century, the business had become highly profitable and was able to hire from a large pool of poor working people in regions such as the Caribbean and Oceania (R. Klein, 2005). As cruise vacations were promoted throughout the latter decades of the twentieth century, the fledgling industry gained popularity among middle-strata vacationers and retirees, especially in North America and Europe. It achieved notoriety through media, for instance, with visits by movie stars covered through private radio and television broadcasts.

Transnational Capital in the Globalizing Cruise Ship Business

The last decades of the twentieth century were a period of growth for cruise line operators as they became ubiquitous in popular culture. Cruise ship companies have become entwined with global capital flows, open to outside capital investments and their shares available on stock exchanges. One ship manufacturer explains that there has been a "shift in the ship financing sector" that "uncovers how fast the traditional financiers to the cruise shipping industry fade away" as a new globalized financial system takes hold (Kuehmayer, 2013, p. 2). With deep pockets and a financial buffer in difficult times, the largest TNCs in the business have become deeply linked with the high-tech global financial system rather than the more nationally rooted financial sectors of the past. Carnival went public on the New York Stock Exchange (NYSE) in 1987, followed by Royal Caribbean in 1993. This reflected in the 1990s and 2000s the boom that occurred alongside major organizational and technological advancements, as well as shifting capital-labor relations. A shipbuilding "frenzy" occurred with larger and larger ships produced (R. Klein, 2005, p. 14). New regions such as in East Asia also started to become major sites of cruise tourism.

Cruise ship companies have initiated stock market launches (also known as initial public offerings [IPOs]) or have partnered with venture capitalists and

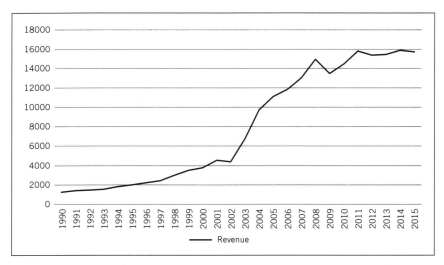

Figure 4.3 Revenue (US$ millions), Carnival Cruise Lines. (Source: Company tax records obtained by the author through the U.S. Securities and Exchange Commission.)

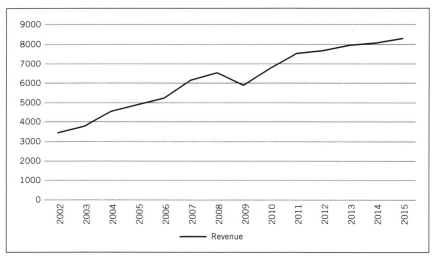

Figure 4.4 Revenue (US$ millions), Royal Caribbean. (Source: Company tax records obtained by the author through the U.S. Securities and Exchange Commission.)

other investors to raise needed capital, in turn allowing for more financial liquidity and growth. Transnational capitalist Leon Black (of Apollo Management) established Prestige Cruise Holding, which now controls Norwegian Cruise Line, Regent Seven Seas, and Oceania. Meanwhile when Carnival went public in 1987, it offered to corporate investors 20 percent of its stocks, which were used for new ships and expansion beyond cruises (as with Carnival Airlines, which took over and merged with Pan Am, and expanded into the hotel business as well). It has since opened up to many more investors. Royal Caribbean's annual revenues of $3.4 billion in 2002 grew to nearly $7.7 billion in 2012. Carnival Cruise Lines revenues of $1.25 billion in 1990 swelled to nearly $15.5 billion by 2013. Far from an anomaly, the cruise ship business's integration into the global financial system continues unabated. (See Figures 4.3 and 4.4.)

The owners and major stockholders of the cruise ship companies became tied to myriad other companies and industries worldwide. As transnational capitalists, they have taken advantage of the scale and financial resources at their disposal to invest in numerous companies and markets. In 2013, major global investment management firms controlled more than a third of Carnival's stocks, including Thornburg, BlackRock, Schroder, Legal & General, M&G, Artemis Investment, and the global asset managers TIAA-CREF, UBS Global Asset, and JPMorgan (Kuehmayer, 2013, p. 16).[3] According to Nasdaq in early 2018 the top five institutional holders had changed to: Suntrust Banks, Bank of America, Vanguard Group, Blackrock Inc., and Northern Trust Corp.

TNCs that invest in the cruise business, such as JPMorgan, are in turn integrated with global markets around the world. As Andrew Gavin Marshall (2013) observes: "A geopolitical force unto itself, and a conglomerate embedded within a transnational network of elite institutions and individuals, JPMorgan Chase goes beyond the financial indicators. Put simply, it is one of the most powerful banks in the world." Transnational capitalists, operating through companies headquartered in the United States (such as with JPMorgan) and in other countries, are geared toward global competitiveness through their holdings in these investment and asset firms and are involved, for instance, in FDI and cross-border M&A in many parts of the world. Furthermore, TNCs, such as those in the cruise business, have increasingly sought out cost-efficient synergies, forming relationships with a variety of other companies (Trade Winds, 2014; Travel Weekly, 2003).

Cruise ship magnates, few in number, have become some of the wealthiest people on the planet, holding investments in numerous globalized industries through a web of transnational finance. In 1992, decades after founding the Carnival Cruise Lines, Ted Arison appeared on the Forbes list of America's hundred wealthiest, worth an estimated $2.8 billion (Garin, 2006, p. 38). After stepping aside and leaving the company to his son Micky in 1990, Ted went on to own Israel's largest construction company as well as massive real estate, technology, and financial holdings. In 1997, he led a corporate buyout of the government of Israel's largest state bank while he also turned down an offer to become Israel's finance minister. At the time of his death, his holdings went to his daughter, instantly making her the wealthiest

Israeli citizen. Micky Arison, current chief executive of Carnival (and owner of the Miami Heat basketball team), was said to be the 32nd richest person in the United States in 2004. As of 2013, he was said to be worth a total of $5.9 billion, the 211th wealthiest billionaire in the world (Forbes, 2013). His investment holdings include companies and stocks that span the globe. In 2008, his reported tax filings were only around $7 million, while his base salary was $880,000, with cash bonus of $2,206,116, stocks granted of $3,618,481, and other compensation totaling $496,513 (Forbes, 2009).

As capitalist owners of the cruise ship corporations have organized to secure massive profits, labor has organized and struggled for improved working conditions. Workers onboard cruise ships have in some instances gone on strike (Oyogoa, 2016a). Ross Klein has written on the conditions of sexual exploitation that women workers face, the restrictions on labor's ability to organize, and deportation of workers who engage in union activities onboard the cruise ships. He has documented also various means of social control and surveillance targeting workers in the business. Cruise lines have typically hired workers from multiple countries, with different languages and ethnic backgrounds, as a strategy for undermining their ability to engage in collective action (R. Klein, 2001–2002): "In those few cases where workers have joined together, they have met with harsh resistance from the companies. In 1981, 240 Central American workers went on strike aboard a Carnival Cruise Line ship in Miami to protest the firings of two co-workers. The company ended the strike by calling the U.S. Immigration and Naturalization Service. The strikers were declared illegal immigrants, bussed to the airport and flown home, unemployed."

In another instance, a cruise company solved a labor dispute by placing South Korean, Jamaican, and Haitian room stewards on buses at the Port of Miami, sending them immediately back to their countries (R. Klein, 2001–2002). Supervisors onboard the ships hold tremendous power over labor, as they can dock pay, which is a real threat to many workers onboard the vessels who have already paid for their return trips. Klein gives the example of a 27-year-old janitor from Saint Vincent. The worker faced a 90 percent reduction, with his "pay reduced from US$452 a month to US$37 while working for Carnival Cruise Line." Even after "five years with the company, he feared his supervisors would brand him a troublemaker if he complained. He endured the reduction in pay without question, rather than risk his job" (R. Klein, 2001–2002).

Fundamental Changes to the Cruise Business under Global Capitalism

Throughout this unprecedented growth and centralization of the business, it has undergone deep changes in a variety of areas. These include the companies becoming highly adept at managing public opinion, the experience of passengers, and the activities of the labor force. Carnival cruise lines, for example, first developed highly focused onboard revenue strategies, where low ticket prices attracted customers who then became consumers at casinos, bars, stores, and spa services. The former head of the Dominican Republic's Chamber of Commerce, who helped bring the cruise business to her country, observes: "The industry has changed completely since the 1970s, when I first became involved with it. It functions totally differently now, growing in volume but also overhauled with everything working so fast, calculated onboard, and immediate with the internet. The customer experience is now an all-inclusive package and everything is tightly customized, with every avenue of profit tapped into" (Rosalinda Thomas, personal communication, 2015).

The cruise businesses links with other economic sectors and the strength of its influence on state officials has become fundamental to its business model. As part of this process, its onboard workforce has become flexibilized with its time commoditized and intensely managed.[4] At the same time, like many other sectors of global tourism, the cruise ship business has obtained more and more value from passenger spending, while maintaining a web of local and regional alliances and relations that benefit from the business (Clancy, 2008). In the context of this phenomenon, I want to highlight five restructuring processes that are taking place:

1. A variety of organizational advancements have been used to restructure the manner in which labor is exploited. For the cruise business, "flags of convenience" are one of the most important elements: this practice allows companies to flag their ships from countries that do not (or are unable to) enforce labor protections.

The flags of convenience serve as a mechanism to allow companies to employ cheap labor and avoid state regulations and pressure from labor unions, as well as gain from lower registration fees, regulations, and taxes, all of which serve to strengthen their position against labor, giving them significant competitive advantages (van Fossen, 2016). As Chavdar Chanev (2015) writes, in regard to cruise ships registered in the Bahamas, Panama, and Liberia, "There are no codes about the number of hours a seafarer may work or his/her days off, no minimum wages, staff can be punished by the captain in case of complaining about issues (such as safety or food quality. . .)." As an example of this: Royal Caribbean maintains its official corporate headquarters in Miami, while officially being incorporated in Liberia. Some trade unions, such as the International Transport Workers' Federation (ITF), have attempted to challenge this practice with campaigns against the cruise companies' use of flags of convenience. In 2002, the ITF launched the "Sweat-

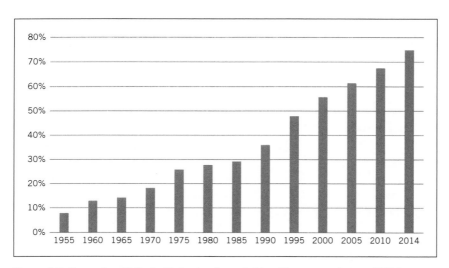

Figure 4.5 Share of world fleet with foreign flagged ships. (Source: van Fossen, 2016.)

ships" campaign (ITF, 2006; War on Want and ITF, 2002), attempting to gain more public attention to the plight of workers onboard the ships. However, the union's campaign was short lived and lacked resources. As Figure 4.5 shows, the share of foreign-flagged ships has continued to soar in recent years.

In the 1960s and 1970s cruise ships and their flags represented national lines, such as the Greek Line, the Italian Line, or the Cunard (Anglo-American) Line. This was reflected in the fact that, often, the largest proportion of the workers were actually from those respective domiciles, and some from nearby countries, as explained to me by a former cruise ship employee who worked in cruise liners in the 1970s and 1980s (Mario Paz, personal communication, 2011). However, we now see an erosion of that relation, as the hiring practices of today's cruise businesses appear to have no significant national orientation but, rather, pull from a global supply of labor (Chin, 2008; Oyogoa, 2016a, 2016b; van Fossen, 2016). The shifting labor-capital relations onboard the cruise ships became visible in the late-1970s and 1980s, coinciding with the growth of companies such as Carnival. Initially, companies such as Royal Caribbean and Norwegian Cruise Line (NCL) retained some of their national character in terms of officers, but even that practice has diminished in recent years. Flags of convenience have served as an important mechanism through which capitalists in the cruise business can exploit a global division of labor.

2. Major technological advancements have been used for restructuring the business. As previously mentioned, new computer technologies allow for instant transactions and more commodification. Another advancement has

been in industrial innovations that, for example, have allowed for larger and larger ships. For comparison, large cruise ships in the 1970s weighed 20,000 to 30,000 tons; in the 1980s, 50,000 to 70,000 tons; in the 1990s, 100,000 to 140,000 tons; while, by the first decade of the twenty-first century, they reached 220,000 tons. This has provided further impetus for the creation of new port facilities able to accommodate the new ships. Expanding capacities (from less than 1,000 passengers in the 1970s to more than 6,000 in the early twenty-first century) have also meant that fewer vessels are required for the same number of tourists. For example, 907,611 passengers visited Jamaica in 2000 onboard 504 different cruise ship visits, also known as "calls." In contrast, in 2010, a similar number of passengers visited during just 325 trips (Caribbean Tourism Organization, 2017).

3. A shifting industry-state relation is taking place. Cruise ship companies have gained unprecedented rights and powers, especially in regions such as the Caribbean, where state officials compete with one another to attract TNCs active in global tourism. According to Carnival chairman Micky Arison, appreciation for the impact of cruise tourism in the region is "far more so than 10 or 20 years ago. But it varies government to government obviously, and country to country. But I think, generally speaking, yes, it is far more recognized today than it was 10 years ago" (Britell, 2013). While this process has occurred unevenly, to attract TNCs active in global tourism, state officials across the Caribbean have lowered taxes and regulations and allowed the industry to operate relatively unhindered. In turn, cruise ship tourism has come to provide only minimal tax income to states in the region, with on average $15 per passenger spent per port of call (Rodrigue, et al., 2013). To understand why this process continues to deepen we need to recognize how business and state elites benefit and connect with one another. Some state policy makers, increasingly oriented toward the global economy, now coordinate closely with organizations that the global tourism industry has set up to help facilitate its activities, such as the Florida-Caribbean Cruise Association.

This transition in the tourism industry's relationship with states, and particularly with regard to the cruise business, has accompanied moves away from traditional ports and their old state-run local port authorities, instead embracing privatized port operations with new enclaves in traditional ports or altogether new installations outside the traditional ports.

A related trend has led to an increasing number of company-run or highly influenced port authorities. While often leased, some ports have actually become the property of cruise ship companies. Carnival owns ports in the Turks and Caicos, Cancún, and Honduras and has plans for a port in Belize. Royal Caribbean Cruises Limited owns the Roatán, a port in Belize City, as well as Falmouth "town" in Jamaica. As the author has witnessed, these cruise ship "towns" are empty when cruise ship tourists are not present.

Even where the companies do not directly own ports, they have considerable influence over port commissions, such as through campaign contributions to local politicians (Dr. Ross Klein, personal communication, 2013). Cruise companies also play countries and ports off one another, demanding better incentives and waterfront overhauls (R. Klein, 2005, pp. 116–117). This in turn has meant that the companies can more easily capture passenger spending at manufactured tourist sites, revenue that in the past would have more directly benefited the region's local economy. The structure of new company-owned ports or enclaves in older ports (with fences and gates) also keeps passengers inside "the port," leaving only on company-controlled bus tours or with approved taxi companies. This is very different from twenty or thirty years ago, when cruise ship passengers had far less controlled experiences (Rosalinda Thomas, personal communication, 2015). "Passengers traditionally wandered around towns more than they do now. However, when they do and spend money, the cruise line still gets its cut (commission). In addition, many of the stores in ports are owned by offshore entities that have cozy relationships with the cruise lines" (Dr. Ross Klein, personal communication, 2013).

4. We also see an expanding TNC-subcontractor relationship playing out through the cruise business. Cruise lines to maximize their profits use a growing number of subcontractors, such as local shore excursion providers, crew management services, and taxi companies. While there are different marketing strategies onboard the ships, all of the cruise companies have devised ways to extract as much money as possible from their passengers. Where a local company (sometimes affiliated with the port agent) might coordinate the shore excursions of visiting cruise passengers, some companies hired by the cruise lines operate in multiple ports (usually within the same country), whereas other subcontractors such as concessionaires operate regionally and onboard the ships (Dr. Ross Klein, personal communication, 2013). Concessionaires manage operations that are less profitable or require an expertise (shops, casinos, photography, spa services, etc.), and these companies in turn pay sizable fees to the cruise ship companies. Importantly, locally based subcontractors and small businesses that have come to link into the globalizing cruise business and depend on it economically have also advocated on its behalf in the Caribbean, with tour excursion providers and taxi operators, for example, mobilizing to lobby in support of the business (Dr. Ross Klein, personal communication, 2013).

5. Mass marketing strategies have also become a key part of the business in the globalization era, latching onto the culture-ideology of consumerism

(Sklair, 2002). Increasingly finely tuned public relations strategies further polish corporate brands, such as in the cruise business. Through advertisement campaigns with slogans such as "untouched, unmatched, unforgettable" or "let your dreams set sail," the business has become adept at public relations and managing perceptions. As Klein observes, "They coin the right words and have the 'right' labels for what they do, even if these labels are at variance with what they actually do" (Dr. Ross Klein, personal communication, 2013).

Public perception is very important for the business. For example, widespread media coverage engulfed the Carnival-operated vessel that sank off the Isola del Gilio in Italy in 2012 that cost the lives of thirty-two people. While the costs from the accident were likely to be relatively low, as the company is insured, negative media coverage catalyzed by such accidents is threatening to the company's reputation. Public relations campaigns thus have proven vital for shaping consumer views.

The Caribbean's Insertion into the Global Cruise Market

Cruise ships have long frequented many Caribbean islands, including some of the lower-income population centers of the region, such as the Dominican Republic, Haiti, and Jamaica. In the 1960s and 1970s, cruise ships traveled between traditional larger ports of call. In recent decades, there has been a rapid development of cruise infrastructure in both traditional and new private ports. Companies have gained more space to operate and exert heightened control under less scrutiny by local authorities. This has occurred as part of a general shift away from indicative models of national economic development and toward a developmental model that hinges on global competiveness and broader market trends. As Carnival's transnational capitalist chairman Micky Arison elaborates, the Caribbean region's economic prospects and the profitability of cruise ship companies have become more broadly "related to the general economic situation around the world." He adds: "20 years ago, it was a North American–centric industry, and now it's a global industry. So the Caribbean has to compete in a global marketplace, and I think that's a challenge that's relatively new recently" (Britell, 2013).

Caribbean state policy makers have meanwhile struggled to take a unified regional position toward the business so that they might obtain a larger share of tourism-generated revenue. They attempted but failed to cooperate in agreeing on a common head tax in the 1990s and early 2000s (R. Klein, 2005, p. 192). Pattullo has explained the way in which the powerful lobbying arm of the cruise companies defeated this effort, illustrating how corporate interests heavily impact the decisions of Caribbean policy makers (2005, pp. 197–199).

State elites oriented toward the TCC compete in a global battlefield for investors, helping keep business costs low. In recent years we can see this playing out regionally, as market shares in the cruise ship business have shifted as more price-competitive areas of the Spanish-speaking Caribbean outpace in growth the traditional English-speaking destinations. In fact, around the world other warm and tropical locations are opening up to the cruise business. As the North American, Mediterranean, and Caribbean markets become saturated, cruise companies are expanding to new markets in Asia (especially in China, Vietnam, and Thailand), Australia, New Zealand, the Middle East (such as in Dubai), and to parts of West Africa.[5]

One clear phenomenon across these regions, and in the Caribbean in particular, has been the shift away from traditional ports toward privatized ports. This has evolved, as previously discussed, through a kind of vertical integration as cruise companies seek to directly or indirectly control the ports of embarkation. In the Dominican Republic, cruise ships previously went to the old ports of La Romana in the country's south and, more importantly, Samaná in the north. In recent years, cruise companies have shifted toward new nontraditional private ports of call or new more privately controlled installations within the old ports. Costa Cruises, for example, visits Casa de Camp, a tropical seaside resort with golf courses in the Dominican province of La Romana. Cruise ship companies that visit the Dominican Republic today include Royal Caribbean (RCL), Norwegian Cruise Line, Seabourn, Holland America (HAL), and Silversea. Not surprisingly, top officials within the Dominican state have close ties with the business and have promoted its development continually over the years (Rosalinda Thomas, personal communication, 2015). Dominican president Daniel Medina, soon after coming into office, pledged to attract 10 million tourists a year to the country and promptly met with executives from Royal Caribbean on one of their ships anchored in the Bay of Samaná (Royal Caribbean, 2013). Marking the first time a Dominican president addressed a cruise ship operator in a press-covered event for Dominican audiences, this meeting showcased the importance of the cruise ship business (Royal Caribbean, 2013).

In 2011, in the Dominican Republic, tourism generated 4.3 billion in revenues, while 3.7 million foreign visitors traveled through the country's airports and 430,000 visited the island onboard cruise vessels (Accessdr, 2012a, 2012b). Tourists visiting the country had grown to 4.56 million in 2012, becoming the region's most highly visited country (Luxner, 2013). Yet as a local tourism specialist, based in Puerto Plata in the Dominican Republic, explains, Amber Cove, the new private Carnival Cruise port, has caused problems locally: "Taxi cab drivers are complaining because many tourists are no longer coming into Puerto Plata (the nearby town). They can't afford their monthly car payments

Figure 4.6 A Royal Caribbean International cruise ship, docked in Frederiksted on the island of Saint Croix in the U.S. Virgin Islands. (Source: Wikimedia Commons.)

even. Carnival operations, running through its newly constructed [privatized] port, keep nearly all the passengers' money [within their own corporate channels]." Protesting the lack of inputs for the local economy, some taxi drivers and local small business owners have begun meeting with government and business officials (tourism industry worker in the Dominican Republic who requested anonymity, personal communication, 2014).

Whereas most visitors to Caribbean countries arrive by plane, new megaprojects look set to heavily expand the number of cruise visitors annually to many countries in the region (Luxner, 2013). While tourists arriving by plane are often navigated into large resorts, those traveling by cruise ships are especially channeled "within the company controlled bubbles," as explained a Jamaican entrepreneur in the tourist industry that I interviewed (business entrepreneur from Ocho Rios, Jamaica, who requested anonymity, personal communication, 2014). This makes it necessary for local businesspeople to form close relations with transnational cruise companies and other TNCs.

Global tourism has become a reality even in the poorest nations of the region. Haiti has served as a laboratory for the privatized cruise port. During the final stages of the Duvalier regime in 1986, Royal Caribbean International began cruises to Labadee, a heavily guarded and fenced-off private resort installation in the north of the country. Cruise operations to Haiti have run smoothly, except for some brief shutdowns during "emergency periods" in the country (Sprague, 2012a). Into the 2010s, Royal Caribbean ramped up its operations at the port, running a high volume of cruises (Booth, 2010). The company leases five beaches and a forested peninsula from the Haitian state. After engaging in watersports, barbecues, and souvenir shopping within the premises, cruise passengers return at night to sleep onboard their cruise vessel (Booth, 2010). Approximately three hundred locals work low-wage jobs at Labadee and a few hundred more are employed indirectly (Booth, 2010). Despite this idyllic and premium setting, Royal Caribbean pays the Haitian state a miserly $6 per visitor. Since 2009, Labadee has been able to receive Oasis class ships, the world's largest class of cruise ships with a maximum passenger occupancy of 5,400. Including staff, this raises the capacity of the new vessel to 6,296 (Royal Caribbean, 2009).

Jamaica, another major population center in the region, is one of the most highly visited cruise ship destinations in the Caribbean. Ocho Rios, its most active cruise port, hosts more than eight hundred thousand cruise visitors annually, followed by Montego Bay, which sees between three hundred thousand and four hundred thousand (Tortello, 2006). Port Antonio has a much smaller cruise presence. Traditional ports of Kingston and Port Antonio are for the most part no longer used by the cruise ship business. Also, whereas the traditional ports can accommodate most ships, new ports and installations have and continue to be developed to accommodate the newer, much heavier ships. This has occurred alongside a trend of cruise lines taking over control of cruise terminals. Presently, cruise companies owe the Jamaican state tens of millions in unpaid taxes, although Jamaica's government has not moved to collect (Dr. Ross Klein, personal communication, 2013).

New nontraditional private port installations have been set up in Jamaica, either as new enclaves within the traditional ports or within new company-owned ports. For instance, Royal Caribbean has developed Falmouth, a private terminal near Montego Bay, allowing for its new "mega-ships" to dock in the country (Williams-Raynor, 2011). The cruise line has promoted the port as unique because of its close access to local city life, allowing passengers to have a "genuine" Jamaican experience. One press outlet describes, "During a Western Caribbean one-week cruise, Falmouth is the only opportunity for passengers to get a look at a real Caribbean island port city. Royal Caribbean and Jamaica have built a modern port facility, with docks and some local shops. Just two blocks away is a real city where residents seem to live much as they did 10 or 20 years ago" (Molyneaux, 2012).

Wealth generated from the cruise ship business goes to a small handful of major capitalist investors, who in turn have allies in state apparatuses and among the local business community. Cruise ship companies hold enormous sway in the region. State elites have become major promoters of the business, with state-sponsored tourism advertisement campaigns targeting wealthy and middle-strata consumers abroad, as well as populations at home, to convince locals of the importance of the business. These government managers in the region are under pressure to integrate their nations into the globalizing capitalist economy, with effects that extend to the broader society.[6] In other words, looking at the cruise ship business as strictly foreign and therefore alien (through a nation-state-centric perspective), incongruously juxtaposes place against space. Instead, we need to understand first and foremost how the changes taking place in the cruise business (and global tourism, more broadly) are linked to the rise of a TCC, which gathers around it a host of allied social forces.

Cruise companies headed by transnational capitalists are deepening their strategies of accumulation in how they deal with states, labor, and passengers. Cruise ship businesses are digging deeper and deeper roots in many parts of the Caribbean to further control the activities of passengers: to limit or control local exposure and keep revenues in their hands thereby increasing the extraction of surplus value. This shows how capitalist expansion is not directed at national economic development. These processes also intensify the fragmentation, splintering, and undermining of the "national," with the help of transnationally oriented forces (some locally based), in effect deepening the integration of the national into the global production/accumulation process and inserting national power blocs into an emerging global power bloc (Robinson, 2014). The point here is that the state is never neutral, nor does the working class necessarily have an ally in the national state, which has a direct interest in the exploitation of labor—hence the importance of waging class warfare to keep the popular classes at arm's length from exercising state power with a view to changing structural conditions.

Ecological Disaster

The cruise business's impact on the environment has been a mounting crisis over recent decades. Cruise ships unleash enormous amounts of waste and trash and have been a contributing factor to the rapid decline of the Caribbean's coral reefs (with more than half of its coral reefs eliminated since the 1970s) (Aldred, 2014; R. Klein, 2009). Much of the waste is disposed of in international waters where no state has jurisdiction, which is a part of the problem. If a company can dispose of its waste freely, then the actual real cost of pollution is not taken into account by state or market forces.

While cruise companies have put into place new waste treatment mechanisms, according to the U.K.'s *The Guardian*, the industry still "consumes millions of tons of fuel and produces almost a billion tons of sewage" (B. Watson, 2015). This includes beryllium, lead, mercury, and other harmful emissions.

The few actions by some stronger states to enforce regional and environmental regulations have been stymied in recent decades as the cruise companies—adept at public relations and lobbying—remain largely unaccountable. Ross Klein (2015) documents how between 1997 and 2014 the cruise ship companies spent over US$52 million on lobbying the U.S. Congress. Caribbean state officials, also targeted by lobbyists, have hesitated to implement or enforce stronger environmental regulations for fear of their destinations losing revenue by becoming less globally competitive. Despite this, cruise companies, as Ross Klein concludes, "would lead us to believe that cruise ships are environmentally neutral. The cruise business projects this image through its lobbyists, public relations campaigns, infiltration of environmental organizations, and advertising" (2005, p. 70). Amid criticism, legal actions, and fines over its environmental impact, cruise companies have sought to mitigate or downplay their environmental impact and risk therein.

Caribbean government elites disposed toward the mass-tourism development projects of TNCs often point to immediate economic benefits, whereas the environmental damage can take a long time to accumulate and be assessed. Even Cuba, the site of the region's most unspoiled coral reefs, has recently become a destination for cruise ships. How this will impact the surrounding reefs and how it will be managed remains to be seen, but over past decades and across the region the cruise business has left a trail of destruction. When we consider the environmental and ecological contradictions, it becomes evident that the cruise ship business is unsustainable.

While there are various "memoranda of understandings" between the cruise industry and the United States over these environmental impacts, these rely only on voluntary compliance (Friends of the Earth, 2014; Walker, 2010). Meanwhile most sanitation codes the companies follow are over thirty-five years old (B. Watson, 2015). Key for cruise ship companies is managing public opinion so that criticism of these types of activities does not grow (R. Klein, 2009).

Conclusion: Cruise Ships, Transnational Capital, Labor, and the State

The cruise ship business increasingly functions as an oligopoly controlled by groups from the TCC, driving smaller competitors out of business or acquiring them. It controls and influences chains of accumulation into which many other business groups and subcontractors have sought to insert themselves. Exploiting labor and poor communities, transnational capitalists profit from the leisurely activities of high-consuming strata in global society. The changing social relations and productive activities that undergird the business have meant massive profits for transnational capitalists, as well as small gains for some managerial, subcontractor, and professional groups. Local markets interacting with cruise passengers have largely come under direct company control or contract as the cruise companies have become proficient in capturing the onshore spending of passengers.

On the other hand, laborers and lower-income communities connected with the cruise ship business are highly exploited (with those onboard the ships often negatively racialized, many of whom are easily deportable due to their citizenship status). As previously pointed out, there are also many gendered dynamics in regard to how labor is exploited in the business. As capital transnationalizes, workers face new flexibilized regimes as they sell their labor power to TNCs and their affiliated businesses (Chin, 2008; Mason, 2010; Oyogoa, 2016a, 2016b; van Fossen, 2016). Labor in the business needs to develop its own transnational infrastructure, mechanisms through which workers from diverse backgrounds can organize and coordinate their struggle.

Governments in the Caribbean region have largely handed over control of port authorities or modified them to operate in conjunction with the business. Reflected in the policies they have promoted, local state officials and elites in the Caribbean actively encourage transnational capitalist investment, due in part to their social reproduction now depending on this type of capital accumulation (H. Watson, 2015). At the same time, officials and managerial strata operating through more powerful state apparatuses, most important, the United States, with the spectacular resources at its disposal, are vital for facilitating networks of global capitalist accumulation (Robinson, 2014a). State managers increasingly behave in ways that extend the rights and power of transnational capital, while diminishing their own ability to act further eroding their loyalty to their own constituencies. State apparatuses never seem as sovereign as when their officials deploy state power in the global arena in the service of transnational capital. This power extends to the right to exploit labor, which involves, for instance, local state managers in the Caribbean leasing land, privatizing ports, or deploying police against labor strikes (Labadee, Falmouth, etc.).

I have attempted to demonstrate that the cruise ship business is organized in keeping with the concentration and centralization of capital under capitalist globalization with the transnational features noted. As mentioned earlier, as national and international circuits of accumulation fragment and undergo an insertion into chains of accumulation that are functionally integrated across borders, many social and material relations are undergoing novel changes. We see this within the cruise ship business, where its globalization not only contributes to ecological crises but also leads to unimaginable wealth for some and to the reproduction of exploitation and contradictory social relations for many more.

5

Migration, Remittances, and Accumulation in the Globalizing Caribbean

During the era of globalization many people in regions around the world have been compelled to export their labor abroad as migrant workers in the global economy. Remittance flows, the money sent from a migrant to her or his family or other relations abroad, now comprise vital revenue for the global poor, however, labor exportation and the increasing reliance on remittances also reflect the desperation and struggles to survive for lower-income people (Gupta Barnes, 2016; World Bank, 2015a).

In 2015, over 250 million people were living outside their country of origin, more than triple the figure from around fifty years prior (Conor, 2016). Consequently, diaspora communities have grown tremendously in recent decades (Portes, 1997). While this chapter focuses on the Caribbean diaspora, this is a global phenomenon that affects poor communities the world over such as the various Indian migrant communities working in exploitative low-wage jobs as noncitizens in areas such as Singapore or the Middle East. How, though, has this process played out in particular with regard to the Caribbean basin?

Immigrants from the Caribbean region, such as Cuba, the Dominican Republic, Haiti, Jamaica, and Puerto Rico, make up one of the largest groups of migrants to North America (as U.S. and Canadian government data indicate). Niimi and Özden observe, "Even if Mexico and the Central American countries tend to top the ranking of migrants in absolute terms, the small Caribbean islands clearly dominate the migration charts when we look at migration flows in relation to each country's population" (Niimi and Özden,

Figure 5.1 A border crossing in Hispaniola between the towns of Mallepasse and Jamani. (Photo by author.)

2008, p. 56). Large diaspora communities from the Caribbean have come to exist in Europe, Canada, and the United States. A Canadian 2001 census, for example, found that the number of Canadian residents that identified as Jamaicans numbered 211,000, whereas another 82,000 as Haitians (with many recruited to jobs in Quebec as professional workers), 60,000 as West Indians, 52,000 as Guyanese, and 50,000 as Trinidadians (Monzon and Tudakovic, 2004, p. 6). Over recent decades, there has also been an uptick in the number of intra-Caribbean migration and Caribbean migration to parts of Latin America (Nurse, 2006; World Bank, 2017). These new diaspora populations not only make return visits and communicate with family in their homelands, but they also take part in economic interactions across frontiers, with remittances as the most important among these. (See Figure 5.1.)

Through the context of the Caribbean, this chapter will examine a part of the undergirding political economy of this process: the way in which migrant remittance flows and the rise of a transnational remittance business (a part of the financial services industry) serve as conduits for transnational social integration and capitalist accumulation.

The connection between globalization and migration has been studied by a number of scholars. Lydia Potts (1990), for example, has shown how migration has been generated by a confluence of factors such as the upturning of populations alongside capitalist expansion, with industrialization in newly integrated areas, and intensive new booms in capital accumulation. Others have shown how, at a microlevel, familial structures often make decisions to migrate based on hardships in the wake of socioeconomic disruption (Brettell and Hollifield, 2007). The decision to migrate is often contested within the family, for instance, with some women choosing to migrate alone, which raises issues of autonomy (Benway, 2000; Hondagneu-Sotelo, 1994).[1] On a macrolevel, the so-called "push" and "pull" factors have long been examined, but endemic to this (and largely ignored) is that expansion in capitalism creates surplus populations, which in turn are compelled to seek out new means of survival. Shortages of local laborers willing to work for low wages also creates incentives for capital to seek out people displaced from other areas.

Alejandro Portes (2013) suggests that processes of capital accumulation and migration in recent decades have been swept up into novel integrative transnational relations. New flexible production and commerce of the global era has opened production spaces for transnational migrant communities (Faist, et al., 2013) through which capital has sought out new routes to exploit transplanted workers with the appropriation of their surplus labor. Major sectors of the global economy have in fact come to depend on the exploitation of migrant sending and receiving communities (Robinson, 2003). Robinson explains how this has occurred as a fundamental shift, where migration has become altered through the transition from the international to the global phase of capitalism: "In the past, immigrants could not hope to maintain fluid and active ties with the homeland. They became assimilated and set up life anew in a new land. But global communications, transportation networks, and the global economic and financial infrastructure increasingly allow immigrants to maintain active and ongoing exchanges between their home country and their country (or countries) of immigration" (Robinson, 2003, p. 272).

Migrant labor and the reverse flow of remittances that it produces have become key structural features of the integrative relations of the global era, especially for lower-income communities. Serving as the basis of a hugely profitable transnational business, as well as a state strategy for the replacement of public redistributive models, remittances now comprise a vital and immediate income source for families around the world. A number of authors have examined remittances as a source of economic development and income for Caribbean nations (Acosta et al., 2008; Fajnzylber and López, 2008; Martínez et al., 2008; Niimi and Özden, 2008; Singh, 2013) and others have looked at remittances as a survival strategy for lower-income communities and families (Nurse, 2006; Sirkeci et al., 2012; Thai, 2014) and in regard to the economic crisis of 2007–2008 (Sirkeci et al., 2012). Scholars have examined the rise of "migrant economic transnational flows" (Trotz and Mullings, 2013) and how they are connected to gendered labor, consumer, and migration patterns (Condon, 1998; Sheller, 2003). As a contradictory relation, remittance flows directly feed into stratification, where certain individuals (and families) in a community benefit, while others do not (Abrego, 2014).

The overarching logic of the mainstream approach, championed by the World Bank (2013) and other institutions, is that remittances are an expanding market, which in global capitalism presents the enormous prospect not only to channel migrants' money through financial intermediaries but also to incorporate receiving households into international finance. What distinguishes migrant labor from other types of cheap labor is that the cost of renewal (the social reproduction, according to Marx) is externalized to sending economies (Burawoy, 1976). "They reproduce, nourish, house, train, and habituate workers, relieving the host country of this cost" (Cross, 2015, citing: Cohen, 1987). Conversely, in the host economy, migrants receive subsistence wages but are excluded from receiving "indirect wages" in the form of family allowance, pensions, unemployment benefits, sick leave, vacation, and often health care. Furthermore, as explained by Maria Mies (1986), this externalized social reproduction falls heavily upon the backs of women workers (who carry out the vast majority of reproductive labor and usually for little to no wages), while often women's surplus labor is transferred to their husbands (Delphy, 2015).

Here I want to argue that new migrant labor relations (bound up with racialized and gendered class relations) and the reverse flow of remittances are a key feature of the new capitalist globalization and the rise of transnational capital.[2] In looking at the formation of the transnational remittance business and the role of Caribbean migrant communities in remittance flows, I want to examine some of the novel structural features of transnationalism and its contradictory nature. A globally competitive and dynamic remittance business has replaced earlier more static money transfer systems. As transnational capital has enveloped more locally oriented business models, pools of labor and a variety of social groups have become bound up with this process.

The global remittance business has formed through new integrative processes and come to function as a transnational circuit of accumulation, syphoning off profits from cross-border money transfers made by migrants (Marini, 1973). As exploited and superexploited workers, migrants often seek to send resources back to their families and communities of origin—where many exist on even lower salaries or in conditions of marginalization. Transnational capital has come to profit tremendously from this relationship. Through the emergence in recent decades of the transnational remittance business, transnational capitalists have used new information technology (IT) and organizational advancements (such as supranational agreements and new firm structures), tapping into and facilitating the massive increase in recent decades of cross-border money transfers worldwide. This has occurred as part of what Cross (2015) describes as the rising power of global financial institutions vis-à-vis productive capital.

This phenomenon has been legitimized and promoted by a wide array of state managers and policy makers, as a central plank of development (Hernández and Coutin, 2006; Rodriguez, 2010). New mechanisms for development have taken shape through the combination of the state's role in facilitating the exportation of labor and the reverse flow of remittances (Portes, 2013). For instance, reports put out by World Bank researchers affirm this as they often portray remittances as synonymous with foreign aid or financial exchange, as just another heightened economic relation of the global economy (Fajnzylber and López, 2008). The World Bank encourages state and global institutions to bolster and formalize remittances, yet increased mass migration and accompanying remittance flows are in themselves an indication of increased displacement, dispossession, and poverty in remittance-receiving countries. If people were thriving at home, why would so many leave? A strategy for economic stability based on ever-increasing remittances presupposes an indefinite increase in poverty and dispossession. As Garni and Weyher (2013, p. 74) critically observe:

> The language of "exporting people" in order to "capture remittances" and "leverage development" while "relieving" an "over-burdened" economy of "surplus labor" (Gammage, 2006, pp. 75–76, 93) obscures the underlying reality that economic elites seek to legitimize the seizure of portions of citizens' private income, differentiated from ordinary income in that it happens to flow across national borders, and that the maximization of such seizures is justified as a matter of economic and development policy when in fact it supports elite interests at the expense of [those] wanting a life for themselves and their families.

So how do new contradictory relations of the global phase of world capitalism undergird migration and the reverse flow of remittances? What general trends do we see manifesting themselves within the Caribbean? This chapter breaks from the TCC/World Bank-official narrative on how migrant remittances simply serve as a useful financial flow and benefit national economies, societies, and particular communities in the developing world. Instead, the argument here is that the remittance business benefits global (financial) capital first and foremost. Furthermore, I look at how this occurs through the unique and contradictory nature of migration and capital accumulation in the global era, arguing that new developments are occurring through capital's transnational expansion and the associated exploitation of world populations. Next, I provide background on migration and remittance patterns in the globalizing Caribbean, explaining the novel relations that undergird these dynamics, and then look in more depth at how the transnational remittance business has formed and penetrates markets in the region.

The Caribbean Migrant Context

Over the past half century, we can see how working people, such as those in the Caribbean, have faced changing economic conditions compelling them to seek out work in other countries. We can also see how this results in a reverse flow of remittances. As shown below, the inflow of remittances into the Caribbean has risen exponentially. In Haiti, over the past half century, remittances grew from a negligible amount to over US$1.715 billion. In Jamaica, a similar process happened—remittances grew from a negligible amount to US$2.259 billion. Remittance growth figures are found throughout the Caribbean.

Worldwide remittances to developing countries increased nearly fiftyfold, from $2 billion in 1970 ($12 billion if taking inflation into account) to $592 billion in 2014 (World Bank, 2015b). By 2006, remittances were valued at more than six times that of developmental assistance, and they were believed to have reached 70 percent of FDI to the developing world (World Bank, 2007). They had far surpassed non-FDI flows, such as portfolio investment and bank and trade-related lending (Acosta et al., 2008, p. 25). Remittances to populations living in "developing countries" (such as those in the Caribbean basin) have dropped off some during economic crises, but they then quickly rebounded (Sirkeci et al., 2012, p. 53; and see Figure 5.2).

With rising out-migration, Latin America and the Caribbean in recent years have become a major source of migrant labor and together make up the largest recipient site for remittances worldwide (after Asia). Robinson (2003, p. 208) describes this as "an arrangement, most likely an emergent structural feature of the global system, whereby the site of labor power and its reproduction have been transnationally dispersed." That is, an increasing percentage of many countries' productive populations live and work abroad and in turn often support young and elderly family members in their country of origin, reducing much of the burden of the state to care for the dependent populations. Part of the value they create thus is inserted, through

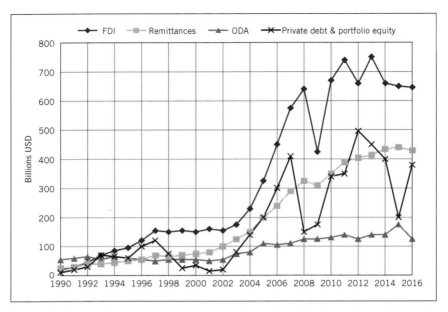

Figure 5.2 Resource flows to developing countries. (Source: World Bank's Development Prospects Group, 2012.)

remittances, into transnational chains of accumulation. We see then the vital contribution of remittances to the broader local social reproduction process, and how this has become entwined with global capitalism.

Whereas Table 5.1 shows the huge increase in the Caribbean-born population living today in the United States, which is by far the largest destination for labor exportation from the region, Table 5.2 indicates that the vast majority of migrants from Caribbean islands living in the United States are from Hispaniola, Jamaica, and Cuba. These tables do not differentiate between the type of labor, nor the familial relations of migrants, but not all the workers are from lower-income backgrounds, as part of these migrant flows are tied to the rising recruitment of professionals (Coles and Fechter, 2007). While Puerto Ricans are not included in this table, they are also among the largest of the Caribbean diaspora populations (with an estimated 1.5 million people of Puerto Rican descent living inside the United States).

Many are trying to leave the Caribbean for the United States and other developed countries at a time of high-technological production and supra-national trade treaties helping drive down domestic demands for simple labor and alongside periods of increasing demand for a variety of types of labor in the global north (Pierce and Schott, 2012; D. Thompson, 2013). The expanding ranks of a global superfluous population, no longer needed by

TABLE 5.1. TOTAL AND CARIBBEAN FOREIGN-BORN POPULATIONS LIVING IN THE UNITED STATES, 1960–2009

Year	Total Foreign-Born	Caribbean-Born	Share of Total
1960	9,738,091	193,922	2.00%
1970	9,619,302	675,108	7.00%
1980	14,079,906	1,258,363	8.90%
1990	19,767,316	1,938,348	9.80%
2000	31,107,889	2,953,066	9.50%
2009	38,517,234	3,465,890	9.00%

Source: Migrant Immigration Source website. Data for 2000 from the 2000 Decennial Census; data for 2009 from the American Community Survey 2009. Data for earlier decades from Gibson and Lennon, 1999.

TABLE 5.2. MIGRANT REMITTANCE INFLOWS, CARIBBEAN COUNTRIES, 1970 TO 2013*

	1970	1975	1980	1985	1990
Barbados	4	9	9	8	38
Dominica	—	—	9	11	14
Dominican Republic	25	28	183	242	315
Grenada	—	—	—	—	18
Haiti	—	59	106	96	—
Jamaica	—	—	96	146	229
St. Kitts and Nevis	—	—	1	1	19
St. Lucia	—	—	—	—	16
St. Vincent and the Grenadines	—	—	—	—	16
Trinidad and Tobago	—	3	6	3	3
	1995	**2000**	**2005**	**2010**	**2013**
Barbados	61	115	94	82	86
Dominica	13	16	22	23	23
Dominican Republic	839	1,839	2,719	3,430	3,706
Grenada	38	46	27	28	31
Haiti	108	578	986	1,474	1,715
Jamaica	653	892	1,762	2,026	2,259
St. Kitts and Nevis	20	27	30	47	45
St. Lucia	23	26	27	29	30
St. Vincent and the Grenadines	17	22	22	29	31
Trinidad and Tobago	32	38	92	91	133

Source: World Bank staff calculation based on data from IMF Balance of Payments Statistics database and data releases from central banks, national statistical agencies, and World Bank country desks. See, also, Orozco, 2006.
*$US millions.

networks of capital, search out those last crevices where they might fare better. At the same time, this migrant labor is more than mere labor export in that it connects and deepens the transnationalization process though myriad ways, including remittances and with attention to the ways that "nations" are being reconfigured—a process that also has cultural implications.

The foreign exchange dimension of remittances and how the state managers see the phenomenon in that context has been an important dynamic for decades, going all the way back to the 1960s. Even prior to the "global era," during the heightened international capitalist period that followed World War II, Caribbean policy makers began to see the benefit in gaining foreign exchange through remittances (Worrell, 1994–1995). Two Barbados Central Bank economists argued, for example, remittances "from abroad accounted for an average of 18 percent of invisible earnings between 1960 and 1963, a period of substantial emigration" (Brathwaite and Codrington, 1982). As recounted to the author by an attendee, during a workshop that was held at the Washington, DC, Hilton Hotel in the early 1990s: "The Ambassador from Barbados to the US/OAS remarked that it was the considered policy of his government to spend the maximum possible on education to educate Barbadians to the best extent possible and encourage as many as possible to migrate to North America and remit money and other resources to help relatives and contribute to the country's development" (personal communication, 2018).

Remittances in money contribute to foreign exchange and help the state pay salaries of the state managers and others that help formulate and implement the policies that force many to try to migrate: the laws of capitalist accumulation drive the process. In some instances, remittances surpass FDI, showing the contribution of remittances to the broader local social reproduction process. Caribbean migrants to the United States, for instance, often utilize "family reunification" provisions in immigration law (which enables family members to immigrate because of the presence of one or more family members in the United States); of course, adults entering under those provisions are often seeking to earn higher wages depending on many circumstances such as employers, education, training, and skills—not normally attainable in many parts of the Caribbean.[3] The low wages they receive, even as superexploited migrant workers, are usually relatively higher to the low wages in a migrant's country of origin.

In the following section, I explain more clearly how a part of the redistributed value created by Caribbean migrant workers has come to be appropriated through the remittance business. I show further how remittance networks have formed through novel material and social relations of the global era. Looking at how this has taken shape in specific countries of the

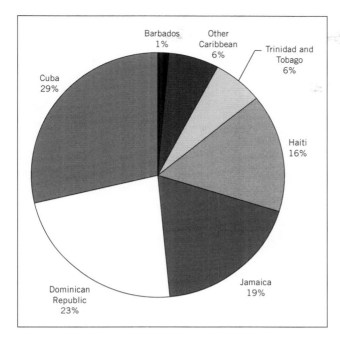

Figure 5.3 Share of Caribbean-born population by country of origin in the United States, 2009. This does not include those born in Puerto Rico. (Source: Migration Information Source website: https://www.migrationpolicy.org/programs/migration-information-source. This data is drawn from the American Community Survey conducted by the U.S. Census Bureau in 2009.)

Caribbean region (the Dominican Republic, Haiti, and Jamaica), I argue that the transformations need to be seen through the context of transnational processes entwined with local, national, and regional dynamics. (See Figure 5.3.)

Surplus Populations, Migration, and the Exportation of Labor

Throughout its existence, capitalism has produced marginalized peoples (those who are structurally locked out). This dynamic continues under globalization, but as a structural feature of a *global* division of labor (Kalleberg, 2009; Marx, 1867/1992, pp. 794–801; Robinson, 2014a; Standing, 2013). As numerous studies have shown, global inequality has intensified in recent decades (Bales, 2012; Holt-Giménez and Patel, 2012; Kloby, 2004), as large parts of the world's population have been reduced to supernumeraries or excess population whose formal labor is not required for the global economy (M. Davis, 2007). While such processes are today occurring on a global level, they are rooted in changes and disruptions caused by the accumulation of capital.

There are also large parts of the population who, though not necessarily permanently marginalized, *are* unemployed, as reserve pools of labor. Under capitalism, as Marx explained, there is a "constant transformation of a part of the working population into unemployed or semi-employed 'hands'"

(1867/1992, p. 786). With the upturning of rural populations through the "primitive accumulation" of early agrarian capitalism, for example, there occurred a growth of surplus labor in towns and cities (Wood, 2002). As Robinson (2004) and others have argued, new waves of primitive accumulation have occurred over capitalism's history, reproducing or forming reserve armies of labor and the disrupting rural livelihoods (M. Davis, 2007; Stark, 1978). One example has been the upheaval of rural populations in parts of the Caribbean, as internal migrants move to the urban areas of their country and outward migrants move abroad (Gowricharn, 2006; Potter, 1989).

Whereas during earlier periods of capitalism, higher volumes of workers were often needed, in the contemporary period fewer and fewer workers are required relative to the productivity achieved (Braveman, 1998).[4] This process under which fewer workers are required to produce more commodities has intensified through the era of globalization with highly advanced technology and new organizational forms.

Through the closing decades of the twentieth century and into the twenty-first century, as discussed in Chapter 1, the phenomenon of flexible accumulation has spread around the world. David Harvey defines this phenomenon as "new systems of production and marketing, characterized by the more flexible labor processes and markets, . . . geographical mobility and rapid shifts in consumption practices" (Harvey, 1991, p. 124). This has occurred as part of a fundamentally new social relation in the globalized economy, as labor power itself is being reconfigured and incorporated into transnational value chains (Robinson, 2014a; Struna, 2009). This flexibility materializes internally within the circuits of capital, such as how it operates within corporations. Although this restructuring process is often portrayed as occurring to the advantage of women doing the double shift, women are actually regularly deprived of promotional opportunities and long-term equity in the workplace (Eisenstein, 2005). Transnationally oriented elites are not generally interested in improving the quality of life for local laboring populations because their own survival is not predicated on a specific country or region; they are free to move their resources around the globe in search of the lowest cost center.

In today's global era, we can see how vast new pools of surplus labor in regions around the world are being marginalized including within the Caribbean. Yet people from every level of society are becoming interconnected with the global economy even in the most remote areas of the region, such as impoverished rural communities in Haiti undergoing a new round of "primitive accumulation," where projects funded by international financial institutions (IFIs) have been set up to ease these population's integration with new accumulation networks (Haiti Grassroots Watch, 2012e). One growing trend has been for governments and supranational organizations to facilitate the involvement of lower-income populations into marketized relations, such as with remittances and microloans, but also through other dynamics such as with land tenure, which, as Howard (2015) points out, in regard to urban areas of Jamaica, has resulted in higher rates of debt and new tensions.

Capitalism in fact is reaching a point where continued growth is becoming more and more difficult. The health of the world economic system and of companies is defined by growth. Indefinite economic growth on a finite planet with finite resources is obviously impossible. Exploiting the poorest of the poor is evidence that the system is trying to wring out every last penny and crumb, but the fact is that we are entering a different phase in the history of world capitalism.

Those who are structurally unemployed or underemployed exist in conditions of misery, uncertainty, constant stress, and pressure to search out other possibilities. Undertaking what are often very difficult or dangerous circumstances for themselves and their families, migrants "export" themselves. The commodity for sale on the global market in this case is their labor power. Pools of surplus labor in regions such as the Caribbean have come to be "marketed" worldwide. A truly global process: from the Caribbean to South Asia, Oceania, parts of Africa, and Central America, elites and their functionaries are promoting the cheapest maquiladora workers, the lowest-wage janitors and cruise ship workers, and globally competitive nannies or nurses (Potts, 1990; Robinson, 2003; Rodriguez, 2010; Sprague, 2011c). As many workers seek to export their labor, migration has become specifically linked to transnational capitalism. Levitt (2001) describes how local communities become "transnational villages," when members go abroad and set up transnational ties. A good deal has been written on the rise of transnational migration, global diasporas, and the transnational family, with populations dispersed across national borders and living through a web of connections, entailing multiple gendered and racialized class dimensions (Cohen, 2008; Condon, 1998; Matthews, 2013; Osuna, 2015; Parreñas, 2005; Thai, 2014).

The ways in which poor people are compelled to export their labor must be seen in light of the gendered and racialized nature of class society in the global era (Eisenstein, 2005; Marable, 2009; Mies, 1986/2014). For example, structural adjustment programs (SAPs), promoted by the IMF and other supranational organizations, use gendered and racialized class relations to exploit free and cheap labor (Harrison, 2013). Often faced with chronic poverty, widespread unemployment, and underemployment, Caribbean people—especially women—have engaged in high rates of migration (Ho, 1999, p. 48). Few Caribbean families have not experienced the departure of friends or family members. Scholars have shown that migratory patterns

have varied for different strata of Caribbean society. While elites and upwardly mobile groups tend to migrate as entire family units and usually
settle permanently, women from lower-income backgrounds often migrate
alone and frequently pave the way for other family members to migrate (p.
39). This process entails many contradictions, such as the undermining of
traditional forms of child-rearing (p. 48; Parreñas, 2005), with many migrants having a "sense of loss, displacement, exile, and alienation resulting
from the destabilizing effects of capitalism" (Ho, 1999, p. 51). Here, it is important to note that labor exportation from the Caribbean has often occurred at a volume higher than any other region worldwide (relative to
population), a trend now for several decades (Deere et al., 1990).

Remittances, the Appropriation of Redistributed Value, and Transnational Circuits of Accumulation

In a literal or geographic sense, the remittance business redistributes value
when someone in one part of the planet sends a portion of his or her income
to someone living in another area. This occurs now through transnational
circuits of accumulation. The more that is sent, the more that TNCs such as
Western Union earn. By controlling chains of distribution, capitalists then
extract value from mostly lower-income people, who, in turn, often resist this
exploitation by finding alternative uncontrolled or illicit routes for transferring goods and money. We can see this in regard to the remittance business
where TNCs charge fees or commissions to send money transfers to individuals in other countries, and, in turn, many people attempt to find alternative
routes, such as transferring money across borders through informal channels.

   Across the region, local banks and remittance businesses operate as
agents for transnational remittance companies. In the Dominican Republic,
for example, this includes Victor Mendez Capellan, owner of the business
Remesas Vimenca of Grupo Vimenca, which operates as an agent for Western Union. Smaller local agents exist, such as Money Corps, owned by Dominican businessperson Ingrid Reyes, which serves as one of the local agents
of Money Gram. Another local remittance business, Caribe Express, is the
in-country agent for Xoom and a subsidiary of a larger globally oriented
conglomerate based in the country. In Haiti, Sogebank, one of the country's
largest banks—owned in part by a few local wealthy elites—operates its Sog-
express chain as a local agent for Western Union. Local companies that process remittances have an interest in maintaining their links with TNCs like
Western Union, MoneyGram, and Xoom; they see themselves strongly
linked transnationally. This reflects the processes through which local businesspeople are integrating into transnational capitalism. (See Figure 5.4.)

Figure 5.4 Remesas Vimenca is a local corporate agent for Western Union in the Dominican Republic. (Photo by author.)

Yet, in the neoliberal environment with few state protections and a minimal social safety net, remittances keep many families afloat and provide a means to consume even in areas where there is no demand for wage labor. Furthermore, remittances are consumed in ways that deepen integration with trade networks, and often boost exports (or reexports) from the United States, especially—contributing to the so-called U.S. trade surplus with states such as Jamaica and the Dominican Republic.

While remittances are important for local consumption and can serve as a lifeline for lower-income and marginalized populations, they also function as a "subsidy to capital," where transnationally oriented elites use them to justify divesting from social programs. As populations undergo disruption brought on by restructuring associated with the global economy, remittance flows can reduce the local social costs for adjustment and promote market relations. In an economic sense, neoliberal state policy makers then can utilize remittances to ease the state's withdrawal from social investment. Remittances thus serve as "'safety nets' that replace governments and fixed employment in the provision of economic security" (Robinson, 2003, p. 208).

At the root of this process is the TCC capturing more of the redistributed value of workers. Remittance flows thus constitute a new functional linkage between people earning wages in one country with people engaging in wage-generated consumption in another country. Throughout the history of capitalism, as dominant groups have sought to decrease the turnover time of capital accumulation and the syphoning of profits, technological changes are used to speed things up and reduce the friction of distance. Faster rates of capital and money flow means more profits can be made in the same amount of time. Whereas reducing the turnover time of these flows has become a crucially important aspect of the global era, we must not overemphasize the role of technology in these phenomena, as this is a process driven by and organized by human beings, and, specifically, by certain class interests.

In recent decades this dynamic has come to exist in an intensive, rapid, and immediate wide-scale manner that occurs through a new functional integration. Whereas capital has long accumulated unevenly with regard to social groups operating in different spaces and places, this process has undergone a qualitative shift through the era of global capitalism, with the rise of transnational networks of accumulation and the associated class relations.

To understand what has happened in the global era, in my view, we need to emphasize as most determinant (of causal priority) the role of social production and how this undergoes change. As Robinson (2014a, p. 111) observes: "The historical forms that are thrown up by the laws of motion of a social order are just that: *historical* and therefore subject to transformation as the system evolves." He explains: "The center-periphery division of labor created by modern colonialism reflected a particular spatial configuration of the law of uneven development that is becoming transformed by globalization" (2008, p. 43). We now increasingly see pools of the Third World in the First World, and vice versa (Robert Cox, 1987). We see high-cost markets for the superrich in some of the poorest countries, just as we see a growth of urban slums in some of the wealthiest nations. While a north-south division continues to be present, we need to understand how a spatial reconfiguration of *social* relations is taking place, or as Robinson elaborates the: "crucial question here is the ways in which globalization may be transforming the spatial dynamics of accumulation and the institutional as well as political arrangements through which it takes place. *The subject—literally, that is, the agents/makers of the social world—is not global space but people in those spaces.* What is central, therefore, is a spatial reconfiguration of social relations beyond a nation-state/interstate framework" (Robinson, 2014a, pp. 108–109).

Rather than capital-labor relations occurring through fixed national social spaces, where social strata are boxed into national communities, or cumbersome back-and-forth international processes, we now increasingly see the role of transnational processes and practices. The global economy is developing through a capillary system, with large arteries and organs entwined with other arteries and smaller bodies (while these often tend to concentrate in the global north, it is clear that major developments are under way in the global south) (Castillo-Mussot et al., 2013). However, this is a contradictory process, with particular national, regional, and international processes entwining with these new transnational processes.

Thus, the emerging transnational integration of material and social life entails major changes for how societies are structured and organized and how value is produced and distributed. In regard to remittance flows, the impact of the scientific and technological revolution based on computers and computer-aided processes like computer-aided design, engineering, and manufacturing led to the creation of new information and communications technology that was used to speed up the flow of money across borders and reduce the demand for telegrams. Western Union, and other companies, used these and other means to restructure their operations and become TNC entities that help advance global capitalist integration. We can also see this motion via the role of internet technology in cross-border money flows and how this development can be used to connect migrant waged workers with populations in their home country. This has, of course, sparked new contradictions: a new dependence on the distribution of remittances by large swaths of humanity serves to fragment local communities and pacify struggle (Garni and Weyher, 2013), heightening stratification within communities where some families receive remittances and others do not (Abrego, 2014). In addition, racialized and gendered disparities are often reproduced through remittance flows, such as through sex work, care work, and other low paid forms of labor where migrants often struggle to send money abroad to loved ones in their homelands (Cabezas, 2009, p. 80).

Yet, across rural communities and urban centers of the Caribbean, some of the barest essentials have often been purchased through the migrant remittances sent home. Faced with high unemployment and a lack of social investment, few other options exist. The point here is not to criticize people who send or receive remittances but rather to evaluate critically the structures that make migration and remittances necessary, as well as those who profit off this necessity.

As a dialectical process, the redistribution of value through remittances creates new objective linkages and networks between people living in different areas. Does this, along with many other processes, create the conditions through which transnational relations among working and popular classes can form? It remains to be seen how the contradictory dynamics of capitalist globalization will yield new avenues of working-class organization and solidarity or help build global consciousness. For instance, Wah and Pierre-Louis (2004) describe how hometown associations (mostly funded by middle strata and upper class in the diaspora) often support specific home communities at the expense of others. This is especially important as hometown associations form key networks for facilitating remittances and other forms of support to certain populations. To understand further the particular and contradictory nature of these changing social and material relations, we now examine their contours in parts of the Caribbean.

Case Studies: The Dominican Republic, Haiti, and Jamaica

The transnational remittance markets have spread worldwide, taking up what are often similar market strategies and patterns. Caribbean nations and their societies have different profiles and backgrounds and varying state policies that greatly impact migrants and their families. U.S. immigration acts, for example, in the mid-1960s and 1970s slowly began easing barriers to visas for Caribbean migrants, as well as admitting certain refugees and asylum seekers (Hernández, 2002).[5] A wide array of formal and informal/unauthorized migration channels developed over the subsequent decades.

In the 1980s, Dominican migration—and, to a larger extent, Haitian migration—accelerated due to economic crises on the island and the decline of the sugar business, as well as economic opportunities that existed abroad. Rising internal migration within the Caribbean also occurred, such as with the rising number of Haitian workers migrating to the Dominican Republic, some of whom also partook in sending remittances. Changing economic conditions also altered the kinds of work and conditions faced by migrant laborers. As one OECD report explained, this period "witnessed a reduction in the importance of sugar production in the Dominican economy, encouraging many Haitian immigrants to move to other sectors including construction, trade, manufacture and domestic service" (OECD Development Centre, 2009, p. 234).

In the global era, the population of the Dominican Republic became an important source of migrant labor in areas of the United States and Puerto Rico. It has had a higher rate of female migration as compared with many nearby countries (Sirkeci et al., 2012, p. 85), reflecting the deepening of gendered forms of exported labor within the country (Mies, 1986). As Benway (2000) found, with respect to both genders, many Dominican migrants living in New York City worked for small-sized and informal businesses, often being paid "under the table," with the majority working alongside Dominicans and others with roots in Latin America and some working within "ethnic enclaves." Just as the out-migration of Dominicans and Haitians intensified, the Caribbean diasporas have grown in significance, especially in terms of remittances. Seeking to support or remain connected with families and others in their country of origin, it has become common for migrants to send back goods or money. As we have seen, concurrent new technology and organizations developed that facilitated and profited from the rapid transfer of these flows. We must, however, point out the contradiction between the benefits provided to families and lower-income communities and the profits gained by transnational capital from these transactions.

The greater contradiction here is that the remittances reduce or eliminate the need of the state to provide a social safety net. This allows the state to reduce taxes on the rich and corporations thus furthering poverty and disenfranchisement and increasing the need for remittances; a vicious circle.

Similar to the experience in many other countries at the time, TNCs began expanding greatly into the Dominican Republic in the 1990s. By the 2000s, money transfers passing through transnational remittance businesses accounted for more than 7 percent of GDP, with an estimated 10 percent of families receiving remittances (Oficina Nacional de Estadísticas de la República Dominicana, 2002). These data suggest that remittances are now fundamental to the nation, as its society and economy are integrated ever deeper into transnational processes. The other major pillar of the Dominican economy has been global tourism, with vast numbers of vacationers from abroad visiting resorts, cruise ports, and privatized beaches and golf courses. According to one prominent local politician interviewed by the author, the country's economic model is now based around "importing foreigners and exporting Dominicans" (interviewee requested anonymity, personal communication, 2015).

As researchers explain, for lower-income populations, remittances have become vital for sustaining demand, stabilizing the economy during downturns, and mitigating the effects of low wage levels and weak social safety nets (Ondetti, 2012). Over recent decades the Dominican Republic has experienced a large growth in remittance inflows, reflecting the significant number of Dominican laborers that have moved abroad. In the Dominican Republic, for example, in 1970, the inflow of remittances amounted to US$25 million. By 2013, it was valued at US$3.706 billion.[6] OECD researchers explain, "Following nearly three decades of large-scale migration to the United States, transnational ties—including but not limited to remittances—have solidified an identity among the Dominicans" through new political, cultural, and social dimensions (OECD Development Centre, 2009, p. 236).

In the Dominican Republic, the major transnational remittance corporations, Western Union and MoneyGram, largely operate through local agents (Suki, 2004). In addition, as Suki (2004, p. 17) explains, "Dominican 'corridor' specialists such as La Nacional, Quisqueyana, BHD Corp. and

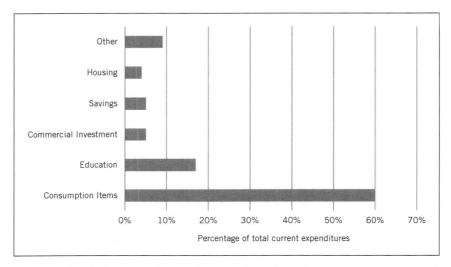

Figure 5.5 Principal use of remittances in the Dominican Republic in 2008 as a percentage of total expenditures by families. (Source: OECD Development Centre, 2009.)

Cibao Express exist because of the concentration of the Dominican community in New York City and the tristate area (New York, New Jersey, and Connecticut). In many cases, the same company owns both the remitting side of the transaction and the distributing agent." While these "Dominican corridor" remittance companies have profited from their special linkages with Dominican diaspora communities in New York and New Jersey, they are also interconnected with global finance and banking interests (Suki, 2004).

The expansion in remittances is reflected in Dominican state policies toward migrants, with policies favoring the diaspora's investment and political and economic interaction in their homeland. Underscoring the importance that Dominican state technocrats assign to economic linkages with the diaspora, in 1994, a constitutional amendment recognized dual nationality; in 1997, the right to vote was extended to overseas Dominicans; and in 2010, the Dominican constitution created overseas congressional seats. Figure 5.5 showcases the importance of remittances on a local level, documenting the spending patterns of remittance receiving communities in the Dominican Republic (OECD Development Centre, 2009, p. 236).

While the Haitian migrant population grew tremendously in the latter part of the twentieth century, especially in the United States, Canada, and France, it was not until the latter part of the 1990s that the reverse flow of remittances began to expand rapidly. Whereas transnational remittance corporations had permeated the Caribbean region in the early 1990s, they lagged behind in Haiti due in part to the instability caused by the 1991 coup d'état. After the constitutionally elected government returned in 1995, the country's economic situation slowly improved, though it was soon plunged into political tumult with another coup in 2004, and then a devastating earthquake struck in 2010. Even under these conditions, the remittance market in the country began to expand, going from $108 million in inflows in 1995, to around $672 million in 2001, to $1 billion in 2006, to nearly $2 billion in 2012 (Orozco, 2006, pp. 5–6; IDB, 2012, p. 20). Compared with other important macroeconomic indicators, a large swath of the country's population has become dependent (or partially dependent) on remittances for their livelihood. Alongside this the state has begun to earn rising tax revenue from remittances. Consequently, the company fees and newly enforced taxes on remittances are highly unpopular among Haitians (Haiti Support Group, 2013).

We can see many contradictions wrapped up in this process. For instance, when we think about the Haitian state taxing remittances without using state funds to engage in significant social investment programs, we see the expanding tentacles of what Robert Fatton (2002) calls the "predatory state"; with Caribbean state managers facilitating and benefiting from these rapidly expanding global industries while disassociating with local needs. Supranational apparatuses have also sought to expand the kinds of labor that can be taxed, looking to further shift the tax burden onto the poor. At one point the WHO, World Bank, and IDB expressed support for taxing the money received by sex workers, on the grounds that sex work represents a form of employment that adds to foreign exchange receipts (Kempadoo, 1999). We can see from this analysis that the workers who remit money and work for low wages are at the lowest rungs of the labor market and therefore are at the mercy of both state managers and transnational capitalists that facilitate transactions. We can see concretely how upgrading and restructuring take place to deepen integration into the process of transnationalization along uneven lines.

The number of Haitian migrants living in the Dominican Republic has also risen rapidly in recent decades, which by 2005 was estimated to number at least six hundred thousand (Orozco, 2006). In recent years, Dominican state elites have enacted xenophobic and racist state policies meant to further repress and contain Haitian migrants as marginalized, reserve, or supraexploited workers (Amnesty International, 2016; S. Martinez, 1996; Wucker, 2000). It is useful here to see recent developments in the context of historical patterns of labor repression in the country. Decades ago, authoritarian regimes in the Dominican Republic developed apparatuses to repress Haitian migrants, even as Dominican policy makers undertook bilateral conventions with the Haitian government to allow entrance to Haitian migrants for a specified time (Wucker, 2000; Trouillot, 2000). This especially occurred during periods when the Dominican Republic faced labor shortages for its large sugar plantations. Yet, as a result of long-term migration patterns, permanent sugar worker settlements called bateyes gradually developed. In spite of this, in recent years, new state policies have meant to further repress migrant workers, such as the 2013 ruling of the Dominican supreme court that revoked the citizenship of Dominican-born children of undocumented migrants dating back generations (Garcia, 2013). These new state policies have clearly diminished the rights of Haitian migrant workers and their communities.

Scholarly studies have examined the changing networks that have emerged between migrant communities and their families abroad, linked by family visits, small investments, organizational connections, and communication over the telephone and internet (Baldassar and Merla, 2014; Orozco, 2006). A variety of cultural connections and hybrid phenomena exist, all of which necessarily affect current class relations. The lack of economic opportunities at home and the lure of economic prosperity abroad, alongside periods of instability, have together shaped Haitian migration trends. Similarly, the increasing communication and connections between domestic and diasporic populations help promote migration.

In this atmosphere, remittances form a vital material linkage but one that alters social relations, producing stratification even as they objectively link populations together through the cross-border redistribution of income. This brings into question: How do remittances affect the social relations of receivers and senders? Recent research suggests that as many as one in five households in Haiti have received remittances, with each recipient family gathering an annual average of nearly $2,000 (Orozco, 2006, p. 6). Thus, these are communities often dependent on the diaspora, and this is sizable, as 59 percent of Haitians lives on less than US$2 per day ($730 per year).[7] Researchers found that Haitians who sent remittances were predominantly under the age of forty and were equally divided along the basis of gender. Since more banks and institutions that serve as agents of the major remittance companies are based in Haiti's cities, rural communities in Haiti have far less access to money transfers (Orozco, 2006, p. 1).

In contrast to migratory patterns from Haiti, out-migration from Jamaica was for many decades geared toward Britain, but with Jamaica's independence, a growing number of Jamaican migrants exported their labor to North American markets, many initially arriving in the United States as "guest workers" (Ness, 2011, pp. 111–149). Jamaican migrants living in the United States have increased from 27,000 in 1960 to 576,000 in 2000.[8] A number of scholarly studies have traced the history and changing patterns of Jamaican migration (Hahamovitch, 2013; Matthews, 2013). Prior to 1990, Jamaica's formal remittance market occurred initially through the government postal services, some commercial banks, and building societies. The penetration of transnational remittance corporations into the country in the early 1990s occurred concurrently with a growing Jamaican diaspora community. The remittance market represented an attractive investment opportunity for TNCs such as Western Union and MoneyGram.

Western Union came to control a significant share of the formal remittance market around the world. Let us look at the case of Jamaica. Western Union first began to operate in Jamaica through a local agent, the Grace Kennedy bank, in late 1990. It was around this time that with the liberalization of capital controls, the possibility for a global remittance market was created. A massive expansion of Western Union took place, laying the foundation for a new transnational circuit of accumulation. Over time, new and older money transfer operators in Jamaica followed suit, seeking to operate as local agents for globally active remittance companies. Today, a number of transnationally oriented remittance companies target Caribbean and Caribbean diaspora markets (Lake, 2005). A study by the Bank of Jamaica explains: "The duopolistic dominance of the Grace Kennedy-Western Union alliance [GKRS-WU] resulted in existing Commercial Banks and Building Societies adopting aspects of their business model. As such, these institutions resorted to acting as agents for the international money transfer companies. By the end of October 2008 there were twelve remittance companies, two building societies and one commercial bank acting as agents on behalf of thirty international money transfer companies" (McLean, 2008, p. 5).

By the time of the Jamaican bank study, the GKRS-WU accounted for over 70 percent of remittance companies' inflows and approximately 50 percent of the entire local remittance market in Jamaica. As Esmond McLean's study explains, "This rapid increase is largely attributed to Western Union's increased economies of scale attributable to its worldwide expansion in the number of agent locations as well as the introduction of electronic money transfer system" (McLean, 2008, p. 6).

The other major player in the remittance market in Jamaica has been the Jamaica National Building Society (JNBS), which in 2002 had nearly 9 percent of the remittance market in Jamaica but by 2008 had increased to nearly 14 percent. In recent decades, the company has realigned itself to capitalize on the Jamaican population and diaspora, serving as a valuable agent for MoneyGram. This relation has been rooted in the significant growth of remittances sent back to Jamaica from the U.K.-based diaspora. Both JNBS and Grace Kennedy have historic roots in the country but are utilized as local agents for remittance TNCs. This allows for transnational capitalists to operate under a local appearance as they appropriate a part of migrant workers' income. JNBS, for instance, was originally founded by business interests in 1874, just over three decades after the abolition of slavery on the island (JNBS, 2010). As the availability and potential profits from small, uncultivated, and abandoned lands were surpassed by the growth of the labor force and larger plantations (Bakan, 1990, p. 18), institutions such as JNBS were important in the process of reconstituting segments of the lower classes as wage dependent. Today, a century and a half later, they are in part an institute serving to connect people into transnational capitalism.

Regulation of remittances did not begin in Jamaica until the twenty-first century. This occurred following the events of September 11, 2001, in the United States and the new emphasis on "global best practice" requirements by the financial action task force (FATF), a supranational organization based out of the OECD headquarters. The Jamaican state extended statutory obligations to the remittance market in 2002. With the passage of amendments to the Bank of Jamaica Act in February 2004, Jamaica then established a regulatory regime that required local remittance companies to be approved by the minister of finance. These reforms complied with the new standards being pushed by a variety of transnationally oriented elites with the aim of standardizing a part of the accumulation process in different nations. World Bank officials, for example, suggested ways to best regulate and tax remittances, and how to best monitor and promote their expansion (Todoroki et al., 2009). The regulations resulted in a few smaller companies exiting the market or merging their operations with larger counterparts, while over time the number of global remittance corporations that used local agencies increased (McLean, 2008, p. 10). By 2007, remittances were around 15.3 percent of Jamaica's GDP (p. 11), approximately equal to earnings from tourism. Remittance flows also averaged more than twice the amount of FDI inflows. By all accounts, remittances have come to represent a major foreign currency source for Jamaica, as well as for Haiti, the Dominican Republic, and other nations in the region.

Advancement of Money Transfers: From Telegram to Telephone to Computer

Transferring money has changed significantly over the past century, shifting from early telegram networks, to telephone and telefax grids, and ultimately to instantaneous internet technology. New fiscal policies encouraging individual debt, companies structured with agents around the world, and instantaneous domestic and cross-border financial services have allowed for widespread individual access to banking and money transfers.

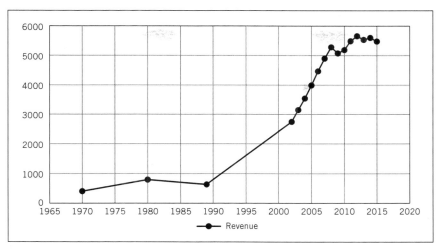

Figure 5.6 Revenue and net income (US$ millions) of Western Union, 1970–2015. (Source: Company tax records obtained by the author through the U.S. Securities and Exchange Commission.)

A key case study in the top owners and controllers of the remittance industry is the role of Western Union, as the company's business model turned toward becoming the premier *global* money transfer company. The dynamics of Western Union have changed over the course of its history, from the leading U.S. telegraph company in the latter nineteenth century and much of the twentieth century, to a company that repositioned and altered its business model with the emergence of globalization. As the data show, Western Union has gone from revenues of $399.5 million in 1970 to $5.664 billion in 2012. (See Figure 5.6.)

During earlier phases of capitalism, the transfer of money or promissory notes that guaranteed payment occurred over long distances through overland and oceanic transportation, which made it difficult and time consuming. Through the early 1860s, the fastest way to send a message from one side of North America to the other was to use the Pony Express, which took about ten days to cross from New York to California. With the completion of the first transcontinental telegraph line in late 1861, that distance could be spanned quickly but through a cumbersome and limiting technology (Nonnenmacher, 2014). Over time improved telegram services as a form of message transfer became widespread, and the technology spread to other parts of the world. Consolidating itself early, Western Union grew rapidly, becoming the premier message transfer company in the United States throughout the latter nineteenth century and into the twentieth century. However, not only was the telegram limited in the amount of information it could transfer; users' access to it was also limited. By the end of World War II, when improvements in telephone technology made direct dialing commonplace and long-distance service relatively inexpensive, the golden age of the telegram was over. People continued to send telegrams for important personal occasions and urgent business throughout the 1950s, but telegraph use dropped off steadily.

Similarly, the transfer of money was done increasingly over telephone or telefax between banks and financial institutions. While this allowed banks and institutions to intensify financial transactions, it also occurred through a hodgepodge of banks and still required a relatively high amount of human labor and repetitive tasks to guarantee the distribution. As international economic activity intensified, by 1974 seven international banks set up SWIFT. This became a global network to facilitate the transfer of financial messages. Using these messages, banks could exchange data for the transfer of funds between financial institutions. The society came to operate as the UN-sanctioned international standards body for the creation and maintenance of financial-messaging standards. In 1977, there were 230 member banks from five countries that started operating through SWIFT. To conduct more rapid transactions and communications, in 1964 it inaugurated a transcontinental microwave radio beam system, and, in 1974, it launched the first domestic communications satellite (Western Union, 2001). Decades later, by 2013, SWIFT had more than 10,000 members worldwide (in more than two hundred countries) and handled more than 15 million messages daily.

Shifting away from its previously U.S.-centric business model (which had operated primarily within the North American market and was facing declining profits and mounting debts), Western Union executives slowly began to divest the company of its telecommunications-based assets beginning in the early 1980s. Using new computer technologies and backing deregulation in the United States and in other countries, Western Union began expanding outside of the United States and European markets.

Reinventing itself as a global brand, Western Union officials set up agent operations internationally to become "the fastest way to send money worldwide." By 1980, Western Union's revenue from domestic money transfers exceeded telegram service revenue for the first time. Then, in 1989, it introduced the quick collect system in which creditors could promptly secure transfers internationally. By 1994, the company was in dire economic straits and declared bankruptcy, which led to a company-wide restructuring, after which it completely dropped its telegram service and became geared toward global financial transactions and money transfers (Covell, 2003). Whereas "the company's message-sending business had become a part of U.S. culture . . . its corporate roots became a thing of the past when all of its telecommunications businesses were divested during the reorganization. Once stripped of these businesses, Western Union was left to concentrate exclusively on financial services" (Covell, 2003). The company's restructuring reflected a larger trend toward financialization in the transnationalizing world economy.

In 1995, Western Union was acquired by First Data Corporation, and, in 2000, it launched its website, providing "fast, convenient ways to send money online" worldwide. Over these years and into the twenty-first century, the company grew extraordinarily. In 2006, Western Union became an independent company and began trading on the NYSE. Its cross-border business-to-business activities expanded greatly, such as with its acquisition of Custom House in 2009 and its acquisition of Travelex Global Business Payments in 2011 (Western Union, 2014). Wide arrays of TNCs and global investors are now major shareholders in the company. For example, Berkshire Hathaway chairman Warren Buffett for a time owned $10 million in shares (Willoughby, 2007). Companies with even larger holdings in Western Union include Schroders, a London-based transnational asset management company; the Los Angeles–based Capital Research Global Investors, one of the largest global investment firms with around $1 trillion under management; Vanguard, which is the world's largest mutual fund company; and the U.S.-based Fidelity Investment, which administers and manages trillions in assets (Fidelity website, 2014). The list goes on, with many of the largest shareholders being U.S.- and U.K.-based financial firms. Yet individual and institutional investors in the company have investments around the world, and many of these larger U.S.- and U.K.-based companies in turn have shareholders from many different countries.

By 2006, Western Union was managing 18 percent of money transfers globally. By 2013, Western Union was operating over the internet and telephone and from more than 115,000 ATMs with over 515,000 agent locations in two hundred countries and territories, with around 9,600 employees.[9] With its economy of scale stretching worldwide, Western Union has secured a competitive advantage in the business. As their website states, their business model "aims to move money anytime, anywhere and anyway our customers choose" (Western Union, 2014).

The largest competitor with Western Union has been MoneyGram International Inc., which was founded in 1940 to process money orders. By the late 1980s, MoneyGram was rapidly expanding its international activities. In 1988, Viad Corp, the parent company of Travelers Express, purchased MoneyGram, only to then spin this off as a publicly traded company (MoneyGram, 2010). As of 2013, MoneyGram had 293,000 agent locations in 197 countries, employing more than 2,350 people around the world. As the data show, MoneyGram's revenues expanded rapidly throughout the final years of the twentieth century and early years of the twenty-first century. Even after its profits declined during the period of the global financial crisis less than a

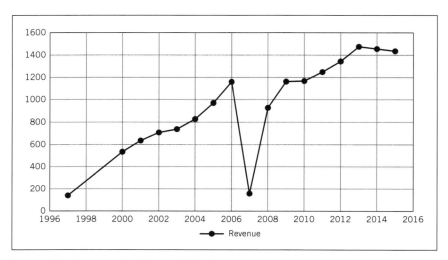

Figures 5.7 Revenue and net income (US$ millions) of MoneyGram, 1997–2015. (Source: Company tax records obtained by the author through the U.S. Securities and Exchange Commission.)

decade ago, MoneyGram has again begun to increase its revenues. Substantial restructuring in recent years has not hindered its growth, and, as of 2013, the company maintained a strong position—cash and cash equivalents of $2.23 billion and net receivables of $767.7 million. These numbers were achieved, while continuing to pay off large loans and expanding into new zones by operating through "domestic" agents (MGI Analyst Report, 2014). (See Figure 5.7.)

In recent decades, a number of new tech firms have entered the remittance market. The most well known of these is Boom Financial Inc., which was founded in 2008, and the Silicon Valley–based Xoom Corp., which was founded in 2001. These major firms, along with other factors, have caused downward pressure on agent's commissions in the business (MGI-Analyst Report, 2014). While Xoom has become active in 30 countries, Boom has grown to reach 130 countries. While these new Silicon Valley–based remittances companies often provide lower surcharges, they operate through smaller networks of local agents, making them less accessible. Without as many agent locations, these companies rely heavily on internet technology. Although the revenues of these companies are small compared to Western Union and MoneyGram, they have good potential to grow, as the data show the rise of Xoom's revenues from $26.2 million in 2009 to $122.2 million in 2013. In 2015, PayPal, the online money transfer company, purchased Xoom. (See Figure 5.8.)

Directors and executive officers of these transnational remittance corporations have worked for a host of other TNCs active in finance, remit-

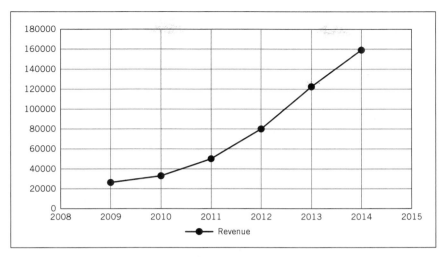

Figure 5.8 Revenue and net income (US$ thousands) of Xoom. (Source: Company tax records obtained by the author through the U.S. Securities and Exchange Commission.)

tances, resource extraction, and other major industries.[10] The owners and managers of the transnational remittance corporations, namely Western Union and its major competitors, form a part of today's transnational capitalist elite (Peetz and Murray, 2012; Robinson, 2014a; Rothkopf, 2009).

TNC Penetration of Caribbean Money Transfers

Through the era of global capitalism, TNCs and financial institutions have penetrated national markets around the world. These transnational enterprises benefit both from economies of scale, which are the cost advantages they obtain due to size, from throughput (the amount of material or items passing through a system), and from the deregulation and privatization of national markets facilitated by policy makers operating through various state apparatuses. Transnational capital has thus been successful at incorporating huge populations into new market relations, including within the Caribbean and its diaspora, such as with the shift toward remittance services of TNCs, instead of traditional banks. Earlier, more static, less accessible, and often more state-linked banking systems came to conflict with transnational realities. The social standpoints and immigration status of workers using these services also often prevents them from using conventional banking. The export of labor and the reverse flow of remittances have become fundamental to the Caribbean's relationship to global capitalism. The cross-border money transfers of the remittance TNCs now surpass the money transfers conducted through bank branches. They are even larger than official development assistance as well as private debt and portfolio equity flows. Remittances represent a third of GDP for many small countries such as Haiti (Sirkeci et al., 2012, p. 5).

Many state elites, meanwhile, have sought to manage the exportation of migrant labor in ways that benefit transnational capital and ensure their own social reproduction in a manner that is linked with the global economy (Parreñas, 2005; Rodriguez, 2010). Often in concert with transnational capital, policy makers promote remittances as vital parts of their economies and global integration. As Segovia (2002) has argued, remittances deposited by their receivers in privatized local banks have helped local state elites gain loans from IFIs. As Ho (1999, p. 34) observes, "Postcolonial Caribbean governments contribute to the transnational traffic by treating immigration as a safety valve for surplus labor and by emphasizing capital rather than human resources in their development plans."

While local businesses and banks still play a role in the remittance of money, often serving as a payout or pickup location for the receiver or sender, they essentially serve as agents for the much larger TNCs that carry out the actual cross-border transfer. For instance, in the Caribbean, the new transnational remittance business now dominates the older bank money transfer systems. This contrasts with the years prior to the 1990s, when the transnational remittance business had not taken shape and traditional banks conducted transfers through a slow and cumbersome process. In the Dominican Republic, for example, only 1 percent of money transfers go through commercial banks, while 92 percent of total remittances pass through licensed money transfer companies.[11] These licensed money transfer companies overwhelmingly are either TNCs, such as Western Union, or operate as the local agents of TNCs.

While at first glance, local agents may appear to be domestically oriented, they are in fact deeply integrated with circuits of global capital accumulation. For example, in the Dominican Republic, the company Caribe Express is the local agent of Xoom. In 2013, as the author found firsthand, Caribe Express/Xoom charged a 5 percent commission on remittances sent through Xoom, whereas Western Union charged approximately 8 percent as a fee. Yet the number of Caribe Express locations was far fewer than those of Western Union. Although Western Union usually charges a higher percentage than its competitors, its agents are more accessible. In addition, Western Union far surpasses its competitors in its name recognition and volume of remittances.

There has been a massive increase of remittance flows in recent decades (as the World Bank data in Table 5.2 shows).[12] Familial connections, as well as cultural and social expectations of reciprocity among senders and receivers, appear to make these flows somewhat resistant to the capitalistic orientation of other financial flows, so much so that remittances are less volatile in relation to other foreign exchange earnings. World Bank researchers have thus argued they serve as an important cushion for local economies and communities. Sirkeci et al. (2012) explain, "At the national level, remittances help offset current account deficits and shore up international reserves" (p. xv). However, evidence suggests that remittances can also add to the depreciation of local currency (p. 5) and be connected to different types of stratification among senders and receivers. However, remittances are wrapped up in an increasingly unequal and unsustainable global system, with its own novelties, contradictions, and crises. This draws attention to the fact that all spheres of social reproduction under capitalism are linked somehow to reinforcing unequal class relations. Clearly capital finds novel ways at each and every turn to extract money from labor, directly and indirectly. Here we see how largely poor working-class Caribbeans become a node in a system that profits TNCs like MoneyGram, Western Union, and others.

Conclusion: Migrant Remittances and the Accumulation of Transnational Capital through Redistributed Value

Through the era of globalization, alongside the major technological and organizational advancements and the increased movement of skilled and unskilled migrants, the remittance business and the exportation of labor have undergone unparalleled growth. New migration patterns have resulted in a reverse flow of remittances that have become a major pillar of the global economy, especially for lower-income communities in many parts of the world. In fact, the magnitude of money transfers stretches beyond the official remittance market, as official data collected on money transfers do not include other forms of "in-kind" remittances, such as goods or money shipped or brought in person to relatives abroad or by people acting as "mules" who are paid to transport goods or money. In Jamaica, the term "barrel children" has come into existence to describe children who "survive on barrels of goodies shipped by migrant parents chiefly from the United States" (Pollard, 2005, p. 24). While a variety of survival and supplemental strategies have been utilized by working people in the global era, remittances have been among the most important. Yet this has also led to ensuring a problematic reality, which Cabezas describes as "dependence on outside relationships to generate an extra cash flow for families or for household survival" (2009, p. 66).

While occurring as a form of transnational social integration, the objective relationship between remittance sender and remittance receiver also occurs through what Garni and Weyher (2013) describe as a "mystified" class relationship, through the separation between the site of wage labor and wage-generated consumption. Furthermore, it is through this relation that transnational capital and transnationally oriented state elites appropriate part of the value being redistributed between migrant labor and migrant-receiving communities, once it is channeled through the remittance business. As dominant groups profit in this uneven and vicious cycle, they seek to "capitalize on the alienation of humanity and their primary response to that alienation—migration and the remittances it generates" (Garni and Weyher, 2013, p. 66). State elites, by facilitating the remittance and other global industries and generating income from their taxation, have come to depend on such transnational processes for their own social reproduction (Rodriguez, 2010; Sprague, 2011c). Transnational capital meanwhile has been able to profit doubly, capitalizing on the surplus labor of migrant workers as well as appropriating part of the value moving through their remittances. In addition to a commission or fee, these companies also often bilk working people by requiring an unfavorable currency exchange rate.

Large swaths of the global population, including many in the Caribbean, have become structurally marginalized or kept in unemployed "reserve pools" of labor. In turn, remittances serve an even more important function for individual and community survival. These communities develop new dependencies that are transnational in nature and can bring about a pacifying effect (Garni and Weyher, 2013). Rather than protest for means of subsistence, there exists now a new pressure to wait for money coming from abroad. Although some may skimp by with remittances sent from family members abroad, they continue to exist in lower-income communities that are structurally marginalized and exploited. Remittance-receiving households and communities survive, yet do so while often separated (or separated in part) from actual processes of waged labor.

Meanwhile, for transnationally oriented elites, this is seen as a means for "freeing up" the state from its obligation to provide a social safety net. The state is then free to reduce taxes and regulations on the TCC, as remittance flows can help dissipate social tensions, providing a small lifeline to some lower-income populations undergoing difficulties associated with global economic restructuring. Among other populations, those living in the Caribbean and in its diaspora have witnessed a complete transformation of the way in which money is transferred across borders. As the Caribbean diaspora has increased exponentially over the latter part of the twentieth century and into the twenty-first century, this has precipitated a significant increase in remittance flows back into the region. Transnational capital has in turn sought to appropriate a portion of the redistributed value changing hands between the global working poor. The contradictory nature of this phenomenon will be undoubtedly bound up in the future ways in which global and Caribbean societies develop.

Globally Competitive Export Processing and Exploitation in the Caribbean

A key part of the globalization process has been the creation of demarcated zones of production for the global market. In the Caribbean by the 1970s and 1980s, as one of the first regions where export process zones (EPZs) evolved, these spaces began to serve as platforms for new relations of production associated with the globalizing economy.[1] As one researcher elaborates, these new productive spaces "in recent decades . . . have been used by many developing countries to help manage a larger strategic transition from a highly protected, inward-oriented domestic economic policy, to a liberalized, globally integrated, outward-oriented domestic economy" (Lang, 2010, p. 7). Known initially as free trade zones (FTZs), these spaces serve as specific-locations where foreign and local industrial tenants receive special tax and trade privileges to compete in the global market. Capital came to move more freely through these new zones, as sites for exploiting and taking advantage of local pools of labor on a wide scale (of course, bound up with many local particularities and historical processes).

In this chapter, I look at: (1) the historical formation of export processing and with regard to the Caribbean, (2) the role of transnationally oriented state elites and the TCC in crafting EPZ legislation through new supranational forums, (3) how the transnationalization (and centralization) of capital occurs alongside a proliferation of contractors enmeshed in TCC accumulation networks, and (4) the flexibilization of capitalist accumulation as it seeks out new advanced ways to exploit gendered and racialized surplus labor. Workers become a "naked commodity," deployed to wherever they are needed, existing alongside various forms of coercion and consent, including paternalistic forms of control—in the process destroying subsistence living and making people more reliant on capital. Throughout this chapter, we see how powerful transnational forces, and through various institutions and businesses, help restructure economies, pushing state apparatuses into line with neoliberal policy prescriptions, always under the mantra of global competitiveness.

A Local and Global Phenomena

A host of euphemisms have been coined to promote EPZs, such as "open-door policy," "investment climate," "free from cumbersome procedures," "an entity with global footmarks," "multiply your value," "renewable production hubs," and so on. By promoting low-wage, compliant labor forces as a "comparative advantage," transnationally oriented state elites and capitalists have used EPZs as a mechanism to reshape and restructure productive relations as an integrated part of the global economy. Through such dynamics, laboring groups around the world have become objectively linked to global chains of production. Horizontally integrated and geographically diffuse global production networks have spread rapidly through EPZs; wherein the labor power of workers is incorporated into transnational value chains, which in turn are controlled by TNCs.

The very geographic essence of the EPZ is changing, including its spatial dynamic as a demarcated special area within a country, as the special benefits and regulations applied to EPZs spread to ever-larger areas and factories, expanding beyond the walls and fences of EPZs. As Lang elaborates, "The notion of an EPZ as a physically limited space has been challenged by the development of 'single factory EPZs' which provide incentives to individual companies regardless of location, as well as by the establishment of EPZs which cover very large geographical areas" (2010, pp. 12–13). Another scholar explains that where "EPZ legislation enables companies to operate within these production enclaves, there is a growing trend for governments to extend these incentives to companies which produce for export but operate outside the designated zones" (L. Dunn, 2010, p. 601). As Willmore (1996, p. 23) earlier observed: "Fenced EPZs inevitably become less important once governments provide incentives for companies located outside special export enclaves." Increasingly, the phenomenon of the EPZ is becoming a generalizable phenomenon across Caribbean nations, where the EPZs have "gradually become indistinguishable from the rest of the country—which is, after all, their final (implicit or explicit) goal" (UNCTC, 1991, p. 332). This fits with the prediction made by Sklair (1989) that a general transformation would take place of the developing world into a vast export-processing plant!

EPZs were meant initially (according to United States and allied policy makers at the time) to help alleviate the problem of unemployment and generate foreign exchange, but over the subsequent decades, they have become part of a deeper developmental model that reshapes societies and economies, orienting them toward globally competitive markets and enriching a small number of capitalists and elites.[2] As spaces within national states linked into global chains of production, they serve as a "form of export promotion, to liberalize and jumpstart their economies and as a way to enter the global economy through international trade" (Virgill, 2009, p. 2). While the ostensible purpose of EPZs is to "invigorate economies' exporting capabilities and capacity" (Virgill, 2009, p. 183), the actual main effect has been an increase in the power of TNCs as they are sheltered from regulations that could potentially uphold labor standards and answer to local constituencies. Business operations within EPZs, for example, are extended preferential tax treatment, preferential duty treatment, a liberal regulatory environment, enhanced physical infrastructure, direct subsidies, as well as other incentives such as export promotion services, and streamlined administration procedures for imports and exports.[3] Often not factored into the EPZ model then is the extra burden on the state apparatus as it invests in infrastructure and subsidies for TNCs and as it is directed away from spending on social policies.

EPZs have been responsible for roughly 20 percent of global trade in recent years (SZ Jug, 2013). As of 1987, there were 175 EPZs in 53 countries, yet, by 1995, there were 500 EPZs in 73 countries (Schrank, 2001, p. 223), and by 2007 there were at least 3,000 EPZs in 135 countries (Singa Boyenge, 2007). Similarly, employment in EPZs grew from 22.5 million people employed in 1997 to 43 million people in 2003 (Sargent and Matthews, 2009). Near the turn of the century, Mexico and the United States had the most EPZs worldwide, with 107 in the former and 213 in the latter (ILO, 1998).

In the United States, EPZs are referred to as FTZs. They take the shape of both industrial parks and smaller sites, allowing advantages such as lessened U.S. regulatory agency requirements for reexport.[4] While FTZs in the United States and many other parts of the global north do often have higher wages and more protections as compared with sites in the Third World—they also serve to push down wages and are used as a launching pad to weaken labor protections. In a league of its own, China has become a center of global capitalist accumulation (Harris, 2009a, 2009b) and the largest site of EPZ production, benefiting from its advanced infrastructure and large low-wage workforce (Fu and Gao, 2007). The epicenter of strikes worldwide, the Chinese state has deployed different strategies for coercing and pacifying labor within the country (Lin, 2016). Whereas nearly half of worldwide EPZ production takes place in these three countries—China, the United States,

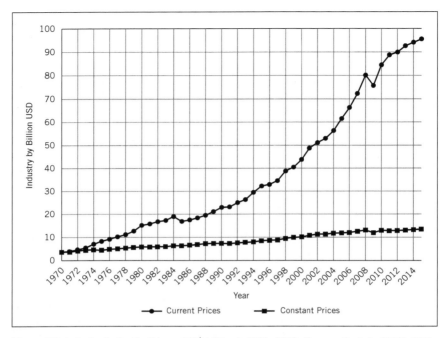

Figure 6.1 Industry in the Caribbean (US$ billions), 1970–2015. (Source: Kushnir, 2013). While this figure does not differentiate between EPZ industry and industry in general, this data, according to Caribbean economists that I spoke with, correlate to the rising role of EPZs in the region.

and Mexico—other regions such as the Caribbean (an early laboratory for the EPZ model) have also seen a growth in the number of zones and continued attempts to deepen the export-processing model.

The importance of the industrial sector for Caribbean economies increased throughout the 1970s, 1980s, and into the early 1990s. Between 1984 and 1990, industrial exports from Caribbean EPZs to the U.S. market grew from 22 percent to 50 percent of the total Caribbean exports to the United States (Klak, 1995, p. 298). Between the mid-1970s and late 1980s, the per capita U.S. dollar value of industrial exports for eight Caribbean countries grew fourfold. Yet, during the 1990s and into the twenty-first century, the region has faced stiff global competition. The Dominican Republic has been one of the most successful in integrating with the global capitalist economy, as the industrial sector's contribution to GDP was 21.92 percent of GDP in 1965, which had grown to 36.36 percent by 1991 (Kushnir, 2013). Dominican economist Ceara Hatton explains: "The expansion of export processing has made up a large part of [the country's] industrial growth over recent decades" (personal communication, 2015). (See Figure 6.1.)

However, over recent decades, with rising global competition and the growing importance of other economic sectors (such as remittances, finance, tourism, and the service sector), industrial production in the region has often faced periods of stagnation and decline. In Jamaica, for instance, the value added by the industrial sector was 37.1 percent of GDP in 1993 but had shrunk to 22.9 percent in 2017 (World Bank, 2017). While Dominican EPZ · production has grown faster than in Jamaica and much of the rest of the Caribbean, it has undergone difficulties in recent years, with the value added by the Dominican industrial sector dropping from 35 percent of GDP in 1991 to 26.1 percent in 2017 (World Bank, 2017). As a reflection of these trends, the number of workers and companies active in Caribbean EPZs has fluctuated over recent decades. In some nations, such as in Jamaica and Haiti, EPZ manufacturing has declined in recent years, while in other parts of the region, such as in Puerto Rico and the Dominican Republic EPZ production has faced ups and downs. Despite the earlier rise and more recent pullback of the sector, export processing remains a vital part of the region's economy and informs planners and policy makers.

This is part of a larger process. The export of capital to the periphery has disrupted many rural zones, causing out-migration to countries abroad and internal migration to areas where work can be found such as in EPZs. As Sassen (1988) argues, bound up with the reorganizing of world finance and manufacturing are migrant flows—where people are compelled to leave those areas of the world starved for capital and to compete in areas of the world where large diasporas have formed.

Large foreign-based TNCs are not the only players in the region's EPZ production. Locally based capitalists have also profited by operating as contractors, local agents, or distributors for TNCs. This underscores the broader reshaping of class society in recent years as local capitalist sectors integrate into transnational production networks. Through integration across borders, many Caribbean businesspeople have become transnational capitalists themselves with global financial portfolios (and often business chains that stretch across the Caribbean and into other regions as well). As Robinson (2009, p. 103) explains: "These forms of participation have opened up space for local investors and small-scale entrepreneurs to integrate into transnational production chains. The industrial activity of TNCs generates demand for a host of suppliers as industrial production is increasingly fragmented and organized through networks of outsourcing and subcontracting."

New regional forums and agreements have been vital for these integrative relations. State policy makers have facilitated these new regional forums in order to allow for transnational capital to continue to take advantage of tax breaks and poor labor standards. Heavy investments from national and supranational state apparatuses have sought continuously to stimulate EPZ operations.

In fact, state practices promoting new policies of regional integration have been pushed for and heavily guided by the TCC (Sprague-Silgado, 2017a). Through the formation of new economic forums, transnational capital has played a decisive role in crafting legislation. Novel and far-reaching policies have set up investment provisions that eliminate many restrictions, performance requirements, and domestic content laws (Ronald Cox, 2008, p. 1537). The formation and expansion of EPZs are not only promoted by local state elites but also a part of the policies pursued by officials from the United States, other states, and supranational institutions. Different institutions, or subunits, within national states and other agencies have served to internalize transnational governance patterns, operated by elites who have become transnationally oriented over recent decades (Jayasuriya, 1999; Sprague, 2010). State policy makers over recent decades have come to see transnational capital as a critical source of investment and tax revenue (Robinson, 2003; Rodriguez, 2010).

For the Caribbean, the first of the major economic forums, meant to deepen the region's integration with the incipient globalizing economy, was the CBI. Launched in 1982, it was facilitated by U.S. policy makers under the Reagan administration. Drafted in Washington, the countries that were eligible to participate had no direct input. In part the CBI was designed to enhance the competitive position of U.S.-based industries doing business in the region at a time, but it also sought to create general conditions that would be conducive for investors. It occurred also as the European Economic Community (EEC) was developing and advancing supranational linkages with the region via the Lomé Convention. The Lomé Convention, first signed in 1975, was a trade and aid agreement between the EEC and seventy-one African, Caribbean, and Pacific countries.

The CBI also stressed military and security matters and was therefore seen as a strategy for staving off alternative and revolutionary tendencies in the Caribbean, while deepening U.S. influence and the region's integration into the globalizing economy (H. Watson, 1991). While some Caribbean state leaders at the time reminded the United States that their problem was not Communism, but intractable economic problems, Reagan was not impressed and evidently believed otherwise. Sandinista Nicaragua, of course, was not invited to participate in the CBI, as it was the target at that time of U.S. economic, political, and military intervention, with U.S. supported death squad insurgents carrying out deadly cross-border raids from their bases in Honduras (Robinson and Norsworthy, 1987). Also, it should be noted that nearly one-third of the $350 million in funds appropriated by Congress for the CBI was used for military intervention in El Salvador (Werner, 2016, p. 33).

The CBI embodied the neoliberal policy agenda in play in the Caribbean to expand and strengthen global capitalist integration through EPZs, with the Washington Consensus institutions, the IMF, World Bank, and U.S. Treasury mediating the process via structural adjustment and related policy measures. The CBI injected dollar loans (used largely to meet payments on existing debt), free trade regimes for a limited number of Caribbean exports, and a new set of tax breaks that were designed to attract the investment of U.S.-based MNCs. Interestingly, Haiti was the first state to accept the CBI, as it had "no genuinely national development program . . . to delay or modify the adoption of the latest U.S. sponsored economic initiative" (Manigat, 1997, p. 87). As other Caribbean states came under pressure, they too soon signed onto the new economic forum.

It should be noted that the earliest incarnation of EPZs occurred before the globalization of high-technology production had incorporated robotics/artificial intelligence and significant amounts of automation; although, this earlier period was a time when the scientific and technological revolution in the United States was making certain industries uncompetitive and when some observers were talking about the rise of the "New International Division of Labor" (H. Watson, 1990). It was during this initial phase of the EPZs that multinational companies manufacturing garments located themselves directly in the Caribbean, taking advantage of the new trade provisions set into motion (Werner, 2016, p. 34).

TNCs benefiting from the exploitation of labor in the region's EPZs soon found it more conducive to rely on subcontractors. Eventually, these large companies decided to disinvest from their direct involvement in production altogether, and instead rely on outsourcing to Caribbean and East Asian businesspeople operating in the region (Werner, 2016, p. 34). Over the decades, with the light manufacturing industries undergoing extraordinary changes through computer and high-tech advancements around the turn of the century and into the twenty-first century, the industry has gone through major changes. Popular movements and the organizing of labor struggles have also sparked challenges for capitalists in the EPZs.

While transnationally oriented elites operating in the Caribbean have at times succeeded in attracting investors through the EPZ model over recent decades, there have also been periods of stagnation and the loss of industrial tenants when lower labor costs have been available elsewhere or when preferential market access has been diluted. Take, for example, the competition from corporations operating through advanced built environments and the exploitation of local labor in East Asia, as well as parts of the Americas and Europe. Often this vicious cycle of competition has led to short life spans for ventures in Caribbean EPZs. For instance, export-processing companies used to assemble garments and electronic components in Barbados subcontracting for U.S. military-industrial corporations. At one point there were fifteen electronic assembly plants in Barbados, none of which exist today. During the 1980s, Intel had a "large plant in Barbados that operated with three shifts, until the movement toward the EU led Intel to close the plant and shift operations to Dublin, Ireland where the state ponied up $500 million in subsidies to attract Intel" (H. Watson, 1992). A large number of problems exist, according to Moberg (2014, p.2), that hinder the success of EPZs in the Caribbean, as they suffer from poor infrastructure quality, bad locations, insufficient zone size, inadequate roads, unreliable power supplies, congestion, inadequate maintenance, lack of effective advertisement to entice companies into the EPZ, poor policy coordination, lack of tax incentives, excessive bureaucracy, and the organizing of labor movements. Even still, under capitalist globalization, with large reserve pools of labor, and in close proximity to the world's largest consumer society, the Caribbean remains an often-eyed site for capitalist export processing.

Although a select few have benefited immensely through capital's reorganization in the region, the vast majority of workers and communities connected with industries, such as those operating through EPZs, face precarious and low-income conditions. Yet with high levels of unemployment, many working people have few options. Those benefiting meanwhile include major transnational conglomerates as well as local factory owners who contract with TNCs and the "emerging transnational class of intermediaries running EPZ promotion agencies" (Neveling, 2014, p. 194). By tethering their own social reproduction to global production networks, some elites directly benefit from maintaining and expanding the export-processing model. Meanwhile, sales and marketing companies push the "culture-ideology of consumerism" (Sklair, 2012), sustaining a consumer base for corporate branded commodities often produced by low-waged workers in these facilities. It is important to note that these consumer groups no longer exist only in so-called developed nations but in the Third World as well (Robinson, 2008). All the while, these processes occur alongside the social alienation and exploitation of labor.

Next, I look at how the EPZ model of development has undergone important changes over recent decades and how EPZs serve as a vital mechanism and integrative space for the reorientation of locally based businesses toward transnational capitalist flows.

Evolution of Export Processing in the Globalizing Caribbean

During the Caribbean's colonial era, as part of the triangular trade, export industries came to specialize in agricultural products such as sugar and tobacco

(Mintz, 1974). In turn, various entry and exit points and warehouses existed where goods were stored and shipped. While plantation capital in the nineteenth-century Caribbean declined, capital received a boost with the completion of the Panama Canal in the early twentieth century. By the mid-twentieth century, agricultural output increased thanks to the advent of new industrial technology; known as the "Green Revolution," this involved the development of high-yielding hybrid crops, new pesticides, herbicides, and fertilizers, and railroads that connected inland hubs and major ports. The highly exploitive relations of the rural economies of the Caribbean during the mid-twentieth century (as part of the advancing international phase of capitalism) have been well documented, such as in the vivid documentary *Bitter Cane* (Arcelin, 1983).

In the postwar period, the Truman administration in the United States through its "Operation Bootstrap" attempted to develop low-wage manufacturing in Puerto Rico. Facilitated by the U.S. government, Puerto Rico's political establishment under the Partido Popular Democrático (PPD) abandoned import substitution policies and instead pushed for export-oriented development (Ayala and Bernabe, 2007). Capital and state policy makers closely oversaw the new initiative (Neveling, 2014).[5] Werner writes: "The garment industry grew rapidly, comprising between one-quarter and one-third of manufacturing jobs on the island from the mid-1950s to the mid-1970s, largely employing women workers" (2016, p. 31).

The so-called Puerto Rican Model (PRM) was advertised for the wider Caribbean. Some well-known figures in the region, such as the Saint Lucian economist William Arthur Lewis (A. Lewis, 1950, 1965, 1978), contributed much to projecting the PRM across the region. In addition, U.S. state managers, through the U.S. Mutual Security Act of 1951, made it clear that alongside these economic developments, securing an anticommunist agenda would take precedence.

Soon a vast new set of experimental policies developed export manufacturing in Puerto Rico by appealing to U.S.-domiciled corporations:

> The Puerto Rican development corporation Fomento contracted the US consulting firm Arthur D. Little in order to convince mainland capitalists of the benefits of investments in Puerto Rico. Significant investment packages including tax and customs holidays, low rate leases of purpose built Fomento factories and so forth were advertised with a full-on marketing operation across the U.S.-nationwide. Already in 1947, Textron, a rising giant in the era of mergers after 1945, relocated spinning mills to Puerto Rico and fired thousands of workers in the U.S. northeast. Other U.S. corporations like General Electrics for example would soon follow. The Truman administration

used the immediate success of Puerto Rican development policies to advertise its Point Four development program globally. Throughout the 1950s and even more so under the Alliance for Progress that the Kennedy administration introduced after the failed invasion in Cuba, thousands of officials from Third World countries were flown to Puerto Rico to visit zones of "modern manufacturing" and learn how similar progress could be achieved. (Neveling, 2014, pp. 8–9)

During the 1960s, similar EPZ models began to develop within the nations of the U.S.-allied regimes in the developing world, such as in Taiwan and in northern Mexico (Neveling, 2014, p. 9). By the 1970s, the Caribbean was an opportune location for manufacturing with its large reserve army of labor and geographic proximity to the North American consumer market. Facilitated largely by U.S.-based MNCs, manufacturing in the region began to expand rapidly.

Initially, EPZs took the form of industrial estates that frequently occupied 100 hectares or less. For the most part, other than functioning as a mechanism for foreign capital to exploit local labor, they were highly isolated from the domestic societies where they operated, specifically in terms of geography, specialized regulations, and sparse linkages to local economies (Lang, 2010, pp. 12–13). During the 1970s and 1980s, state officials closely controlled who could operate in the zones. Focused on industrial production, businesses in the EPZs engaged primarily in light manufacturing and processed apparel, textiles, and footwear for export to foreign markets. Lower-income populations in developing nations were traditionally excluded from the consumption of EPZ products (Lang, 2010, pp. 12–13).

By the early 1980s, both ISI and traditional export industries underwent significant difficulties, as states in the developing world faced rising debts and financial pitfalls. As a response to these economic instabilities, in nations across the developing world there was an expansion of nontraditional exports and the development of EPZs. EPZs grew as manufacturing hubs and attracted global investors, through their provision of "low-cost production, easy market access, and a business climate conducive to foreign direct investment" (Long, 1987, p. 64). Suiting both the interests of transnationally oriented capitalists and transnationally oriented state elites, EPZs have since become a central part of developmental strategy. Not just in the global south; EPZs are now becoming linked forward and backward into globalizing local markets. As the data illustrate, Puerto Rico (closely integrated for more than a century with the U.S. market) is by far the most industrialized of the Caribbean islands. The Dominican Republic, which in recent decades has developed a robust network of EPZs, now has the region's second largest industrial sector.

TABLE 6.1. INDUSTRIAL PRODUCTION AND RATINGS OF INDUSTRY IN THE CARIBBEAN, 2013		
Countries	Industry, billion dollars (total: 90.4)	% of Production
Puerto Rico	50.6	56
Dominican Republic	14.5	16
Trinidad & Tobago	11.4	12.6
Cuba	9.1	10.1
Jamaica	1.7	1.9
Haiti	0.83	0.92
Bahamas	0.57	0.63
Barbados	0.36	0.4
Aruba	0.25	0.28
Cayman Islands	0.17	0.19
St. Lucia	0.086	0.095
St. Kitts & Nevis	0.075	0.083
Grenada	0.06	0.066
St. Vincent & the Grenadines	0.054	0.06
British Virgin Islands	0.052	0.058
Dominica	0.043	0.048
Turks & Caicos Islands	0.042	0.046
Anguilla	0.018	0.02
Montserrat	0.0032	0.0035
Source: Kushnir, 2013.		

Since 1997, EPZs have also been set up in Cuba, a trend that looks set to intensify as the country integrates more over the coming years with the global capitalist economy (Willmore, 2000). (See Table 6.1.)

As low-cost platforms for companies seeking to exploit cheap labor, EPZs have also developed through standardized laws and practices, such as cuts in tariffs and other duties. Export processing has been promoted as boosting FDI and foreign exchange, encouraging employment, leading to the transfer of technology, upgrading workforces with new skills, fostering entrepreneurial practices, and encouraging a "demonstration effect" wherein domestic firms learn from foreign firms.

A problem that the export-processing model has in the Caribbean is the lack of infrastructure (in industry, supply chains, and education), which significantly harms its global competitiveness for capital. While light manufacturing can be set up easily with machines moved around from country to country, there is hardly any EPZ type of commodity (good or service) that can be produced in the Caribbean that cannot be more efficiently produced in China, India, and other locations, in terms of an advantage in wage and price competitiveness. By contrast, more advanced manufacturing and high-tech industries have difficulty getting off the ground in the region.

Without a capital goods sector and a base in research and development (R&D) and dynamic and adaptable manufacturing (that integrates modern technology and incorporates vast amounts of information through machines), it is very difficult for Caribbean policy makers and elites to know what to anticipate. This puts Caribbean-based capitalists at a disadvantage that means they must work to integrate with transnational forces. Meanwhile, policy makers in the region either lack the resources or the political capacity to invest in educating and training professional and technical labor at a time when machines (robots and other smart tools) are becoming cheaper to produce and maintain than certain types of cheap labor, in effect reinforcing an uneven and combined transnational development. Businesses active in the region must not only import technology but also purchase imported fuel. In this difficult climate, many highly educated Caribbeans leave their countries in search of higher-paying jobs in the global economy. While some institutions in the region have been developed to maintain professional groups and use them locally, this remains a structural problem throughout the Caribbean. These dynamics add to the difficulties for the region in moving beyond light manufacturing and labor-intensive production toward more high-tech alternatives. The anarchy of capitalist production, especially for regions that lack advanced built economic environments, is reflected in how policy makers will advocate a deepening insertion into transnational accumulation networks through whatever means necessary. All of this puts more into question capitalist development, as the internal contradictions of capitalism mean that it is never going to work how its proponents claim it will work.

In this situation, deepening transnational links are indispensable for Caribbean-based and diasporic businesses, not only via subcontracting and banking but also by attempting to form strategic alliances with TNCs and thereby develop a realistic presence in Europe, North America, and other locations. The new export-processing model of the global era is thus instructive for understanding the transnationalization of capitalist production networks (Jequier, 1988). Businesses based in many different countries and with investors from around the world have become active in the Caribbean region through EPZs, often setting up or contracting out operations with other companies both domestically and abroad. Likewise, companies based in the Caribbean have sought out profits abroad or sought locally to integrate with large flows of transnational capital. A UN report from the mid-1990s illuminates the web of capitalist interests involving Caribbean EPZs:

> Export processing has attracted considerable local investment in the Dominican Republic and Jamaica . . . More than a quarter of the free zone companies in the Dominican Republic are owned by nationals of that country; they also employ approximately a quarter of the labour force. Jamaican entrepreneurs own nearly half the export processing establishments in that country, but the locally owned companies are much smaller on average than foreign-owned companies and therefore account for less than a quarter of total employment in the export processing sector. The absence of local ownership of export processing companies in Saint Lucia is due not to discrimination against native investors, but rather to a lack of interest on the part of local entrepreneurs . . . The United States, the main market for products of export processing plants in the subregion, is also the main source of overseas investment. The three countries have also attracted investment from the Republic of Korea, Hong Kong and several European countries. Only the Dominican Republic is host to investment from Taiwan, province of China. (Willmore, 1996, p. 11)

In Jamaica, EPZ reforms have been promoted in recent years; the country's half dozen FTZs expanded in 2015 into a network of sixteen special economic zones (SEZs), with a key difference being that the new SEZs no longer have the 15 percent cap on how much of the zone's production can be sold within the country (Reggie Nugent, personal communication, 2014). This means that the capitalists and policy makers promoting the zones are now seeking deeper linkages between transnational capitalists and the local economy, a model that follows the example of other countries, such as the Dominican Republic, where EPZs have established a wider presence and become more integrated into the country's social fabric. Officials promote EPZs to connect TNCs with local companies in order to produce for global, regional, and local markets. This new trend of producing for local markets in the EPZs is a reverse enclave development model, which fosters capitalist development that both integrates with the global economy and links directly with local consumption. This occurs at a time when global consumer markets and cultural products are establishing a growing niche among many Caribbean populations.

In Haiti's EPZs, meanwhile, companies operate with zero taxes and tariffs and are facilitated by UN-, World Bank–, and U.S.-provided subsidies, including, for example, the South Korean–based apparel manufacturer

TABLE 6.2. NUMBER OF EPZs IN SELECTED CARIBBEAN NATIONS						
	1969	1978	1988	1995	2005	2015
Dominican Republic	1	N/A	7	23	46	56
Haiti	0	0	1	1	2	3
Jamaica	0	1	2	5	6	16
Trinidad & Tobago	N/A	N/A	N/A	N/A	N/A	17
Sources: Willmore, 1994; U.S. Department of State, 2014; World Bank, 1992, 2003.						

Sae-A (IDB, 2011; Shamsie, 2009). In recent decades, political crises and the January 2010 earthquake in Haiti have been used to leverage and to develop new EPZs. This initially occurred, for example, in 2002 when Haiti's hamstrung and aid embargoed government was pushed by IFIs to agree to develop the Ouanaminthe EPZ and with the postearthquake government in 2010 going along with U.S. and UN plans to develop another zone in Caracol. Many other similar types of zones have come about in the region and nearby. Most recently, for instance, new SEZs have been developed in Veracruz and Oaxaca in Mexico. (See Table 6.2.)

Concurrent with the growing number of EPZs, the actual functions of EPZs are changing. Seeing the emergence of this trend early on, Willmore explained in the mid-1990s how sales to domestic consumers in the region had increased (Willmore, 1996, pp. 16–18). The evolving transnational production model has become part of the shifting flows of global capitalism, with its manufacturing sites (EPZs) representing vital spaces through which global production processes penetrate and transform domestic economies. Next, I discuss this interactive process in more detail.

Intensification of Local-Transnational Business Linkages

Through the context of the transnationalization of material production and the changing social and class relations at its core, we can better see how national economies are enmeshed with the global economy. We can understand such a relationship by looking at Caribbean EPZs and the capital operating through them. In this section, I look specifically at the growing interaction between TNCs and subcontractors that operate in Caribbean EPZs.

From a sociological class analysis, we can understand how capitalist formation and relations have congealed through processes of export processing. During research in Port-au-Prince, Kingston, Santiago de los Cabelleros, and Santo Domingo, the author met with foreign as well as local capitalists operating in the country, with many involved in start-ups in the EPZs. According to one young businessperson, of Dominican-Swiss origin, his company has purchased "entire prefabricated factories from China" that are then shipped directly to the Dominican Republic. This individual, whose family company has been heavily involved in road construction throughout Hispaniola (and a new road project that will link Port-au-Prince to the Dominican border), explains "major changes are taking place in how the island's economy is becoming one with the global economy. We have investors from around the world here, and so much money can be made" (Christian Murmann, personal communication, 2015).

A structural feature of export processing has been both the role of local or foreign-based transnational companies and locally (or regionally) based subcontractors who are seeking linkages with large transnational capitalist chains of accumulation. In this way, we can see how locally based capitalists are obligated to become transnationally oriented. Already the banks and financial systems they use and rely on have become entwined with transnational capital. As Robinson observes, "The spread of diverse collaborative arrangements and interim partnerships . . . are a major mechanism of class integration across nation borders" (Robinson, 2004, p. 67).

Gildan Activewear and Groupo M in Hispaniola

Some of the largest TNCs in the clothing industry contract out production with companies based in the Caribbean. Here we can see the local-transnational connections of capital and the labor exploitation that is tied up with this process. Peoples on the island of Hispaniola have experienced the ups and downs of export processing. As of 2012, 584 companies operated in EPZs within the Dominican Republic. Completely exempt from taxes, duties, charges, and fees affecting production and export activities in the EPZs, slightly more than 40 percent of the companies were domiciled in the United States, with many of the other companies active in the zones based in the Netherlands, Canada, Puerto Rico, the United Kingdom, and Korea. Dominican exports, over half of which come from the nation's EPZs, totaled $4.99 billion in 2012, compared with $4.8 billion in 2011 (U.S. Department of State, 2014). In Haiti, by contrast, there are far fewer EPZs and a smaller number of active companies. Indeed, manufacturing in Haiti has declined since its heyday of the 1980s. However, it was during the heyday of EPZs in Haiti, when many of the country's socioeconomic indicators went into decline (Emersberger, 2015).

At a factory run by a company named Genesis, which is owned by local Haitian industrialists and located near the Port-au-Prince airport in Haiti, operations are contracted out by the Canada-based TNC Gildan Activewear. Since the late 1990s, Gildan has become the top distributor of 100 percent cotton T-shirts in the United States and many other countries worldwide. In 2013, Gildan Activewear had total sales of $1.9 billion annually and has been publicly listed on the NYSE since 1999. Gildan has bought up a number of competitors and older firms in the textile industry and operates through an expanding network of contractors. In turn, some of the top investors within Gildan include major financial firms and hedge funds such as: Fidelity Investments (a TNC with $48.0 billion under management); Janus Enterprise, a publicly traded "smart growth" hedge fund that invests mostly in equity securities worldwide; and Vanguard Total International Stock Index, a hedge fund that "tracks stock markets all over the globe" and invests heavily in emerging and developing markets. Gildan operates and subcontracts with production plants in Bangladesh, Honduras, and other impoverished countries, and a growing part of its manufacturing takes place in Haiti and the Caribbean. Violations of workers' rights at the plants where Gildan's clothing is produced have been well documented (Porter, 2014). The company has tried to sideline criticism and workers' voices by rebranding itself and engaging in corporate responsibility publicity campaigns.

With readily available surplus labor, new infrastructure, and no taxes, EPZs in Haiti, for instance, appear to provide benefits for local Haitian capitalists, most important through the increased access to global investors. At one EPZ, the Caracol Industrial Park, founded after the 2010 earthquake, the U.S. government, UN, and Haitian state have worked to entice potential tenants to set up business operations (CEPR, 2012). So far, these include a Korea-based garment company (S&H Global), a Haitian paint manufacturer (Peinture Caraibe), and a number of Dominican- and Haitian-based textile, candle, door, and construction material companies.

In Ouanaminthe, Haiti, the location of an EPZ founded in 2003, the Dominican-domiciled company, Grupo M, employs local workers through its CODEVI factory. Clothing produced at the plant is sold to TNCs such as Nautica, Dockers, Fruit of the Loom, and Levi Strauss. Among some of the largest global clothing brands, these companies are infused with transnational capital. For example, in 2013, the TNC Levi Strauss had annual sales of $4.68 billion among more than 110 countries. While the company has expanded globally through business relations with companies worldwide, its ownership structure has become extremely centralized—a fact for almost every publicly traded company. The Haas family owns 45 percent of the company's stock and another 250 relatives own nearly 43 percent. Family members' charitable foundations and nonfamily directors and officers of Levi Strauss hold the remainder of the company's stock (Forbes Staff, 2014).

Grupo M is just one of the many contractors that Levi Strauss uses. Currently, Grupo M employs 3,600 workers in the Dominican Republic and 7,000 workers in Haiti. As of 2004 its workers were paid a minimum of \$12 for a six-day, 48-hour working week (Regan, 2004). By 2017, after significant labor organizing, this had increased to \$27 for the entire workweek (Connel, 2017). The main owner of Grupo M, Dominican citizen Fernando Capellán, has explained how the company has undergone fundamental changes over the past three decades and become linked with high-tech and transnational networks of production. Forbes featured this evolution of Grupo M in a 2014 article:

> [His company's] concerns transcend borders, being the first Dominican investor who settled in the Republic of Haiti, installing the CODEVI industrial park for the operation of manufacturing companies. Over the years it has also ventured into other sectors like real estate, besides being part of the board of the Metropolitan Hospital of Santiago and the Cibao International Airport, among other companies. He is also a member of the executive committee of the National Council of Private Enterprise (CONEP) and leads the Association of Industries of the Dominican Republic (AIRD) . . . In his almost 30 years, the business management model has changed: "We started with factories that, solely, were assemblies. Then we moved to modular systems, giving way today to technology with more sophisticated management systems and planning programs" . . . [He] highlights the importance of *lean manufacturing*, a production model focused on creating flow to deliver maximum value to clients, using minimal resources . . . "Moreover, as technology progresses, we have to adapt to these models and we have to do things that would never have crossed my mind. For example, until recently our volume we could produce was based on long runs, which increasingly has become shorter [runs] . . . more repetitions of the orders are made. Before we would charge orders six months in advance, [now] we do not know what we will produce in the next three months."[6] (Forbes Staff, 2014)

New local-transnational accumulation networks are emerging in Hispaniola, which are based on functional integration across borders alongside the exploitation of deeply impoverished local communities. Yet these industrial ventures also face many difficulties and contradictions as they occur in a part of the global economy with relatively low levels of development.

Jamaica and GraceKennedy

A host of other types of companies are active in Caribbean EPZs, such as those in Jamaica, many of which use the population's "cultural capital" with a large pool of capable, low-wage, English-speaking workers. According to a senior adviser in Jamaica's ministry of industry, current businesses operating in Jamaica's EPZs are in "knowledge oriented businesses, back office, legal, contract, call center, and assembling component parts of printers" (Reggie Nugent, personal communication, 2014).

Some of the leading transnational capitalists from the region operate factories in the EPZs. One of the most well-known TNCs based in Jamaica, GraceKennedy Limited, is active in Jamaica's EPZs. GraceKennedy's EPZ operations, though, comprise only a small portion of its business portfolio. Reflecting the interwoven nature of finance and production capital (with financial accumulation more and more dominant) in the global era, the company is active in banking, remittances, insurance, manufacturing, retail, and distribution.[7] GraceKennedy's main role in Jamaica's EPZs has been through the packaging of foodstuffs, such as fruit juices, packaged soups, instant porridges, hams, sausages, and a variety of yogurts and cheeses.[8] In addition to some investors from outside the Caribbean, many of the company's CEOs and investors have come from the Anglophone Caribbean wing of the TCC, including some of the wealthiest Jamaican, Trinidadian, and Barbadian families (Gordon, 2006). Many of these elites have transitioned from nationally and internationally oriented capitalists to transnationally oriented capitalists, adapting to changing market conditions as their businesses have become rooted in flows of capital operating functionally across borders.

With a long history in Jamaica, GraceKennedy has transitioned from a small trading establishment to an international importer and now to a major Caribbean-based TNC. Leading regionally based transnational capitalists, such as the owners of GraceKennedy, are not interested in operating solely as local agents for foreign-based TNCs. Rather, they are expanding their own operations and intertwining with transnational capital, seeking out new synergies and profits worldwide. In 1995, GraceKennedy developed its "2020 Vision" plan that aimed to "transform the company from a Jamaican trading company to a global consumer group by 2020" (Jackson, 2014). The company that had been listed on the stock exchanges of Jamaica, Trinidad, Barbados, and the Eastern Caribbean is now eyeing the NYSE and has more than sixty subsidiaries and divisions in the Caribbean, North America, Central America, and the United Kingdom. In 2008, the company advanced into mainland Europe, becoming a "serious player in Europe's specialist juice market" when it bought the Dutch juice and smoothie manufacturer, Hoogesteger Fresh Specialist BV (Gordon, 2008). In recent years, the company has looked toward expansion into Eastern Europe and Africa. The company has profited greatly through its expansion phase; its market value of $183 million in 2005 had increased by 1,500 percent from its value ten years prior (GraceKennedy, 2005).

As of 2014, the company continued to grow, achieving an annual revenue of $375 million in Jamaica, $97 million in Europe, $78.5 million in North America, $34 million from other areas of the Caribbean, and $700,000 in Africa (Jackson, 2014).[9] Many other Caribbean-based companies, such as Goddard Enterprises Limited (domiciled in Barbados), have also forged global linkages (Brathwaite, 2008).

The fact that leading capitalists in the Caribbean region, like Goddard Enterprises Limited and GraceKennedy and their Trinidad and Tobago, or Dominican, or Haitian counterparts have to forge transnational linkages signals that they do not stand a chance of competing globally by going it alone in the region. In addition to those major transnational capitalists with domestic backgrounds who operate in EPZs and the TNCs contracting out operations in the EPZs, a number of smaller businesses operate through these settings as well and are attempting to deepen their ties with global capital. This is especially true in the technology and telecommunications sectors.

The IT Sector

New telecommunication technologies have allowed for instant real-time communication and coordination. In turn, EPZs connect with new tech-oriented industries, which are often linked to large North American and European markets, such as data entry and processing, data conversion, software programming and development, geographic information services, image processing, indexing, automated mapping, electronic publishing, medical transcription, and video conferencing (L. Dunn, 2010, p. 603). The IT sector has taken root in EPZs in the Caribbean, but it has also heavily fluctuated over the years, with both foreign-based TNCs and smaller contractors operating in Caribbean EPZs; groups that are easily able to relocate their business operations to various locations (depending on labor and market conditions). This trend reflects the expansion of EPZs beyond the traditional light manufacturing sectors (Engman and Farole, 2012; Kaplinsky, 1993). Many EPZs have come to host "high technology industries, electronics and chemicals companies, financial services firms, IT and software services companies—as well as a range of commercial operators providing services of all kinds to these companies and their employees" (Lang, 2010, pp. 12–13).

Not only utilizing technology to expand its profits; the IT sector also hinges on the use of technology in reaction to worker struggle, as capitalists seek to develop new forms of social control. Workers in the IT sector can be more thoroughly monitored and are often relatively easy to replace (depending on the populations' language and infrastructure). New technologies then can function to clamp down on labor militancy. Investors in Caribbean EPZ production also face the difficulty that production costs in other parts of the world are often more competitive, and with more disciplined labor regimes and/or highly developed production and supply chain infrastructure (such as in China, Mexico, and Vietnam). Yet with large reserve pools of labor, geographic proximity to the North American consumer market, and continued attempts to construct supranational policies that encourage transnational economic integration with the region, the Caribbean will continue to be a site for global capitalist production and exploitation.

Transnationally Oriented Elites, Supranational Economic Forums, and State Apparatuses: Promoting Export-Processing-Led Development

The role of the state in EPZs has shifted over recent decades, from being primarily government-run and -funded operations to zones increasingly directly run by private sector management or highly influenced by transnational capital. As nodes meant to smoothly facilitate the production and movement of goods, transnationally oriented policy makers have sought to facilitate "tax holidays, unrestricted repatriation of profits, duty-free imports and exports, special low-cost infrastructure, good communications facilities and access to sea or air ports," and, in addition, promote "an abundant supply of low-cost" labor that is either nonunionized or represented by compliant union bureaucracies (L. Dunn, 2010, pp. 601–602). At the same time, faced with intense unemployment and other negative structural conditions, many Caribbean policy makers see EPZs as an important tool at their disposal. This result exemplifies how transnational capital has become an internalized logic of Caribbean policy makers aiming to map out the best—and seemingly only—route for economic development.

Furthermore, emphasis on economic development through incorporation with global capital is a strategy that many state elites have pursued to transfer state resources from "program oriented ministries (social services, education, labor, etc.) to central banks, treasuries and finance and economic ministries, and the foreign ministry" (Robinson, 2001, p. 186). Sharing in this overarching project, many state elites have promoted policies in the interest of transnational capital. To entice global investment, especially into regions of the developing world such as the Caribbean, transnationally oriented state technocrats and elites have promoted new integrative economic policies.

The transnational elite policy makers of major powers, especially the United States, play a key role in facilitating regional economic initiatives and frameworks and bilateral agreements (that in turn facilitate EPZ production); helping lead to shifts in Caribbean production strategies away from

Figure 6.2 State and business attendees at the Caribbean Forum listened to panel discussions on global banking in the region. The above gathering in part was funded by the IMF, and it had a keynote talk by the president and CEO of Massy Group, a Trinidad-based TNC. (Source: Wikimedia Commons.)

traditional exports and domestic production and instead toward financialization, new forms of export-oriented production, real estate, and tourism. This can be seen in the negotiations and ratification of the NAFTA and CAFTA-DR, as economic forums crystallizing through the activities of a "transnational interest bloc" of state and business leaders, with U.S. policy makers playing a major role (Ronald Cox, 2008, p. 1528). Regulatory frameworks established in one forum often have been integrated into later agreements, for example, with provisions in NAFTA incorporated into rules establishing the WTO (Ronald Cox, 2008). (See Figure 6.2.)

In the Caribbean, during the 1980s, it was the CBI that marked a significant ramping up of the EPZ model for the region. In the Dominican Republic, the CBI achieved the "desired effect of stimulating manufactured exports and reducing dependence on primary commodities (for example, by 1990 agricultural exports accounted for less than 20% of Dominican exports by value)," while it catapulted apparel manufacturing to become the dominant business model for the region (Werner and Bair, 2009, p. 7). Supranational forums thus serve the purpose of further opening up national economies and propelling state apparatuses in-line with neoliberal policy prescriptions and a constant enhancement of global competitiveness. Such forums, however, provide neither long-term solutions nor any attempt to deal with the deep problems facing low-income communities. Even so, policy makers across the region continue to promote EPZs as a central plank of economic development. Although they might be successful in stimulating investment in the EPZs in the short or medium term, the global spread of the apparel industry has shifted through different market and regulatory conditions, with Caribbean producers facing the contradiction of losing their competitive edge as East Asian, Mexican, and Central American production has intensified.

Whereas the temporary and limited free trade agreements (of the CBI and the Lomé Convention) had deepened during the 1980s, into the twenty-first century policy makers have put in place what are increasingly all-inclusive trade agreements (and which are treaties that in fact expand beyond trade, such as with copyright law). This has been the case with CAFTA-DR, which eliminates tariffs and reduces barriers to services. The nations of CAFTA-DR have since become increasingly interconnected with the U.S. market and the global economy, with TCC fractions profiting tremendously. As the Office of the United States Trade Representative (2014) explains: "Total two-way goods trade between the U.S. and our six CAFTA-DR partners has increased over 71% . . . from $35 billion in 2005 to $60 billion in 2013. In 2013, U.S. exports to the CAFTA-DR countries totaled $30 billion; imports totaled $30 billion." During this period under which the Dominican Republic has been the only Caribbean basin nation within the agreement, the Dominican Republic has become the leading site of foreign investment among all Caribbean island nations.

These new forums, encouraging cross-border investment and production are not just promoted by government officials but also lobbied for by capital. For example, leading Dominican "business groups supporting CAFTA-DR are located in the fast-growing export processing zones, which have seen a tenfold growth in employment over two decades" (Ronald Cox, 2008, p. 1537). These include transnationally oriented Dominican firms, such as Grupo M, Interamerican Products, and D'Clase Corporation, who are closely connected with North American-based corporations as both importers of capital and suppliers of apparel. Transnational banks, financial services, and telecommunications industries utilizing the advantages they have gained through new forums have deepened their penetration into the Caribbean basin's markets. For instance, banks and insurance firms that are highly active in global finance have gained full rights to establish subsidiaries, joint ventures, and branches through forums and new agreements. Long-standing barriers are in the process of being broken down, ranging from limitations on foreign insurance companies, to the regulatory licensing of foreign professionals, to local partner requirements in sectors such as financial services, to

Figure 6.3 Small-scale textile production in the home of a Dominican family in Santiago de los Caballeros, June 2013. (Photo by author.)

many other restrictions and requirements (Ronald Cox, 2008, p. 1538). While many small and nationally oriented businesses have been upended by the trend toward monopolization, centralization, and transnationalization of capital, some entrepreneurs especially from upper-class and middle-strata backgrounds have been able to successfully navigate the changing conditions by tapping into niche markets, and by seeking to tether their business operations to transnational circuits of accumulation.

Interestingly, even some small-scale entrepreneurs, without the advanced organizational structure of major businesses, are channeled into transnational markets. In the Dominican city of Santiago, for instance, I interviewed proprietors of a small home business, where a limited number of locals worked behind sewing machines producing specialized clothing for a local firm. The wife of the household ran the operation through the labor of poorer local women. The textiles were then sold to a local company. In turn, this firm sells the clothing to a transnational conglomerate that then offloads the textiles in nearby Puerto Rico. The family owning the small business explained how the implementation of CAFTA-DR made it easier to operate with companies based abroad such as in Puerto Rico (interviewees requested anonymity, personal communication, 2015). (See Figure 6.3.)

Yet those most benefiting from and those designing and largely responsible for pushing forward these new transnational frameworks have been major TNCs. Many pharmaceutical TNCs based in the United States, for example, have lobbied for the supranational forums to strengthen intellectual property rights provisions to increase profits. In the Caribbean, expanding upon the rights already gained through WTO frameworks, new forums have shielded Big Pharma from many safety tests and other forms of regulatory oversight (Ronald Cox, 2008, pp. 1537–1538). Another sector to benefit from new supranational forums and treaties has been the global agribusiness industry and commodity producers from across the region and in the United States. As Ronald Cox argues, "The rise of non-traditional agro-exports has been a trend that has integrated US-based TNCs with suppliers in the region" (2008, p. 1539). The textile industry, also active in lobbying for these treaties and forums, has worked to maintain conditions (such as preferential tax and duty treatments) that keep the Caribbean a competitive site for export-processing production. With coalitions of large business associations involved in lobbying, TNC representatives have crafted legislation of economic forums and trade agreements (Ronald Cox, 2008, pp. 1539–1540).[10] The final protocols and legislation of these forums, as Cox observes, make up "a hodgepodge of investment guarantees reflecting the particular interests of those investors closest to the process of negotiation and ratification" (p. 1542).

The interest groups crafting and helping propel these forums and treaties have privileged the dominant fractions of transnational capital. In the case of CAFTA-DR, for example, TNCs based in the United States played a leading role yet were "complemented by the growth and expansion of transnational firms in Mexico, Central America and the Dominican Republic." These firms, Cox adds, "have developed extensive ties to the U.S. market and have in turn developed transnational lobbying networks that are part of the transnational blocs that mobilized politically for NAFTA and CAFTA-DR" (2008, p. 1541). As I found in my research, wealthy elites in parts of the Caribbean have also banded together to support lobbyists in Washington, DC.

One example of this is right-wing businessperson Reginald Boulos, the president of the National Chamber of Commerce and Industry of Haiti, and a third-generation Lebanese-Haitian. He has financed in part the DC-based lobbyist group *The Haiti Democracy Project*, which was an important voice supporting the U.S.-orchestrated coup d'état of the country's democratically elected government in February 2004 (Esser, 2006). Also, as I found during an interview at the DC-based right-wing "think tank" *The Heritage Foundation*, their expert on Latin America and the Caribbean listed as his main contacts in the region an array of sweatshop owners and ultra-right-wing bourgeoisie, such as Boulos.

A number of other corporate interest groups active in the Caribbean play important political roles and play a role in influencing various state officials, not just those operating within U.S. state apparatuses but also from among the EU, the Mercosur states, China, and Taiwan, all of which have sought special legislation and investment privileges for fractions of the TCC in recent years. Ronald Cox explains how this reflects how globalization has entailed transnational integration and conflict:

Intensified competition among transnational interest blocs to better position themselves within regional markets in ways that give them an often temporary edge over their global competitors. Within this framework sectors of the most competitive transnational capital work with both the USA and the EU to advance their interests in penetrating Latin American markets, and where possible to forge alliances with complementary networks of producers in Latin America. In opposition are often domestic interests and competing fractions of capital, as well as a broad array of civil society groups, whose interests would be harmed by the specific provisions included in these investment agreements. Narrowly economic and narrowly political accounts of this process obfuscate the deep interconnectedness between the power of transnational capital and the process of globalisation, as well as the increasingly contested terrain that has emerged over the terms of globalisation. (2008, pp. 1541–1542)

Often, new legislation and policies intended to foster EPZ manufacturing in the region have not been enough to overcome global competition (Werner and Bair, 2009, p. 9). Job losses have occurred in countries, sometimes after a certain period of job growth or after the elapsing of certain treaty conditions. Creating a vicious cycle, in turn, business interests have threatened factory flight, pushed for a constant lowering of taxes, and advocated for currency devaluation or reductions in labor protections (Werner and Bair, 2009, pp. 9–10).

We can see the TCC at work operating within their corporations and with various economic and political forums to set the global agenda by drafting proposals, lobbying, and defining priorities for advancing their interests.[11] This capitalist class (heterogeneous though it is) consciously builds its advantage: programmed to undermine the competition but ready to lock arms where necessary and where possible to defend their class interests against organized labor, civil society, and any progressive forces that make their way into the state. This class has become enabled by more extensive and supportive transnational strategies and infrastructure that are in place.

Labor and Caribbean Export-Processing Zones

In a race to the bottom for labor, companies seek out manners of control (through various forms of coercion, paternalistic practices, and so on) as well as ways to bring down costs by employing workers in those areas with corporate-friendly regulatory environments. For example, companies with production lines composed of light equipment can easily move to other locations with more exploitive labor conditions that benefit capital.

The labor-capital relationship has undergone novel changes in the age of globalization. As labor power has become inserted into transnational value chains, this creates the objective conditions for globally oriented proletarian fractions (Lin, 2016; Stuna, 2009). As an important part of this process, capital operating through EPZs have brought labor under the umbrella of ever more flexible labor regimes and intensified relations of global competitiveness. Many have examined the specific ways in which abstract human labor has been objectified through manufacturing and sweatshop factories (Neveling, 2015). Tasks performed by labor have increasingly become broken up and dispersed over geographic areas, so that, for example, a clothing item might have its fabric sewn, its separate parts attached, and embroidering done in different locations and by workers with different backgrounds and cultures. Here a "deskilling" of workers is occurring, which contributes to their precarity. Scholars have shown how new precarious conditions have evolved, with workers more easily replaced and disciplined in areas around the world (L. Dunn, 2010, p. 604; Standing, 2013). There are, though, many countervailing trends, as certain workers have special skills—a part of the hierarchy and status among labor. These are divisions that dominant groups also can seek to play upon and exploit. Scholars have written studies on the historic role of labor in the region, and, as mentioned in Chapter 3, the concerted effort to destroy and undermine leftist and socialist currents within labor unions in the region. Yet advancing forms of exploitation and integration are creating a dialectical foundation for transcending the relations and processes that global capitalism has created. Some recent studies have begun to look at how transnational accumulation creates new opportunities for workers to organize and alter the ways in which they interpret the world (K. Moody, 2018; Robinson, 2014a).

New complex and dispersed business networks create difficulties as well as opportunities for labor. While creating the objective conditions for labor to struggle transnationally (Struna, 2009), the challenge now is for labor, social, and political movements from below to develop the infrastructure to coordinate transnationally from below. Many workers can clearly articulate how their struggles are increasingly connected through finance and broader struggles, but many other dynamics exist that lead (often) to divisions and social alienation. For workers to successfully organize locally and on a transnational level, it remains to be seen how the subjective conditions and institutional structures will evolve.

Scholars have begun to consider the different structural features of how labor interconnects transnationally with the global capitalist economy. For example, Struna argues compellingly that:

> the fractions of the global working class are divided into two broad segments: transnational fractions, including the dynamic-global, the

static global, and the diasporic-global; and national or local fractions, including the dynamic-local, the static-local, and the diasporic-local. Fractional determinations are based first, on workers' physical mobility relative to nation-states and regions, and second, on the geographic scope of workers' labor-power expenditure relative to the circuits in which they are engaged. By using a fractionated perspective of the global proletariat we can continue to make meaningful the concept of class relative to commodity production regardless of (but respectful of, in many senses) the overwhelming occupational, cultural, and social complexity that conditions the labor-capital relation in the global era. (Struna, 2009, p. 253)

It remains to be seen, though, when and how organized labor will effectively mobilize transnationally (Bieler, 2012), with the local, regional, historical, and institutional contradictions it faces, and which I now discuss.

A number of reports have been published examining the general dynamics of labor in the Caribbean (ILO, 2014). In recent years, the number of companies active in the region's EPZs has grown. New production technologies, though, have often allowed for the reduction of the number of workers required for certain tasks. Governments across the region have carried out rounds of market-oriented "reforms," as elites seek to improve the global competitiveness of their EPZs (a constant mantra of policy makers). This has resulted in a difficult situation for labor, as the real wages of workers have declined or stagnated in most sectors. Trinidad and Tobago, a nation considered one of the most globally competitive in the region, recognized early on the importance of the race to the bottom in terms of EPZ labor protections. Indeed, in the 1980s, Trinidad and Tobago eagerly launched "a process that included a wage freeze and accelerated depreciation on equipment imported duty-free for export production" (Gomes, 2013). Research shows how state elites in other Caribbean nations have also worked to keep wages artificially low (Regan, 2013).

As the data show, the number of laborers in Caribbean EPZs varies by country, with some boasting more EPZs and larger manufacturing sectors than others. In Jamaica, for instance, overall employment tripled between 1975 and the late 1980s, while during this time in the Dominican Republic employment grew from 6,500 to 112,000 jobs (Schopfle and Perez-Lopez, 1992, p. 142). Yet, at other times, the number of jobs has fallen. Policy makers and business groups have sought to amend labor laws to compete with the conditions that workers face in other locations. The social basis of these chains of production thus revolves around a flexibilized extraction of surplus labor from workers in the EPZs. (See Table 6.3.)

TABLE 6.3. NUMBER OF WORKERS AND FIRMS ACTIVE IN EPZs IN SELECTED CARIBBEAN COUNTRIES, 2007		
Country	Workers	Firms
Dominican Republic	154,781	556
Haiti	10,000	90
Jamaica	20,000	N/A
Puerto Rico	340,000	2,800
Trinidad & Tobago	19,350	N/A
Source: Singa Boyenge, 2007.		

Labor protests and ongoing grassroots and union organizing continues in the region and in the EPZs specifically (Caribbean Newslink, 2014).[12] Rodriguez-Garavito (2008) has looked, for example, at numerous maquiladora labor organizing campaigns across the Caribbean and how they are intertwined with events in the United States. Marion Werner (2016) has elaborated upon the struggle of workers in Hispaniola's industrial parks, such as with the EPZ factories on the northern side of the Haitian and Dominican border (in Ouanaminthe and Dajabón), looking at the contested way in which EPZ production is formed and took shape within a community facing extremely desperate circumstances (Werner, 2016). Labor upheavals in the island's textile plants have been a recurring phenomenon, achieving positive gains for the local workers. However, these struggles over recent decades have increasingly occurred as disparate campaigns and, at times, have even been influenced by right-wing and dominant groups or by state-connected institutions from abroad, such as with the role of the AFL-CIO's Washington-based American Center for International Labor Solidarity (ACILS), also known as the "Solidarity Center" (Scipes, 2011; Sprague, 2008; Werner, 2016, pp. 126–129). Problematically, then, and occurring as part of a desperate competition over limited resources and political infighting, labor struggles can become unlinked from broader popular political struggles or be entwined with interests that are not immediately clear (Hallward, 2008). We then need to pay attention to labor struggles as not just contained to local struggles within EPZs, but also how they play out more broadly through hegemonic struggles in the "extended state" (or what Gramsci [1971] saw as the social power relations encompassing the political plus civil society).

The business union model, keeping its distance from broader popular struggles, has been heavily promoted in fact by many of today's largest labor federations. Well-resourced state, capitalist, and important regional and global institutions and forums also clearly prefer this approach. It reflects often into the lack of cross-sector solidarity among labor and the lack of labor's connection to broader political projects to challenge structures of class and elite power. I see this also as related to the historic defeats faced by Marxist, socialist, leftist, and progressive forces in the region and worldwide, undermining long term the potential capacity for concerted struggles.

While there have been some cross-border campaigns among some labor unions in the region (Frundt, 1999), as well as inspiring examples of joint community-labor mobilizations, as in many sectors and parts of the world, business unionism has become dominant.

International labor federations and bodies active in the Caribbean tend to focus on combating the most egregious human rights problems, such as child labor. Yet cross-sector and cross-border organizing remains underdeveloped. Furthermore, states and corporations have sought to promote compliant labor union bosses and support nonthreatening labor organizing. Here it is important to recognize, as Scipes (2011) shows, labor agencies connected with the United States and other wealthy Western states often privilege unions and union officials that are unthreatening to the political agenda of transnational elites. Yet a general tendency in many parts of the world (especially during and after the Cold War) has been the rise of business unionism, winning out often over more populist and left-wing labor. This process played out violently in the Caribbean, such as with the crushing of leftist labor organizing in Jamaica (Post, 1978), the Duvalierist state's attack on organized labor in Haiti, or the government assaults on labor movements in the Dominican Republic for many decades now. Often the sacking of labor receives little coverage, as I found was the case in postcoup Haiti when thousands of public sector workers were fired and received next to no international support (Sprague, 2008). It should be said there has been a rise in recent decades in wildcat strikes in many parts of the world, as well as large-scale mobilizations of marginalized and excluded populations (M. Davis, 2007).

With a large base of unemployed and underemployed workers forming a "reserve army of labor" (Marx, 1867/1992), those with formal employment face numerous difficulties and pressures. Challenges also include the bureaucratization of labor unions, the low percentage of organized workers in the region in general, patriarchy and the harassment of women workers, an overall lack of resources, sectarian divisions, a dependence on foreign donors, the constant sacking and repression of militant workers, and the lack of cooperation between labor with popular and leftist political currents. Caribbean states also play a role in disciplining labor in the EPZs, mobilizing police and security forces to surround or suppress labor strikes.

In reaction to continued struggles from below, managerial developments put into place in the EPZs in recent decades have meant to further regiment and disempower labor. As scholars have documented (Jones et al., 2015), new

Figure 6.4 Women workers in a textile factory in Haiti. (Source: Haiti Support Group.)

managerial techniques and processes have promoted more tightly disciplined and monitored labor regimes for workers in the global era. A goal of these new labor regimes has been for capitalists to avoid the responsibilities related to direct employment while also helping create labor environments that are more precarious and insecure. While in earlier eras it was common for "local supervisors, technicians and plant managers" (Willmore, 1996, p. 22) to operate plants (and they still do often), a recent trend has been outsourcing to production management companies that specialize in EPZ factories. These companies and their professionals move between different locations in both the Caribbean and beyond. This has facilitated more standardized labor regimes and practices for globalized production management (Jones et al., 2015). In this stringent system, the only workers that remain employed are those who remain uninjured, continually achieve cost, time, and production targets, and display themselves as compliant and loyal to management (Jones et al., 2015). (See Figure 6.4.)

The exploitation of Caribbean labor, and, for that matter, Third World labor in general, is also rooted in gendered and racialized dynamics (Ortiz, 1996; Werner, 2016). The harshest labor conditions of export processing overwhelmingly impact negatively racialized and gendered groups. These are peoples often in the Third World but also in the so-called developed world where supraexploited workers, often migrants, are used as sweatshop labor. Women workers in these settings operate under intensely exploitative conditions. During the 1970s and 1980s a heightened feminization of waged labor in the EPZs was observed (Gray, 1986; Werner, 2016), the trend in which women composed a growing segment of the labor force within EPZs and were channeled into particular jobs. Among Caribbean EPZ workers there has also existed a gendered division of labor (Freeman, 2000; Safa,

2002; Thorin, 2001). Werner explains: "In Latin America and the Caribbean, women in export factories were often taking on the 'breadwinner' role under dramatically eroded wage conditions as their male kin faced the indignities of decline in import substituting industrial sectors" (2016, p. 4). Disempowered and channeled into low-paying and exploitive work, women workers are constantly victims of patriarchal and abusive relations in the workplace, targeted especially by male managers and bosses.

The treatment of labor in the Caribbean region is consistent with the strategy to defend the interests of capital as the first priority of the state, signaling once more that so-called national development is not the vocation of capital in its various configurations and iterations in any spatial context. Downplaying the poor working conditions and the inspiring history of popular organizing in the region, policy makers have placed much effort in promoting EPZs to both investors and local populations in a compliant and positive light. To do so, promotional and advertisement campaigns have been well honed over the years.

During visits (sometimes supervised visits) to EPZs in the region, the author was provided numerous advertisement and promotional pamphlets highlighting the advantages of EPZ production. A pamphlet in Jamaica that I received promoted the "Buy Jamaica" campaign, with sales points about the English-speaking and dynamic capabilities of Jamaican workers. Key selling points were the new high-speed internet that had been installed and the work experience of local laborers in telecommunications. Advertising campaigns have reframed countries as platforms for global capital, with the EPZ representing a fundamental part of this rebranding (Tornhill, 2010, pp. 74–75). Onboard air flights in the region one can flick through glossy brochures with titles such as: "Honduras is open for business!" These efforts aim not just to attract global investors but also to provide a degree of local legitimacy for a developmental strategy in which the main people profiting are transnational capitalists.

Cuba's Contradictory Integration with the Global Economy

A contradictory reality unfolds in Cuba as its policy makers attempt to maintain a socialist project while compelled (out of numerous necessities and pressures) to make overtures and compromises with transnational capital. Starting during the Special Period of the late-1990s, four EPZs were opened (two in Havana, one in the nearby port of Mariel, another in the southern port of Cienfuegos). Garnering little investment, these early EPZs in Cuba served mainly as "bonded warehouses for goods in transit to the domestic economy" (Willmore, 2000). However, more than a decade later,

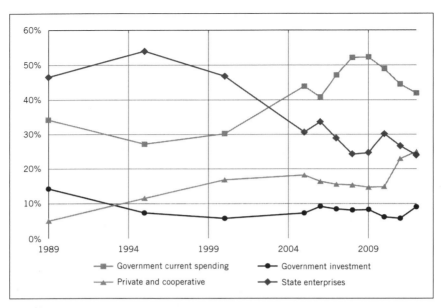

Figure 6.5 Estimated GDP composition of Cuba, by sector. (Source: Desilver, 2015.)

with Cuba facing an economic crisis (including the fall in the price of nickel, its number one export) the state slashed around one million jobs. Since 2010, a growing proportion of Cuba's economy has become rooted in small private and cooperatively run businesses, a phenomenon that has skyrocketed in recent years.

Seeking to entice foreign investors while maintaining a collectivist ethos, Cuban policy makers have sought to expand an independent (or semi-independent) cooperative sector, seeing this as a way to harness market forces to encourage productivity (while maintaining strict controls, such as allowing foreign capitalists to own only up to 49 percent of a hotel enterprise). It remains to be seen how successful Cuba's market socialist model will be, or if it will serve rather as a transitory stage into a more capitalistic society and future regime change efforts. (See Figure 6.6.)

Under recent market reforms, Cuban state officials have launched a new EPZ strategy, one meant to be globally competitive (BBC, 2010). They have sought especially to work with non-U.S.-based TCC fractions, such as with TNCs from Brazil and Singapore. This is also, of course, due to the more than fifty years of illegal embargo by Washington upon Cuba, where companies based in the United States and around the world have been restricted from doing business on the island. The embargo only began to loosen in 2016.[13] Cubans have seen increased access to consumer goods and foreign currency,

Figure 6.6 Two men play chess inside a large government-sponsored tourist bazaar in Havana where artists, artisans, and small businesses sell their goods. Note the container ships anchored in the distance. (Photo by author.)

especially with a boost in tourism. Tourism to Cuba has also become linked to a growing racialized inequality that had previously become more and more eroded following the 1959 revolution (Roland, 2010). While having political and developmental capabilities that other Caribbean states do not have, as Edmonds (2013) observes there are also fundamental contradictions and pitfalls for Cuba's engagement with global capital, such as through the new investments in its supply chain and production capacities:

> The shift of the primary port facilities from Havana to Mariel is part of a massive project that seeks to turn Mariel into Cuba's most important hub for cargo and light manufacturing. The $900 million project has largely been funded by Brazilian capital and will be managed by the Singaporean firm PSA. . . . Unlike the regulated and heavily state-owned tourism model, the adoption of EPZs provides a space similar to export processing zones elsewhere in the world where foreign corporations pay no tariffs on imported material and machinery, and where they enjoy a 10 year tax holiday where they may transfer all of their profits abroad without paying any property or sales taxes. The

Cuban government has publically defended the EPZ project, stating that "the Zone will function on the basis of special policies with the goal of promoting sustainable economic development by stimulating international and domestic investment, as well as technological innovation and the concentration of industry." . . . Whether the construction of the EPZ at Mariel will be an isolated occurrence, or the start of a shift towards a Chinese/Vietnamese EPZ-based economy, remains to be seen. Perhaps the decision to turn over a portion of Cuban territory to the demands of international capital is an overture of economic reform intended to bolster relations with the U.S. What is clear is that if Cuba does decide to embrace EPZs as a major part of its economy without establishing numerous economic linkages to the domestic economy, the pro capital policies that are demanded by this model will pose a significant threat to Cuba's progress in the areas of genuine and sustained human development. If Cuba, like so many others who have embraced the EPZ model, is not careful on this new economic path, it may end up sacrificing its self-determination and human development only to receive increased levels of poverty in return.

Conclusion: Export Processing in a Dynamic Transnational System of Production, Finance, and *Exploitation*

Capitalists seeking to escape the barrier of national frontiers and thus shape a new objective reality have come to utilize new spaces for manufacturing and other forms of production under which they exploit waged labor. Likewise, state policy makers have supported the creation of these special economic zones, so as to further integrate their local economies with the global economy. Here, new nontraditional export-oriented industries could operate supposedly unhindered by local pressures. Expected to expand and diversify industrial production, EPZs continue down this path "designed to facilitate the insertion of a country into the global trading system" (Lang, 2010, p. 15). Many changes are on the horizon that may impact the businesses operating in Caribbean EPZs, such as the new deepwater ports planned or under development in Cuba, Haiti, Jamaica, the Dominican Republic, and other countries in the region. In both scope and scale, this will allow Caribbean economies to further integrate with the global trade system. The very spatial nature and role of the EPZs is becoming more pliable, as a wider range of companies become active in EPZs and TNCs seek new consumer markets from among upwardly mobile and middle strata in the region.

The successes and failures of the EPZ model have varied, even within lower-income countries. In some parts of the region the model has failed or stagnated, but in other areas production has grown. Attempts to renew and expand the export-processing model have gone through fits and spurts. State policy makers and a host of elites active in the region have come to depend on the expansion of transnational capitalist networks for their own social reproduction. Trade and investment agreements between Caribbean governments and other states—most important, the United States—have advanced a host of bilateral as well as regional economic forums.

It must be noted, though, that often what is referred to as "trade" is made up in part by transfers within the same company. Different economic forums and state negotiations have thus reflected the power of a "hodgepodge" of powerful interests, from transnationally oriented elites operating through different state apparatuses to fractions of transnational capital. They have sought to override "outdated laws" that protected certain industries and workforces, which therein hindered cross-border investment and synergies between local and offshore companies (Willmore, 1996, p. 2). The future of the EPZ-centered developmental model in the region, while continually promoted by elites, remains unclear as it underlays an unsustainable and crisis prone system. It is replete with risk. As transnational elites face crises of legitimacy within the United States and many other nations, policies may be enacted that appear in apparent contradiction and may favor one set of elites over another. Yet, as I have argued elsewhere, today's political-economic restructuring is broadly consolidating power in the hands of a transnational bourgeoisie (with its different fractions).

Neoliberal policies have been formulated to help speed up capitalist globalization by getting state managers and others to adopt strategies that advance transnational capitalist accumulation partly by reducing and eliminating policies and practices that constrain the global movement of capital. This is abundantly clear from export processing as part of the drive for globally competitive production in the Caribbean. Yet this is a messy process, with various elite groups promoting different strategies, while also facing struggles from below.

In the Caribbean, contrary to the constant claims, I do not see countries becoming competitive through EPZ-type strategies. While national governments adopt policies to attract and keep portions of transnational capital within their borders, we need to see TNCs as competing with one another and operating through uneven social relations and also uneven built environments. Yet the territorial division of the world into separate nation-states corresponds less and less with the spatial (economic) organization of production, hence our emphasis on the rise of transnational material and social relations.

We know that capitalist globalization does not *create* the integration of countries into capitalism, rather it restructures, reconfigures, and accelerates this in a new cross-border functional manner. Through this process certain portions of a society's population are exploited (while others are marginalized), and this occurs in relation to the geographic zones where these populations are centered as the capitalist process is based on uneven and combined development. We can see, though, how these processes of "zoned" exploitation and exclusion take place now in a globally structured economy that is integrated through numerous transnational processes.

It is not so-called national economic development that motivates capital, as capital does all it can to render labor as flexible, insecure, and disposable as possible. EPZs are strategic in this regard. Of course, the fragmentation of the production process is inevitable where the drive is to lower the cost of production by intensifying the exploitation of labor. There is also a constant drive to fragment the large pools of workers that are required—in order to keep them divided and crushed. Bourgeois neoliberal ideology aside, the capitalist order cannot compel workers to commit themselves to the production process by investing their full energies to produce at the level capital expects, as production is for private accumulation, so the approach ultimately is to make workers superfluous to the production process (Perelman, 2011).

A long-forged internationalized history characterizes the Caribbean, but we now see, in addition to this, new transnational processes. Clearly, outsourcing and subcontracting are important for expanding the capitalist process and integrating certain investors and others into global capitalism, based on the needs of the TCC, thereby intensifying the fragmentation of the production process within the global division of labor. Major players include not just TNCs and states but also powerful financial institutions and supranational agencies. The pressure on national state policy makers in the Caribbean is significant and state managers regularly operate as willing agents—once more confirming that protecting the interests of capital dominates much of what national states do within regional and global contexts. Although manufacturing has grown during certain time periods, it has occurred alongside rising inequality and other deepening crises (Bales, 2012; Emersberger, 2015; Kloby, 2004). History has shown that sweatshop manufacturing in general and the EPZ model in particular have not yielded the benefits that its proponents have claimed.

7

From International to Transnational Mining

*The Industry's Shifting Political Economy
and the Caribbean*

Since the emergence of capitalist globalization, industrial mining has undergone significant changes in many parts of the world (R. Moody, 2007). The Caribbean is one such region, where TNCs have reaped extraordinary profits for their owners and stakeholders by harnessing new technologies and other advancements. In contrast, mining companies earlier in the twentieth century operated through circuits of international production and were heavily impacted by the internationally and domestically geared policies of state officials. This earlier form of production took place within and sometimes across national frontiers, and within colonies or countries where state elites often were closely aligned with the state in which the company was domiciled. Through the context of the Caribbean, this chapter examines the historical trajectory through which industrial mining has shifted from nationally and internationally oriented practices toward transnational ones. I contend that globally competitive mining corporations, entwined with transnational capital and promoted by transnationally oriented state elites, have supplanted earlier international corporate models and statist developmental policies. At the same time, workers in the industry have been rendered increasingly flexibilized and managed by more advanced labor regimes, often with the aid of subcontractors seeking out new inputs into the globalizing industry. These developments occur alongside continued environmental damage and often shrinking benefits for Caribbean states and local communities (Ramírez, 2012).

Historical Background

The history of capitalist mining is also a history of exploitative labor and the appropriation of land, from the forced mining by indigenous and African slaves during earlier colonial periods (van Dijk, 2009, pp. 132–133) to the industrialized mining of the late nineteenth and twentieth centuries. Large-scale industrial mining in the Caribbean began in Suriname and Guyana in the early twentieth century (Jong and Boersema 2006), with the industry's early formation in the region dependent on British capital. Over time, inter-nationalizing capital in North America provided the impetus for growth in export-oriented mining and some domestic manufacturing. By the 1950s, North American capital had ramped up mining operations in Jamaica, geared toward the extraction of bauxite, a dry mineral that is converted into aluminum through electrolysis. In fact during the postwar period, U.S. pol-icy makers supported national mining policies in order to build up resources for the U.S. military-industrial complex, through which the bauxite industry in the Caribbean would come to supply "nine-tenths of the raw-material needs of the aluminum industry of North America, which in turn produces 50 per cent of world aluminum output" (Girvan, 1967, p. 1). In fact, the U.S. Mutual Security Act (1951) and the Point IV Program (established in 1949) set the stage for decisions regarding the treatment of raw materials, such as bauxite, crude oil and their derivatives, to be seen as matters of "national security." U.S. government initiatives came to facilitate large-scale mining in the Caribbean through U.S.-based companies during the 1950s and 1960s.

Resource extraction became a central pillar of development for former British colonies in the region. Whereas labor in the mines came primarily from local communities, there was a heavy reliance on European and North American specialists and engineers. In other areas of the Caribbean, such as the Dominican Republic and Cuba, mining developed at a slower pace dur-ing the latter half of the twentieth century but would eventually receive sig-nificant foreign capital investment. Despite this growth, local inputs in mining consisted primarily of low-wage jobs. Caribbean policy makers wrestled over how to engage with the industry.

By the mid-twentieth century and in the decades following World War II, in many areas of the world, corporate policies were heavily impacted by the national and international policies of state policy makers, a factor especially within the nations in which these companies were domiciled. In my view, it has been the case that most local (national) capitalists have never seriously embraced so-called economic nationalism. Rather, alongside the social rela-tions, it was the organizational and technological capabilities of capital, in earlier historical periods, that kept it bound to national and international arrangements. The state then was key for helping ease along these built economic environments. Powerful states, such as the United States, facilitated the international operations of associated capitalists (Panitch and Gindin, 2013). Yet state officials, especially in many developing nations, sought at times to manage or control (at least partially) industries operating in their nation. In developing regions such as the Caribbean, many state managers (often pressured by movements from below or influenced by different political currents) began promoting policies meant to incubate in some form domestic production, albeit through limited forms of ISI and partial state ownership of some economic sectors, such as bauxite mining.

As capital began to transnationalize (Robinson, 2004) during the closing decades of the twentieth century, it sought to break free from national restraints and regulations (Harvey, 1991, 2005). A fractionation of elites meanwhile occurred, with new transnational fractions emerging within the power blocs of nations around the world, including the Third World (Robinson, 2003). It was during this period that new polyarchic arrangements were established: as segments of local and foreign dominant groups (most important, U.S. policy makers) pushed for tightly managed electoral systems in which political contestation was narrowly confined to competing elites. This helped solidify the rise of transnationally oriented state managers and technocrats (Domínguez, 1996; Robinson, 2012).

These new elite groups, as part of an emergent globally oriented historic bloc, have promoted development through the breakup of formerly insulated markets. Alternatively, in this way, neoliberal restructuring, through privatization and the imposition of austerity measures, has further led to the development of global networks of production (Dicken, 2007) and finance (CARICOM, 2005; Körner and Trautwein, 2014; H. Watson, 1985). To guarantee their own social reproduction, state managers have promoted deeper integration with the global economy. Yet as they abandon national forms of development, this leads to crises of legitimacy. This has been a contradictory process, as transnationally oriented elites must maintain national political legitimacy; they must deal with the local alignment of forces even as they seek out a transnational agenda.

Consistent with many other global industries, mining has become reorganized along increasingly flexible lines and highly entwined with financial interests. Capitalist production has become more attuned to fluctuating markets, reflected in the rise of operational intervals, where mines shutter and then reopen at a faster pace. These new instruments have strengthened the hand of management and created new pressures on state policy makers, labor, and local communities (R. Moody, 2007). In mining as in other industries, through capitalist globalization, the very labor power of workers has become incorporated into transnational (rather than national or international) value chains (Struna, 2009). Therefore, while residues of the previous national and international arrangements remain, the political economy of mining needs to be understood in light of the changes associated with the cross-border functional integration of global capitalism.

Industrial Mining in the Epoch of Global Capitalism

The contemporary history of mining is part of the expansion of capital, through its international expansion and *later* transnational expansion. Through this expansionary process capital breaks down national barriers, connecting nations and places. This, however, is inherently contradictory, as it displaces and creates conditions of marginalization and landlessness (where many workers are structurally excluded from the increasingly mechanized labor market). For centuries mining has involved significant displacement with major contradictory consequences for working people—driving many rural people into the ranks of unemployed or highly marginalized working class without access to the means to reproduce themselves. At the same time, since the minerals extracted from mining operations are vital to an array of goods, mining has long been a socially determined process in which society determines how the properties that generate income are economically realized (Marx, 1993b, p. 756). By this I mean that minerals do not have some kind of natural predetermined economic value, but, rather, the value of this commodity is determined through human social relations.

With the collaboration of powerful states and comprador elites, international monopolies dominated the mining industry during much of the twentieth century (Fine, 1994; Nwoke, 1987), including in many parts of the developing world. Throughout the twentieth century, mining became more and more interconnected with international monopoly capital, developing new sites by the middle of the century in the postcolonial Third World, usually with the support of powerful foreign states.

In the late twentieth and twenty-first centuries mining has become contingent on new chains of transnational capitalist accumulation. This has meant its restructuring as it links into globally competitive markets, and a global division of labor with its flexibilized workforces, alongside the rising role of subcontractor and exploratory companies. New, more market-oriented laws began to take shape across the region (General Secretariat of the OAS, 1984; Gobierno de Republica Dominicana, 1997), and by the early twenty-first century transnationally oriented state elites were busy facilitating global competitive policies in the region.

TNC mining operations has come to develop through a series of phases. First, transnational mining firms or smaller globally active exploration companies locate and assess mineral deposits. When positive results are obtained, a larger transnational mining conglomerate usually takes over, often buying out or gaining a controlling position over smaller exploratory firms. Once political and contractual guarantees have been secured, the second phase begins—the development and operation of the mine. Market pressures have thus pushed state managers (looking for global investors) to standardize their regulatory and contractual processes. As discussed further below, TNCs are using a growing array of exploratory companies and are developing mining sites by relying on numerous contractors and subcontractors. This is in marked contrast to the mining operations of decades ago.

With the rise of capitalist globalization, new waves of mining projects have been spurred for a number of reasons: (1) technological advancements, (2) organizational innovations with the rise of mining TNCs, (3) the growing concentration of global capital through corporate M&As, which has further propelled transnational mining corporations, (4) the rise of successful smaller mining exploratory companies that try to link into the massive accumulation of the large mining TNCs, (5) the rising value of mineral ores as a finite resource (at times offset by new technologies), and (6) the role of transnationally oriented state elites and technocrats in promoting policies of global competitiveness and investor confidence to entice new mining projects. Together these factors, in conjunction with various specific local conditions, have resulted in the renewal of old mining sites, the upgrading of existing locations, and the launching of new operations. (See Figure 7.1.)

The volume of cross-border corporate M&As in the mining industry has increased at unprecedented levels in recent decades, raising capital for new megadeals to smaller buyouts (Ernst and Young, 2012). Cross-border financial integration and the industry's growing global orientation has led to new "synergies, bolt-on growth and acquisitions that enabled companies to utilize competitive advantages" (Ernst and Young, 2012). As the industry transforms into a globally competitive battleground for oligopolies, it is infused with transnational finance capital. The trend toward financialization among ruling groups, in regard to mining, even impacts which sites get exploited and when—as financial markets come to play a big role in determining mineral markets (Dr. Vladimir Pacheco, personal communication, 2013). Concomitant with this, the role of smaller exploratory companies and subcontractors in the industry has grown, many becoming active around the world, filling niches and providing specialized services. Mining expert

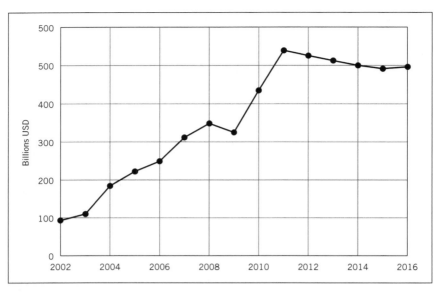

Figure 7.1 Total revenue of top mining companies, 2002–2016. (Source: Xie, 2012; Statista, 2017.)

Dr. Vladimir Pacheco, who has worked as a research fellow at the University of Queensland's Centre for Social Responsibility in Mining, explains:

> Over the recent decades [mining companies] have had a trend toward cross-border investment and monopoly. In gold, for example, just around half a dozen companies now process the vast majority of gold. The amount of capital is just huge, but in many ways it's like other global industries. They don't want to get caught up with local peculiarities and problems, so everything is standardized and tightly managed as compared to the past, such as the agreements with states, the operations, the construction. It's a turnkey, finely tuned process, with lots of subcontractors, hundreds. Some subcontractors are active globally, others regionally, and others only operate locally (Dr. Vladimir Pacheco, personal communication, 2013).

Transnational mining corporations, highly attuned to cyclical processes in the market, are competing over new markets and economies of scale in production. As diversified large companies continue to ramp up mining production through acquisitions and expansion, smaller start-up companies' fill a niche by pioneering new deposits. Focused on "frontier" locations, "companies that have traditionally been national champions are globalizing, using their domestic scale and often privileged access to capital" (Accenture, 2011). As identified in this chapter, the industry's global orientation has occurred through rising values in stocks and earnings, an attractive investment for transnational finance capital. While exhibiting caution after global economic crises, TNCs are benefiting from new sources of capital, spanning sovereign wealth funds to strategic partnerships and private wealth (Ernst and Young, 2012).[1]

Investment in production and exploration has also expanded into locations with fragile local conditions and with only a marginal history of mining. This is because as capitalism expands intensively it has an incentive to launch or renew mining ventures in the developing world, reassessing areas previously viewed as unprofitable or too risky. Between 2002 and 2012, GDP tripled in the mining industry in Latin America, the industry gaining importance in most of the countries of the region (Bamrud, 2012). Many areas of the Caribbean, such as Hispaniola, are viewed as ripe for growth. Yet at the same time, the industry's operations in the Caribbean present a stark example of how the modern mining industry exists within the extremely unequal dynamics of the global economy and in a manner disconnected from locally geared development.

While mining companies have shifted toward an ever-greater reliance on private contractors, many contractors themselves have become active on a larger scale, becoming themselves more deeply integrated with global financial systems. Large amounts of credit and loans are required for contractors, especially when active regionally or globally (Roger Moody, personal communication, 2013), obtained through banks that are entwined with global chains of finance. Newer mining operations (such as Barrick Gold's Pueblo Viejo mine in the Dominican Republic) involve a higher number of contractors than the mining operations of previous decades. This new trend is important because contractors and diverse economic arrangements serve as important spaces for local capital and small-scale entrepreneurs to integrate into transnational production chains, a mechanism of class integration across frontiers.

To varying degrees of success, in recent decades state policy makers in the Caribbean have sought to craft conditions that promote transnational investment, including in the mining industry. Regional and supranational bodies, such as institutions of the UN and the World Bank (R. Moody, 2007, pp. 16–42), and CARICOM and CARIFORUM in the Caribbean context, have pushed for heightened transnational standards and policy regimes to create conducive climates for investment (Bernal, 2013). As Pacheco observes, there has been an expanding reliance by "national governments and private companies on transnational mining policy regimes in order to secure legitimacy" and "to demonstrate they are globally competitive" (Dr. Vladimir Pacheco, personal communication, 2013). Transnational juridical frameworks and standards, as other scholars have examined, have deepened structural disparities where an "increasing technicisation of decision-making processes" sideline and depoliticize local input (Campbell, 2012, p. 140).

The quest for global competitiveness compels capitalists to embrace neo-liberal policies as a way to promote TCC interests within a transnational framework (Sprague, 2015). Transnationally oriented policy makers advocating neoliberal restructuring have lowered levies on mining companies and widely abandoned the previous statist policy initiatives. World Bank studies have advocated these neoliberal reforms, a fact that explains how such policies have been "successful in generating substantial interest in attracting exploration to the [Latin American] region which, for the first time in 1994 and 1995, was ranked as the first region in the world in terms of mining exploration expenditures" (World Bank, 1996, p. viii). With heavy capital and technological investment involved in mining operations, many governments in the Caribbean and Latin America have altered laws, lowered taxes and levies, and in general promoted conditions enabling TNC investment. This has resulted in a period of rapid expansion in mining, as one World Bank publication explains: "Between 1990 and 1997, while global exploration investment went up 90%, it increased fourfold in Latin America" (McMahon and Remy, 2001, p. 2). In regard to regulation and controls, "the recently diminished role of the state in the mining industry" (p. 2) has had far-reaching effects, such as in how environmental regulations and negotiations with local communities now feature TNCs in a more central role.[2]

In regard to labor, transnational corporate mining has required fewer and fewer labor inputs. In 1990, there were nearly 25 million workers in the mining industry worldwide, but as organizational advancements and mechanization has intensified, there were only 5.5 million working in the industry by 2000 (R. Moody, 2007, p. 69). The shrinking number of employees in Caribbean mining operations, such as in Jamaica and the Dominican Republic, reflects the global decline of labor inputs that industry requires. Furthermore, the power of *minero* labor unions has declined as the industry became increasingly less tethered to state enterprises. Roger Moody explains, "The proportion of ill-paid, disempowered, subcontracted mineworkers has significantly increased" over recent years (p. 69). Thirty years ago, Caribbean miners were often paid directly through state-owned enterprises, even when an MNC managed operations. This is almost unheard of today. Contemporary mining workers are paid directly by TNCs or through contractors/subcontractors, forming a more flexibilized labor regime where work is more tightly managed, standardized, and monitored.

One former miner from the town of Maimón in the Dominican Republic, who worked at Pueblo Viejo between 1973 and 1993 (when mining operations were owned and more directly influenced by the state), spoke to me about his career and the changes that have taken place in the mining industry. In contrast to current workers at the Pueblo Viejo mine paid directly by

Barrick Gold, during the earlier period of the mine's operations it was the Rosario Dominicana state enterprise that paid workers' salaries (S. A. Ramírez Beltne, personal communication, 2013). He explained further how workers, as they have come to labor directly for TNCs, have faced less stable and predictable duties, now being required more often to adapt to fluctuations and changes in production and efficiency.

Going back through the history of the Spanish and Portuguese colonies in the Americas, it was enslaved Africans and their descendants that early on labored in mines that were set up (Lane, 2011). While other groups have been brought into mining through the international and, now, global division of labor, racialized class relations continue to play an important role in mining. Such social and material relations are reproduced, though, in a dynamic manner, as racialized low-waged workers now more and more move around to different locations and some across borders, and many workers deposit their pay checks into accounts with banks that are interlinked with global finance (S. A. Ramírez Beltne, personal communication, 2013). In regard to Pueblo Viejo, more experienced Bolivian, Peruvian, and Chilean workers were brought in to do much of the highly skilled work and Dominicans were hired only for the more menial tasks and support (Tim Shenk, personal communication, 2016). Managers and experts in the industry, even more so, move around often to different geographic sites. Whereas these managerial and specialist groups overwhelmingly come from privileged and positively racialized strata and usually from nations in the global north, as compared to earlier decades, a rising number do hail from the global south and from negatively racialized strata.

Shifting labor regimes in the industry, alongside rising environmental and local concerns, have been reflected in the large number of protests occurring across Latin America and the Caribbean, with antimining movements protesting 218 mining projects in 2015 (Observatorio de conflictos mineros de América Latina, 2015). Next, I examine the historical trajectory and political economy of the earlier international models of industrial mining and the role of the state. I then consider the transnationalization of the industry and the increasingly facilitative role of state elites as they abandon forms of national development in place of transnational engagement and global competitiveness. I will discuss how these complex processes have played out, through the examples of Jamaica, the Dominican Republic, and Haiti.

Jamaica: From International to Transnational Mining

Bound up with specific conditions and historical legacies, industrial mining in the Anglophone Caribbean developed at a more rapid pace than elsewhere in the Caribbean. With the allied nations during World War II and the postwar period requiring resources for their military industries, new state-guided investments emerged with a focus in resource extraction industries. The commercial discovery of bauxite in Jamaica occurred in the early 1940s, and soon thereafter North American investors purchased and leased large areas of land containing deposits of ore (Hughes, 1973, p. 3). With the defeat of Jamaica's militant labor and left-wing political forces in 1938, dominant groups solidified their relative hegemony (Post, 1978). In turn, the island's independence in the mid-twentieth century opened further opportunities for international investment. Jamaica's situation and experience with a relatively late independence, after a period of political tutelage, contrasted greatly with the historical context of other nearby islands.

Motivated in part by U.S. Cold War policies in the 1950s, North American capital invested heavily in developing bauxite mining in Jamaica (Hughes, 1973, p. 1). Between 1950 and 1966, the vast majority of foreign capital into the country went to bauxite mining, a magnet of economic growth that served as the single largest source of tax revenue for the country. By the beginning of the Korean War, the United States sought to double its capacity in aluminum through the auspices of national security. The U.S. Defense Production Act of 1950 provided generous financial support for this new policy (Hughes, 1973). U.S. international corporations, such as Kaiser and Reynolds, acquired deposits in Jamaica and in fact received a majority of the act's money allocated for building U.S. metal capacity (Hughes, 1973): "The United States Government had a particular interest in introducing the Jamaican deposits as the chief source of incremental supplies. In the first place, the large size of the reserves made large-scale production over time feasible; secondly, the proximity of Jamaica to the Gulf Coast ports made the strategic route easier to defend" (Girvan quoted in Sprague, 2015, p. 82).

Initially it was the strategic requirements of the U.S. government (building up its National Strategic Stockpile) that prompted the creation of the bauxite industry in Jamaica. At the time U.S. policy makers stated that the "development of the West Indies deposits is important as a security measure" (Girvan, 1971, p. 20). By the 1960s the burden of financing the operations had switched to the private sector. Jamaica's bauxite was near the surface, so it could be mined with conventional mining equipment (p. 26). Low extraction costs, local accessibility, and importantly, the proximity to the United States, were all important features (p. 21). U.S. reliance on Jamaican bauxite grew tremendously during this period; in 1951, imported bauxite from Jamaica supplied 61 percent of U.S. needs, and by 1965 the U.S. imported 86 percent of its bauxite from Jamaica (p. 30).

Growing production in the 1960s included the advent of local mining subsidiary companies. Owned largely by foreign corporations, these subsidiaries allowed for taxation, regulation, and liability benefits for international capital. Their emergence reflected the growing international-orientation and organizational capacity of mining corporations and their capitalist owners and investors (Girvan, 1971, p. 15). Mimi Sheller explains, though, how "there were few strikes or unrest associated with the Jamaican bauxite mines, largely because they employed a relatively small numbers of workers, these workers were relatively well paid compared to other local industries, especially agriculture, and were thus easily replaceable" (Sheller, 2015, p. 195).

Jamaica's national independence in 1962, with the conservative JLP first coming to power, signaled a turning point for the role of the mining industry in the country. Social and political tensions heightened during the 1960s, especially as the popular classes faced hardship while major economic sectors, such as mining, reaped extraordinary profits. Jamaica's independence and the onrushing of North American capital led to shifts within Jamaica's class structure, with business interests and state elites turning increasingly outward toward international financial markets. British finance capital and London's oversight had dominated Jamaica for many years. However, by the 1960s, following the island's independence, London's guarantees on financial support began to evaporate. Internationalizing U.S. finance capital, and, to a lesser extent, internationally geared Canadian finance capital grew more active in the Anglophone Caribbean (Sheller, 2015, pp. 152–159). Besides the U.S.-based Kaiser and Reynolds, Alcoa established bauxite mining operations in Jamaica as well as in the Dominican Republic.

As international capitalism expanded beyond the restraints of the earlier colonial orders, it faced new challenges with the formation of postcolonial states.

In 1972, the center-left People's National Party (PNP) swept the nation's elections, gaining a majority in Jamaica's parliament. In order to fund social programs and facilitate national production, a major plank of the PNP's political platform was to increase revenues from the bauxite sector. This meant higher taxes on mining operations and partial state ownership of the sector. Under Prime Minister Michael Manley, the PNP government acquired a sizable stake of local mining subsidiaries, with the government purchasing 51 percent of the local subsidiary of Kaiser and Reynolds, as well as 6 percent of Alcoa's and 7 percent of Alcan's operations. The government also repurchased most of the ore reserve lands owned by the companies. Mining companies, in return, received forty-year mining leases.

By 1974, Jamaica became the world's fourth largest producer and second biggest exporter of alumina. That same year, following the dramatic rise of worldwide oil prices, the state increased bauxite taxes through a production levy. In effect, the levy indexed the price of bauxite to the price at which the aluminum companies sold aluminum ingots.

The Manley administration developed new agencies to manage the state's enlarged role in the industry. The Jamaica Bauxite Institute began operating in 1976 to monitor, regulate, conduct research, and advise the government on all aspects of the industry. Yet local and international conditions and the structural contradictions therein made it extremely difficult for the PNP's project to succeed. International capital and the United States strongly opposed statist developmental policies. To assuage its opponents, Manley's government sought to position itself as nonaligned during the Cold War. Yet exaggerating Jamaica's relations with Cuba and the Soviet Union, hard-line militarists in Washington sought to undermine Manley's government. U.S. intelligence apparatuses and various business interests—including those connected with the mining industry—engaged in a campaign to destabilize Manley's first administration (Blum, 1995/2003, pp. 263–267). The defeat of the PNP's initial platform was symbolized by its loss in violence-marred elections held in late 1980. Washington and its allies vastly exaggerated the role of the left in Jamaica. The small Marxist party the Workers Party of Jamaica had tried to pull the PNP to the left during the 1970s but was eventually pushed out of the PNP and later collapsed. The hollowing out of Jamaica's political landscape was made easier by the fact that the socialist left within Jamaica's labor movement had been marginalized and brutally crushed decades prior (Post, 1978). Left-wing Jamaican journalist John Maxwell (2008a) later observed how many of the country's former radicals had since become "intellectual leaders of free market theology."

To subvert future progressive and leftist movements, elites and allied policy makers sought in an increasingly concerted effort to restructure political systems in developing regions, such as the Caribbean (Robinson, 1996). This is clearly reflected by events in Jamaica. Throughout the 1980s and 1990s under the JLP and then under a reconstituted PNP, the earlier statist mining policies were largely dismantled. Alongside an economic restructuring of Jamaica during the global era, policy and ideological differences between the two major parties have diminished (Sprague, 2014c). Foreign investment in mining has grown somewhat, which industry experts estimated resulted in increased output of 1.5 million metric tons of bauxite production per annum. Over recent decades the Jamaican state's macroeconomic policies have increasingly run in-line with the Washington Consensus promoted by IFIs, encouraging state budgetary austerity alongside borrowing to boost capital investment and local consumption. This has led to a multilateral debt trap, in which the country's long-term economic development has stagnated, social inequality has increased, and a small number of businesspeople have become extremely wealthy (Johnston, 2013).

Policies meant to promote global competitiveness can be seen in the withdrawal of the Jamaican state from its former role in domestic mining operations.[3] In 1999, the government agreed to a further reduction of the bauxite levy. Since then, the levy has been eliminated altogether, as local policy makers seek to make Jamaica competitive and in-line with proindustry conditions established in many other parts of the world. Transnational capital clearly has held powerful influence over policy makers in Jamaica's state apparatus, as state managers have sought to accommodate investors by opening up local markets and eliminating barriers to capital mobility. Barclay and Girvan explain how officials operating through Jamaica's state apparatus have dropped earlier indicative planning policies (or so-called national development) in regard to the industry, even abandoning taxation:

> Since the late 1970s, the Jamaican government has progressively changed its policy stance vis-à-vis the Transnational Corporations (TNCs) operating in its bauxite industry from relatively confrontational to relatively accommodating. A controversial bauxite production levy was replaced by a fiscal regime based on corporate profits taxes and royalties. The changes were due to a steep decline in the government's bargaining power in relation to the traditional TNCs players and to the new players in the global industry; manifested in a dramatic fall in Jamaica's global bauxite and alumina market share and the perceived need to restore international competitiveness. Also playing a part were the deteriorating economic situation of the country and the changing ideological climate associated with the Washington Consensus. The policy changes, in the context of the global restructuring of the aluminum industry; resulted in new investment with increases in plant capacity and production; but aggregate returns from the industry have not grown significantly as per unit returns have declined; and the recent global economic slowdown has resulted in plant closures. (2008, p. 1)

To be clear, mining has become a more globally competitive industry. By the early 1970s, bauxite production in Australia had overtaken Jamaica, with some 27 million tons a year produced as opposed to Jamaica's 11 to 12 million tons. By 2010, bauxite mining in Jamaica was producing 9 million tons per anum, in comparison to 70 million tons produced in Australia and with the mining of bauxite expanding worldwide. In total, mining and quarrying contributed 8.6 percent to Jamaica's GDP in 1995, with 98 percent of that coming from bauxite and alumina. Bauxite has remained among the country's leading industries well into the twenty-first century. Alumina and bauxite have remained the two leading export commodities, accounting for more than 50 percent of the total value of exports in 2000.

Bauxite mining (though in a slow decline, as it is a finite resource being depleted) appears set to continue for many more decades on the island. There are at present four bauxite mining and refining operations in Jamaica. Half of the mined bauxite is processed on the island in the four alumina refineries, which have a combined capacity of some 2.7 million tons a year. The alumina is exported mainly to Europe and North America, but in recent decades exports have expanded to other nontraditional locations. (See Table 7.1.)

Whereas mining companies in the mid-twentieth century were closely identified with their domicile nation, in recent years, mining companies have become more transnationally oriented, operating through global chains of production and financial systems functionally integrated across borders. For instance, the TNC United Company Rusal, now the largest alumina producer worldwide, recently acquired the Jamaica operations of WINDALCO and ALPART. The company, with operations around the world, is headquartered in Moscow but incorporated on the island of Jersey, a British crown dependency and tax haven in the Channel Islands. The company initially formed in 2007 through a merger of the Switzerland-based Glencore's alumina assets and the Russian companies RUSAL and SUAL. Major transnational capitalists hold large shares in the company, such as the American tycoon Nathaniel Rothschild and Chinese billionaire Robert Kuok (Kuok Hock Nien). Rusal's hedge funds meanwhile are managed by U.S. billionaire John Paulson and Moscow-based state bank Vneschekonombank (Gopalan, 2009).

Jamaica's mining industry, like mining operations around the world, has become integrated with transnational circuits of production and finance. In the 1980s and 1990s, as circuits of production and finance transnationalized through new organizational and technological advancements, major capitalists around the world shifted from a national or international orientation toward a transnational one. Mining companies no longer operate in Jamaica as an extension of U.S. state policies or subsidies, nor in the interests of a particular fraction of national capitalists; rather, they thrive in a globally competitive and integrated market benefiting transnational capitalists.

Transnational mining firms, like earlier multinational firms, have often operated through subsidiaries. In Jamaica these have included: Alumina Partners

TABLE 7.1. BAUXITE AND ALUMINUM PRODUCTS AS A TOTAL OF JAMAICAN EXPORTS						
	1972	1980	1991	2001	2010	2015
Aluminum oxide and hydroxide	38.7	57	43.8	51.8	28.7	44.1
Bauxite and concentrates of alum	24.2	21.1	9.1	7.5	9.1	10.3
Source: ECLAC-CEPALSTAT, 2018.						

of Jamaica, Noranda Jamaica Bauxite Partners, URS Jamaica Ltd., Lydford Mining Co., and Windalco's West Indies Alumina Company. As a case study, Alumina Partners operates a bauxite refinery in the southern part of Jamaica. As of 2007, the company exported 1.65 million tons of alumina overseas per year, and earned gross revenues of $1.3 billion. In 2011, however, Rusal bought out others in the company to assume a 100 percent stake. Rusal also has gained majority shareholder status in the Windalco West Indies Alumina Company. Windalco produces 1.2 million tons of alumina annually at its two plants, Kirkvine and Ewarton (see Figures 7.2 and 7.3).

Another TNC, Noranda Aluminum, previously based out of Quebec, Canada, also operated bauxite mining in Jamaica. In 2006, Xstrata purchased Noranda. Headquartered in Zug, Switzerland, Xstrata is registered in London, and holds operations in nineteen countries across Africa, Asia, Australia, Europe, North America, and South America. Among the numerous shareholders of Xstrata, the largest is Glencore International PLC (with a stake of approximately 34 percent). In turn, Glencore, a transnational commodity trading and mining company, with shareholders from around the world, is headquartered in Baar, Switzerland, but registered on the island of Jersey. The world's largest commodities trading company, Glencore, had a

Figure 7.2 Sign in front of the Windalco mine in Jamaica, owned in November 2014 by RUSAL. (Photo by author.)

Figure 7.3 Part of the Windalco operations in Jamaica. (Photo by author.)

2010 global market share of 60 percent in the internationally tradable zinc market, 50 percent in the internationally tradable copper market, 9 percent in the internationally tradable grain market and 3 percent in the internationally tradable oil market. Glencore has production facilities around the world and supplies metals, minerals, crude oil, oil products, coal, natural gas, and agricultural products to global customers in the automotive, power generation, steel production, and food-processing industries.

A number of other transnational enterprises have large holdings in Xstrata. The Qatari sovereign wealth fund, Qatar Holding, has a 12 percent stake in Xstrata. Glencore also has ties with the U.S.-based Century Aluminum Co., and it has a 70.5 percent stake in one of the top three nickel producers based in Australia (Minara Resources Ltd.), and an 8.8 percent share in Rusal. Another transnational mining firm, the Australian-headquartered Ausjam Mining, began the first recorded gold-mining operation in Jamaica in 2000, in Pennants. Subsumed in a global whirlpool of finance capital, many long-standing industrial operations, such as mining in Jamaica, have continued into the contemporary era but as part of the global strategies and accumulation platforms of TNCs.

Local Jamaican elites have become deeply interconnected with the global economy through the sale of imports, export processing, tourism inputs, and financial flows. Despite the integration of local elites into the global economy, economic activity around mining has remained largely within the sphere of foreign transnational conglomerates. Local Jamaican subcontracting ties with the industry have remained primarily through port logistic services and transportation (Jamaican Ministry of Trade official, personal communication, 2014). While the operations of mining corporations have shifted over recent decades, one long-standing dynamic persists: the lack of local inputs. This can be seen also in the continued lack of technological transfers, with Jamaica still lacking local aluminum smelters.

Yet, transnationally oriented state elites and technocrats operating through state apparatuses have played a significant role in ushering along TNC mining projects in recent decades. In Jamaica, officials from both major political parties, the JLP and the PNP, have promoted the dismantling of the state's direct role in mining while undertaking policies conducive to transnational mining capital. In one ongoing project that encourages future TNC mining operations, the Jamaican state's mining agency collaborates with the mining agency of the government of the Czech Republic to identify local nonmetallic mineral deposits "for rapid economic development" as well as other projects focused on new and continuing mining operations. While attempts to promote mining in Jamaica continue, taxation levels are dropping and repatriation of local earnings continues unabated. It now appears that the last remaining "national goal" is to maintain a minimal level of low-waged jobs in the sector so as not to exacerbate the high level of unemployment in the country. In late 2014, the Jamaican state agreed to cease for two years the last remaining levies on companies active in mining bauxite within the country. With levies dropped and local operations almost completely privatized, the few thousand low-wage jobs that are left appear to be one of the few benefits left for the local population. As the host government and local business interests benefit only marginally from the global mining industry, the more important overarching concerns of elites and policy makers in Jamaica appear to be in maintaining a globally competitive, investor-friendly climate—as a withdrawal of mining corporations could be seen as a bad signal to other transnational capitalist investors.

The Dominican Republic and Transnational Mining: A New El Dorado?

By the late nineteenth century, both the Dominican and Haitian states had passed mining laws, yet the industry remained barely existent in Hispaniola (Aitkens, 1931, pp. 1–2). With the United States occupations of the Dominican Republic (1916–1924) and Haiti (1915–1934), U.S. policy makers, and eventually, the regimes they put in place, assumed the task of expanding private property rights, improving road networks, managing the money supply, and fostering development of credit institutions. By 1930, the dictatorship of Rafael Leonidas Trujillo in the Dominican Republic had consolidated power through the military and state apparatuses. Yet suffering from fragmentation and economic fragility, few local mechanisms existed through which political negotiations and a legalistic distribution of power could occur. With a weak and repressed civil society, the Trujillo regime consolidated power, in turn reproducing exclusion and inequality. As foreign capital controlled the country's most dynamic sectors, officials and families close with the leadership of the regime took over the role as local counterpart to foreign investors and businesses active in the country. As Trujillo and his nepotistic coterie owned many of the largest businesses in the country, this slowed the formation of local productive capital (Espinal, 1986). Over time, buying out some of the most profitable local monopolies, and excluding foreign capital, Trujillo promoted a particular brand of ISI policies.

Not only did the island lack the infrastructure and social and political cohesion best suited for the mining industry's development; international mining companies focused on easier to reach mineral deposits and usually in countries with more developed infrastructure. With limited success, local officials worked to entice foreign capital to invest, offering sweetheart deals to potential foreign investors that required mines pay as little as 2 percent of the gross product to the public treasury.[4] During the decades after World War II, international corporate investment in the "imperial frontier" expanded. Though to a lesser extent than in Jamaica, U.S. state policies helped the Alcoa mining corporation begin mining bauxite in the Dominican Republic by 1959.

Deepening international economic activity occurred alongside transformative political and social processes in the Dominican Republic. Soon after a group of conspirators ambushed and did away with the dictator Trujillo in 1961, a short-lived democratically elected center-left government came to power under Juan Bosch. When a right-wing coup overthrew Bosch, an armed conflict ensued between constitutionalist and putschist factions, which U.S. policy makers then used as justification to occupy the country and back the local putschist and reactionary forces. Ultimately, the Trujillista leader Joaquín Balaguer came to power, strengthened by the force of U.S. bayonets. However, learning from the failures of Trujillo and advised by U.S. officials, the Balaguer regime while it offered some space for foreign and local business elites, especially those linked to productive industry, construction and finance (many providing kickbacks to the regime)—it continued to promote a clientilistic form of ISI through some limited industrial subsidies and protections (Werner, 2016, p. 32). The Dominican state under

Balaguer also continued to repress labor and grassroots movements (Espinal, 1986). Years later it would be revealed that Balaguer had long been an asset of the FBI U.S. intelligence agency (Weiner, 2013).

The early 1970s saw the construction of large-scale dams on the island, such as the Péligre Dam in Haiti in 1971 and the Yaque del Norte in the Dominican Republic in 1973. These infrastructure projects were important steps for capitalist development, permitting the expansion of the electrical grids and incremental improvements to the overall quality of life, primarily in urban areas. With new export-processing initiatives, economic relations strengthened between certain local and foreign capitalists, especially with the influx of private investment promoted by the U.S. state.

As part of what would later become a broader regional and international trend (Robinson, 1996), a managed democratic transition occurred in the late 1970s with the election of the Partido Revolucionario Dominicano (PRD), the party founded by Bosch. Fractions of the business community, once excluded from the paternalistic system of business-government relations under Balaguer, built alliances and collaborated with PRD politicians. Yet while the political system modernized and enshrined more basic rights, the socioeconomic conditions of the poor remained backward and the role of labor unions was marginal. Espinal explains: "Despite the democratic opening, which has largely consisted of holding freer and more competitive elections and more protection of basic human and political rights, the working class continues to be highly excluded from power and a fair share of the wealth produced in society" (1986, p. 228). In turn, segments of the local bourgeoisie became increasingly linked with foreign investors and helped foster local conditions conducive to the expanding global economy.

During this period, the mining industry began to expand in the Dominican Republic. One study explains: "Mining in particular took on a greater role, as that sector's share of exports grew from an insignificant level in 1970 to 38% by 1980" (Library of Congress, 1986). While mining has continued on in recent decades its share as a percentage of "national exports" has dropped, as export processing and other production has intensified. As mining ramped up in the 1970s, state managers sought a role in managing, facilitating, and taxing operations in order to assure greater revenues for the government. By the early 1980s the Dominican state levied a 5 percent export tax and charged a 40 percent annual income tax on the net profits of private mining operations (with, however, various exemptions).

In time, international pressure urged state policy makers to drop the state's heavy role in various industries, including mining. Neoliberal policies called for leveraging local assets, such as mineral resources, to entice investment from abroad. These policies began to percolate during the 1980s, as the

Dominican state relied on the mining expertise of corporations abroad while maintaining ownership and a partial role in management (S. A. Ramírez Beltne, personal communication, 2013). In the 1990s, as capitalist globalization intensified, a new administration under the rightist Partido Reformista Social Cristiano (PRSC), headed once again by Joaquín Balaguer, issued new mining decrees, bringing the country's mining laws in step with proinvestment regimes such as in Mexico (Gobierno de República Dominicana 1997), an important step toward deepening the confidence of capitalist investors in local mineral extraction. Under the subsequent Partido de la Liberación Dominicana (PLD) and PRD administrations, officials negotiated new contracts with transnational mining companies, though only some reached full-scale production. By the new century, structural dynamics developed that had turned the nation into an easily accessible node for transnational capital.

To understand the novel role of mining TNCs in the country, it is especially useful to look at the development of the Pueblo Viejo mine, founded in 1972 as a concession from the Dominican state. Between 1975 and 1999, the New York– and Honduras-based Rosario Mining Company with support from Dominican state authorities, initiated operations on what would become a vast 7.5 million square meter open-pit mine, containing gold, silver, zinc, and copper. Open-pit mining is a surface mining technique for extracting rock or minerals through their removal from an open pit, rather than through a shaft into the ground. Grullón and Antares (2012) observe, "The operations of Rosario Dominicana were disastrous in environmental, social and financial terms." They add, "At least four rivers of the area were polluted with Acid Mine Drainage (AMD) and with discharges from the tailings of dams, one of which overflowed in 1979 during a hurricane; and more than 600 families were displaced" to make way for the project. It is estimated that hundreds of millions of dollars would be required to clean up the environmental damage (Grullón and Antares, 2012, pp. 27–28).

Despite the mine's closure at the turn of the century, and the extensive environmental damage it caused, production resumed nearly ten years later, with the restarted operations greatly benefiting from new technology and techniques. In 2002, a Vancouver-based transnational mining company, Placer Dome, signed mining contracts with the Dominican government, including a 25-year lease (extendable to 75 years) for the Pueblo Viejo mining area (Austen, 2005). However, in 2006, Placer Dome was acquired for $10.4 billion by another Canadian-based transnational mining corporation, Barrick Gold, the largest gold mining company in the world.[5] Placer Dome's interests in the gold and silver mines of La Coipa and Pueblo Viejo were passed to Barrick Gold, potentially growing Barrick's output of gold tremendously.[6] That same year, another transnational mining corporation, Goldcorp, acquired 40 percent of

TABLE 7.2. PRODUCTION OF SELECTED MINERALS IN THE DOMINICAN REPUBLIC								
	1990	1998	2009	2010	2011	2012	2013	2014
Gold/kg	4,350	1,421	173	494	490	4,106	23,019	35,081
Silver/kg	21,600	7,409	450	20,300	18,300	27,296	78,228	127,712
Copper	—	—	11,500	9,000	11,700	11,737	*	*
Nickel	28,700	40,300	500	—	1,143,000	1,301,694	*	*

Sources: Wacaster, 2010, 2011, 2012, 2013, 2014; Barrick Gold website, 2015; Goldcorp website, 2014.
*= data not available.
Values in metric tons unless otherwise specified.

the Pueblo Viejo venture from Barrick.[7] Despite these corporate maneuvers, Barrick remained the sole operator, through its local subsidiary, the Pueblo Viejo Dominicana Corporation (PVDC).

Consistent with its unparalleled presence in gold mining worldwide, Barrick Gold Corporation has investors from around the world. Headquartered in Toronto and founded by Canadian real estate magnate Peter Munk, it has four regional business units located in Australia, Africa, North America, and South America, with mining and exploratory projects that span the globe, from Papua New Guinea, to the United States, Canada, the Dominican Republic, Australia, Peru, Chile, Russia, South Africa, Pakistan, Colombia, Argentina, and Tanzania. Major investors in the company include Van Eck Associates Corp (a U.S.-based investment firm with global coverage, including much of the "developing world"), the Bank of Montreal (one of the largest banks in Canada, with investments around the world), First Eagle Investment Management (a U.S.-based investment management firm whose global fund has assets totaling almost $50.92 billion invested in 172 different holdings), Allianz Asset Management (a financial assets company based in Munich, Germany, with $624.95 billion in total assets and with investors from around the world), and the Bank of New York Mellon (the largest deposit bank in the world, with $27.9 trillion in worldwide assets under custody or administration). All these institutional investors are themselves interconnected with a wide variety of global industries, active with investors around the world.

Barrick Gold's mining operation at Pueblo Viejo began in 2011, with the extraction of gold and other minerals and production growing since that time. According to Barrick and Goldcorp, the proven reserves of the Pueblo Viejo mine numbered 20 million ounces of gold, 117 million ounces of silver, and 424 million pounds of copper. All told, however, the total output of the mine will likely be much higher than this initial assessment (Nicomedes Acevedo, personal communication, 2013). (See Figures 7.4 and 7.5.)

Figure 7.4 Barrick Gold's operations at Pueblo Viejo, Dominican Republic. (Photo by author.)

Figure 7.5 The Pueblo Viejo open pit mine operated by Barrick Gold. (Photo by author).

Heightened contractor and subcontractor arrangements can also be seen at Pueblo Viejo. Whereas earlier state connected mining operations at Pueblo Viejo involved very few private subcontractors, this has changed in recent years. Barrick Gold Employee Nicomedes Acevedo explains, "We've had a huge expansion in the volume of relations with subcontractors. We've worked with around thirty subcontractors here in the Dominican Republic, but we have five main subcontractors that have around 3,000 permanent employees" (Nicomedes Acevedo, personal communication, 2013). One of the subcontractors operating at Barrick Gold's Pueblo Viejo facilities is Fluor, employing not just Dominicans but also workers from Colombia, Peru, the Philippines, and other countries. Fluor, a FORTUNE 500 company with sixty office locations on six different continents, serves a variety of industries for engineering, procurement, construction, maintenance, and project management for "governments and clients in diverse industries around the world."[8] "A global company," as Fluor's website describes, it boasts, "core strengths in strategic sourcing, material management, and contract management" that enable it to "effectively manage supplier and subcontractor information on a global basis for both . . . commercial and government clients."[9]

Another globally active subcontractor at the Pueblo Viejo mine is Sodexo, a company that provides meals for labor and management. As with Fluor, investor shares in Sodexo are publicly traded in the NYSE, among other exchanges. Headquartered in Paris, the TNC Sodexo is one of the largest employers in the world with 380,000 employees, representing 130 nationalities, present on 34,000 sites in 80 countries. Reflecting the gendered relations of the workforce, Sodexo workers at Pueblo Viejo are overwhelmingly women and are paid low wages. As Barrick officials explain, they take pride in their increased use of women workers in comparison to past operations in which few women were employed. Gendered social relations now entwine with capitalist flexibilization and the intense monetization of the lives of workers. Whereas in the past, for example, "workers ate lunches at the mine that their wives packed for them at home," today workers all eat the same lunch provided to them in plastic containers and cooked on-site by Sodexo employees (who are mostly women). The growing standardization of the industry and role of subcontractors is reflected in these changing social relations.

Many smaller local subcontractors active at Pueblo Viejo are based in towns nearby, exemplifying how some local businesses do have direct, albeit limited, connections with transnational mining capital. One contractor, Presecon, is based in the small town of Cotuí. With the company's owners seeking to expand across the country, leveraging the global investment they have tapped into, its website states that it aspires to "become one of the most important and recognized nationwide, seeking to be the leader in the area of sub-contracting human resource services."[10] Another local subcontractor, Adesco, is also based in the nearby town of Cotuí and has approximately eighty local employees doing seasonal work reforesting former mining sites.[11] Another Cotuí-based subcontractor, Agencia Navarro, provides surveying resources and equipment—such as chain saws and compactors—providing transportation services for workers and management at the mine.[12]

State elites and technocrats operating through Dominican state apparatuses have worked to stimulate the global mining industry. For instance, as companies seek mining rights, they must first gain concessions for extraction, which requires approval from the National Assembly. State officials in the assembly and other government bodies have thereby served as vital conduits through which TNCs secure concessions. Industry insiders regularly hold important government posts and vice versa (Dominican Today, 2012).[13] One social justice activist in the Dominican Republic, commenting on the Pueblo Viejo contract, writes, "This was actually a rubber stamp exercise by the neoliberal deputies, most of which were from the corrupt PLD of President Leonel Fernández. There were some votes against the contract, but few in comparison to the yes votes" (local antimining activist who requested anonymity, personal communication, 2013) (see also Shenk, 2009). Similar processes were undertaken during the preceding PRD administration of Hipólito Mejía, which oversaw the construction of a deepwater megaport and facilitated the ramping up of the global mining industry (Gregory, 2006).

Beyond Barrick Gold, it is important to note that other mining TNCs are active on the island. Whereas Barrick owns 60 percent of the Pueblo Viejo, another company, Goldcorp, owns the rest. This is also significant given that Goldcorp had its mining operations in Guatemala suspended by the Inter-American Commission on Human Rights (IACHR) in 2010, shuttering for a period its Marlin mine due to human rights violations and extensive environmental damage (Guatemala Times, 2010).

In addition to these operations, nickel has been another prominent mineral mined in the Dominican Republic. From the 1970s, industrial scale nickel mining has taken place in the country, a process known for its legacy of environmental damage. By the mid-2000s the Dominican Republic ranked eleventh in the world in nickel production (Wacaster, 2010).

New mining operations are on the horizon, aimed largely at the mountains of the Massif du Nord Metallogenic (the northern mineralization belt) that stretches from Haiti's north through to the southeast of the Dominican Republic. In mid-2012, the TNC GoldQuest Mining, operating in the western Dominican Republic, released results of a new massive gold-copper exploratory operation (Wacaster, 2013; Keen, 2012b). Another transnational mining emporium based out of Canada, Everton Resources Inc., holds the concessions in the perimeter areas adjoining the Barrick Gold/Goldcorp Pueblo Viejo operation.[14] In addition, two other transnational companies, Novus Gold and Unigold, hold lucrative concessions in western areas of the Dominican Republic, closer to the border with Haiti, generally in the northwestern area of the country (Keen, 2012a). One of these concessions is nearly 1,000 square kilometers, including areas within the J. Armando Bermúdez reserve (a protected tropical forest). In 2012, a mining TNC based out of Australia, Perilya Limited, acquired the exploitation and exploration rights for a number of copper, silver, and gold operations in the Maimón area. The mining TNC, Xstrata Nickel, also continues to be active in the country. As one mining expert explains, the "Dominican Republic is shaping up to be a new mining district that should not be underestimated" (Bassteam, 2012).

The overall role of mining in the region has fluctuated, especially as other economic sectors have grown in recent decades. In recent years there has occurred a shuttering of some operations and a reopening or starting up of others. The transnational mining company, Xstrata Nickel (based in the U.K.), after shutting down temporarily its Falconbride Dominicana Corporation, which accounted for much of the nickel mining in the country, began new nickel mining operations near Bonao (Wacaster, 2010). Another TNC, GlobeStar Mining Corp., in 2009 began producing copper, gold, and silver from open pit mining at its wholly owned Cerro de Maimón operations, also located near Bonao (Wacaster, 2010).

These new operations have been met by protests carried out by locals, students, and environmentalists in the country, as solidarity activist Tim Shenk observes:

> A half-dozen protestors were injured and several more were jailed Sunday during a peaceful rally for the preservation of Loma Miranda, a mountain in the Dominican Republic's central range. The protest was called after arsonists allegedly set fires May 7 on the mountain under exploration for ferronickel extraction. Government officials were opaque in their response. On Sunday, Dominican National Police and the Army fired shots attempting to disperse the environmental rally at Loma Miranda. They wounded six, including university professor Juan Alberto Benzan and Sixto Gabín, president of the Asociación Dominicana de Profesores in the city of San Francisco de Macoris.
>
> Mobilizations were led on Sunday by Catholic priests Rogelio Cruz and Nino Ramos, as well as participants in a long-standing protest camp on the mountain. Protestors denounced that forest fires had been set intentionally at three or four strategic points on Loma Miranda last Thursday, May 7 at around 9 a.m. Facts in the unfolding case of alleged arson seem to implicate agents tied to FALCONDO, the Dominican subsidiary of the transnational mining company Glencore Xstrata, with potential complicity or cooperation from government agencies. (2015)

Community and social movements in the Dominican Republic have repeatedly launched protests over the environmental damage and the high profits that TNCs make from mineral extraction in the country (local anti-mining activist who requested anonymity, personal communication, 2013).

Figure 7.6 A protest held by popular organizations in Cotui near the Pueblo Viejo mining operations of Barrick Gold. (Source: Global Justice.)

One group, the peasant movement Movimiento de Trabajadores Campesinos las Comunidades Unidas, has organized against La Cementera, a proposed cement factory that would have extracted minerals from Los Haitises National Park in the northeast of the Dominican Republic. While in some instances these groups have had successes, the overall trend has been toward an intensification of environmentally harmful resource extraction (Global Justice, 2010). (See Figure 7.6.)

Most indications, though, suggest that the industry in the region will continue to expand, as activist organizing has occurred sporadically and with little infrastructure and resources. Incentives for continued growth of the mining industry meanwhile include heightening values of minerals, growing investment in the industry worldwide, and the continued drive toward global competitiveness by transnationally oriented elites insulated from popular pressures. Over the next decade, the share of the Dominican Republic's GDP from mining will likely surpass 3 percent (Bamrud, 2012). Reports suggest that Barrick's recently renegotiated Pueblo Viejo contract will pay out to the Dominican State $377 million from the $8 billion of gross revenue between 2012 and 2016 (Medina Herasme, 2014).

Declared by one commentator as the "investment jewel of the Caribbean," mining operations in the Dominican Republic are rapidly becoming a major spigot for the TCC entry into the country. As discussed below, moreover, mining contracts pushed through after the 2010 earthquake in Haiti have been aimed at a similar outcome. Junior mining exploratory companies active in the Dominican Republic have seen their values rise, as have large mining TNCs such as Barrick. As one industry watcher explained, "Their new high-grade gold (and copper) discoveries in the Dominican Republic have caught the attention of investors, both retail and institutional" (Bassteam, 2012). Today, the Dominican Republic has become a major site of FDI in the Caribbean, as companies from around the world have set up shop, including companies based in the United States, the EU, Canada, Australia, Brazil, Colombia, and Venezuela (Pellerano, 2012). As the Dominican case illustrates, mining increasingly reflects the speculation, demands, capabilities, and rent seeking of transnational capital, rather than statist developmental projects, locally oriented policies, or the international models of the past.

Haiti and the New Disaster Mining

U.S. government researchers explained in the late 1940s (U.S. Tariff Commission, 1949, p. 4) that mining in Haiti had only developed to a very small degree. Sheller explains how over the decades the U.S.-based corporation Reynolds Metal then ramped up its operations in the country, and "from 1956 to 1982 exported 13.3 million tons of bauxite from Haiti to its alumina refinery in Corpus Christi, Texas." She adds: "Haitian bauxite accounted for almost one-fifth of Reynolds' bauxite acquisition in that period, and Reynolds was given access to 150,000 hectares, expelling thousands of Haitian families" (Sheller, 2015, pp. 195–196).

During the first four years of François "Papa Doc" Duvalier's dictatorship, the Reynolds company held a monopoly on bauxite mining in the country, paying a mere 7 percent of its earnings to the Haitian state. Similarly, in the 1970s under Jean-Claude "Baby Doc" Duvalier, a small amount of copper mining was undertaken by a U.S. company.[15]

Over the last quarter of the twentieth century, supranational agencies and state agencies initiated mineral exploratory operations around the world, especially where local investors or governments were unable. In Haiti, for example, the UN Development Program carried out exploratory drilling in the northwest of the country in the 1970s. During the 1980s, West Germany's Bundesanstalt fur Geowissenschaften und Rohstoffe ran feasibility studies of mining in Haiti's northeast. That same decade, the area was explored again by the UNDP and also surveyed by the French Bureau de Recherches Géologiques et Minière. In the 1990s, a Canadian exploratory mining venture also conducted drilling in Haiti's north (T. Niles, 2012). For a number of reasons—lack of infrastructure, political instability, and a mineral market that did not yet justify the costs—the findings of these projects were not pursued at the time. Rural communities in Haiti's north have also protested mining operations, viewing them as providing little to the local population (Sprague, 2006b).

With the end of the Duvalier dynasty in 1986 and the failure of successive attempts by the military and elites to crush popular protests, democratic elections were ultimately allowed at the behest of "enlightened" U.S. officials and other powerful international interests. Whereas elites and their foreign backers (most important, U.S. policy makers) attempted to manipulate the electoral process, their plans backfired when the popular-progressive government of former priest Jean-Bertrand Aristide was elected with wide support. Yet only seven months into his term in office, in September 1991, a military junta overthrew Aristide. Rooted in the country's traditional power structure, the coup regime received support from those sectors of the elite and army who had rejected the democratic transition (and backing from some of the more conservative sectors within the United States). Yet the military regime, heavily involved in narcotics and widespread repression, soon faced international isolation. It faced widespread protests in the country, and even grassroots protesters when mining initiatives were attempted in the north of the country (Sprague, 2006b).

Attempting to gain foreign investors, the de facto regime granted some mining concessions (Prepetit, 2000),[16] but only after the restitution of the constitutional government in 1994 were new mineral exploratory operations begun. In 1995, a Canadian mining company, Saint Genevieve Resources, began prospecting in the north of the country (Prepetit, 2000). The following year, the U.S.-based company Newmont Mineral Exploration gained prospecting licenses for areas of north and central Haiti (Prepetit, 2000). A number of small-scale exploration operations continued on throughout the late 1990s and early 2000s (Wacaster, 2010). However, renewed efforts to undermine Haiti's government and popular movement by sectors of the upper class, with some local disaffected groups, and their allies abroad and former members of the disbanded military led to another coup d'état, this time carried out by the U.S. George W. Bush regime in February 2004. Supported by other powers, a UN military occupation was deployed in mid-2004 and lasted officially until late-2017 (Blumenthal, 2004; Fenton and Engler, 2005; Hallward, 2008; Sprague, 2012a; Podur, 2012).[17] Dominant groups working with and through various state and supranational agencies have since sought to press forward with the country's economic restructuring, while blocking free and fair elections and engaging in mass voter suppression and other strategies to remake the country politically.

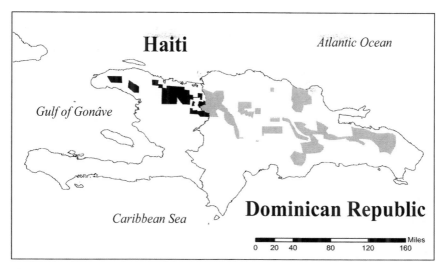

Figure 7.7 A rough map of the major gold, silver, and copper mineralization belt in Hispaniola, and the areas that have been cordoned off in Haiti and the Dominican Republic for potential mining operations. (Created by the author and based upon: Haiti Grassroots Watch, 2012b; Immomexx-Demaria Land Consultants, 2011.)

Haiti's fragility creates a risk that any new mining operations will result in few tangible benefits for the Haitian people, such as investment in the country's public infrastructure. In mid-2005, new mining concessions were granted by the postcoup regime of Gérard Latortue, such as with the mineral rights to the SOMINE (Society Minière du Nord-Est S.A.) area, leased through a Mining Convention (valid until 2020) for Majescor, a Canadian-based transnational mining company. As one researcher explains, after the 2004 coup, "It did not take long for Haiti's mountains to start to glitter. For example, an exploration of the Faille-B prospect in 2007 found a gold vein that averaged 42.7 grams of gold per ton of ore (g/t) over 6 meters, including values of 107.5 g/t of gold over one meter" (Chery, 2012). Leopoldo Espaillat Nanita, former head of the Dominican Petroleum Refinery explains bluntly: "There is a multinational conspiracy to illegally take the mineral resources of the Haitian people. Haiti's mineral wealth is immense, with gold, valuable strategic metals such as iridium and other minerals as well" (Espacinsular, 2009). (See Figure 7.7.)

The immensity of this resource wealth came into view following the earthquake of 2010, when a new wave of donor-facilitated exploratory operations began. Heightened penetration by global capital has thus gone hand in hand with disaster relief, deepening the country's structural inequalities alongside so few immediate options for economic development. One commentator explains: "Mining companies appear to know that now is likely the best time in years to move into Haiti: the country has a low royalty rate, there are peacekeepers stationed throughout the country, a giant free trade zone and new deepwater port are being built in the north, minimum wage is the lowest in the hemisphere, and all signs indicate that the new government will write business-friendly laws" (Haiti Grassroots Watch, 2012a).

With the ramping up of capitalist globalization after the earthquake of 2010, the mining industry began to show signs of major expansion in Haiti. Global corporations and their allies in governments have become adept at taking advantage of situations in which natural disasters have thrown societies and their political systems into disarray. In such situations, corporate planners have learned to skirt long-standing laws, renegotiate various contracts, and remake property relations (N. Klein, 2009/2018). Economic development in postquake Haiti has been intentionally channeled through transnational capitalist chains of accumulation. One group of researchers found, "If geologists' calculations are correct, Haiti's northern mountains contain hundreds of millions of ounces of gold . . . one estimate puts the eventual take at $20 billion" (Haiti Grassroots Watch, 2012b).

Shifting political dynamics in the country, furthermore, are reflected in the recent push to create large mining zones across the country. In the decade following the coup and especially in the years following the 2010 earthquake, the country's right wing has reestablished itself as the dominant force within the country's political scene (Weisbrot, 2011, Sprague-Silgado, 2018a). In the years following the earthquake, under the right-wing regimes of Michel Martelly and Jovenel Moïse, the country's constitutional process has been violated in order to set into motion new mining concessions (Haiti Grassroots Watch, 2012c). Here it is important to note the close ties between government officials with the industry, as state managers abandon national models of development in place of transnational engagement. As one researcher explained in 2012: "Haiti's new prime minister—Laurent Lamothe—is very probusiness. A telecommunications and real estate entrepreneur with companies in Africa and Latin America, he has pledged to push through business-friendly legislation in all sectors, including mining" (Haiti Grassroots Watch, 2012a). In another case, former Haitian finance minister Ronald Baudin, instrumental in approving the Martelly government's new mining convention, became a consultant for the transnational mining firm Newmont immediately after leaving office. This was one of the companies for which he had helped to get the convention enacted while in office (Haiti Grassroots Watch, 2012c).

Two mining companies Majescor and Eurasian/Newmont have looked to fast-track mining operations in the years following the earthquake. In

April 2012, the Eurasian/Newmont venture and the Haitian government agreed for exploratory drilling to take place as a new mining convention was being ratified to permit the company's new projects. Under a memorandum of understanding, the Savane La Place gold prospect is the first project slated for drilling. The convention will cover a huge amount of land, 1,350 square kilometers (Haiti Grassroots Watch, 2012c). The Eurasian/Newmont operation, through its local partner Marien Mining, is believed to hold more mining licenses in Haiti than any other company, so much so that their holdings amount to one-tenth of the country's landmass. All the while collusion between state and corporate officials appears to be widespread.[18] Looking to stimulate mining operations after the earthquake, the World Bank's private sector agency, the International Finance Corporation, has invested $5 million in the Eurasian/Newmont operation (Haiti Grassroots Watch, 2012c).

Another mining company, the Canada-based transnational, Majescor, has pursued mining at the copper-silver-gold rich mountain ridge in the north of the country.[19] Specializing in mineral surveys, Majescor's investments could potentially lead to huge profits.[20] Majescor and its Haitian partners hold licenses for at least 450 square kilometers. As one investigative report explains, "Taken together, foreign companies are sitting on research or exploration permits for one-third of Haiti's north, 15% of the country's territory" (Haiti Grassroots Watch, 2012b). The same report observes:

> Majescor is ahead of its rivals, having recently moved to the "exploitation" phase for one if its licenses. But VCS and Newmont/Eurasian are close on its heels. All of the companies recognize Haiti's potential. "Haiti is the sleeping giant of the Caribbean!" a Majescor partner said recently, while Eurasian president David Cole boasted on a radio show: "We control over 1,100 square miles of real estate." . . . Because in most locations the copper, silver and gold deposits are mostly spread out as tiny specks in the dirt and rock—what is sometimes called "invisible gold"—expensive pit mining will often be the only option, but Eurasian's partner Newmont knows its pits. The gold giant opened the world's first pit mine in Nevada in 1962 and later dug in Ghana, New Zealand, Indonesia, and other countries. (Haiti Grassroots Watch, 2012c)[21]

Majescor operates in Haiti through a local affiliate, SOMINE, which is 66.4 percent owned by Majescor, while Haitian business interests own the rest of the company. In one example of Haitian and diaspora elite involvement in local mining ventures, a former Haitian prime minister (Jean Max Bellerive) and a president of the Haitian Diaspora Federation (Joseph Baptiste) sit on the advisory committee of VCS Mining, a company based out of the United States that currently holds (with its partner Delta Mining) licenses for over 300 square kilometers in the north of Haiti. From this we might ascertain that in those built economic environments where transnational mining companies have not yet begun operations, it might be easier for locally based capitalists to seek out future rentier profits in the industry, for instance, through their knowledge of local land deeds and connections with local state officials. This is not the case in some other localities, such as in Jamaica, where earlier international operations have transitioned into transnational operations. It might be the case that it is at the beginning phases of such operations that locally based dominant groups are best situated to profit (especially through the gaining of rents).

One clear indicator of how little the state and general population will gain from the mining is illustrated by the country's new mining convention. Christian Aid researcher, Claire Kumar, observes that Haiti's two previous conventions on mining appeared to have been positive, since they aimed to secure a 50/50 split of profits and put a cap on the state's expenses. Yet the problem with the new convention is that it places Haiti's royalty rate at an extremely low 2.5 percent (Haiti Grassroots Watch, 2012d; Kumar 2009), among the lowest worldwide.

Major components of the postearthquake development strategy in Haiti have been centered on drawing in global investors, a practice seen in the United States and World Bank facilitation of export-processing ventures, a new deepwater port, and the new mining developments discussed above. Policy makers and investors view Haiti as an emergency situation for which the solution is to deepen the country's integration with the global economy. The political corollary to this economic restructuring, alongside the natural and man-made disasters that have occurred over recent years, has been a UN occupation and a deepening political exclusion of the poor. Yet even the most well-laid plans of policy makers have faced difficulties. Electoral uncertainties and continued organizing from below by popular and grassroots forces, in mid-2015 had pushed transnational mining corporations to put on hold plans for operations in the country (Fox, 2015).[22] The most likely policy of transnational oriented elites will be to continue to undermine or marginalize any alternatives to the status quo, deepening polyarchy in the country in order to secure local political alignment with their interests and intensify the country's integration with global capital.

Conclusion: Mining and Capitalist Globalization in the Caribbean

The mining industry's structure during the era of global capitalism has developed unevenly and in conjunction with novel transnational processes. The very nature in which landed property is economically realized has been modified: from statist-oriented policies of development and international corporate models to a globalized industry of transnational capitalists, new labor regimes, and a host of subcontractors and exploratory firms. State interaction with the industry has changed from directing or maintaining partial control of local operations, with particular attempts at enticing international investors toward policies of global competitiveness and standardization to attract transnational capitalist investors. The newest rounds of mining have been propelled further through technological advancements, rising mineral prices, and the global scope of TNCs (in both finance and production). We see all these changes occurring through this period of restructuring, through this shift from an international to a transnational phase of capitalism.

Whereas top dominant groups connected with the industry have profited tremendously, management has worked to push mineworkers into more globally standardized operations. They have sought to enforce flexibilized labor regimes, even as labor inputs overall have declined (R. Moody, 2007). In some parts of the region, such as in the Dominican Republic, there have been a number of protests aimed at the mining industry in recent years by labor and local community groups (Díaz, 2010). Criticism has also grown over the Haitian government's role in pushing through mining contracts that violated the nation's constitution. This and other antipopular policies are an important reason for the Haitian state's ongoing effort to rebuild the country's army as a tool of internal repression (previously disbanded in 1995). Meanwhile, state managers in Jamaica appear to have completely abandoned levies and taxes upon the industry.

The mining industry has come to use a rising number of subcontractors, ranging from globally oriented corporations to smaller locally based businesses. Yet, these contracting relations, which are more intensive than in earlier decades, do not appear to be a major source of value for leading capitalists based in Caribbean nations or the wider Caribbean diaspora. They, however, do appear to serve as a way in which some local and large businesses are seeking to link into transnational chains of accumulation, and some massive TNCs such as SODEXO are becoming active in the region.

Transnational capitalists and global investors, though they mostly hail from wealthier nations, now operate through globally competitive relations, transitioning from the earlier international phase to the global phase of world capitalism (Robinson, 2003). At times in recent decades, mining projects in the Dominican Republic and Jamaica, as well as mining excavation in Haiti, have received new infusions of transnational capitalist investment. A number of mining excavation firms and larger TNCs have proposed new or restructured projects in the region, and received the backing of top state officials.

From the 1980s and especially into the 1990s, Caribbean states undertook policies to contract out and privatize state mining operations, which by the twenty-first century resulted in local conditions highly conducive for exploratory firms and transnational mining conglomerates. Even as state apparatuses have increasingly disengaged from a direct role in mining, resource extraction remains a major "developmental strategy" for transnationally oriented policy makers in the Caribbean region. State apparatus and supranational agency officials are seeking to jumpstart mining in economically fragile areas, even if it means violating domestic constitutional law, as in Haiti. On both sides of the Dominican-Haitian border, resource extraction zones are being cordoned off for mining TNCs and exploration companies.

A number of untapped mineral deposits remain in the region. Gold and silver are so highly valued and rare that some neoliberal state policy makers, facing protests and demands from local populations, might renegotiate contracts for these most resource rich zones, such as has occurred recently in the Dominican Republic (Jiménez, 2013). In general, however, transnationally oriented state elites and technocrats, bypassing input from local communities and overlooking issues of sustainability, have promoted increasingly accessible juridical and regulatory frameworks to entice transnational capitalist investors. Across the Caribbean, TNCs have come to dominate mining operations. Mining in the region looks set to continue and in some locations intensify over the coming decades as extractivist programs deepen, whereas in some areas (such as in Haiti) it remains unclear how local conditions will impact the industry. How these material relations unfold will ultimately be determined by social struggles and new initiatives on the ground.

Transnational capitalists in many industries, including mining, have developed by operating under new globally competitive conditions. This will continue to be a historical process replete with contradictions, as changing phases of capitalism eventually develop economic crises and stagnation or upsurges from working people and other marginalized groups (as can be seen in the many struggles against mining corporations by labor, activists, and local communities in the Caribbean and Latin America). The different historical phases of mining in the region have been replete with labor and community protests, such as with the recent strike by open pit miners in Cerrejón on Colombia's Caribbean coast (Vieira, 2013). Recognizing the shifting political economy of the industry, researchers and activists need to consider how local communities, labor, environmentalist campaigners, and social and political movements can best organize to generate progressive reforms and alternative structural conditions. As others have argued (Liodakis, 2010; Robinson,

2014a), in the face of capitalist relations that are integrating transnationally across borders, movements and projects from below need to seek out new forms of organizing that will coordinate and link their efforts across frontiers.

It remains to be seen how a structural alternative can come about, how a humanistic alternative to the exploitative nature of the global mining industry can come into existence. One thing is clear: successful challenges to global industry require that movements from below transnationalize their struggle, working in coordination with social, political, labor, and environmental movements across frontiers.

Conclusion

Transnational Processes and the Restructuring of the Caribbean's Political Economy

This book focuses on the Caribbean region's contradictory integration into global capitalism in recent decades. I have explored the structural processes that led to its transition into the new global stage of world capitalism by examining four major areas—tourism, export processing, mining, and migration and the reverse flow of remittances. Markets once segmented by national frontiers or connected externally through international trade are fragmenting and becoming functionally integrated across borders.

At the core of this transition is the transformation of relations of production. Whereas earlier class relations were rooted largely *within* international production relations, we now see the rise of class relations rooted in transnational production. As outlined in the conclusion of Chapter 1, I see five strategic traits as unfolding across the region: (1) the rise of a transnational financial system into which Caribbean society has become integrated, (2) the envelopment of the region by transnational networks of production, (3) the exploitation and marginalization of the popular classes in relation to global capitalism, (4) the emergence of transnationally oriented state elites in the Caribbean, and (5) new subcontractor networks through which, for instance, local business groups are deepening their transnational orientation.

Many powerful interests operating through big businesses and state apparatuses have had a role in influencing developmental patterns (away from previous indicative models and toward transnational accumulation), to ensure their own self-reproduction and to expand market profits. This has included U.S. state and other top elites seeking the breakup of political projects promoting ISI in the late twentieth century (as ISI policies were meant in different ways to promote nationally oriented development). Similarly, U.S. officials, many top elites, and their allied strata in different parts of the world have worked to undermine alternatives (such as the ALBA alliance and attempts at endogenous development in the early twenty-first century). Today's most powerful forces have helped instead to facilitate capitalist economic integration that is transnational in nature and in many ways unmoored from local needs and local control. Yet, this remains a process riven with internal tensions.

Ultimately, capitalist development is geared to capital accumulation as an end in itself rather than toward social transformation according to socially determined goals. While many factors exist, the main variable determining developmental options is the organization of production toward private capital accumulation. It is class power that masks what transpires in the global division of labor, around which the right to exploit and accumulate capital are organized.

This historical process has not been smooth but has in fact entailed a number of significant crises, including: (1) social polarization, with transnational capitalists obtaining unimaginable levels of wealth while working and lower-income people face exploitation, marginalization, and exclusion; (2) a crisis of political legitimacy as state policy makers seek to maintain the loyalty of their local constituencies even as they intensify policies meant to benefit transnational capital; (3) as discussed briefly in Chapter 2, this also occurs alongside catastrophic climate change propelled by industrialization and carbon intensive consumption; and, (4) as also briefly discussed in Chapter 2, the endemic instability of capitalism through its overaccumulation and cyclical crises.

The global capitalist system thus is tenuous and conflict ridden. National circuits of accumulation are being subsumed to transnational ones. Fierce resistance continues to occur, and in what is becoming a globalizing class struggle from below (from the Seattle protests in 1998 to the worldwide protests over the rising cost of rice in 2009).

On both the regional and global levels, the goal of transnational capitalists is to overtake the competition and to get rid of workers whenever possible. We see this with the rise of "Toyotism" (Dohse et al., 1985), the flexibilized and computerized oligopolistic lean manufacturing of recent decades, and now the emergence of "Uberism," a highly flexibilized and increasingly computerized oligopolistic service sector. Of course, there are different issues at play here. One is automation, which capital uses to break resistance and eliminate jobs, another is the drive for efficiency in manufacturing (in the drive to create more surplus value). Efficiency and automation are not entirely bad things, as they can lead to better uses of resources and less wasted labor time. However, we must ask: efficiency and automation for what? This is because under capitalism these are used primarily to expand profits for a small ruling elite.[1] Raising the development of productive forces can lead to improved conditions for some, but without an alternative to capitalism they occur as part of a system of growing inequality and environmental destruction. While capital during earlier historical phases also waged war on the poor and upon nature, this has taken on new dynamics under globalization. Alongside these global fissures, though, are major organizational and technological advancements, allowing for so many new kinds of products, and with increased access to important goods and services.

However, global competition ultimately is felt throughout the lives of workers, as workers have less and less control over the conditions of their social reproduction. Heavy investment in robotics, artificial intelligence, and other smart tools brings this reality increasingly to light, as CEOs of various companies are charting out future plans to eliminate more and more labor or re-create more precarious workforces. Any interest capital has shown in "national economic development" in the past is now at odds with its aims under capitalist globalization.

While many state officials claim to be promoting so-called national economic development this is not capital's priority, and surely not *transnational* capital's priority. Although some state leaders, seeking to offset the crisis of legitimacy they face, implement some domestically geared policies or pay lip service to their local constituents, their allegiance to the accumulation networks of transnational capital is made clear by their backroom trade deals made between corporations and with states, the protection of intellectual property rights globally to protect certain transnational capitalist interests, and so on. Many differences within the TCC exist, and we can often see these contradictions playing out within the political scene of the national state.

Globalization has demonstrated the inevitable consequences of the development of capital's internal dynamics to freely roam the earth—an ugly race to the bottom for many, fought through class struggle and whereas many trying to survive are desperate for the crumbs left by the rich and powerful. This has all taken place against the backdrop of uneven and combined development that occurs increasingly through transnational processes that envelop many dynamics in our global society and global economy. Caribbean-based ruling elites, as well as elites from other regions around the world are compelled to forge transnational alliances to ensure their survival. Similarly, workers from the Caribbean and elsewhere fight to survive or to migrate, with expectations of a better livelihood for themselves in a globalizing economy.

What we have then is a relationship of states and classes to the global system that is transforming as transnational business interests articulate interests that are tied less and less to the territoriality of nation-states, even while built environments do remain important. While the significance of the north-south divide continues in a major way, powerful transnational capitalist groups have emerged throughout both the global south and the global north, whose interests lie in the transnational over national economies and the older international processes. Rather than core and peripheral nation-states, I have argued that the core and periphery can be seen more as denoting social groups in a transnational setting.

Globalization of the Caribbean: Summation of Findings

This book is rooted in a historical materialist approach, but one that calls into question the state-centrism inherent in many interpretations of production relations. Taking a "global capitalism school" approach, and specifically relying on the theory of transnational processes (Robinson, 2003, pp. 10–27), this book argues that global capitalism is in a new stage of its ongoing evolution. This new stage is characterized by the transnational reorganization of production and finance and the transnationalization of class relations. This book breaks from the many studies that rely on an international monopoly-capital, new imperialism, or world systems view of nation-state competition forming the core organizing principle of the world economy and the institutional framework through which global social forces operate. Rather than viewing social and material relations as constrained within the nation-state and the back-and-forth relations of the interstate system, we need to consider how many of these relations are undergoing a process of transnationalization in this new stage of capitalism. As transnational capital subsumes former national and international circuits of accumulation, deep structural shifts occurring in regions such as the Caribbean are cutting across traditional frontiers and barriers in novel ways. Yet, at the same time, Caribbean policymakers face a dilemma as many businesspeople operating within the region find themselves facing a distinct disadvantage in competing with capital operating out of more advanced built environments abroad, and as large parts of Caribbean society are marginalized from the global economy.

The chapters in this book have shown how capital is reorganizing accumulation in the Caribbean region into new transnational circuits. For example, Chapter 7 observed how in the decades following World War II, U.S. capital subsidized through the "national security" Cold War policies of the U.S. government, began mining operations in the Caribbean. Some local Caribbean state policy makers, especially during the 1970s, meanwhile attempted to control portions of the new international operations that came about. Yet with the onset of the global era, U.S. government subsidies for mining in the region dried up and over time Caribbean governments were compelled (and advised by IFIs) to privatize their mining assets. This fragmentation of the earlier model gave way to the rise of transnational mining corporations in the region, who operate globally and are cross invested with TNCs and transnational capitalists around the world.

These changes have occurred through dominant groups facilitating new accumulation networks, in the process compelling workers to incorporate their labor power into transnational value chains. Chapter 4, for instance, discussed the problematic socioeconomic transformation of the cruise ship industry over recent decades and in the context of the Caribbean region. The industry's new era of cross-border integration and global competitiveness has occurred alongside new flexibilized labor regimes, a standardization of the passenger experience, and new business strategies seeking to exploit and finely manage local inputs. The owners and executives of major cruise companies have come to epitomize transnational capitalists—implicated functionally across borders in transnational processes and of circuits of capital accumulation.

Chapter 5 explained how Caribbean migrants living abroad have become objectively linked to their families and communities at home in a new manner through transnational remittances. Yet, this objective relation takes place through circuits of capital that are controlled by TNCs. These corporations operate by expropriating in a *new* way a portion of the value produced by migrant workers. Here again we see a qualitative shift in the region's political economy: the replacement of *national* and *international* circuits of accumulations by *transnational* circuits of accumulation. Previously, during the international phase of world capitalism, small levels of money transfers occurred through local banks across cumbersome international circuits. This has now exploded into a transnational phenomenon. Moreover, migration has come to serve as a mechanism for lower-income communities to export their labor from "underdeveloped countries," with the remittances they send home serving as part of a new developmental model linking local business interests, state elites, and wide swaths of the population in the region to transnational finance capital. Global finance not only immerses regional businesses into transnational capital flows but also connects exploited working-class people to each other across borders via these remittance networks. However, as Caribbean people become embedded within transnational remittance networks, new inequalities have emerged among community members. Politicians in the region meanwhile have justified withdrawing the state from its social responsibilities, claiming that remittances provide a sufficient cushion for lower-income populations.

Chapter 6 looked at the novel export-processing model of the global era and emphasized how dynamic new production networks have come about in the region. This chapter demonstrated how capital is no longer motivated by or conducive to contributing to a so-called national objective, contrary to the argument of Karagiannis and Polychroniou (2015). Capital is not interested in national job creation or transforming the productive powers of labor. Instead, transnational capital and transnationally oriented state policy makers promote globalized production mechanisms through which the interests of labor and local communities are regularly eschewed. Yes, some workers gain jobs through different developments, and new consumer options come about, but the overriding drive of capital is to make profits. While capital in previous historical periods also exploited labor and local communities, the national and international process through which it existed could make it appear as if it were engaged in "national development." So, one could more easily be led to falsely believe that capital's interests were one and the same with the nation. Under globalization the mask has fallen.

As I point out in Chapter 6, transnational capital and elites promoting export processing in the Caribbean, face significant difficulties—as, in addition to other factors, the built economic environments in the region remain less developed in comparison to other areas more conducive to capitalist production, such as in parts of Mexico or areas of East Asia, China, most notably (Bernal, 2014). Also, as I point out, the globally competitive export-processing model depends heavily on flexibilized, feminized, and negatively racialized labor.

It has been my argument here, echoing Robinson (2003), Harris (2006), Liodakis (2010), and H. Watson (2013), that there is emerging a gradual disembedding of social classes, structures, and institutions from the nation-state context. My argument is not that nation-states, borders, or uneven development are not important. Rather, I suggest that the social configuration of space is shifting as production relations become transnationalized (this includes the role of technologies such as the internet). With in-depth research in three Caribbean countries (the Dominican Republic, Haiti, and Jamaica) and with some brief research visits and notes on other parts of the region I have illustrated the unevenness and particularities of this new configuration. Groups operating through regions such as the Caribbean, and nations and zones within and across them, have developed their own profiles in the global era, with their own special niches in the global economy. I have suggested in this book that we need to reconsider political economy in light of a qualitative shift in social formation, without disregarding continuities and differentiations.

The tensions and contradictions of global capitalism in the region are apparent, aggravating new class dynamics as well as leading to state policies that are increasingly disconnected from the interests of local communities and locally oriented development. These developments in the Caribbean occur alongside intensifying global inequalities. Around the world we see a trend toward growing social polarization, as wealth becomes concentrated in the hands of the global "1 percent" (or, more accurately, the "0.01 percent"), a sector of global society that includes a rising number of transnational capitalists from or active in the region. Yet the nationally aggregated data we have for understanding social polarization, such as GDP, present an indication of "national wealth." The problem here is that this deemphasizes the interconnected nature of a country's population with the global economy. It does not take into account, for instance, the transnational spread of capital flows and many segments of the global investment portfolios and cross-border M&A of local and diasporic capitalists or foreign-based capitalists active in the region, nor the way in which working-class populations have their life savings in accounts at banks linked into transnational financial chains.

Nationally aggregated data remain an indicator (and as most data sets remain aggregated in this way), for examining social polarization empirically. According to World Bank data, for instance, in the Dominican Republic as of 2013, the poorest quintile of the population had a 3.8 percent share of the nation's GDP, whereas the richest quintile had 53.5 percent share (ECLAC, 2014). Yet looking at social polarization through the scope of this nationally aggregated data ignores how these "national populations" have become entwined with a diaspora and other social groups active in the global economy. An accurate picture of global wealth, with, for example, the complex transnational spread of investments and use of tax havens by the TCC, would better demonstrate the dramatic nature of inequality, skewed in favor of the planet's top quintile. In addition to the many studies on the TCC that I have cited in the previous chapters, many other recent studies of the wealth and power of the "super class" show the extreme concentration of capital among the highest echelons of global society (Rothkopf, 2009).

Another major contradiction associated with capitalist globalization is the crisis of legitimacy, which in part stems from the abandonment by state managers of national development as they seek transnational integration. Their growing detachment from locally oriented development has been made possible as a restructuring of the world economy has occurred alongside political restructuring. Emphasizing economic development through incorporation with global capital, state functionaries increasingly have come to work to transfer state resources from "program oriented ministries (social services, education, labor, etc.) to central banks, treasuries and finance and economic ministries, and the foreign ministry" (Robinson 2001, p. 186). Over recent decades, more and more state elites have shared in this project, which is ultimately in the interest of the TCC. While state functionaries still engage in long-established functions (taxation, public works, etc.), these are now geared in many ways toward global accumulation (such as creating deepwater ports or supply chains and infrastructure to benefit first and foremost transnational capital). The very social reproduction of many state elites has come to depend on transnational, rather than national or international, circuits of capitalist accumulation (Robinson, 2014a). Increasingly, state technocrats believe that to develop they must insert their national states and institutions into global circuits of accumulation (Robinson, 2010b; Domínguez, 1996). They need access to capital, and capital is in the hands of the TCC. However, state elites must still appeal to their home audiences. They still interact with a variety of locally based communities.

Of course, globalization creates new spaces for rethinking the political paradigm, as the theme "workers of the world unite" is perhaps more apt now than in Marx's time. We need to understand furthermore how the difficulties that the working and popular classes face now are also rooted in the victories and defeats of earlier historical eras and the processes this has set into motion. In regard to victories, we can see how many of the social programs and laws benefiting working people in the region were put in place after major struggles from below, pressuring dominant groups. In regard to defeats: a magnificent and malevolent job, for instance, was done in the late 1940s to early 1950s to undermine the fledgling working-class movements in many parts of the Caribbean, with the crushing of the CLC by Cold War enthusiasts from abroad and within the region, the consequences of which are still evident today. This is the historical climate on top of which EPZ production formed in the latter twentieth century.

To get more at the context of the difficulties facing popular and grassroots forces in the region, it is important to note how already during the twentieth century radical labor unionism was overpowered in many nations by business unionism, a strategy heavily facilitated by U.S. Cold War policies. The ongoing strategies of amending labor laws to accommodate the demands of the TCC is a logical extension of strategies of many labor organizations and mainstream political parties that have been consistently anti–working class for most of the decades following World War II. In some instances, unions have even come to rely on funding sources traced back to powerful U.S. agencies (Scipes, 2011; Sprague, 2008), as part of a larger trend of many groups from below becoming compromised and undermined over recent decades.

Numerous progressive and leftist social and political movements do exist across the Caribbean, but cross-border coordination and solidarity remains largely underdeveloped as does the development of long-term structural alternatives. Caribbean movements in particular suffer from a lack of infrastructure and resources. The antineoliberal state alliance ALBA had begun to forge some small new forms of cross-border infrastructure in the region, yet in recent years this project has been weakened, for a number of factors, among them being intensively targeted through destabilization strategies (many hatched or backed by Washington), through advanced economic, political, and media measures. The "pink tide" countries in Latin America, and especially Bolivarian Venezuela and revolutionary Cuba have faced many structural problems (such as the massive decrease in commodity prices, revenues from which these projects had invested in social spending). It is unclear how these social and political forces will weather the mounting right-wing counteroffensive taking shape across the hemisphere—but whatever the case the struggle *will* continue.

Future Research

The Caribbean and regions around the world are now entangled in the novel production relations of capitalist globalization. Beyond the case studies in this book, what other economic sectors in the Caribbean do we need to examine in light of the new class relations? Future research could look at the structural features of transnational banking and tax havens (especially with the rise of cryptocurrencies), real estate, logistics and supply chains, import sales industries, and the narco trade.

These sectors are also important because their interests become embedded in many state apparatuses, such as the relationship of real estate businesses to local state actors, playing an important role in blocking local grassroots initiatives.

We might think more strategically, for instance, about "logistics" in the Caribbean, given that Cuban policy makers are trying to position their country as a "logistics hub" in the region, and whereas Jamaican officials and business leaders have also been "making noise" for such an option for themselves as well.

Each of these areas of research is a major site of transnational penetration, undergoing major changes in the global phase of world capitalism and of prime import for the lives of many people, and becomes a potential site of labor protest and organizing from below. Studies of these sectors through the "global capitalism school" approach would continue to enrich our understanding of transnational capitalism in the region. Any ongoing research agenda into global capitalism in the Caribbean needs to look also at additional data and research on capital flows, inequality, and gendered and racialized class relations, as well as on sexuality in the transnational era.

While I have only skimmed the surface of some of these topics, further research needs to examine also the connection of transnational capitalism to environmental crisis and in the context of the Caribbean. More work needs to be done on contemporary political, labor, and social movements and their struggles in the Caribbean during the transition to globalization, as examining these in more detail would prove imperative for a further understanding of the phenomena examined here. So too we need to look more at those marginalized and sidelined in global society and at how they are being targeted in new ways by state authorities and dominant groups. How do their lives connect and disconnect with the global economy? These research topics are central for understanding a way out of the crises facing human civilization and the planet and for thinking more about *what can be* and *what needs to be done*. The topics in this study and future studies can help us understand how dominant groups are reproducing themselves. Ultimately, class struggles, along with democratic socialist, environmentalist, feminist, antiracist, and antihomophobic struggles, bring forward the emancipatory role of human agency in the context of the global era, and lead us to consider how a global consciousness can be brought about. It forces us to consider the linkages and forms of solidarity between working and popular classes that need to be formed, and the institutions and infrastructure that is required. Just as the TCC has increasingly come to see itself as a self-conscious class, how too can working and popular classes achieve a transnational or global class consciousness? A global consciousness from below.

In this book I have applied the theory of *transnational processes* to the Caribbean in an original way and in doing so help advance the theory. My empirical study is, of course, open to distinct interpretations. My case studies have been largely based on a structural analysis but have also engaged in a relational analysis of historical processes. I have found bringing these forms of analysis together useful for understanding the underlying causality of the processes we are examining. While a number of critical political economy studies have examined nations in the Caribbean and long-term historical process, no broad studies of the region's socioeconomic and political economic structural features as of yet have used the theory of transnational processes. Here, I have aimed to look critically at how these dynamics have taken root and reproduced in the region.

The spatially (and even more important, the *socially*) uneven basis of capitalist production and accumulation and the need to cover the entire globe, drives capital into areas and population centers that might otherwise seem marginal—places with small populations, small landmasses, small labor forces, and limited means to expand production. Capital is compelled to try to drive downward to reduce the average global price of labor, unsatisfied until it covers and dominates the entire world, and this is where it is now poised; however, capital is not victorious. Of course, if you were to ask many people in the world about this point you might get answers from more than a few who reflect resignation, cynicism, and defeatism. Alienation stalks everything, chauvinism and conservative religious forces become a salve, and the tendency to read history backward becomes pervasive, blaming others (or ourselves) for all the contradictions in our lives, without any clear sense of capitalism and what it entails.[2] Global capitalist integration and exploitation necessitate repressive and manipulative responses, and it soon becomes very clear that the options before us are either a postcapitalist progressive world or barbarism.

Once the slave-plantation outposts of European colonialism and then a domain of U.S. imperialism, over recent decades the Caribbean has become engulfed in novel forms of accumulation and social relations as transnational capitalists have descended upon and sprouted in the region. This book has offered an account of the Caribbean's integration into today's novel global capitalist system, as a product of the interplay of class dynamics and institutional apparatuses operating on local and global levels over the closing decades of the twentieth century and the early decades of twenty-first century. The emergence of globalizing transnational capitalism carries extraordinary consequences for regions around the world, including the Caribbean basin.

As working and lower-income populations in their labor and consumption are more and more entwined with transnational circuits of accumulation, they are beginning to become functionally integrated across borders through their productive relations, remittance networks, global communications, and other activities. Social forces in the region, while conditioned in many ways by local particularities, are entering a qualitatively new era of transnational integration and inequality. Working and popular classes in the Caribbean and worldwide must move toward new forms of solidarity and organizing, not only within nations but also functionally across borders— seeing how our struggles for justice and equality are interlinked. Even when surrounded by intensely negative conditions, we must not forget that human society and its future is what we make of it.

Notes

CHAPTER 1

1. International Bank for Reconstruction and Development and the World Bank. (2014). Investing in people to fight poverty in Haiti (p. 8). Washington, DC. Retrieved from http://documents.worldbank.org/curated/en/222901468029372321/pdf/944300v1 0REPLA0sment0EN0web0version.pdf.

2. The circuit of capital occurs through ruthless competitive processes where the capitalists function to promote an integration and spread of the system, but as agents, they have only a certain level of autonomy within this process. Exploitation of labor is central to the process (Marx, 1867/1992, chapter 2; Wright, 1980). The technologies and the primacy of one form of capital over another change, but the exploitation of labor continues.

In some instances, earlier classes and social groups have been reconfigured, even while maintaining many of their previous dynamics and appearances. They may remain tied to the national state in various ways (such as through their subjectivity or various activities), even while becoming objectively rooted in globalized chains of accumulation. For example, many in the region's popular classes, while locally rooted in many ways, are entering into transnational chains of accumulation through businesses such as those involved in global tourism, mining, remittances, and export processing. Banking, communications, and consumer activities further link vast populations into globalizing economic and societal relations. Transformation and preservation are thus dialectically (mutually) constitutive. The nation form, for instance, is a means to an end rather than an end in itself.

3. The term "transnational" has become quite popular in academic parlance and is sometimes, in my view, mistakenly used to describe processes occurring in earlier historical periods under which transnational processes were not yet emergent. The term is often used interchangeably with "international," ignoring how they describe fundamentally different dynamics.

One might argue that embryonic transnational processes occurred *quantitatively* in earlier times (with people moving around and being displaced more often and over wider distances, with the rise of earlier, slower remittance systems such as during the post–World War II years, and with the spread of laboring diasporas long before that). However, in my view, we do not see transnationalism qualitatively emerging (and continuing to heighten into its open-ended and uncertain future) until the shift in productive forces and social relations during, roughly, the last quarter of the twentieth century and into the twenty-first century.

In my view, the term "transnational" might be useful to describe some subjective dynamics occurring in earlier periods, for example, in the way that Basch, Schiller, and Blanc (1993) and others deploy transnationalism to think about how migrants and others form subjective bonds across nations, developing a particular kind of consciousness. Yet this subjective dynamic becomes all the more pronounced in recent decades as transnational *objective* processes begin to form.

One way of seeing the distinction between international and transnational objective processes is in relation to the world economy. "Internationalization," Robinson (2004) argues, "involves the simple extension of economic activities across national boundaries and is essentially a quantitative process that leads to a more extensive geographical pattern of economic activity . . . [whereas] transnationalization differs qualitatively from internationalization processes, involving not merely the geographical extension of economic activity across national boundaries but also the functional integration of such internationally dispersed activities" (p. 14). Many factors have contributed to this, among them, the unprecedented technological revolution made possible by the development of the microprocessor, leading to leaps in coordinative and labor-eliminating computer technologies across sectors, but especially in communications, transportation, and capital-intensive production (Baptist and Rehmann, 2011). While playing an important role, technology is not *the* driving force of the changes that are occurring. The most important factor has been the *human* role in constructing our shifting social and material relations. How this will play out in the future, though, is uncertain (with the rise of artificial intelligence).

4. As Marx and Engels write in the *German Ideology*: "We set out from real, active men, and on the basis of their real life-process we demonstrate the development of the ideological reflexes and echoes of their life-processes" (1998, p. 47).

5. The unfolding of different phases of the capitalist mode of production in the region can be seen not just in the new technologies and other productive forces but also through changing labor-capital relations. Importantly, during certain periods, while a mode of production dominates, other earlier kinds of production can still be found. A case in point is the shift from slave labor to private peasant production and ultimately to waged labor in the Caribbean, each representing a new form of capitalist exploitation. There are many instances of overlap between these forms of exploitation: for example, when alongside the emergence of waged labor there still existed pockets of peasant production, as Post (1978) mentions in regard to Jamaica.

While in slavery the laborer is unfree, his or her oppression is open, not hidden or veiled as in free labor. There is, of course, a distinction between "owning" workers outright as property (chattel slavery) and "renting" workers (wage labor). With the abolition or overthrow of slavery, many former slaves moved into small-scale peasant production. While peasants do not live under formal slavery, they are tied to the land in different ways. By contrast, waged workers are not tied to the land and are formally free, as their work does not consist of physical enslavement (though the demands on their time can be systematic, having to clock in and being ensured of their indebtedness). The waged workers' true lack of freedom is hidden because capital rules over him or her, while human social relations and the peculiar forms of exploitation under capitalism are portrayed as commodities for exchange. Instead of the creators of objects, working people are treated as objects themselves.

Workers "undergo a dialectical inversion" as they suffer the effects of capitalist development; they become disconnected from the reproduction of their own existence (Marx, 1869/1994, p. 798). As Marx writes, "They distort the worker into a fragment of a man; they degrade him to the level of an appendage of a machine; they destroy the actual content of his labor by turning it into a torment; they alienate from him the intellectual potentialities of the labor process" (p. 798). He describes this process of "social alienation" as occurring on four levels: (1) alienation from production, (2) alienation from process, (3) alienation from human being, and (4) alienation from species being.

Elites in the region also face changing circumstances. Initially, planter elites (the slave-plantation owners) became the dominant class in the region under colonialism. But, at different instances, they were displaced by other factions of capital, were overthrown by revolutionary movements, or reconstituted themselves and helped facilitate political and economic transitions. Other changes took place as well. Whereas the colonial systems had often privileged metropole-based enterprises, the decline of colonialism (or its restructuring as a less insular enterprise) occurred alongside the rise of international monopoly capital. In the decades after World War II, policy makers operating through U.S. government apparatuses and the new Washington Consensus institutions helped to further facilitate the integration of many former and transitioning European colonies into international webs of finance and debt (Panitch and Gindin, 2013). The larger backdrop to the turbulence of recent decades has been the integration of the region into the new global capitalism, with novel rearrangements taking place among its social groups and classes. The objective social and class conditions that have formed can thus be understood as rooted in the capitalist mode of production and its altered phases.

6. Along similar lines, Arrighi (1983; Robinson, 2010a) argued that international monopoly capitalism and Lenin's theory of nation-state imperialism held firmly for the period from 1875 to 1945. It was also roughly during this period that British imperialism, as Arthur W. Lewis (1978) argues, retarded in different ways the economic development of its colonies. Meanwhile, Anievas (2014) helps us consider how the rise of Nazism and Fascism was linked into the broader containment and interventionist policies launched by the Western imperial states and international monopoly capital targeting the Soviet Union from its very early days. In the decades following World War II, a heightened internationalization of capital occurred, with the U.S. state apparatus fundamental to pushing this process forward (Panitch and Gindin, 2013).

7. Within each historical phase of world capitalism it can be useful to identify different subphases. For instance, within the phase of international monopoly capitalism there have been subphases: (1) an initial subphase during the late nineteenth and early twentieth centuries when international monopolies blocked free enterprises from growing in a number of branches of national economies, (2) the decades following World War I during which national governments stopped representing the interests of the entire capitalist class and instead worked on the interests of monopoly capitalists in order to impose conditions favorable for their monopolies' growth, and (3) the period after World War II when vast arrays of state mechanisms were created for developing international markets and financial growth, becoming a springboard into a new phase (Panitch and Gindin, 2013; Regalado, 2007, p. 19).

8. For more on these internal contradictions, see the work of Moshe Lewin (2016), Richard Sakwa (2013), and Michael Lebowitz (2012). They discuss the problems that the Soviet project faced, such as the centralization of decision making, periods of budget crisis, problems associated with attempts to integrate more deeply into the world economy, and a structurally militarized economy with a high proportion of resources needed to service the military as the eastern bloc was under constant aggression from the West (see also Agee and Wolf, 1988; Blum, 1995/2003).

9. Panitch and Gindin (2013) argue that the U.S. national state and "American MNCs" found key allies abroad among many dominant groups, as various state elites and dominant class fractions worldwide stood to gain through neoliberal reforms. This can be seen with regard to China, where local neoliberal elites and businesspeople saw as advantageous many of the U.S.-promoted policies. As these domestic class forces gained power within the Chinese Communist Party in the final decades of the twentieth century, the authors explain that this allowed for the United States and China to become deeply interlocked, with "American MNCs" buying up privatized Chinese assets, as Chinese enterprises invested heavily in U.S. treasury bonds.

10. See among numerous other studies, Burnham et al., 2006; Pilger and Lowery, 2000.

11. Many important questions have been raised about how to best substantiate the changes taking place (Embong, 2000).

12. Breaking into these protected markets situated in the Atlantic world, pirates and others would at times attempt to pillage them (Linebaugh and Rediker, 2013).

13. Sidney Mintz writes in more detail: "There grew up, in effect, two so-called triangles of trade, both of which arose in the seventeenth century and matured in the eighteenth. The first and most famous triangle linked Britain to Africa and to the New World: finished goods were sold to Africa, African slaves to the Americas, and the American tropical commodities (especially sugar) to the mother country and her importing neighbors. The second triangle functioned in a manner contradictory to the mercantilist ideal. From New England went rum to Africa, whence slaves to the West Indies, whence molasses back to New England (with which to make rum). The maturation of this second triangle put the New England colonies on a political collision course with Britain, but the underlying problems were economic, taking on political import precisely because they brought divergent economic interests into confrontation" (Mintz, 1986, p. 43).

14. One problem in the scholarly literature on the Caribbean has been the isolation of scholarly studies, as researchers with different backgrounds and languages and in different academic settings often do not take into account the works of others writing on similar phenomena. For instance, research on the Anglophone Caribbean tends to ignore the Francophone and Hispanophone, and vice versa. While part of this is a simple problem of different languages, it is also in part a reflection of a cultural hangover from imperialism. For instance, within the Anglophone Caribbean this takes on the shape of British imperialism's "moral epistemology," which cultivated the notion that others must study English because it is the universal language of commerce (A. Thompson, 1997).

Gordon Lewis examined the moral epistemology of empire, how it spanned the Caribbean from English- to French- and Spanish-speaking areas of the West Indies (G. Lewis, 1968, 1987). The cultural hangover from imperialism was so strong that, for instance, European policy makers were pleasantly shocked and surprised to see how easy it was to deal in the postcolonial moment with the leaders of the people they had colonized and dehumanized for so long (Kiernan, 1969). British imperialists expressed amazement and great satisfaction that they had succeeded in creating black and brown men who they felt had so fully internalized British values and cultural norms (Kiernan, 1969).

15. While merchant enterprises had already existed for many centuries, the labor-capitalist relation and the associated relations of production ultimately developed as a fundamentally new relation, and in part as a response to the crisis of feudalism (H. Watson, 2015, p. 384). In the Caribbean, rural conflicts of "primitive accumulation" also occurred, such as through the struggle between landlords and peasants (Hilton, 1990; Linebaugh and Rediker, 2013). Dupuy (2015) makes important points with regard to the capitalist underdevelopment of Haiti's countryside and the international forces arrayed against its people. He elaborates on changing rural social patterns and shows how, with the rise of a landed peasantry, efforts by the landed bourgeoisie to defeat, expropriate, and proletarianize the population were to some extent stymied. He argues that this limited the ability of local dominant groups to develop national infrastructure and a more diversified economy and led to their procuring wealth primarily by the distribution rather than the production of goods (Dupuy, 2015). Eventually, it was the intensification of foreign capital investment that imposed proletarianization on many of Haiti's small and subsistence farmers, creating a pool of surplus labor for businesses operating in the cities and compelling many to export their labor abroad.

Here it is useful to briefly trace the historical background of inequality and provide some signposts toward understanding a class analysis. Archaic *Homo sapiens* evolved to anatomically modern humans in Africa between one hundred thousand and two hundred thousand years ago. Some began leaving Africa around sixty thousand years ago. For tens of thousands of years humans mainly lived in small egalitarian nomadic and subsistence societies. It was only around fifteen thousand to eight thousand years ago that some small fishing and agricultural settlements appeared, where archeologists believe that some small levels of surplus began to lead for the first time to a very, very low level of inequality (Pringle, 2014). The earliest civilization rose between forty-five hundred and five thousand years ago in lower Mesopotamia and along the Nile, Indus, Yellow, and Yangtze Rivers. Inequality became structured in qualitatively new ways through the rise of new modes of production, of which the capitalist mode of production is only the most recent (Harman, 2008). As such, large-scale inequality—and class systems especially—is a fairly recent phenomenon in human history.

16. Often so busy and worn down from working—not to mention competing with one another—they largely eschew union organizing (much like modern-day Uber drivers).

17. This was part of the plantation system's architecture, as large slave populations were required for intensive plantation production. In the West Indies a low slave population could mean disastrously low productivity. For example, when British forces briefly occupied parts of Cuba during the eighteenth-century Seven Years' War, some officials complained that the island was too lightly populated with slaves and that more slaves would be required to expand agricultural productivity on the island (Horne, 2014b).

18. Marx gets at this process when he writes: "The fact that we now not only call the plantation owners in America capitalists, but that they *are* capitalists, is based on their existence as anomalies within a world market based on free labour" (1869/1994, p. 513). As is clear, capitalist slavery functioned in ways fundamentally different to the slavery of the ancients (O. Patterson, 1982; Snowden, 1983; Williams, 1944; and see this excellent critique of Patterson: Fleming, 2016).

19. Countries in the periphery, Clive Thomas argued, had more fragile social orders as compared to countries in the core (1984, p. 56). He added that the popular classes in poorer regions, such as the Caribbean, were larger and regularly faced harsher conditions due to the lack of industrial production, manufacturing, and assembly of consumer goods for urban and high-income markets. By the 1980s although the service sector employed a growing part of the labor force, most businesses were small, except for some government enterprises (p. 56). Women workers were often relegated to households and tax haven export zones. With most businesses employing small numbers of people, working-class unionized action was underdeveloped (p. 56).

20. For example, in his analysis of class warfare in mid-nineteenth century Paris, Marx defined fractions within the French bourgeoisie class as (1) unproductive finance capitalists and (2) productive industrial capitalists. Within the French working class, he identified an unproductive lumpenproletariat and a productive proletariat. Describing the class fractions and strata aligned against the Paris Commune of 1871, he listed the "aristocracy of finance, the industrial bourgeoisie, the middle class, the petit bourgeoisie, the army, the lumpenproletariat organized as the Mobile Guard, the intellectual lights, the clergy and the rural population" (Marx, 1869/1994).

21. It is important to note that other approaches do exist for studying structural features of society, most important, the Weberian perspective (Weber, 1958), which describes different spheres of society (such as status groups, public officials, and pluralist interest groups). Weber does not look at the nature of the interactions and interdependencies generated by the use of resources in productive activity. Instead, he directs his analysis of social relations toward a set of normative concerns centered, above all, on business communities' interests, such as the efficiency and rationalization of business relations (though he does, in passing, recognize problems that workers face). Rather than understanding society as divided according to humanity's relation to the production and acquisition of goods, Weber describes "status groups" as being stratified according to the "principles of their consumption of goods" as represented by special "styles of life," and so on.

22. On the labor regime used in the Spanish colonies to exploit the Caribbean's indigenous, Patricia Seed writes: "Trusteeships were in fact deliberately constructed differently from slavery or serfdom because royal interests were at stake. While [Queen] Isabel was perfectly willing to coerce native to mine gold with little or no payment, she drew the line at slavery because slavery involved *private* ownership of labour, whereas she wanted to establish *public* control. 'Custodial' Indians were mining gold, a public property which 'the people' owned and which only the queen or her representative could administer. In similar fashion, Spanish settlers could similarly only hold native labour or quotas in trust from the Crown. The custodianship of labour could be transferred or inherited but never sold. Finally, tutelage signified a right to use, not an individual's labour, but that of a community" (Seed, 2015, p. 72).

23. As Sheena Jolley (2015) writes, Irish began to be transported to the Caribbean in 1637: "In all, more than 50,000 Irish were transported from Ireland to Barbados (more were sent to other islands in the West Indies), many of them prisoners captured by Oliver Cromwell during the wars in Ireland and Scotland and following the Monmouth Rebellion. . . . [They] became known as Redlegs, almost certainly a reference to the sunburn they picked up in the hot tropical sun."

24. We should note that urban and rural populations in Europe had a long history with and deep understanding of the local upper classes. Through centuries of uprisings, various customary rights had been achieved and evolved over time—making it unfeasible for elites to force local subaltern populations into chattel slavery.

25. Linebaugh and Rediker (2013, pp. 138–139) describe a similar process that played out in Virginia, where "The planters' fear of multiracial rebellion was replaced by fear of the slave revolt, as expressed in two acts aimed at preventing 'Negro insurrections,' passed in 1680 and 1682. The transition was completed with 'An Act Concerning Servants and Slaves' (1705), which guaranteed the rights of servants and defined slaves as a form of property that would constitute the basis of production in Virginia . . . The defeat of the servants and slaves and the recomposition of the plantation proletariat coincided with the origins of scientific racism."

26. The nineteenth-century French anthropologist and white supremacist eugenicist Paul Topinard explained, when he ultimately admitted defeat later in life, that "race in the present state of things is an abstract conception, a notion of continuity in discontinuity, of unity in diversity. It is the rehabilitation of a real but directly unattainable thing" (as quoted in Jackson and Weidman, 2005, p. 92).

27. It is important here to note the historic role that philanthropy has played in securing the social order of advancing capitalism, not just in regard to the modern-day "NGO complex" but also through the altruistic projects that elites have developed within civil society in the metropole states. See the excellent study on this topic by Michael Barker (2017).

28. Racialization and the way in which so many contemporary identities have come to form can be understood as heavily structured and built up through the emergence, expansion, and reproduction of world capitalism—with its many particularities. Ideological constructs and justifications are constantly developed to justify material relations (and the dominant order). This is not a static situation but one that is constantly reproduced and in flux. Among the most important of these has been liberal multiculturalism (and what in academia is described as "privilege theory"). While it criticizes racial prejudice, liberal multiculturalism fails to see racialized social relations as existing and coming about *through* the structural features of the class system (Choonara and Prasad, 2014; Malik, 1996; Žižek, 1997). Instead it focuses on a multitude of unmoored identities, treating them in very ahistorical ways. In recent years, neo-fascistic groups (the so-called alt-right) have sought to co-opt identitarian language to promote "white identity," inverting history to promote a new kind of reactionary and racist agenda for the twenty-first century (Haider, 2017). Racism, though, does not exist as just a subjective and ideological dynamic but also requires that this dynamic be materialized in an objective sense.

29. While media outlets and political officials in the United States and many other countries regularly downplay or completely ignore the historical violence associated with five hundred years of capitalism (Sprague, 2006a), discussion on the violence associated with the twentieth-century state socialist projects can be reported on in an exaggerated manner without regard for evidence. See, Norton, 2017.

30. It must be noted that Fanon specified that his argument was geared toward the particular situation of black people in the Caribbean. Further studies, he argued, would need to be undertaken to understand the life process of African descendent peoples in other regions.

31. Fanon interestingly also wrote about how some middle-strata Caribbeans of African descent who were able to study abroad in the metropole, such as in France, often became pitted (through a class dynamic) against low-income peoples in the region.

32. Rather than address the exploitation at the core of this relation, mainstream economists writing for the World Bank (Díaz and Rodriguez-Chamussy, 2016) by contrast attempt to understand how the labor, as "unused human capital," of young Caribbean women who have not entered the formal workforce can be better tapped into by global capitalist forces.

CHAPTER 2

1. A number of works have attempted to address some of the lingering problems of nation-state centrism but have often reified it in part (see, i.e., Anievas and Nisancioglu, 2015; Kay, 1975; Sender, 1987; Warren, 1980).

2. The post–World War II international division of labor, as Mies (1986/2014) explained, deepened as labor in the Third World was no longer restricted to extractive industries but now also expanded into productive industries. This also occurred in connection with an intensified "sexual division of labor" that feminized many economic sectors, such as within the EPZs that began to develop after World War II (S. James, 2012).

3. See especially Robinson's (2010, 2011) critical overviews of the world systems approaches of Wallerstein and Arrighi.

4. See, for example, the post-structuralist approach of Spivak, 1996, which is well critiqued in Chibber, 2013.

5. See also my review (Sprague, 2011b) of Peter Dicken's *Global shift*.

6. Denis O'Brien also holds major investments in commercial aircraft, oil, gas, and a number of other industries. For more information, see his profile on the Forbes magazine website; retrieved from: http://www.forbes.com/profile/denis-obrien/.

7. In recent years the Caribbean has seen a massive increase in the number of cell phone users, dynamically altering consumerism and communication in the region.

8. See also my interview (Sprague, 2014a) with Ietto-Gillies.

9. To see the continual growth in the number of cross-border M&A deals over recent decades one useful source is the United Nations Conference on Trade and Development (UNCTAD). See, for example: "Annex table 10. Value of cross-border M&As by region/economy of purchaser, 1990–2015," in the World Investment Report 2016: Annex Tables. Retrieved from: http://unctad.org/en/Pages/DIAE/World%20Investment%20Report/Annex-Tables.aspx. To see the fluctuating value of cross-border M&As over recent years see "Statista: The Statistics Portal" at: https://www.statista.com/statistics/964025/value-cross-border-mergers-acquisitions/.

10. FDI is measured as stock and flows. FDI stock can refer to either: (1) "outward FDI stock," the value of the investors' equity in and net loans to enterprises in foreign countries, or (2) "inward FDI stock," the value of foreign investors' equity in and net loans to enterprises inside a particular country. FDI flows, by contrast, refer to: (1) "FDI inflows," the value of inward direct investment made by foreign investors inside a country, and (2) "FDI outflows," the value of outward direct investment made by the resident of a country into a foreign country.

11. It must be mentioned that I have emphasized in my work the role of "transnationally oriented elites" operating through state apparatuses, rather than Robinson's focus on the transnational elites operating through the "transnational state" and its apparatus (2010b). This is largely because I feel that the analytical abstraction of the "transnational state" has so often been misportrayed and appears to be confusing for many scholars (Sprague, 2012b).

12. See also my review (Sprague, 2014b) of Panitch and Gindin's *The making of global capitalism*.

13. These "nationalist backlashes" have provoked thoughtful discussion in the literature around transnational capitalism. See, for example, the round table held by the Great Transition Initiative; retrieved from: http://www.greattransition.org/publication/roundtable-global-capitalism.

14. For my thoughts on Trump's termination of the TPP read my coauthored article: Rangel and Sprague-Silgado, 2017.

15. One of the most recent examples of this being the $1 billion a year weapons supply and training program, known as Timber Sycamore, which was launched to support Islamist antigovernment fighters in Syria, backed by the CIA alongside Persian Gulf and Turkish intelligence agencies (Norton, 2016).

16. Such as with U.S. imperialism's reaction to the Cuban Revolution, or the violent reaction of large rural landowners to the creation of socialist cooperatives in Bolivarian Venezuela, or the reaction of right-wing elites to the disbandment of the army under the Fanmi Lavalas political project in Haiti, or the right-wing reaction to the call for a constitutional assembly in Honduras in 2009, and so on.

17. Even while some capitalist interests, such as in the prison-industrial complex, do profit from criminalizing, jailing, and deporting migrant waged-labor, these interests still exploit waged labor (such as with prison guards, prison labor, and others).

18. Yousef Baker (2014), in the context of Iraq, elaborates upon how a transnationally oriented multinational security apparatus has evolved. He explains his own experience walking daily through a Baghdad Green Zone, through a "hotel manned by private security of the British company that was overseeing the hotel at the time, Georgian soldiers outside the hotel and the middle of the main road, Salvadoran private security guards outside an adjacent building and Nepalese private security guards outside the entrance to the prime minister's office employed by an Australian private security company. In between American soldiers from the Third Infantry Division looked on" (Baker, 2014, pp. 121–122).

19. See also the numerous videos published by Jamaican leftist Lloyd D'Aguilar; retrieved from: https://www.youtube.com/user/lgdaguilar/videos.

20. Numerous human rights investigations (from Harvard Law School, Miami University, the *Lancet Medical Journal*, the National Lawyers Guild, and the Quixote Centre) documented and decried the postcoup state-sponsored campaign of violence and persecution. Ironically, the donors and mainstream media that had been so often critical of the ousted Aristide government now exhibited restraint and silence. Some of the larger Washington, DC–based human rights groups, such as Human Rights Watch, said virtually nothing. For more on this, see Macdonald, 2008; Emersberger, 2008; Danticat, 2017.

21. U.S., OAS, and UN officials methodically integrated four hundred paramilitaries into the state's police force following the 2004 coup d'état (Sprague, 2012a, pp. 235–274).

22. In today's global media landscape many in the Caribbean consume media from outside of the region. There also exists a broad array of TV, radio, internet, and print news media produced in or geared toward the region.

While journalists around the world face the contradiction of working for private media that are not run democratically, in the Caribbean especially journalists face a severe lack of resources. This is reflected in the dependence often on foreign global media outlets, and how some important stories receive little to no local coverage. Looking over coverage of the "anthropocene" on the websites of over two dozen Caribbean based news outlets, I have found that some of the few articles produced by authors in the region on this topic came out of a small paper in Trinidad, an environmental NGO in Haiti (which is dependent on foreign grantees) and the Communist Party and its youths' wing newspaper in Cuba where some limited infrastructure does exist for journalists to cover important stories.

While media in the region, especially grassroots and critical media, has gone through difficult times, we can point to a number of important outlets over recent years. I have excluded here many of the media that are heavily funded by wealthy donor groups or agencies of capitalist states heavily active in the region. This does not mean that these do not put out valuable reports (such as the excellent environmental news reports published by the United Nations funded Inter Press Service; retrieved from: www.ipsnews.net), but

I want to emphasize here grassroots alternatives to monopoly, donor, and corporatist-oriented media.

In the Dominican Republic, the main leftist media outlet has been the worker cooperative-run *El Grillo*, with its website; retrieved from: www.elgrillo.do. In Haiti there exists the left-wing newspaper *Haiti Liberté* run out of offices in Brooklyn, New York, and Port-au-Prince, with their website located at: haitiliberte.com/. Solidarity campaigners also run outlets supporting the Haitian poor's struggle for justice and equality, such as the California-based Haiti Action Committee with its publication *Haiti Solidarity*, located at: haitisolidarity.net/. Excellent articles on the region have also been published by the Center for Economic and Policy Research (CEPR): http://cepr.net/ and in The Intercept: https://theintercept.com and Grayzone Project: https://thegrayzone.com.

Fewer leftist outlets exist in the English-speaking Caribbean, but some useful blogs do exist, such as that of Jamaican organic intellectual Lloyd D'Aguilar at: lookingback-lookingforward.com. A wide variety of other useful new online media outlets exist, with the class struggle and all of its contradictions constantly playing out through social media and the web. For more English-language outlets with Caribbean-related material, see the websites run by U.K. activists, "Caribbean Labour Solidarity," and Global Women's Strike; retrieved from, respectively: http://www.cls-uk.org.uk or www.globalwomenstrike.net/.

Over the past decade we have also seen the rise of important international websites that cover news in the region. This includes leftist media such as Spain-based Rebelión, which publishes a large number of stories about the region on its website; retrieved from: https://www.rebelion.org/. Another website, América Latina en movimiento, based in Ecuador, publishes numerous stories related to the Caribbean in English, French, and Spanish: alainet.org/

Also evolving over the past decade are well-resourced regional media outlets support-ed by the ALBA bloc, most important, TeleSUR, with a TV channel and website; retrieved from: http://telesurtv.net. Socialist Cuba has long maintained radical outlets, many of which continue to produce a large amount of material. One such outlet *Contrainjerencia,* founded by the late Jean-Guy Allard, is currently defunct: www.contrainjerencia.com, but numerous other websites, periodicals, and blogs exist dedicated to anti-imperialism and Cuba's over-fifty-year-long struggle.

The long-standing difficulty that grassroots media (oriented toward the interests of the popular classes) has had in the region is the lack of resources and lack of infrastructure, as popular forces are always outgunned and far surpassed by the wealth of media barons, U.S. state backed outlets, and the numerous business media start-ups that now operate so many websites. Many leftists have long sought to reach larger audiences by publishing through mainstream outlets (a strategy that Marx also undertook). Private media outlets have largely obtained a stranglehold on the news that most people consume. For a critical study of how private media functions in capitalist society, see Chomsky and Herman (2002).

23. The scientific consensus is clear. As the *Washington Post* (Oreskes, 2004) reports: "We read 928 abstracts published in scientific journals between 1993 and 2003 and listed in the database with the keywords 'global climate change.' None of the papers disagreed with the consensus position that current climate change is caused by human activity. There have been arguments to the contrary, but they are not to be found in scientific literature, which is where scientific debates are properly adjudicated. The message is clear and unambiguous."

24. See also my full review (Sprague-Silgado, 2017c) of H. Watson's book *Globalization, sovereignty and citizenship in the Caribbean.*

25. See, for example, my criticism of the approach toward understanding recent political developments in Haiti through the scholarly works of Alex Dupuy and Robert Fatton (Sprague-Silgado, 2017c).

26. See the excellent coverage of events in Venezuela on the website; retrieved from: http://www.venezuelanalysis.com.

CHAPTER 3

1. The Haitian invasion of Santo Domingo also raised fears among Cuban elites that Haitians would invade the country.

2. Williams's (1984, p. 350) entire remark is as follows: "Only four territories in the Caribbean in the nineteenth century did not participate in the vast demographic revolution which was in operation in the area as a whole: independent Haiti, Spanish Santo Domingo, which became independent in 1844, Spanish Puerto Rico, and British Barbados. Elsewhere the simple population pattern at the end of the eighteenth century—a few white people of the metropolitan country, some mulattoes, and a majority of Negroes—became a heterogeneous mixture which included Indians, Chinese, Javanese, and Portuguese, with all the infinite gradations, shadings and mixtures produced by miscegenation."

3. Thomas wrote that social relations could "overlap in one person or in one family, creating a complex intertwining of feudal, other precapitalist, and capitalist property relations" (Thomas, 1984, p. 58). Yet, Thomas never parted ways with the dependency/state-centric analysis, and his approach did not necessarily indicate a careful reflection on the changes that were beginning to occur in the late twentieth century.

4. Much earlier (from late 1940s) the U.K. promotion of federation was the earliest postwar initiative that emphasized limitations of smallness. Eric Williams's *Economics of nationhood* at the time of the Federation was a statement on why integration of very small Caribbean states was an absolute necessity (Williams, 1959). Keep also in mind that Arthur Lewis's short booklet *The Agony of the Eight* in the aftermath of the collapse of the Federation also addressed smallness (Lewis, 1965). His earlier work also looked at economic development in the Caribbean where the size/scale argument was seen as central (Lewis, 1950).

5. These include the treaties set in place through the tutelage of the U.K. and under the intensified economic relations with the United States in the post–World War II period.

6. Clive Thomas argues that "the emergence of this [statist] sector of the petty bourgeoisie constitutes the most important postcolonial development in the class structure of the peripheral capitalist societies. It has been variously described as the 'state petty bourgeoisie,' the 'state bourgeoisie' or the 'bureaucratic bourgeoisie'" (1984, p. 60).

7. The leading form of social control utilized by the Cuban state is through the Comités de Defensa de la Revolución (CDR).

8. See, for example, the important research produced by CovertAction Quarterly, a U.S.-based publication that focused on CIA operations, often on those occurring in the Caribbean and Latin America. It was published between 1978 and 2005. It was relaunched in 2018.

CHAPTER 4

1. While a number of scholarly works have examined the cruise ship business (Chin, 2008; R. Klein 2005, 2009; Oyogoa, 2016b; Pattullo 2005), none have looked at it in regard to the rise of a TCC.

2. This research is based on analysis of business and governmental data, including company tax records of the U.S. Securities and Exchange Commission, secondary accounts of the industry, and semistructured interviews with experts and workers involved with the cruise ship business. My views were also shaped through a significant amount of time spent in the region, in the Dominican Republic, Haiti, and Jamaica.

3. For more on this deepening relation, view the "Ownership and Insiders" page on the website for the financial services TNC, fidelity.com, where one can see details on the major institutional and mutual fund stockholders.

4. Another increasingly flexibilized workforce linking into the business is in the call centers. Like many other large TNCs, cruise companies exploit offshore telephone center labor to answer its customers' reservation calls. Royal Caribbean is currently in the process of moving its British call center to Guatemala (McNeil, 2013). Carnival, on the other hand, now has its call center labor work from home, where their activities can be easily monitored through new internet marketing technology (Heilman, 2012).

5. A map, updated in real time, of the position of most major cruise ships around the world; retrieved from: http://www.cruisemapper.com.

6. Even in the particular case of Cuba, as it adapts and faces new contradictions, and as it integrates with the global capitalist economy, a major overhaul of the port of Havana is being undertaken in order to bring in transnational cruise ships and tourism.

CHAPTER 5

1. Benway, for example, writes: "One of the critical transmogrifications in migrant women's experience in the United States is from primarily reproductive roles to more heavily productive ones. This is not to say that Dominican women are not economically active in the Dominican Republic, nor that their roles as mothers and wives are necessarily diminished as part of the immigration and acculturation process. Rather, women's productive and reproductive roles differentiate in meaningful ways during the process of establishing North American lives. . . . While changes to the traditional power dynamics of Dominican households are adopted to respond to an urban labor market in which jobs are unstable and wages are low, the social consequences have been to alter gender and generation dynamics such that women, by virtue of their labor force participation, and children, by virtue of their English-language and North American cultural fluencies, challenge and sometimes permanently depose their benevolent dictators—husbands and fathers. This 'coup' prompts changes in the economic structure and strategies of Dominican families in the United States; significant changes are reported in the household division of labor as well" (Benway, 2000, p. 3).

2. This framework for studying migrant remittances with attention to transnational integration/accumulation in the Caribbean is consistent with Marx's method. In Marx's statement on method in *The Grundrisse* he takes exception to the valorization that is indicative of fetishization and alienation found in the work of mainstream economists, arguing that when we study the social relations of production it is necessary to avoid beginning with the "real and concrete . . . with e.g. the population, which is the foundation and the subject of the entire social act of production. However, on closer examination this proves false." Marx continues: "The population is an abstraction if I leave out, for example, the classes of which it is composed. These classes . . . are an empty phrase if I am not familiar with the elements on which they rest, e.g. wage labour, capital, etc. These latter in turn presuppose exchange, division of labour, prices. . . . For example, capital is nothing without wage labour, without value, money, prices, etc. Thus, if we were to begin with the population, this would be a chaotic conception . . . of the whole, and I would then by means of further determination, move analytically towards ever more simple concepts . . . , from the imagined concrete towards ever thinner abstractions until I had arrived at the simplest determinations" (Marx, 1973, pp. 100–101).

3. The moral imperative in liberal ideology leads some to object to the idea that workers aim to become more skilled and go abroad to have their labor more intensely exploited.

Many thinkers do not see exploitation in terms of the capital-wage labor relation; they see it subjectively in terms of how one feels personally about being exploited given that the dominant notion is about a fair day's work for a fair day's wage.

4. Here it is useful to consider the distinction that Marx made between constant capital as the value of goods and materials required to produce a commodity and variable capital as the wages paid for the production of a commodity (Marx made this distinction to explain how *labor-power* creates new value).

5. Whereas in 1965, 120,000 migrants from the Western Hemisphere were allowed to enter the United States, by 1976, each country in the hemisphere was given a quota of 20,000.

6. This really is astonishing growth. Compounded at an annual rate of 12 percent for forty-four years, an increase of 14,800 percent.

7. This is according to World Development Indicators; retrieved from: http://databank .worldbank.org/data/reports.aspx?source=2&country=HTI&series=&period=.

8. As of 1990, the U.S. Census placed the total number of documented Jamaican Americans at 435,025.

9. This information is from the website Transnationale; retrieved from: http://www .transnationale.org/companies/western_union.php.

10. See, for example, MoneyGram International Inc., 2012.

11. This is according to data released by the Dominican agency ENHOGAR (La Encuesta Nacional de Hogares de Propósitos Múltiples).

12. While remittances *outflows* from these countries were much smaller than inflows, some countries such as Jamaica, Haiti, and the Bahamas all had sizable outflows in 2012. These were $232 million, $310 million, and $140 million, respectively.

CHAPTER 6

1. Different terminology has been used to name (or emphasize) specific kinds of zones that have been spaces through which production has been geared toward the global economy. Though often serving similar roles, these zones have been termed at different points: free trade zones, free zones, free customs zones, international commerce zones, free ports, free warehouses, EPZs, special economic zones, industrial free zones, and others. For this chapter, I have preferred to use the term "export-processing zone," emphasizing the outward orientation of the zones.

2. It is important to note that there were critics of the policy at the time who in many ways accurately predicted the downward spiral the EPZ sweatshop model would create for workers (see, e.g., Gray, 1986).

3. Sometimes incentives are provided unconditionally, while at other times they are conditionally provided based on criteria such as export-performance, technology transfer requirements, local employment, or local content requirements.

4. Website with a list of many of these "Free Trade Zones" in the United States; retrieved from: http://enforcement.trade.gov/ftzpage/letters/ftzlist-map.html#puerto%20Rico.

5. EPZs were also initially formed in Ireland in the postwar period (Virgill, 2009, p. 2) and an earlier version of the model had begun to be developed even earlier, with the United States' Foreign Trade Zones Act of 1934.

6. This is the author's translation of excerpts from an article that appeared in the Español version of *Forbes* magazine.

7. Companies, divisions, and subsidiaries within the GraceKennedy group include in banking (First Global Bank Limited, First Global Financial Services Limited, FG Funds Management Limited, First Global Trinidad and Tobago Limited, Signia Financial

Group Incorporated); in remittances (with divisions located in Jamaica, the United States, Trinidad and Tobago, and Guyana); in life and general insurance (Allied Insurance Brokers Limited, EC Global Insurance Company Limited, First Global Insurance Brokers Limited, Jamaica International Insurance Company Limited, Trident Insurance Company Limited); and in manufacturing, retail, and distribution (Dairy Industries (Jamaica) Limited, Grace Foods and Services Company GraceKennedy (Belize) Limited, Grace Food Processors Limited, Grace Food Processors (Canning) Limited, Grace Kennedy (United States) Incorporated, Grace Foods International Limited, National Processors Division, World Brands Services Limited, Hi-Lo Food Stores (Jamaica), GK Foods (UK), GraceKennedy (Ontario) Incorporated, Hardware and Lumber Limited).

   8. See the GraceKennedy website; retrieved from: http://www.gracekennedy.com. Also see the GraceKennedy 90th Anniversary website (2012). "GraceKennedy Timeline"; retrieved from: http://www.grace90thanniversary.com/History.

   9. I converted these numbers (provided by Jackson, 2014) that were originally in Jamaican dollars to the U.S. dollar. I used the currency exchange rate of April, 7, 2015, which was US$1 for J$114.390.

   10. As Ronald Cox writes, in regard to CAFTA-DR, through the "top tier lobbying network for transnational firms in the textile industry, representing more than $100 billion in annual textile production and sales" the "final agreement gave US firms a competitive advantage over their Chinese competitors in the exportation of textiles, cotton, fibre, machinery, carpets and rugs, and fabrics to Central America and the Dominican Republic" (2008, p. 1539).

   11. Clearly the TCC has come to represent itself as a class "for itself" rather than a class "in itself" (meaning that, for the former, they have developed an awareness of themselves and become organized as a social class, rather than, as with the latter, only sharing a common social relation to the means of production and being conscious of sharing some common grievances or views).

   12. See, for example, the excellent website of Caribbean Labor Solidarity; retrieved from: http://cls-uk.org.uk/.

   13. This occurred as U.S. president Barack Obama, with support from more "enlightened" groups within the U.S. elite and TCC fractions, sought to pursue a "soft power" strategy, one that seeks to build up local market forces (which eventually could promote regime change from within) rather than continue to promote the failed embargo strategy.

CHAPTER 7

   1. As one industry report observes: "By the end of the second half of 2011, the mining and metals sector had successfully ridden the storm of global economic uncertainty, emerging financially stronger and poised for growth. Balance sheets are stronger, with many companies faced with the challenging but positive decision of how best to utilize their capital—the dilemma of buy, build or return is back on many boardroom tables" (Ernst and Young, 2012).

   2. Unable to discuss much the ecological impact of industrial mining and the new contradictory protocols that have been developed to regulate environmental impacts, readers should view other studies that discuss this, for example, R. Moody, 2007.

   3. Such as its 7 percent share in 2011 in the West Indies Alumina Co. (Wacaster, 2012).

   4. In the case of mines situated on land owned by others, companies were required to pay an additional 2 percent to owners of the topsoil. Officially all land beneath topsoil

was owned by the government, so mining companies (domestic or foreign) had to obtain a permit from the government to undertake mining operations and excavate. Laws on the ownership of land beneath topsoil can be traced back to the legal codes of the European monarchies that colonized the Caribbean (Aitkens, 1931, pp. 2–3, 7).

5. See Barrick Gold's official website; retrieved from: http://www.barrick.com.

6. Placer Dome at the time of being acquired was the world's sixth largest producer of gold, with many of its most successful operations in Australia, South Africa, and North America. Prior to the merger, around 60 percent of Placer Dome's production came from mines in North America. Other top gold mining TNCs include Newmont mining of Denver, and AngloGold Ashanti of Johannesburg.

7. See Goldcorp's official website; retrieved from: http://www.goldcorp.com.

8. "A Letter to Suppliers and Contractors," Fluor website; retrieved from: http://www.fluor.com/services/ procurement/supplier_ and_contractor_registry/pages/a_letter _to_ suppliers_and_contractors.aspx. Accessed July 2014.

9. "A Letter to Suppliers and Contractors," Fluor website; retrieved from: http://www .fluor.com/services/ procurement/supplier_ and_contractor_registry/pages/a_letter_to _ suppliers_and_contractors.aspx. Accessed July 2014.

10. Presecon, "¿Quiénes Somos?" Retrieved from: http://presecon.blogspot.com /p /que-es-presecon-vision-convertirnos-en.html. Accessed July 2013.

11. Adesco stands for Agencia de Empleo y Servicios Cotuí.

12. Agencia Navarro S.R.L., company's Facebook website; retrieved from: https://www.facebook.com/pages/ Agencia-Navarro-SRL/136580319725075. Accessed July 2013.

13. Illustrating well the revolving door between elites operating through government and global industry, former U.S. ambassador to the Dominican Republic (nominated by President George W. Bush), Hans Hertell, a Puerto Rican and member of the U.S. Republican Party, while the sitting ambassador lobbied extensively for Barrick Gold and Goldcorp during the companies' negotiations over Pueblo Viejo with the Dominican state. After he finished his ambassadorship in Santo Domingo, a law firm representing Barrick Gold in the Dominican Republic hired Hertell.

14. See the Everton Resources website; retrieved from: http://www.evertonresources .com.

15. Also, in the mid-1980s a marble quarry briefly operated. (Prepetit, 2000).

16. See, for example, Prepetit's (2000) discussion on Société minière Citadelle's silver deposit concessions in the Grand-Bois and Morne Bossa.

17. Ancillary evidence suggests that at least one mining interest provided financial support to antidemocratic ex-army paramilitaries. In his investigation into Haiti's 2004 coup, Hallward explained: "In Cap-Haïtien I spoke to people who say they were party to meetings of leading local businessmen, for instance at the Hotel Saint Christophe, which served to raise funds on [Guy Philippe and the FLRN's] behalf. I was also told that some international companies, for instance the Québec-based mining firm Saint Geneviève Resources (with gold-mining interests in northeastern Haiti), contributed money to [the paramilitaries] cause." See Hallward, 2007.

18. The authors add that: "Eurasian and Newmont Mining, its partner and the world's Number 2 gold producer, are also drilling illegally in one area—La Miel, in the northeast— in collusion with certain government members."

19. Observing the property's underdevelopment, Chery (2012) explains: "The official story is that an abundance of copper had until recently obscured the fact that the area's ore is also rich in silver and gold, and this was discovered from Majescor's recent prospects of

Douvray, Blondin and Faille-B. However, the story could just as well be that the mining executives were biding their time and waiting for a 'stable' non-nationalistic government to take effect before initiating their projects."

20. Chery (2012) explains that, "The SOMINE property is surrounded by other mining properties owned jointly by Majescor and much larger concerns like Eurasian Minerals and Newmont Mining. Once Majescor's surveys are complete, it plans to find a big partner, like Eurasian, Newmont or Barrick (or some partnership of these like EMX-Newmont), to handle the extractive part of the project."

21. Haiti Grassroots Watch (2012a) lists some of the recent allegations made against Newmont: "In Peru, Newmont runs one of the world's largest open pit gold mines: the 251-square kilometer Yanacocha mine. Not long ago, Newmont was accused of influence peddling there when it was linked to former Peruvian spymaster Vladimiro Montesinos. After allegedly assisting Newmont negotiate favorable terms, a former U.S. State Department employee ended up on the Newmont payroll. The company was also accused of mercury and cyanide spills."

22. For my brief perspective on the current political and social struggles in Hispaniola and Jamaica, see my recent pieces Sprague, 2013, 2014c, 2018; Sprague-Silgado, 2016. See also my two other relevant recent journal articles Sprague-Silgado, 2018b; Sprague, 2019.

CONCLUSION

1. Though this can also lead to "Javon's paradox," where the increasing efficiency in using a resource occurs alongside a growing rate of consumption of that resource as demand increases.

2. See Balibar (2015) who also makes this point.

References

Aarseth, Tori. (2012). *Private military companies: Assisting the transnational capitalist class in accumulation by dispossession.* (Master's Thesis). American University in Cairo.

Abbassi, Jennifer, and Sheryl L. Lutjens. (Eds.). (2002). *Rereading women in Latin America and the Caribbean: The political economy of gender.* Lanham, MD: Rowman and Little-field.

Abrego, Leisy J. (2014). *Sacrificing families: Navigating laws, labor, and love across borders.* Stanford, CA: Stanford University Press.

Accenture. (2011). Mining executive series: Global operating models for mining companies. Retrieved from http://www.accenture.com/SiteCollectionDocuments/PDFAccenture _Mining_Global_Operating_Models_POV_FINAL.pdf.

Accessdr. (2012a). New Dominican president will encourage more investment in tourism industry. Retrieved from http://www.accessdr.com/2012/08/new-dominican-president -will-encourage-more-investment-in-tourism-industry/.

Accessdr. (2012b). 430,000 cruise ship tourists visit the Dominican Republic. Retrieved from http://www.accessdr.com/2012/04/430000-cruise-ship-tourists-visit-the-domin ican-republic/.

Acosta, Nelson, and Sarah Marsh. (2018). U.S. trade embargo has cost Cuba $130 billion, U.N. says. *Reuters.* Retrieved from https://www.reuters.com/article/us-cuba-economy -un/us-trade-embargo-has-cost-cuba-130-billion-un-says-idUSKBN1IA00T.

Acosta, Pablo, Cesar Calderón, Pablo Fajnzylber, and J. Humberto López. (2008). Do remittances lower poverty levels in Latin America? In Pablo Fajnzylber and J. Humberto López (Eds.), *Remittances and development: Lessons from Latin America* (pp. 87–134). Washington, DC: World Bank.

Agamben, Giorgio. (2005). *State of exception.* Chicago: University of Chicago Press.

Agee, Philippe. (1975). *Inside the company: CIA diary.* New York: Farrar, Straus and Giroux.

Agee, Philippe, and Louis Wolf. (Eds.). (1988). *Dirty work: The CIA in Western Europe.* New York: Dorset Press.

Agencia Navarro S.R.L. (2013). Company's facebook website. Retrieved from https://www .facebook.com/pages/Agencia-Navarro-SRL/1365803 19725075.

Agnew, John. (2009). *Globalization and sovereignty*. Lanham, MD: Rowman and Littlefield.

Aitkens, Irene. (1931). *Information circular: Mining laws of the Dominican Republic*. Washington, DC: Department of Commerce, United States Bureau of Mines.

Aldred, Jessica. (2014). Caribbean coral reefs "will be lost within 20 years" without protection. *The Guardian*. Retrieved from https://www.theguardian.com/environment/2014/jul/02/caribbean-coral-reef-lost-fishing-pollution-report.

Allahar, Anton. (2005). *Ethnicity, class, and nationalism: Caribbean and extra-Caribbean dimensions*. Lanham, MD: Lexington Books.

Allen, Theodore W. (2012). *The invention of the white race*. London: Verso.

Amin, Samir. (1978). Unequal development: An essay on social formations of peripheral capitalism. *Science and Society, 42*(2), 219–222.

Amnesty International. (2016). Haiti/Dominican Republic: Reckless deportations leaving thousands in limbo. Amnesty International. Retrieved from https://www.amnesty.org/en/latest/news/2016/06/haiti-dominican-republic-reckless-deportations-leaving-thousands-in-limbo/.

Anderson, Benedict. (1991). *Imagined communities: Reflections on the origin and spread of nationalism*. London: Verso.

Anderson, Kevin. (2010). *Marx at the margins: On nationalism, ethnicity, and non-western societies*. Chicago: University of Chicago Press.

Anderson, Perry. (1974). *Lineages of the absolutist state*. London: Verso.

Anievas, Alexander. (2014). *Capital, the state, and war: Class conflict and geopolitics in the thirty years' crisis, 1914–1945*. Ann Arbor: University of Michigan Press.

Anievas, Alexander, and Kerem Nisancioglu. (2015). *How the West came to rule: The geopolitical origins of capitalism*. London: Pluto Press.

Apter, Andrew, and Lauren Derby. (Eds.). (2010). *Activating the past: History and memory in the black Atlantic world*. Newcastle upon Tyne, U.K.: Cambridge Scholars.

Arbasetti, Joel Cintron, Carla Minet, Alex V. Hernandez, and Jessica Stites. (2017). Who owns Puerto Rico's debt, exactly? We've tracked down 10 of the biggest vulture firms. *In These Times*. Retrieved from http://inthesetimes.com/features/puerto_rico_debt_bond_holders_vulture_funds_named.html.

Arcelin, Jacques. (1983). *Bitter cane*. New York: Crowing Rooster Arts.

Arendt, Hannah. (1966). *The origins of totalitarianism*. San Diego, CA: Harcourt Brace and World.

Arrighi, Giovanni. (1983). *The geometry of imperialism: The limits of Hobson's paradigm*. London: Verso.

Arrighi, Giovanni. (1994). *The long twentieth century: Money, power, and the origins of our times*. London: Verso.

Associated Press. (2018). Tourism booming in Cuba despite tougher new Trump policy. Retrieved from https://www.voanews.com/a/tourism-booming-in-cuba/4218262.html.

Atkinson, Rowland, and Sarah Blandy. (2005). Introduction: International perspectives on the new enclavism and the rise of gated communities. *Housing Studies, 20*(2), 177–186.

Austen, Ian. (2005). Placer Dome agrees to sweetened Barrick bid. *New York Times*. Retrieved from http://www.nytimes.com/2005/12/23/ business/worldbusiness/23gold.html.

Ayala, Cesar J., and Rafael Bernabe. (2007). *Puerto Rico in the American century*. Chapel Hill: University of North Carolina Press.

Bakan, Abigail B. (1990). *Ideology and class conflict in Jamaica: The politics of rebellion*. Montreal, Canada: McGill-Queen's University Press.

Baker, Gordon. (Ed.). (2007). *No island is an island: The impact of globalization on the Commonwealth Caribbean*. London: Chatham House.

Baker, Yousef. (2014). Global capitalism and Iraq: The making of a neoliberal state. *International Review of Modern Sociology, 4*(2), 121–148.

Baldassar, Loretta, and Laura Merla. (Eds.). (2014). *Transnational families, migration and the circulation of care: Understanding mobility and absence in family life*. London: Routledge.

Bales, Kevin. (2012). *Disposable people: New slavery in the global economy*. Berkeley: University of California Press.

Balibar, Étienne. (2015). *Citizenship*. Cambridge, U.K.: Polity Press.

Ball, Laurence M., Nicolás De Roux, and Marc Hofstetter. (2011). Unemployment in Latin America and the Caribbean. NBER Program. Retrieved from http://www.nber.org/papers/w17274.

Bamrud, Joachim. (2012). Mining GDP contribution triples in Latin America. *Mining Weekly*. Retrieved from http://www.miningweekly.com/article/mining-gdp-contribution-triples-in-latin-america-2012-10-11.

Baptist, Willie, and Jan Rehmann. (2011). *Pedagogy of the poor*. New York: Teachers College Press.

Barclay, Lou Anne, and Norman Girvan. (2008). Transnational restructuring and the Jamaican bauxite industry: The swinging pendulum of bargaining power. Conference paper, The global economic history of bauxite, Paris, France. Retrieved from http://www.normangirvan.info/wp-content/uploads/2009/05/transnational-restructuring-and-the-jamaican-bauxite-industry-final-version11.pdf.

Barker, Michael. (2017). *Under the mask of philanthropy*. Scotts Valley, CA: CreateSpace Independent Publishing Platform.

Barnet, Richard J., and Ronald E. Muller. (1974). *Global reach: The power of the multinational corporation*. New York: Touchstone.

Barrick Gold. (2014). Barrick Gold website. Retrieved from http://www.barrick.com/operations/dominican-republic/pueblo-viejo/default.aspx.

Barrow-Giles, Cynthia, and Tennyson S. D. Joseph. (2010). *General elections and voting in the English-speaking Caribbean 1992–2005*. Bogota, Colombia: Autores editores.

Basch, Linda, Nina Glick Schiller, and Cristina Szanton Blanc. (1993). *Nations unbound: Transnational projects, postcolonial predicaments and deterritorialized nation-state*. London: Routledge.

Bassteam, Jack. (2012). GoldQuest mining unigold precipitate Barrick Gold. *Amp gold and precious metals portfolio*. Retrieved from http://ampgoldportfolio.com/2012/08/20/goldquest-mining-unigold-precipitate-gold-barrick-gold/.

BBC. (2010). Cuba to cut one million public sector jobs. Retrieved from http://www.bbc.com/news/world-latin-america-11291267.

BBC. (2015). Britain's forgotten slave owners: Profit and loss. Retrieved from http://www.bbc.co.uk/programmes/b062nqpd.

Beckford, Clinton L., and Kevon Rhiney. (Eds.). (2016). *Globalization, agriculture and food in the Caribbean: Climate change, gender, and geography*. London: Palgrave Macmillan.

Beckford, George. (1999). *Persistent poverty: Underdevelopment in plantation economies of the third world*. Kingston, Jamaica: University of West Indies Press.

Beesley, Arthur. (2007). Digicel sells $1.4bn of high-yield bonds. *The Irish Times*. Retrieved from http://www.highbeam.com/doc/1P2-24869644.html.

Beeton, Dan. (2006). What the World Bank and IDB owe Haiti. *Global Policy Forum*. Retrieved from https://www.globalpolicy.org/component/content/article/97/32135.html.

Bell Lara, Jose. (2008). *Cuba: Socialism within globalization*. La Habana, Cuba: Editorial Jose Marti.

Benway, Gaelan Lee. (2000). *Quisqueya* unbound: Gender roles among Dominican women in Providence, RI. Paper given at the Latin American Studies Association.

Bernal, Richard L. (2013). *Globalization, trade, and economic development: the CARIFORUM-EU economic partnership agreement*. London: Palgrave Macmillan.

Bernal, Richard L. (2014). *Dragon in the Caribbean: China's global re-dimensioning—challenges and opportunities for the Caribbean*. Kingston, Jamaica: Ian Randle.

Best, L. (1968). Outlines of a model of the pure plantation economy. *Social and Economic Studies, 17*(3), 283–323.

Best, L., K. Levitt, and N. Grivan. (2009). *Essays in the theory of plantation economy*. Press study. Kingston, Jamaica: University of the West Indies.

Best, Lloyd. (1966). Size and survival. *New World Quarterly, 2*(3).

Bhattacharya, Tithi. (Ed.). (2017). *Social reproduction theory: Remapping class, recentring oppression*. London: Pluto Press.

Bieler, Andreas. (2012). "Workers of the world, unite?" Globalisation and the quest for transnational solidarity, *Globalizations, 9*(3), 365–378.

Bieler, Andreas, and Morton, Adam David. (Eds.). (2006). *Images of Gramsci: Connections and contentions in political theory and international relations*. London: Routledge.

Bigwood, Jeremy. (2014). Why USAID's Cuban Twitter program was secret. *NACLA*. Retrieved from http://nacla.org/news/2014/4/14/why-usaid's-cuban-twitter-program-was-secret.

Bilgin, Pinar, and Adam David Morton. (2002). Historicizing representations of "failed states": Beyond the cold-war annexation of the social sciences. *Third World Quarterly, 23*(1), 55–80.

Bishop, Louis. (2013). *The political economy of Caribbean development*. Palgrave Macmillan U.K.

Blake, Jillian. (2014). Haiti, the Dominican Republic, and race-based statelessness in the Americas. *Georgetown Journal of Law and Modern Critical Race Perspectives*.

Blum, William. ([1995] 2003). *Killing hope: U.S. military and C.I.A. interventions since World War II*. Monroe, ME: Common Courage Press.

Blumenthal, Max. (2004). The other regime change. *Salon*. Retrieved from http://www.salon.com/2004/07/17/haiti_coup/.

Blumenthal, Max. (2018). US gov. meddling machine boasts of "laying the groundwork for insurrection in Nicaragua." *Grayzone*. https://grayzoneproject.com/2018/06/19/ned-nicaragua-protests-us-government/.

Blumenthal, Max, and Jeb Sprague. (2018). Facebook censorship of alternative media "just the beginning," says top neocon insider. *Grayzone Project*. Retrieved from https://grayzoneproject.com/2018/10/23/facebook-censorship-of-alternative-media-just-the-beginning-says-top-neocon-insider/.

Bolland, O. Nigel. (2001). *The politics of labour in the British Caribbean. The social origins of authoritarianism and democracy in the labour movement*. Kingston, Jamaica: Ian Randle.

Booth, Robert. (2010). Cruise ships still find a Haitian berth. *The Guardian*. Retrieved from http://www.theguardian.com/world/2010/jan/17/cruise-ships-haiti-earthquake.

Boyce, Hayden. (2003). Cruise liners seeking to divide and rule the Caribbean. *Nassau Guardian*, October.

Boyenge, Jean-Pierre Singa. (2007). *ILO database on export processing zones* (Rev ed.). Geneva, Switzerland: Sectoral activities programme, Working Paper, International Labor Organization.

Brathwaite, Carlos, and Harold Codrington. (1982). The external sector of Barbados 1946–1980. In DeLisle Worrel (Ed.), *The economy of Barbados 1946–1980* (48–150 passim). Bridgetown, Barbados: Central Bank of Barbados.

Brathwaite, Cecilia Karch. (2008). *Corporate culture in the Caribbean: A history of Goddard Enterprises Limited*. Bridgetown, Barbados: Goddard.

Braveman, Harry. (1998). *Labor and monopoly capital: The degradation of work in the twentieth century*. New York: Monthly Review Press.

Brennan, Denise. (2004). *What's love got to do with it? Transnational desires and sex tourism in the Dominican Republic*. Durham, NC: Duke University Press.

Brenner, Robert. (2003). *Merchants and revolution: Commercial change, political conflict, and London's overseas traders, 1550–1653*. London: Verso.

Brettell, Caroline B., and James F. Hollifield. (Eds.). (2007). *Migration theory: Talking across disciplines*. London: Routledge.

Brewer, Anthony. ([1980] 1990). *Marxist theories of imperialism: A critical survey* (2nd ed.). London: Routledge.

Brewster, Havelock, and C. Y. Thomas. (1967). *The dynamics of West Indian economic integration*. Mona, Jamaica: Institute of Social and Economic Research, University of the West Indies.

Bridgman, Benjamin. (2012). What ever happened to the Puerto Rican sugar manufacturing industry? Federal Reserve Bank of Minneapolis. Research department staff report 477. Retrieved from https://www.minneapolisfed.org/research/sr/sr477.pdf.

Britell, Alexander. (2013). Interview with Micky Arison, chairman of Carnival Corporation. *Caribbean Journal*. Retrieved from http://www.caribjournal.com/2013/12/17/interview-with-micky-arison-chairman-of-carnival-corporation/.

Brouwer, Steve. (2011). *Revolutionary doctors*. New York: Monthly Review Press.

Budd, Adrian. (2007). Gramsci's Marxism and international relations. Retrieved from http://isj.org.uk/gramscis-marxism-and-international-relations/.

Bueno, Ramón, Cornelia Herzfeld, Elizabeth A. Stanton, and Frank Ackerman. (2008). *The Caribbean and climate change: The costs of inaction*. Retrieved from http://ase.tufts.edu/gdae/Pubs/rp/Caribbean-full-Eng.pdf.

Bulkan, Janette. (2014). REDD letter days: Entrenching political racialization and state patronage through the Norway-Guyana REDD-plus agreement. *Social and Economic Studies, 63*(3–4), 249–279.

Burawoy, Michael. (1976). The functions and reproduction of migrant labor: Comparative material from Southern Africa and United States. *American Journal of Sociology, 81*(5), 1050–1087.

Burnham, Gilbert, Riyadh Lafta, Shannon Doocy, and Lee Roberts. (2006, October 21). Mortality after the 2003 invasion of Iraq: A cross-sectional cluster sample survey. *The Lancet, 368*(9545), 1421–1428.

Business Research and Economic Advisors. (2015). Economic contribution of cruise tourism to the destination economies. Retrieved from https://www.f-cca.com/downloads/2015-cruise-analysis-volume-1.pdf.

Butler, Smedley. ([1935] 2003). *War is a racket: The antiwar classic by America's most decorated soldier*. Los Angeles: Feral House.

Cabezas, Amilia L. (2009). *Economies of desire: Sex and tourism in Cuba and the Dominican Republic*. Philadelphia: Temple University.

Callinicos, Alex. (1995). *Race and class*. Bookmarks.

Camp, Stephanie M. H. (2004). *Closer to freedom: Enslaved women and everyday resistance in the south*. University of North Carolina.

Campbell, Bonnie. (2012). Corporate social responsibility and development in Africa: Redefining the roles and responsibilities of public and private actors in the mining sector. *Resources Policy, 37*, 138–143.

Caribbean Newslink. (2014). Newsletter of the ILO decent work team and Office for the Caribbean. July–December. Retrieved from http://www.ilo.org/wcmsp5/groups /public/---americas/---ro-lima/---sro-port_of_spain/documents/publication/wcms _331138.pdf.

Caribbean Tourism Organization. (2017). Tourism statistical tables. Retrieved from http:// www.onecaribbean.org/statistics/historical-data-1970-2015/.

CARICOM. (2005). Transnationalization in the financial services sector. In CARICOM (Ed.), *Caribbean trade and investment report: Corporate integration and cross-border development*. Retrieved from http://www.caricom.org/jsp/community/regional_issues /CTIR2005/Chapter%20VI%20CTIR%202005.pdf.

Carmona Baez, Antonio. (2004). *State resistance to globalisation in Cuba*. London: Pluto Press.

Carroll, William K. (2013). *The making of a transnational capitalist class: Corporate power in the 21st Century*. London: Zed Books.

Castells, Manuel. (2009). *The rise of the network society: The information age: Economy, society, and culture*. Wiley-Blackwell.

Ceballos, Gerard, Paul R. Ehrlich, Anthony D. Barnosky, Andrés García, Robert M. Pringle, and Todd M. Palmer. (2015). Accelerated modern human-induced species losses: Entering the sixth mass extinction. *Science Advances, 1*(5).

CEPR. (2012). Environmental, labor concerns overlooked in rush to build Caracol Park. Retrieved from http://www.cepr.net/index.php/blogs/relief-and-reconstruction-watch /environmental-labor-concerns-overlooked-in-rush-to-build-caracol-park.

Césaire, Aimé. (2010). *Discourse on colonialism*. Delhi, India: Aakar Books.

Chacko, Priya, and Kanishka Jayasuriya. (2017). A capitalizing foreign policy: Regulatory geographies and transnationalized state projects. *European Journal of International Relations*.

Chailloux, Graciela, Rosa López Oceguera, and Silvio Baró Herrera. (1999). *Globalization and Cuba-US conflict*. La Habana, Cuba: Editorial Jose Marti.

Chang, Grace. (2000). *Disposable domestics: Immigrant women workers in the global economy*. Brooklyn, NY: South End Press.

Chase, Gregory Lee. (2002). *The economic impact of cruise ships in the 1990s: Some evidence from the Caribbean*. (Unpublished doctoral dissertation). Kent State University Graduate School of Management, Kent, Ohio.

Chavdar, Chanev. (2015). Cruise ship registry, flag state control, flag of convenience. *CruiseMapper*. Retrieved from http://www.cruisemapper.com/wiki/758-cruise-ship -registry-flags-of-convenience-flag-state-control.

Chery, Dady. (2012). Poor little rich Haiti to be fleeced of copper-silver-gold via Caracol deep-water port. *San Francisco Bay View: National Black Newspaper*. Retrieved from http://sfbayview.com/2012/poor-little-rich-haiti-to-be-fleeced-of-copper-silver-gold -via-caracol-deep-water-port/.

Chew, Sing C. (2006). *The recurring dark ages: Ecological stress, climate changes, and system transformation*. Lanham, MD: Rowman and Littlefield.

Chibber, Vivek. (2013). *Postcolonial theory and the specter of capital*. Penguin Random House.

Chin, Christine B. N. (2008). Labor flexibilization at sea. *International Feminist Journal of Politics, 10*(1), 1–18.

Chomsky, Noam, and Edward Herman. (2002). *Manufacturing consent: The political economy of mass media*. New York: Pantheon.

Choonara, Esme, and Yuri Prasad. (2014). What's wrong with privilege theory? *International Socialism*. Retrieved from http://isj.org.uk/whatsDwrongDwithDprivilege Dtheory/.

Ciccariello-Maher, George. (2016). *Building the commune: Radical democracy in Venezuela*. London: Verso.

Clancy, Michael. (2008). Cruisin' to exclusion: Commodity chains, the cruise industry, and development in the Caribbean. *Globalizations, 5*(3), 405–413.

COHA. (2009). The U.S. military's presence in the greater Caribbean basin: More a matter of trade strategy and ideology than drugs. Retrieved from http://www.coha.org /the-u-s-militarys-presence-in-the-greater-caribbean-basin-more-a-matter-of-trade -strategy-and-ideology-than-drugs/.

Cohen, Robin. (1987). *The new helots: Migrants in the international division of labour*. Aldershot, U.K.: Avebury.

Cohen, Robin. (2008). *Global diasporas: An introduction*. Abingdon, Oxon: Routledge.

Coles, Anne, and Anne-Meike Fechter. (Eds.). (2007). *Gender and family among transnational professionals*. London: Routledge.

Condon, Stephanie. (1998). Compromise and coping strategies: Gender issues and Caribbean migration to France. In Mary Chamberlain (Ed.), *Caribbean migration: Globalised identities*. London: Routledge.

Connel, Tula. (2017). Haiti garment workers demand wage boost to survive. *AFL-CIO Solidarity Center*. Retrieved from https://www.solidaritycenter.org/haiti-garment-workers -demand-wage-boost-survive/.

Conor, Phillip. (2016). International migration: Key findings from the U.S., Europe and the world. Pew Research Center. Retrieved from http://www.pewresearch.org/fact -tank/2016/12/15/international-migration-key-findings-from-the-u-s-europe-and-the -world/.

Covell, Jeffrey. (2003). Western Union financial services, Inc. *International directory of company histories*. Retrieved from http://www.encyclopedia.com/topic/Western_Union_ Telegraph_Company.aspx.

Cox, Oliver C. (1948). *Caste, class, and race*. New York: Monthly Review Press.

Cox, Robert. (1987). *Production, power, and world order: Social forces in the making of history*. New York: Columbia University Press.

Cox, Ronald W. (2008). Transnational capital, the US state and Latin American trade agreements. *Third World Quarterly, 29*(18), 1527–1544.

Cross, Hannah. (2015). Finance, development, and remittances: Extending the scale of accumulation in migrant labour regimes. *Globalizations, 12*(3), 305–321.

Crouch, Luis Arturo. (1981). *The development of capitalism in Dominican agriculture*. (Doctoral dissertation). University of California Press, Berkeley.

Cruise Market Watch website. (2016). Retrieved from https://www.cruisemarketwatch.com/.

Curtin, Philip D. (1990). *The rise and fall of the plantation complex: Essays in Atlantic history*. Cambridge: Cambridge University Press.

Cusack, Asa. (2019). *Venezula, ALBA and the Limits of Postneoliberal Regionalism in Latin America and the Caribbean*. London: Palgrave Macmillan.

Cushion, Stephen. (2016). *A hidden history of the Cuban revolution: How the working class shaped the guerillas' victory*. New York: Monthly Review Press.

Cwerner, Saulo, Sven Kesselring, and John Urry. (Eds.). (2009). *Aeromobilities*. London: Routledge.

Dangl, Ben. (2010). *Dancing with dynamite: Social movements and state in Latin America*. Oakland, CA: AK Press.

Danticat, Edwidge. (2017). A new chapter for the disastrous United Nations mission in Haiti? *New Yorker*. Retrieved from https://www.newyorker.com/news/news-desk /a-new-chapter-for-the-disastrous-united-nations-mission-in-haiti.

Danticat, Edwidge. (2018). Haitians want to know what the government has done with missing oil money. *New Yorker*. Retrieved from https://www.newyorker.com/news /news-desk/haitians-want-to-know-what-the-government-has-done-with-missing -oil-money.

Davis, Diane E. (2009). Non-state armed actors, new imagined communities, and shifting patterns of sovereignty and insecurity in the modern world. *Contemporary Security Policy, 30*(2), 221–245.

Davis, Mike. (2007). *Planet of slums*. London: Verso.

Daye, Marcella, Donna Chambers, and Sherma Roberts. (Eds.). (2011). *New perspectives in Caribbean tourism*. Oxford: Routledge.

Dayen, David. (2015). The scariest trade deal nobody's talking about just suffered a big leak. *New republic*. Retrieved from http://www.newrepublic.com/article/121967/whats -really-going-trade-services-agreement.

Deere, Carmen Diana, Peggy Antrobus, Lynn Bolles, Edwin Melendez, Peter Phillips, Marcia Riversa, and Helen Safa. (1990). *In the shadows of the sun: Caribbean development alternatives and U.S. policy*. Boulder, CO: Westview.

de la Fuente, Alejandro. (2001). *A nation for all: Race, inequality, and politics in twentieth-century Cuba*. Chapel Hill: University Press of North Carolina.

del Castillo-Mussot, Mercelo, Jeb Sprague-Silgado, and A. de la Lama García. (2013). Global capitalism and "north-south" unevenness: In light of ranking, statistical correlations, and profits of Forbes world list of top 2000 firms. *Perspectives on Global Development and Technology, 12*, 219–245.

Dellink, Rob, Elisa Lanzi, Jean Château, Francesco Bosello, Ramiro Parrado, and Kelly de Bruin. (2014). Consequences of climate change damages for economic growth: A dynamic quantitative assessment. OECD Economics Department Working Papers.

Delphy, Christine. (2015). The core enemy: The political economy of patriarchy. *Revista Brasileira de Ciência Política, 17*, 99–119.

Derby, Lauren H. (2009). *The dictator's seduction: Politics and the popular imagination in the era of Trujillo*. Durham, NC: Duke University Press Books.

Desai, Manisha. (2009). *Gender and the politics of possibilities: Rethinking globalization*. Lanham, MD: Rowman and Littlefield.

Desilver, Drew. (2015). What we know about Cuba's economy. Pew Research Center. Retrieved from http://www.pewresearch.org/fact-tank/2015/05/28/what-we-know -about-cubas-economy/.

De Ste. Croix, G.E.M. (1981). *The class struggle in the ancient Greek world: From the archaic age to the Arab conquests*. Ithaca, NY: Cornell University Press.

Díaz, Mercedes Mateo, and Lourdes Rodriguez-Chamussy. (2016). *Cashing in on Education: Women, children, and prosperity in Latin America and the Caribbean*. Washington, DC: World Bank.

Díaz, Rocio. (2010). Dominican Republic: Opposition to Barrick Gold mining operations. *Global voices*. Retrieved from http://globalvoicesonline.org/2010/03/28/do minican-republic-opposition-to-barrick-gold-mining-operations/.

Diaz del Castillo, Bernal. (2003). *The discovery and conquest of Mexico*. Cambridge, MA: Perseus.

Dicken, Peter. (2007). *Global shift: Mapping the changing contours of the world economy.* New York: Guilford Press.

Dikotter, Frank. (1997). *The construction of racial identities in China and Japan.* Honolulu: University of Hawai'i Press.

Dirzo, Rodolfo, Hillary S. Young, Mauro Galetti, Gerardo Ceballos, Nick J. B. Isaac, and Ben Collen. (2014). Defaunation in the anthropocene. *Science, 345,* 401–406.

Dohse, Knuth, Ulrich Jürgens, and Thomas Malsch. (1985). From "fordism" to "toyotism"? The social organization of the labor process—in the Japanese automobile industry. *Politics and Society, 14*(2), 115–146.

Domhoff, William G. ([1967] 2013). *Who rules America? The triumph of the corporate rich.* New York: McGraw-Hill Education.

Domínguez, Jorge I. (1996). *Technopols: Freeing politics and markets in Latin America in the 1990s.* University Park: Pennsylvania State University.

Dominican Today. (2012). New mining regulators for Santo Mining Corp. SanDominicanToday.com. Retrieved from http://www.dominicantoday.com/dr/economy/2012/10/27/45578/New-mining-regulators-for-Santo-Mining-Corp.

Donaldson, Mike. (2012). "The riddle of history solved": Socialist strategy, modes of production and social formations in capital. *Journal of Australian Politicale, 70,* 130–143.

Dowling, Ross K. (2006). *Cruise ship tourism.* Boston: CABI.

Du Bois, W. E. B. ([1935] 1998). *Black reconstruction in America, 1860–1880.* New York: Free Press.

Dunn, Hopeton S. (1995). *Globalization, communications, and Caribbean identity.* Kingston, Jamaica: Ian Randle.

Dunn, Leith. (2010). Export processing zones: A Caribbean development dilemma. *Development in Practice, 9*(5), 601–605.

Dupuy, Alex. (1996). Race and class in the postcolonial Caribbean: The views of Walter Rodney. *Latin American Perspectives, 23*(2), 107–129.

Dupuy, Alex. (2015). From revolutionary slaves to powerless citizens: The unresolved contradictions of the Haitian revolution. In Hilbourne Watson (Ed.), *Globalization, sovereignty and citizenship in the Caribbean.* Mona, Jamaica: University of the West Indies Press.

ECLAC. (2013). *European Union and Latin America and the Caribbean: Investments for growth, social inclusion and environmental sustainability.* Chile, Santiago: United Nations. Retrieved from http://www.cepal.org/en/publications/european-union-and-latin-america-and-caribbean-investments-growth-social-inclusion-and.

ECLAC. (2014). *Social panorama of Latin America.* Santiago, Chile: United Nations. Retrieved from http://www.cepal.org/en/publications/37626-social-panorama-latin-america-2014.

ECLAC-CEPALSTAT. (2018). Databases and statistical publications. Retrieved from http://estadisticas.cepal.org/cepalstat/web_cepalstat/estadisticasindicadores.asp.

Edgell, Stephen. (2012). *The sociology of work: Continuity and change in paid and unpaid work.* Thousand Oaks, CA: Sage.

Edgeworth, Matt, Dan Richter, Colin Waters, Peter Haff, Cath Neal, and Simon James Price. (2015). Diachronous beginnings of the Anthropocene: The lower bounding surface of anthropogenic deposits. *Anthropocene Review, 2*(1), 33–58.

Edmonds, Kevin. (2012a). Beyond good intentions: The structural limitations of NGOs in Haiti. *Critical Sociology, 39*(3), 439–452.

Edmonds, Kevin. (2012b). Selling citizenship in the Caribbean. *NACLA.* Retrieved from https://nacla.org/blog/2012/12/21/selling-citizenship-caribbean.

Edmonds, Kevin. (2013). Cuba's reforms favor foreign investment, create low-wage sponge. *NACLA*. Retrieved from https://nacla.org/blog/2013/10/31/cuba%25E2%2580%2599s-reforms-favor-foreign-investment-create-low-wage-sponge.

Edmonds, Kevin. (2014a). After 34 years, Watler Rodney's assassination in Guyana now under review. *NACLA*. Retrieved from https://nacla.org/blog/2014/5/7/after-34-years-walter-rodneys-assassination-guyana-now-under-review.

Edmonds, Kevin. (2014b). Race, class, and cannabis in the Caribbean. *NACLA*. Retrieved from https://nacla.org/blog/2014/10/23/race-class-and-cannabis-caribbean.

Edmonds, Kevin. (2014c). The creeping decriminalization of marijuana in the Caribbean. *NACLA*. Retrieved from https://nacla.org/blog/2014/5/23/creeping-decriminalization-marijuana-caribbean.

Edwards, Lucy E. (2015). What is the anthropocene? *Eos*, 96.

Eisenstein, Hester. (2005). A dangerous liaison? Feminism and corporate globalization. *Science and Society, 69*(3), 487–518.

Elie, Janise. (2017). "It feels like Dominica is finished": Life amid the ruins left by Hurricane Maria. *The Guardian*. Retrieved from https://www.theguardian.com/global-development/2017/nov/01/it-feels-like-dominica-is-finished-life-amid-the-ruins-left-by-hurricane-maria?CMP=share_btn_fb.

Ellner, Steve. (Ed.). (2014). *Latin America's radical left: Challenges and complexities of political power in the twenty-first century*. Lanham, MD: Rowman and Littlefield.

Ellner, Steve. (2017a). The campaign against the economic war and corruption in Venezuela. *MROnline*. Retrieved from https://mronline.org/2017/10/20/the-campaign-against-the-economic-war-and-corruption-in-venezuela/.

Ellner, Steve. (2017b). Venezuelans hold demonstrations for and against OAS effort to isolate Venezuela. *The Real News Network*. Retrieved from http://www1.therealnews.com/t2/index.php?option=com_content&task=view&id=31&Itemid=74&jumival=18830.

Elmaazi, Mohamed. (2019). Trump wanted "war with Venezuela" in 2017, says former FBI director. *The Canary*. Retrieved from https://www.thecanary.co/trending/2019/02/21/trump-wanted-war-with-venezuela-in-2017-says-former-fbi-director/.

Embong, Abdul Rahman. (2000). Globalization and transnational class relations: Some problems of conceptualization. *Third World Quarterly, 21*(6), 989–1000.

Emersberger, Joe. (2008). The failure of Human Rights Watch in Venezuela and Haiti. *MRonline*. Retrieved from https://mronline.org/2008/02/24/the-failure-of-human-rights-watch-in-venezuela-and-haiti/.

Emersberger, Joe. (2015). Kicking away the ladder in Haiti. *TeleSUR*. Retrieved from http://www.telesurtv.net/english/opinion/Kicking-Away-the-Ladder-in-Haiti-20150220-0027.html.

Emersberger, Joe. (2017). Lenin Moreno steers Ecuador rightward and betrays the revolution that elected him. *Counterpunch*. Retrieved from https://www.counterpunch.org/2017/12/26/lenin-moreno-steers-ecuador-rightward-and-betrays-the-revolution-that-elected-him/.

Engels, Friedrich. ([1884] 1972). *The origin of the family, private property, and the state*. International.

Engman, Michael, and Thomas Farole. (2012). Export processing zones. In G. Ritzer (Ed.), *The Wiley-Blackwell encyclopedia of globalization*. Malden, MA: Blackwell.

Ernst and Young. (2012). *Mergers, acquisitions and capital raising in mining and metals: 2011 trends, 2012 outlook, recognizing value in volatility*. Retrieved from http://s2.pulso.cl/wp-content/uploads/2012/02/1465351.pdf.

Espacinsular. (2009). *Recursos mineros del pueblo haitiano: Espaillat Nainta revela en Haiti existen grandes recursos de oro y otros minerals.* Santo Domingo, Republica Dominicana: Espacinsular. Retrieved from http://www.espacinsular.org/spip.php?article8942.

Espinal, Rosario Rafaeline. (1986). *Classes, power, and political change in the Dominican Republic* (Unpublished doctoral dissertation). Washington University, St. Louis, Missouri.

Esser, Dominique. (2006). Haiti democracy project: Supporting coup plotters since 2002. Indy bay. Retrieved from https://www.indybay.org/newsitems/2006/06/20/18281608.php.

Faist, Thomas, Margit Fauser, and Eveline Reisenauer. (2013). *Transnational migration.* Cambridge, U.K.: Polity.

Fajnzylber, Pablo, and J. Humberto López. (Eds.). (2008). *Remittances and development: Lessons from Latin America.* Washington, DC: World Bank.

Fanon, Frantz. (1967). *Black skin, white masks.* New York: Grove Press.

Fanon, Frantz. (1968). *Wretched of the earth.* New York: Grove Press.

Farmer, Paul. (2005). *The uses of Haiti.* Monroe, ME: Common Courage Press.

Farmer, Paul, and Amartya Sen. (2004). *Pathologies of power: Health, human rights, and the new war on the poor.* Berkeley: University of California Press.

Fatton, Robert. (2002). *Haiti's predatory republic: The unending transition to democracy.* Boulder, CO: Lynne Rienner.

Fatton, Robert. (2013). *Haiti: Trapped in the outer periphery.* Boulder, CO: Lynne Rienner.

Fawthrop, Tom. (2010). Cuba's aid ignored by the media? *Al Jazeera.* Retrieved from http://www.aljazeera.com/focus/2010/01/201013195514870782.html.

Federici, Silvia. (2004). *Caliban and the witch: Women, the body and primitive accumulation.* New York: Autonomedia.

Feldman, David. (2013). Trouble brewing in South America: NATO sets its sights on Colombia. *Spectrezine.* Retrieved from http://spectrezine.org/trouble-brewing-south-america-nato-sets-its-sights-colombia.

Fenton, Anthony, and Yves Engler. (2005). *Waging war on the poor majority: Canada in Haiti.* Winnipeg, Canada: Red, Fernwood.

Ferguson, James. (2003). Migration in the Caribbean: Haiti, the Dominican Republic and Beyond. Minority Rights Group International. Retrieved from http://minorityrights.org/wp-content/uploads/2015/07/MRG_Rep_Caribbean.pdf.

Fernandes, Sujatha. (2006). *Cuba represent! Cuban arts, state power, and the making of new revolutionary cultures.* Durham, NC: Duke University Press Books.

FIAS (Foreign Investment Advisory Service). (2008). Special economic zones. performance, lessons learned, and implications for zone development. Washington, DC: World Bank.

Fidelity website. (2014). Fidelity by the numbers: Corporate statistics. Retrieved from https://www.fidelity.com/about-fidelity/fidelity-by-numbers/corporate-statistics.

Fields, Karen E., and Barbara Fields. (2014). *Racecraft: The soul of inequality in America.* London: Verso.

Finch, Aisha K. (2015). *Rethinking slave rebellion in Cuba: La escalera and the insurgencies of 1841–1844.* Chapel Hill: University of North Carolina Press.

Fine, Ben. (1994). Coal, diamonds and oil: Towards a comparative theory of mining? *Review of Political Economy, 6*(3), 279–302.

Fleming, Crystal M. (2016). Kindler, gentler pathologizing: Racial asymmetries in the cultural matrix. *Ethnic and Racial Studies, 39*(8), 1436–1444.

Fluor. (2012). A letter to suppliers and contractors. Fluor website. Retrieved from http://www.fluor.com/services/procurement/supplier_ and_contractor_registry/pages/a_letter_to_suppliers_and_contractors.aspx.

Flynn, Karen. (2011). *Moving beyond borders: A history of black Canadian and Caribbean Women in the diaspora.* Toronto, Canada: University of Toronto Press.

Forbes. (2009). The 400 richest Americans: #56 Micky Arison. Retrieved from http://www.forbes.com/lists/2009/54/rich-list-09_Micky-Arison_OAU8.html.

Forbes. (2013). Micky Arison net worth $5.9B as of September 2013. Retrieved from http://www.forbes.com/profile/micky-arison/.

Forbes, Marcia. (2015). Caribbean youth and unemployment. *Caribbean Journal.* Retrieved from http://www.caribjournal.com/2015/01/06/caribbean-youth-and-unemployment/#.

Forbes Staff. (2014). Grupo M, el gigante textil del Caribe. *Forbes magazine.* Retrieved from http://www.forbes.com.mx/grupo-m-el-gigante-textil-del-caribe/.

Fornari, Ariel. (2019). Haitian and Dominican governments betray Venezuela at the OAS; Popular sectors mobilize for resistance. HaitiAnalysis. Retrieved from http://haitianalysis.com/2019/02/11/haitian-and-dominican-governments-betray-venezuela-at-the-oas-popular-sectors-mobilize-for-resistance/.

Fox, Ben. (2015). Mining in Haiti on hold amid uncertainty and opposition. *Associated Press.* Retrieved from http://www.msn.com/en-us/news/world/mining-in-haiti-on-hold-amid-uncertainty-and-opposition/ar-AAaV9Zn.

Franco Pichardo, Franklin. (2009). *Historia del pueblo Dominicano* (8th ed.). Santo Domingo, Dominican Republic: Editora mediabyte, S.A.

Frank, Andre Gunder. (1967). *Capitalism and underdevelopment in Latin America.* New York: Monthly Review Press.

Frank, Dana. (2016). *Bananeras: Women transforming the banana unions of Latin America.* Chicago: Haymarket Books.

Fraser, Nancy. (1997). Heterosexism, misrecognition, and capitalism: A response to Judith Butler. *Social Text,* (52/53), 279–289.

Fredrickson, George M. (2002). *Racism: A short history.* Princeton, NJ: Princeton University Press.

Freed, Kenneth. (1994). MREs falling hardest in new Haiti. *Los Angeles Times.* Retrieved from http://articles.latimes.com/1994-10-22/news/mn-53261_1_morally-repugnant-elite.

Freeman, Carla. (2000). *High tech and high heels in the global economy: Women, work, and pink-collar identities in the Caribbean.* Durham, NC: Duke University Press.

Frezzo, Mark. (2015). *The sociology of human rights.* Cambridge, U.K.: Polity Press.

Friends of the Earth. (2014). *2014 cruise ship report card.* Retrieved from http://www.foe.org/cruise-report-card.

Frundt, Henry. (1999). Cross-border organizing in the apparel industry: Lessons from Central America and the Caribbean. *Labor Studies Journal, 24*(1), 89–106.

Fu, Xiaolan, and Yuning Gao. (2007). Export processing zones in China: A survey. *ILO.* Retrieved from http://www.ilo.org/public/french/dialogue/download/epzchineeng lish.pdf.

Gafar, John. (1998). Growth, inequality and poverty in selected Caribbean and Latin American countries, with emphasis on Guyana. *Journal of Latin American Studies, 30*(3), 591–617.

Galeano, Eduardo. (1997). *Open veins of Latin America: Five centuries of the pillage of a continent.* New York: Monthly Review Press.

Gammage, Sarah. (2004). Exercising exit, voice and loyalty: A gender perspective on transnationalism in Haiti. *Development and Change, 35*(4), 743–771.

Gammage, Sarah. (2006). Exporting people and recruiting remittances: A development strategy for El Salvador? *Latin American Perspectives, 33*(6), 75–100.

Gane-McCalla, Casey. (2016). *Inside the CIA's secret war in Jamaica.* Los Angeles: Over the Edge Books.

Garcia, Marcela. (2013). Haitians without a nation: A ruling in the Dominican Republic divides immigrants in Boston. *Boston Globe.* Retrieved from http://www.boston globe.com/opinion/2013/12/30/haitians-dominican-republic-immigration-ruling -leaves-communitystateless/7XLAA20GHC4RV5No9fw26 M/story.html.

García Muñiz, Humberto, and Glorida Vega Rodríguez. (2002). La Ayuda Militar como Negocio: Estados Unidos y el Caribe 1791–2001. San Juan, Puerto Rico: Ediciones Callejon.

Garin, Kristoffer A. (2006). *Devils in the blue sea: The dreams, schemes and showdowns that built America's cruise-ship empires.* New York: Penguin Group.

Garni, Alisa, and L. Frank Weyher. (2013). Dollars, "free trade," and migration: The combined forces of alienation in postwar El Salvador. *Latin American, 40*(5), 62–77.

Gaskins, Joseph, Jr. (2013). "Buggery" and the Commonwealth Caribbean: A comparative examination of the Bahamas, Jamaica and Trinidad and Tobago. In C. Lennox and M. Waites (Eds.). *Human rights, sexual orientation and gender identity in the commonwealth: Struggles for decriminalisation and change.*

General Secretariat of the OAS. (1984). *Mining and petroleum legislation in Latin America and the Caribbean.* New York: Oceana.

Gibson, Campbell, and Emily Lennon. (1999). *Historical census statistics on the foreign-born population of the United States: 1850 to 1990.* Washington, DC: U.S. Government Printing Office, U.S. Census Bureau, Working Paper No. 29.

Gilmore, Ruth Wilson. (2007). *Golden gulag: Prisons, surplus, crisis, and opposition in globalizing California.* Berkeley: University of California Press.

Girvan, Norman. (1967). *The Caribbean bauxite industry.* Mona, Jamaica: Institute of Social and Economic Research, University of the West Indies.

Girvan, Norman. (1971). *Foreign capital and economic underdevelopment in Jamaica.* Mona, Jamaica: Institute of Social and Economic Research, University of the West Indies.

Girvan, Norman. (1978). *Corporate imperialism, conflict and expropriation: Essays in transnational corporations and economic nationalism in the third world.* New York: Monthly Review Press.

Girvan, Norman. (2011). Existential threats in the Caribbean: Democratising politics, regionalizing governance. C.L.R. James memorial lecture, Cipriani College of Labour and Cooperative Studies.

Global Justice. (2010). Barrick Gold and Cisneros Group: Two threats to the Dominican people. Retrieved from www.justiciaglobal.com.

Gmelch, George. (2003). *Behind the smile: The working lives of Caribbean tourism.* Bloomington: Indiana University Press.

Gobierno de Republica Dominicana. (1997). *Ley minera de la república Dominicana y regulaciones ambientales relacionadas / Mining law of the Dominican Republic and regulations relative to the environment.* Panama: S.A. Russin, Vecchi and Miner Mount Isa.

Golash-Boza, Tanya. (2016). *Due process denied: Detentions and deportations in the United States.* New York: Routledge.

Goldcorp website. (2014). Retrieved from http://www.goldcorp.com/English/Unrivalled -Assets/Mines-and-Projects/Central-and-South-America/Operations/Pueblo -Viejo/Overview-and-Development-Highlights/default.aspx.

Goldenberg, Shira M., Jill Chettair, Paul Nguyen, Sabina Dobrer, Julio Monaner, and Kate Shannon. (2014). Complexities of short-term mobility for work and migration among sex workers: Violence and sexual risks, barriers to care, and enhanced social and economic opportunities. *Journal of Urban Health, 91*(4), 736–751.

Goldwyn, David L., and Cory R. Gill. (2014). *Uncertain energy: The Caribbean's gamble with Venezuela*. Washington, DC: Atlantic Council.

Golinger, Eva. (2005). *The Chavez code: Cracking U.S. intervention in Venezuela*. Havana, Cuba: Editorial Jose Marti.

Gomes, Anthony. (2013). The Caricom trade imbalance—Jamaica/T&T. *Jamaica Observer*. Retrieved from http://www.jamaicaobserver.com/columns/The-Caricom-trade-im balance---Jamaica-T-T_14266396.

Gopalan, N. (2009). Rusal IPO draws initial investors. *Wall Street Journal*. Retrieved from http://online.wsj.com/article/SB10001424052748703510304574625452262729652 .html.

Gordon, Susan. (2006). GraceKennedy's chairman, past best before date. *Jamaica Gleaner*.

Gordon, Susan. (2008). Producers group buys Dutch juice company. *Jamaica Observer*.

Goudge, Paulette. (2003). *The whiteness of power: Racism in third world development and aid*. London: Lawrence and Wishart.

Gowricharn, Ruben. (2006). *Caribbean transnationalism: Migration, socialization, and social cohesion*. Lanham, MD: Lexington Books.

GraceKennedy. (2005). *Annual report*. Kingston, Jamaica: GraceKennedy. Retrieved from http://www.gracekennedy.com/.

Gramsci, Antonio. (1971). *Selections from the prison notebooks*. New York: International.

Gramsci, Antonio. (2000). *The Antonio Gramsci reader: Selected writings 1916–1935*. New York: New York University Press.

Grandin, Greg. (2007). *America's workshop: Latin America, the United States, and the rise of the new imperialism*. New York: Holt Paperbacks.

Gray, Lorraine, dir. (1986). *The global assembly line*. Wayne, NJ: New Day Films.

Gregory, Steven. (2006). *The devil behind the mirror: Globalization and politics in the Dominican Republic*. Berkeley: University of California Press.

Grell-Brisk, Marilyn. (2018). Eluding national boundaries: A case study of commodified citizenship and the transnational capitalist class. *Societies 8*(35).

Griffin, Tom. (2004). Haiti human rights investigation: November 11–21, 2004. University of Miami School of Law. Retrieved from http://ijdh.org/CSHRhaitireport.pdf.

Griffith, Ivelaw L. (2000). *The Political Economy of Drugs in the Caribbean*. London: Palgrave Macmillan.

Grugel, Jean. (2004). State power and transnational activism. In Nicola Piper and Anders Uhlin (Eds.), *Transnational activism in Asia: Problems of power and democracy* (pp. 26–42). London: Routledge.

Grullón, Rodríguez, and Virginia Antares. (2012). *Tras el oro de Pueblo Viejo: Del colonialismo al neoliberalismo. Un análisis crítico del mayor proyecto minero dominicano*. Santo Domingo, Republica Dominicana: Academia de Ciencias de República Dominicana.

Guatemala Times. (2010). IACHR calls on the Guatemalan government and Goldcorp to halt mining. *Guatemala Times*. Retrieved from http://www.guatemala-times.com/ news/guatemala/1668--iachr-calls-on-the-guatemalan-government-and-goldcorp -to-halt-mining.html.

Gupta Barnes, Shailly. (2016). Migration, money, and modinomics. *Kairos: The center for religions, rights, and social justice*. Retrieved from https://kairoscenter.org/migration -money-and-modinomics/.

Hahamovitch, C. (2013). *No man's land: Jamaican guestworkers in America and the global history of deportable labor*. Princeton: Princeton University Press.

Haider, Shuja. (2017). The safety pin and the swastika. *Viewpoint Magazine*. Retrieved from https://viewpointmag.com/2017/01/04/the-safety-pin-and-the-swastika/.

Haiti Grassroots Watch. (2012a). What's in Haiti's hills? Retrieved from http://haitigrass rootswatch.squarespace.com/18_02_ENG.

Haiti Grassroots Watch. (2012b). Gold rush in Haiti! Who will get rich? Retrieved from http://haitigrassrootswatch.squarespace.com/18_01_ENG.

Haiti Grassroots Watch. (2012c). Haiti's mines—"open for business"? Retrieved from http://haitigrassrootswatch.squarespace.com/18_04_ENG.

Haiti Grassroots Watch. (2012d). Haiti lags in the royalties race. Retrieved from http://haitigrassrootswatch.squarespace.com/18_03_ENG.

Haiti Grassroots Watch. (2012e). World Bank "success" undermines Haitian democracy. Retrieved from http://haitigrassrootswatch.squarespace.com/23_2_eng.

Haiti Support Group. (2013). National education fund: The promise, politics, and profit of primary education for all. Retrieved from http://www.haiti-liberte.com/archives /volume6-30/National%20Education%20Fund.asp.

Hall, Stuart, Chas Critcher, Tony Jefferson, John Clarke, and Brian Roberts. (Eds.). ([1978] 2013). *Policing the crisis: Mugging, the state and law and order* (35th anniversary ed.). London: Palgrave Macmillan.

Hallward, Peter. (2007). Insurgency and betrayal: An interview with Guy Philippe. *HaitiAnalysis*. Retrieved from http://haitianalysis.blogspot.com/2013/03/insurgency -and-betrayal-interview-with.html.

Hallward, Peter. (2008). *Damming the flood: Haiti, Aristide, and the politics of containment*. London: Verso.

Hameiri, Shahar, and Lee Jones. (2015). *Governing borderless threats: Non-traditional security and the politics of state transformation*. Cambridge: Cambridge University Press.

Hamilton, Carrie. (2012). *Sexual revolutions in Cuba: Passion, politics, and memory*. Durham: University of North Carolina Press Books.

Hardt, Michael, and Antonio Negri. (2001). *Empire*. Cambridge, MA: Harvard University Press.

Harman, Chris. (2008). *A people's history of the world: From the stone age to the new millennium*. London: Verso.

Harris, Jerry. (2006). *The dialectics of globalization: Economic and political conflict in a transnational world*. Newcastle upon Tyne, U.K.: Cambridge Scholars.

Harris, Jerry. (2009a). Outward bound: Transnational capitalism in China. *Race and Class, 54*(1), 13–32.

Harris, Jerry. (2009b). Statist globalization in China, Russia and the Gulf States. *Science and Society, 73*(1), 6–33.

Harris, Jerry. (2016). *Global capitalism and the crisis of humanity*. Atlanta: Clarity Press.

Harrison, Faye V. (2013). The gendered politics and violence of structural adjustment: A view from Jamaica. In Margaret Hobbs and Carla Rice (Eds.), *Gender and women's studies in Canada: critical terrain* (pp. 561–568). Toronto, Canada: Women's Press.

Hart, Richard. (1989). *Rise and organize: The birth of the workers and national movements in Jamaica*. London: Karia Press.

Hart, Richard. (2013). *Occupation and control: The British in Jamaica 1660–1962*. Arawak.

Harvey, David. (1991). *The condition of postmodernity: An enquiry into the origins of cultural change*. Hoboken, NJ: Wiley-Blackwell.

Harvey, David. (1997). *A brief history of neoliberalism*. Oxford: Oxford University Press.

Harvey, David. (2005). *The new imperialism*. Oxford: Oxford University Press.

Heilman, Wayne. (2012). Carnival moving springs call center workers to homes. *The Gazette*. Retrieved from http://gazette.com/article/138073/.

Herman, Edward S., and Frank Brodhead. (1984). *Demonstration elections: U.S.-staged elections in the Dominican Republic, Vietnam, and El Salvador*. Brooklyn, NY: South End Press.

Hernández, Éster, and Susan Bibler Coutin. (2006). Remitting subjects: Migrants, money, and states. *Economy and Society, 35*(2), 185–208.

Hernández, Ramona. (2002). *The mobility of workers under advanced capitalism: Dominican migration to the United States*. New York: Columbia University Press.

Hilferding, Rudolf. ([1910] 2006). *Finance capital: A study in the latest phase of capitalist development*. London: Routledge.

Hilton, Rodney. (1990). *Class conflict and the crisis of feudalism: Essays in medieval social history*. London: Verso.

Hirst, Paul, and Grahame Thompson. (1999). *Globalization in question*. Cambridge, U.K.: Polity Press.

Ho, Christine G. T. (1999). Caribbean transnationalism as a gendered process. *Latin American Perspectives, 26*(5), 34–54.

Ho, Christine G. T., and Keith Nurse. (2005). *Globalisation, diaspora and Caribbean popular culture*. Kingston, Jamaica: Ian Randle Publishers.

Hobsbawm, Eric. (1996a). *The age of revolution: 1789–1848*. New York: Vintage Books.

Hobsbawm, Eric. (1996b). *The age of capital: 1848–1875*. New York: Vintage Books.

Hobsbawm, Eric. (1996c). *The age of empire: 1875–1914*. New York: Vintage Books.

Hobsbawm, Eric. (1996d). *The age of extremes: A history of the world, 1914–1991*. New York: Vintage Books.

Hogue, John S. (2013). *Cruise ship diplomacy: Making U.S. leisure and power in the Anglophone Caribbean, 1900–1973*. Ann Arbor, MI: ProQuest.

Holt-Giménez, Eric, and Raj Patel. (Eds.). (2012). *Food rebellions: Crisis and the hunger for justice*. Oakland, CA: Food First Books.

Hondagneu-Sotelo, Pierrette. (1994). *Gendered transitions: Mexican experiences of immigration*. Berkeley: University of California Press.

Hoogvelt, Ankie. (2001). *Globalization and the postcolonial world: The new political economy of development*. Baltimore, MD: John Hopkins University Press.

Horne, Gerald. (2007). *Cold war in a hot zone: The United States confronts labor and independence struggles in the British West Indies*. Philadelphia: Temple University Press.

Horne, Gerald. (2014a). *The counter-revolution of 1776: Slave resistance and the origins of the United States of America*. New York: New York University Press.

Horne, Gerald. (2014b). Six-part interview with the real news. Retrieved from https://www.youtube.com/watch?v=UH_Fi6403nM&list=PL0yL-pgxqmYONuAKbIm 5Gq5KylkoyOKpI.

Horne, Gerald. (2015). *Confronting black jacobins: The U.S., the Haitian revolution, and the origins of the Dominican Republic*. New York: Monthly Review Press.

Horne, Gerald. (2018). *The apocalypse of settler colonialism: The roots of slavery, white supremacy, and capitalism in seventeenth-century North America and the Caribbean*. New York: Monthly Review Press.

Howard, David J. (2015). Talk at invited session—states, markets, and the political economy of the Caribbean. Latin American Studies Association (LASA) conference, San Juan, Puerto Rico.

Hristov, Jasmin. (2009). *Blood and capital: The Paramilitarization of Colombia*. Athens: Ohio University Press.

Hudson, Peter James. (2017). *Bankers and empire: How Wall Street colonized the Caribbean*. Chicago: University of Chicago Press.

Hughes, Iorwerth Gwyn. (1973). *The mineral resources of Jamaica* (Bulletin no. 8). Kingston, Jamaica: Geological Survey Department.

Hymer, Stephen. (1971). The multinational corporation and the law of uneven development. In J. W. Bhagwati (Ed.), *Economics and world order* (pp. 113–140). London: Macmillan. Reproduced in H. Radice (Ed.). (1975). *International firms and modern imperialism* (pp. 113–135). Harmondsworth, U.K.: Penguin.

Hymer, Stephen. (1972). The internationalization of capital. *Journal of Economic Issues, 6*(1), 91–111.

Hymer, Stephen. (1976). *The international operations of national firms: A study of direct foreign investment*. Cambridge, MA: MIT Press.

Hymer, Stephen. (1978). International politics and international economics: A radical approach. *Monthly Review, 29,* 10.

Hymer, Stephen. (1979). The multinational corporation and the international division of labour. In R. B. Cohen, N. Felton, M. Nkosi, and J. Van Liere (Eds.), *The multinational enterprise: A radical approach.* Papers by Stephen Herbert Hymer. Cambridge: Cambridge University Press.

Ietto-Gillies, Grazia. (1992). *International production: Trends, theories, effects.* Cambridge, U.K.: Polity Press.

Ietto-Gillies, Grazia. (2012). *Transnational corporations and international production: Concepts, theories and effects.* Cheltenham, U.K.: Edward Elgar.

Immomexx-Demaria Land Consultants. (2011). Mines for sale Dominican Republic: lime stone, sand, gravel, marble. Retrieved from http://www.elcatey.com/minesand miningforsale.

Inter-American Development Bank (IDB). (2011). *Haiti and its partners lay the foundation for the Caracol Industrial Park.* Retrieved from http://www.iadb.org/en/news /news-releases/2011-11-28/caracol-industrial-park-in-haiti,9724.html.

Inter-American Development Bank (IDB). (2012). *Remittances to Latin America and the Caribbean in 2012: Differing behavior across subregions.* Washington, DC: Inter-American Development Bank. Retrieved from http://idbdocs.iadb.org/wsdocs/getDocument .aspx?DOCNUM=37735715.

International Labour Organization (ILO). (1998). Export processing zones growing steadily. Geneva, Switzerland: ILO News. Retrieved from http://www.ilo.org/global /about-the-ilo/media-centre/press-releases/WCMS_007997/lang--en/index.htm.

International Labour Organization (ILO). (2014). *2014 Labor overview: Latin America and the Caribbean.* Lima, Peru: Regional office for Latin America and the Caribbean. Retrieved from http://www.ilo.org/wcmsp5/groups/public/---americas/---ro-lima/docu ments/publication/wcms_334089.pdf.

International Monetary Fund (IMF). (2018). Chart of the Week: Crime, Joblessness, and Youth in the Caribbean. *IMF Blog.* Retrieved from https://blogs.imf.org/2018/02/12 /chart-of-the-week-crime-joblessness-and-youth-in-the-caribbean/.

International Organization for Migration (IOM). (1996). Trafficking in women from the Dominican Republic for sexual exploitation. Geneva, Switzerland: International Organization on Migration. Retrieved from http://www.itfglobal.org/flags-convenience /sub-page.cfm.

Itzigsohn, Jose. (2000). *Developing poverty: The state, labor market deregulation, and the informal economy in Costa Rice and the Dominican Republic.* University Park: Penn State University Press.

Ives, Stephen. (2012). *American experience: Panama Canal.* Arlington, VA: PBS Documentary. Retrieved from http://www.pbs.org/wgbh/americanexperience/films/panama/.

Jackson, John P., and Nadine M. Weidman. (2005). *Race, racism, and science: Social impact and interaction.* New Jersey: Rutgers University Press.

Jackson, Steven. (2014). Grace mulls London stock exchange. *Jamaica Observer.* Retrieved from http://www.jamaicaobserver.com/business/Grace-mulls-London-Stock-Exchange _16745532.

Jamaica National Building Society (JNBS). (2010). Longest serving agent in Jamaica. Retrieved from http://www.jnbs.com/jnbs-gets-moneygrams-outstanding-agent -award.

James, C. L. R. (1980). *Spheres of existence: Selected writings.* London: Allison and Busby.

James, C. L. R. (1989). *The black jacobins: Toussaint L'Ouverture and the San Domingo revolution.* New York: Vintage.

James, Selma. (2012). *Sex, race, and class: The perspective of winning: A selection of writings, 1952–2011.* Oakland, CA: PM Press.

Jayasuriya, Kanishka. (1999). Globalization, law, and the transformation of sovereignty: The emergence of global regulatory governance. *Indiana Journal of Global Legal Studies, 6*(2), 425–455.

Jayasuriya, Kanishka. (2005). *Reconstituting the global liberal order: Legitimacy and regulation.* London: Routledge.

Jeffries, Stuart. (2016). *Grand hotel abyss: The lives of the Frankfurt school.* London: Verso.

Jequier, Nicolas. (1988). Export processing zones and the role of TNCs. *The CTC Reporter* No. 25 (Spring 1988), UNCTC. Retrieved from http://unctc.unctad.org/data /ctcrep25f.pdf.

Jilani, Zaid. (2015). Elite lawyers now selling Caribbean tax havens as havens from terror, too. *The Intercept.* Retrieved from https://theintercept.com/2015/12/19/elite-lawyers -now-selling-caribbean-tax-havens-as-havens-from-terror-too/.

Jiménez, Manuel. (2013). Barrick gold shipment released by Dominican Republic. *The Global and Mail.* Retrieved from https://www.theglobeandmail.com/globe-investor /barrick-gold-shipment-released-by-dominican-republic/article9931919/.

Johnson, Adam. (2017). WaPo's one-sided cheerleading for coup and intervention in Venezuela. FAIR. Retrieved from https://fair.org/home/wapos-one-sided-cheerleading -for-coup-and-intervention-in-venezuela/.

Johnson, Cedric. (2017). The Panthers can't save us now. *Catalyst, 1*(1). Retrieved from https://catalyst-journal.com/vol1/no1/panthers-cant-save-us-cedric-johnson.

Johnson, Diana. (2018). Trotskyist delusions: Obsessed with Stalin, they see betrayed revolutions everywhere. *Consortium News.* Retrieved from https://consortiumnews .com/2018/05/04/trotskyist-delusions-obsessed-with-stalin-they-see-betrayed-rev olutions-everywhere/.

Johnson, Janagan Emmanuel, and Dylan Kerrigan. (2013). Human trafficking and forced prostitution: A channel carrier of HIV. In R. Mangaleswaran (Ed.), *Working with youth, women and children with HIV/AIDS: Strategic intervention for inclusive development* (pp. 279–286). New Delhi: AuthorsPress.

Johnston, Jake. (2013). *The multilateral debt trap in Jamaica.* Washington, DC: Center for Economic and Policy Research. Retrieved from http://www.cepr.net/documents /publications/jamaica-debt-2013-06.pdf.

Jolley, Sheena. (2015). The Irish of Barbados. *Irish America.* Retrieved from http://irishamer ica.com/2015/10/the-irish-of-barbados-photos/.

Jones, Robert, Samir Shrivastava, Christopher Selvarajah, and Bernadine Van Gramberg. (2015). Lean production as a tool of global capitalism in Asia: The transnational capitalist class in action. In Jeb Sprague (Ed.), *Globalization and transnational capitalism in Asia and Oceania* (pp. 73–88). London: Routledge.

Jong, Lammert de, and Douwe Boersema. (2006). *The kingdom of the Netherlands in the Caribbean, 1954–2004.* West Lafayette, IN: Purdue University Press.

Kalleberg, Anne L. (2009). Precarious work, insecure workers: Employment relations in transition. *American Sociological Review, 74*(February), 1–22.

Kaplinsky, Raphael. (1993). Export processing zones in the Dominican Republic: Transforming manufactures into commodities. *World Development, 21*(11), 1851–1865.

Karagiannis, Nikolaos., and C. J. Polychroniou. (2015). The scourge of dependency and globalization in the Caribbean. *Truthout.* Retrieved from http://www.truth-out.org/opinion/item/29951-the-scourge-of-dependency-and-globalization-in-the-caribbean.

Katznelson, Ira, and Aristide R. Zolberg. (Eds.). (1987). *Working-class formation: Nineteenth-century patterns in western Europe and the United States.* Princeton, NJ: Princeton University Press.

Kay, Geoffrey. (1975). *Development and underdevelopment: A Marxist Analysis.* London: Palgrave Macmillan U.K.

Keen, Kip. (2012a). GoldQuest drills monster gold-copper hole in the Dominican Republic. *Mineweb.* Retrieved from http://www.mineweb.com/mineweb/view/mineweb/en/page67?oid=152050&sn=Detail&pid=67.

Keen, Kip. (2012b). Chasing GoldQuest in the Dominican Republic. *Mineweb.* Retrieved on December 13, 2013, from http://www.mineweb.com/mineweb/view/mineweb/en/page67?oid=158042&sn=Detail&pid=67.

Kempadoo, Kamala. (Ed.). (1999). *Sun, sex, and gold: Tourism and sex work in the Caribbean.* Lanham, MD: Rowman and Littlefield.

Kempadoo, Kamala. (2004). *Sexing the Caribbean: Gender, race and sexual labor.* London: Routledge.

Kerrigan, Dylan. (2015). Transnational anti-black racism and state violence in Trinidad. *Cultural Anthropology* website. Retrieved from https://culanth.org/fieldsights/692-transnational-anti-black-racism-and-state-violence-in-trinidad.

Kerrigan, Dylan. (2016). "Who ent dead, badly wounded": The everyday life of pretty and grotesque bodies in urban Trinidad. *International Journal of Cultural Studies, 21*(3), 257–276.

Kerrigan, Dylan, Peter Jamadar, Elron Elahie, and Tori Sinanan. (2017). *Securing equality for all: The evidence and recommendations.* Caribbean judicial dialogue. Retrieved from https://www.dylankerrigan.com/uploads/2/4/3/4/24349665/cjd_paper_1_-_kerrigan.pdf.

Kiely, Ray. (1996). *The politics of labour and development in Trinidad.* Mona, Jamaica: University of the West Indies Press.

Kiernan, Victor G. (1969). *Lords of human kind: European attitudes towards the outside world in the imperial age.* London: Weidenfeld and Nicolson.

Kim, Dong-Hun. (2013). Making or breaking a deal: The impact of electoral systems on mergers and acquisitions. *Kyklos, 63*(3), 432–449.

Klak, Thomas. (1995). A framework for studying Caribbean industry policy. *Economic Geography, 71*(3), 297–317.

Klak, Thomas. (1997). *Globalization and neoliberalism: The Caribbean context.* Lanham, MD: Rowman and Littlefield.

Klak, Thomas. (1999). Globalization, neo-liberalism and economic change in Central America and the Caribbean. In Robert N. Gwynne and Kay Critsobal (Eds.), *Latin America Transformed. Globalization and Modernity*. London: Routledge.

Klapper, Bradley. (2015). United States loosens embargo against Cuba. *Associated Press*. Retrieved from https://www.pbs.org/newshour/nation/united-states-loosens-embargo-cuba.

Klein, Naomi. (2009). *The shock doctrine: The rise of disaster capitalism*. New York: Picador.

Klein, Naomi. (2014). *This changes everything: Capitalism vs. the climate*. New York: Simon and Schuster.

Klein, Naomi. (2018). *The battle for paradise: Puerto Rico takes on the disaster capitalists*. Chicago: Haymarket Books.

Klein, Ross. (2001–2002). High seas, low pay: working on cruise ships. *Our Times: Canada's Independent Labour Magazine*. Retrieved from http://www.cruisejunkie.com/ot.html.

Klein, Ross. (2005). *Cruise ship squeeze: The new pirates of the seven seas*. Gabriola, BC, Canada: New Society.

Klein, Ross. (2009). Environmental impacts of cruise tourism. *Prows edge cruise magazine and guide to cruising*. Retrieved from http://www.prowsedge.com/views-ross-klein.html.

Kloby, Jerry. (2004). *Inequality, power, and development: Issues in political sociology*. Amherst, NY: Humanity Books.

Koerner, Lucas. (2017). Marco Rubio threatens El Salvador, Haiti, and DR to Vote for Venezuela OAS suspension. *Venezuelanalysis*. Retrieved from https://venezuelanalysis.com/news/13008.

Koerner, Lucas. (2019). The global left and the danger of a dirty war in Venezuela. *MintPress*. Retrieved from https://www.mintpressnews.com/global-left-danger-dirty-war-venezuela/255501/.

Kolbert, Elizabeth. (2014). *The sixth extinction: An unnatural history*. New York: Henry Holt.

Körner, Finn Marten, and Hans-Micheal Trautwein. (2014). Sovereign credit ratings and the transnationalization of finance—evidence from a gravity model of portfolio investment. *Economics-ejournal, 31*.

Kuehmayer, J. R. (2013). Cruise ship owners/operators and passenger ship financing and management companies. Austrian Marine Equipment Manufacturers. Retrieved from http://www.amem.at/pdf/AMEM_Cruise-Ship-Owners-And-Operators.pdf.

Kumar, Claire. (2009). Undermining the poor: Mineral taxation reforms in Latin America. *Christian Aid Report*. Retrieved from http://www.christianaid.org.uk/images/undermining-the-poor.pdf.

Kushnir, Ivan. (2013). *World macroeconomic research, 1970–2013*. Self-published e-book. Retrieved from http://kushnirs.org/store/wmr2013.html.

Lake, Lisa. (2005). Remittances and the Jamaican economy: From fundamentals to effective policy recommendations. Bank of Jamaica Working Paper.

Lamrani, Salim. (2013). *The economic war against Cuba: A historical and legal perspective on the U.S. blockade*. New York: Monthly Review Press.

Landau, Saul. (1988). *The Dangerous Doctrine: National Security and U.S. Foreign Policy*. Boulder, CO: Westview Press.

Lane, Kirs. (2011). Mining, Gold, and Silver. *Oxford Bibliography*. Retrieved from http://www.oxfordbibliographies.com/view/document/obo-9780199730414/obo-9780199730414-0084.xml.

Lang, Andrew. (2010). Trade agreement, business and human rights: The case of export processing zones. Corporate Social Responsibility Initiative, Working Paper No. 57. Cambridge, MA: Harvard University.

Layne, Christopher. (2006). *The peace of illusions: American grand strategy from 1940 to the present*. Ithaca, NY: Cornell University Press.

Leacock, Eleanor, and Helen I. Safa. (Eds.). (1986). *Women's work: Development and the division of labor by gender*. New York: Berin and Garvey.

Lebowitz, Michael. (2012). *The contradictions of "real socialism": The conductor and the conducted*. New York: Monthly Review Press.

Lenin, Vladimir. ([1917] 1969). *Imperialism, the highest stage of capitalism: A popular outline*. New York: International Publishers.

Leonard, Adrian, and David Pretel. (Eds.). (2015). *The Caribbean and the Atlantic World Economy: Circuits of trade, money and knowledge, 1650–1914*. London: Palgrave Macmillan.

Levitt, Peggy. (2001). *The transnational villagers*. Berkeley: University of California Press.

Lewin, Moshe. (2016). *The Soviet Century*. London: Verso.

Lewis, Arthur W. (1950). *Industrialization of the British West Indies*. Bridgetown, Barbados: Government Print Office.

Lewis, Arthur W. (1965). *The agony of the eight*. Bridgetown, Barbados: Advocate Commercial Printery.

Lewis, Arthur W. (1978). *The evolution of the international economic order*. Princeton, NJ: Princeton University Press.

Lewis, Gordon K. (1968). *Growth of the modern West Indies*. New York: Monthly Review Press.

Lewis, Gordon K. (1987). *Main currents in Caribbean thought: The historical evolution of Caribbean society in its ideological aspects, 1492–1900*. Baltimore, MD: Johns Hopkins University Press.

Lewis, Gordon K. (2004). *Puerto Rico, freedom and power in the Caribbean*. Miami: Ian Randle.

Lewis, Linden. (Ed.). (2012a). *Caribbean sovereignty, development and democracy in an age of globalization*. New York: Routledge.

Lewis, Linden. (2012b). The dissolution of the myth of sovereignty in the Caribbean. In Linden Lewis (Ed.), *Caribbean sovereignty, development and democracy in an age of globalization*. New York: Routledge.

Library of Congress. (1986). *Dominican Republic-growth and structure of the economy*. Washington, DC: Library of Congress. Retrieved from http://www.mongabay.com /history/dominican_republic/dominican_republic-growth_and_structure_of_the _economy.html.

Liechty, Mark. (2003). *Suitably modern: Making middle-class culture in a new consumer society*. Princeton, NJ: Princeton University Press.

Limitone, Julia. (2019). Venezuela regime change big business opportunity: John Bolton. *Fox Business*. Retrieved from https://www.foxbusiness.com/politics/venezuela-regime -change-big-business-opportunity.

Lin, Kevin. (2016). Global capitalism and the transformation of china's working class. In Jeb Sprague (Ed.), *Globalization and transnational capitalism in Asia and Oceania*. London: Routledge.

Linebaugh, Peter, and Marcus Rediker. (2013). *The many-headed hydra: Sailors, slaves, commoners, and the hidden history of the revolutionary Atlantic*. Boston: Beacon Press.

Liodakis, George. (1990). International division of labor and uneven development: A review of the theory and evidence. *Review of Radical Political Economics*, 22(2–3), 189–213.

Liodakis, George. (2010). *Totalitarian capitalism and beyond*. Surrey, U.K.: Ashgate.

Long, Frank. (1987). "New Exports" of the Caribbean to the international economy. *Development Policy Review, 5,* 63–72.

Lumsdon, Les M., and Stephen J. Page. (Eds.). (2003). *Tourism and transport: Advances in tourism research.* New York: Routledge.

Luxner, Larry. (2013). Dominican Republic leads Caribbean in tourist arrivals. Retrieved from http://newsismybusiness.com/dominican-republic-leads-caribbean-in-tourist-arrivals/.

MacCannell, Dean. (1976). *The tourist: A new theory of the leisure class.* Berkeley: University of California Press.

Macdonald, Isabel. (2008). "Parachute journalism" in Haiti: Media sourcing in the 2003–2004 political crisis. *Canadian Journal of Communication, 33,* 213–232.

Maher, JaneMaree, Sharon Pickering, and Alison Gerar. (2014). *Sex work: Labour, mobility, and sexual services.* Abingdon: Routledge.

Maingot, Anthony P., and Wilfredo Lozano. (2005). *The United States and the Caribbean: Transforming hegemony and sovereignty.* London: Routledge.

Mair, Lucille Mathurin. (2006). *A historical study of women in Jamaica, 1655–1844.* Mona, Jamaica: University of the West Indies Press.

Malik, Kenan. (1996). *The meaning of race: Race, history, and culture in western society.* New York: New York University Press.

Manigat, Sabine. (1997). The popular sectors and the crisis in Port-au-Prince. In A. Portes, C. Dore-Cabral, and P. Landolt (Eds.), *The urban Caribbean: Transition to the new global economy* (pp. 87–123). Baltimore, MD: John Hopkins University Press.

Mann, Charles C. (2011). *1943: Uncovering the new world Columbus created.* New York: Vintage.

Marable, Manning. (2009). Globalization and racialization. *Znet.* Retrieved from http://zcomm.org/znetarticle/globalization-and-racialization-by-manning-marable/.

Marable, Manning, and V. Agard-Jones. (2008). *Transnational blackness: Navigating the global color line.* London: Palgrave Macmillan.

Marcuse, Herbert. (1964). *One-dimensional man: Studies in the ideology of advanced industrial society.* Boston: Beacon Press.

Marini, Ruy Mauro. (1973). *Dialectica de la dependencia.* Mexico City, Mexico: Ediciones Era.

Mars, Perry, and Alma H. Young. (2004). *Caribbean labor and politics: Legacies of Cheddi Jaggan and Michael Manley.* Detroit, MI: Wayne State University Press.

Marshall, Andrew Gavin. (2013). Global power project, part 4: Banking on influence with JPMorgan Chase. Occupy.com. Retrieved from http://www.occupy.com/article/global-power-project-part-4-banking-influence-jpmorgan-chase.

Martinez, Osvaldo. (1999). *Neoliberalismo en crisis.* La Habana, Cuba: Editorial de Ciencias Sociales.

Martínez Peria, Maria Soledad, Yira Mascaró, and Florencia Moizeszowiz. (2008). Do remittances affect recipient countries' financial development? In Pablo Fajnzylber and J. Humberto López (Eds.), *Remittances and development: Lessons from Latin America,* Washington, DC: World Bank.

Martinez, Samuel. (1996). *Peripherial migrants: Haitians and Dominican Republic sugar plantations.* Knoxville: University of Tennessee Press.

Martinez-Vergne, Teresita, and Franklin W. Knight. (Eds.). (2005). *Contemporary Caribbean cultures and societies in a global context.* Chapel Hill: University of North Carolina Press.

Marx, Karl. (1973). *The grundrisse.* London: Lawrence and Wishart.

Marx, Karl. ([1867] 1992). *Capital: A critique of political economy* (Vol. 1). London: Penguin Classics.

Marx, Karl. (1993a). *Capital: A critique of political economy* (Vol. 2). London: Penguin Classics.

Marx, Karl. (1993b). *Capital: A critique of political economy* (Vol. 3). London: Penguin Classics.

Marx, Karl. ([1869] 1994). *The eighteenth brumaire of Louis Bonaparte.* New York: International.

Marx, Karl, and Friedrich Engels. (1998). *The German ideology.* Great Books in Philosophy. Amherst, NY: Prometheus Books.

Mason, Paul. (2010). *Live working or die fighting: How the working class went global.* Chicago: Haymarket Books.

Matthews, Lear. (Ed.). (2013). *English-speaking Caribbean immigrants: Transnational identities.* Maryland: University Press of America.

Mawby, Spencer. (2012). *Ordering independence: The end of empire in the anglophone Caribbean, 1947–1969.* Basingstoke: Palgrave Macmillan.

Maxwell, John. (2008a). A pigeon among the cats. *Jamaica Observer.* Retrieved from http://www.jamaicaobserver.com/news/John-Maxwell-is-dead.

Maxwell, John. (2008b). Scott McClellan's road to Damascus and Cuba's internationalism. *Jamaica Observer.* Retrieved from https://blackagendareport.com/content/scott-mcclellan's-road-damascus-and-cuba's-internationalism.

McAuley, Christopher. (2001). A comment on capitalist origins. *Solidarity: A socialist, feminist, anti-racist organization.* Retrieved from http://www.solidarity-us.org/node/1007.

McLean, A. Esmond. (2008). An investigation of recent trends in the remittance industry: Evidence from Jamaica. Bank of Jamaica. Retrieved from http://www.boj.org.jm/uploads/pdf/papers_pamphlets/papers_pamphlets_An_Investigation_of_Recent_Trends_in_the_Remittance_Industry__Evidence_from_Jamaica.pdf.

McMahon, Gary, and Felix Remy. (2001). *Large mines and the community: Socioeconomic and environmental effects in Latin America, Canada, and Spain.* Washington, DC: World Bank.

McMichael, Philip. (1996). *Development and social change: A global perspective.* Thousand Oaks: California. Pine Forge Press.

McNally, David. (2011). *Global slump: The economics and politics of crisis and resistance.* Oakland: PM Press.

McNeil, Linsey. (2013). Royal Caribbean to move its call centre to Guatemala. *TravelMole.* Retrieved from http://www.travelmole.com/news_feature.php?news_id=2008068.

Medina Herasme, Alexander. (2014). *Mining tax regime as development tools.* UNCTAD. Retrieved from http://unctad.org/meetings/en/Presentation/SUC_MEM2014_100414_MEDINA.pdf.

Meeks, Brian. (2007). *Caribbean reasonings: Culture, politics, race and diaspora—the thought of Stuart Hall.* Kingston, Jamaica: Ian Randle.

Melander, Veronica. (1999). The hour of God?: People in Guatemala confronting political evangelicalism and counterinsurgency (1976–1990)(Doctoral Dissertation). Uppsala, Sweden: Uppsala Universitet.

Merrill, Dennis. (2009). *Negotiating paradise: U.S. tourism and empire in twentieth-century Latin America,* Durham: University of North Carolina Press.

MGI Analyst Report. (2014). MoneyGram earnings top, lays growth plans. Yahoo Finance. Retrieved from http://finance.yahoo.com/news/moneygram-earnings-top-lays-growth-135948525.html.

Michaels, Walter Benn. (2016). *The trouble with diversity: How we learned to love identity and ignore inequality*. London: Picador.

Mies, Maria. ([1986] 2014). *Patriarchy and accumulation on a world scale: Women in the international division of labour*. London: Zed Books.

Miles, Tom. (2014). Top tax haven got more investment in 2013 than India and Brazil: U.N. *Reuters*. Retrieved from http://www.reuters.com/article/us-tax-havens-idUSBREA0R 1KF20140128.

Miller, Todd. (2014). *Border patrol nation: Dispatches from the front lines of homeland security*. San Francisco: Open Media Series, City Lights Book.

Mills, C. Wright. ([1956] 2000). *The power elite*. Oxford: Oxford University Press.

Mills, Charles. (2010). *Radical theory, Caribbean reality: Race, class and social domination*. Mona, Jamaica: University of the West Indies Press.

Mintz, Sidney W. (1974). *Caribbean transformations*. Chicago: Aldine.

Mintz, Sidney W. (1986). *Sweetness and power: The place of sugar in modern history*. London: Penguin Books.

Mintz, Sidney W. (1989). *Caribbean transformations*. New York: Columbia University Press.

Moberg, Lotta. (2014). The political economy of special economic zones. In R. Hernandez (Ed.), *Mobility of workers under advanced capitalism: Dominican Migration to the United States* (pp. 1–25). New York: Colombia University Press.

Mohan, Preeya, and Patrick Kent Watson. (2010). CARICOM cross-border equity flows. First Caribbean International Bank and St. Augustine, Trinidad and Tobago: Sir Arthur Lewis Institute of Social and Economic Studies University of the West Indies. Retrieved from http://www.cavehill.uwi.edu/bdoffice/documents/CARICOM CrossBorderEquityFlo ws.pdf.

Molyneaux, David G. (2012). Cruise lines: Developing destinations. *Miami Herald*. Retrieved from http://www.miamiherald.com/2012/10/20/3057708/developing-destinations.html.

Moneygram. (2010). Our company. Retrieved from http://moneygram.com/MGICorp /MediaRelations/OurCompany/index.htm.

Moneygram International Inc. (2012). Form 10-K filed with the U.S. Securities and Exchange Commission. Retrieved from http://ir.moneygram.com/annual-reports.

Monzon, Luis E., and Emina Tudakovic. (2004). Remittances: A preliminary research. *FOCALPoint* (Special ed., March, pp. 5–7). Retrieved from http://www.focal.ca/pdf /migration_Nurse_diaspora%20migration%20development%20Caribbean_Sep tember%202004_FPP-04-6.pdf.

Moody, Kim. (2018). Modern capitalism has opened a major new front for strike action-logistics. *The Conversation*. Retrieved from https://theconversation.com/modern -capitalism-has-opened-a-major-new-front-for-strike-action-logistics-89616.

Moody, Roger. (2007). *Rocks and hard places: The globalization of mining*. London: Zed Books.

Morales Dominguez, Esteban. (Ed.). (2012). Race in Cuba: Essays on the revolution and racial inequality. New York: Monthly Review Press.

Morrissey, Marietta. (1989). *Slave women in the new world: Gender stratification in the Caribbean*. Lawrence: University of Press of Kansas: Studies in Historical Social Change.

Morton, Adam David. (2007). *Unravelling Gramsci: Hegemony and passive revolution in the global economy*. London: Pluto Press.

Mowforth, Martin, and London Munt. (2008). *Tourism and sustainability: Development, globalisation and new tourism in the Third World*. London: Routledge.

Moya Pons, F. (1986). *El pasado Dominicano*. Santiago, República Dominicana: Universidad Católica Madre y Maestra.

Muggah, Robert, Victoria Walker, Ilona Szabo, and Antoine Hanin. (2013). Study on EU support to justice and security sector reform in Latin America and the Caribbean. *The International Security Sector Advisory Team*. Retrieved from http://issat.dcaf .ch/download/38585/573411.

Munroe, Michelle Angela. (2013). *The dark side of globalization: The transnationalization of garrisons in the case of Jamaica.* (Thesis). Florida International University.

Murray, Georgina, and David Peetz. (2010). *Women of the coal rushes.* Sydney, Australia: UNSW Press.

Murray, Georgina, and David Peetz. (2012). The financialisation of global corporate ownership. In Georgina Murray and J. Scott (Eds.), *Financial elites and transnational business: Who rules the world?* Cheltenham, U.K.: Edward Elgar.

Murray, Georgina, and J. Scott. (Eds.). (2012). *Financial elite and transnational business: Who rules the world?* Cheltenham, U.K.: Edward Elgar.

NACLA. (1977). The Cane Contract: West Indians in Florida. *Report on the Americas, 11*(Nov./Dec.), 11–17.

NASA. (2010). How will global warming change earth? Retrieved from http://earthob servatory.nasa.gov/Features/GlobalWarming/page6.php.

Ness, Immanuel. (2011). *Guest workers and resistance to U.S. corporate despotism.* Chicago: University of Illinois Press.

Neveling, Patrick. (2014). *How the historical geography of capitalism is made: Area studies, commodity chains, export processing zones and the spatial reconfiguration of the capitalist world-system after 1947.* University of Berne, Switzerland: Working Paper for Historical Institute/Contemporary History in Global Perspective.

Neveling, Patrick. (2015). Export processing zones and global class formation. In James G. Carrier and Don Kalb, *Anthropologies of class: Power, practice and inequality,* Cambridge: Cambridge University Press.

Nienaber, Georgianne. (2017). China extends her silk road to Haiti. Huffington Post. Retrieved from http://www.huffingtonpost.com/entry/china-extends-her-silk-road-to -haiti_us_5984927ae4b0bd8232029723.

Niimi, Yoko, and Çaglar Özden. (2008). Migration and remittances in Latin America: Patterns and determinants. In P. Fajnzylber and J. Humberto López (Eds.), *Remittances and development: Lessons from Latin America* (pp. 51–86). Washington, DC: World Bank.

Niles, Bertram. (2006). Are Guyanese welcome in Barbados? BBC. Retrieved from http://www.bbc.co.uk/caribbean/news/story/2006/09/060906_guyaneseinbdos .shtml.

Niles, Ted. (2012). Shock waves—Majescor flourishes in post-quake Haiti. *Financial Post.* Retrieved from http://business.financialpost.com/2012/05/01/shock-waves-majescor -flourishes-in-post-quake-haiti/.

Nonnenmacher, Tomas. (2014). History of the U.S. telegraph industry. Retrieved from https://eh.net/encyclopedia/history-of-the-u-s-telegraph-industry/.

Norton, Ben. (2016). CIA and Saudi weapons for Syrian rebels fueled black market arms trafficking, report says. *Salon.* Retrieved from https://www.salon.com/2016/06/28/ cia_and_saudi_weapons_for_syrian_rebels_fueled_black_market_arms_trafficking_report_says/.

Norton, Ben. (2017). Why are the Trump White House and media citing an anti-semitic book's claims to demonize Communism? *Alternet: Grayzone Project.* Retrieved from https://www.alternet.org/grayzone-project/trump-media-antisemitic-black-book -communism-whitewash-nazis.

Norton, Ben. (2018). Every Single Member of the US Congress Approved Crushing Sanctions on Nicaragua. *Grayzone Project*. Retrieved from https://grayzoneproject.com/2018/12/14/congress-sanctions-nicaragua-nica-act/.

Nurse, Keith. (2006). Diaspora, migration and development in the Caribbean. Focal. Retrieved from http://www.focal.ca/pdf/migration_Nurse_diaspora%20migration%20development%20Caribbean_September%202004_FPP-04-6.pdf.

Nwoke, Chibuzo. (1987). *Third world minerals and global pricing: A new theory*. London: Zed Books.

Observatorio de conflictos mineros de América Latina. (2015). Mapa de conflictos mineros, proyectos y empresas mineras en América Latina. Retrieved from https://basedatos.conflictosmineros.net/ocmal_db/.

OECD Development Centre. (2009). Dominican Republic. In *Latin American Economic Outlook* (pp. 233–236). Retrieved from http://www.oecd.org/dev/americas/44535785.pdf.

Office of the United States Trade Representative. (2014). CAFTA-DR (Dominican Republic-Central America FTA). Retrieved from https://ustr.gov/trade-agreements/free-trade-agreements/cafta-dr-dominican-republic-central-america-fta.

Oficina Nacional de Estadisticas de la Republica Dominicana. (2002).

OilVoice. (2018). China and Russia remain key allies for Venezuela but more financial support will come at the price of sharing an increasing control of the country's oil and gas sector, says GlobalData. Retrieved from https://oilvoice.com/Opinion/22464/China-and-Russia-Remain-Key-Allies-for-Venezuela-But-More-Financial-Support-Will-Come-at-the-Price-of-Sharing-an-Increasing-Control-of-the-Countrys-Oi.

Ondetti, Gabriel. (2012). International migration and social policy underdevelopment in the Dominican Republic. *Global Social Policy, 12*(1), 45–66.

ONPES and World Bank. (2014). *Haiti: Investing in people to fight poverty*.

Oreskes, Naomi. (2004). Undeniable global warming. *Washington Post*. Retrieved from http://www.washingtonpost.com/wp-dyn/articles/A26065-2004Dec25.html.

Orozco, Manuel. (2006). Understanding the remittance economy in Haiti. Washington, DC: Inter-American Dialogue.

Ortiz, Altagracia. (Ed.). (1996). *Puerto Rican women and work: Bridges in transnational labor*. Philadelphia: Temple University Press.

Osuna, Steven. (2015). Intra-Latina/Latino encounters: Salvadorian and Mexican struggles and Salvadorian-Mexican subjectivities in Los Angeles. *Ethnicities, 2*(15), 234–254.

Oxfam. (2017). An economy for the 99%. Retrieved from https://www.oxfam.org/sites/www.oxfam.org/files/file_attachments/bp-economy-for-99-percent-160117-en.pdf.

Oyogoa, Francisca. (2016a). Cruise ships: A triumph of global capitalism and exemplar of racialized servility. Paper presented at the annual meeting of the American Sociological Association Annual Meeting, Chicago, August 20.

Oyogoa, Francisca. (2016b). Cruise ships: Continuity and change in the world system. *Journal of World-Systems Research, 22*(1), 31–37.

Padget, Tim. (2008). A new cold war in the Caribbean? *Times*. Retrieved from http://content.time.com/time/world/article/0,8599,1826161,00.html.

Paley, Dawn. (2014). *Drug war capitalism*. San Francisco: AK Press.

Palmer, Colin A. (2014). *Cheddi Jagan and the politics of power: British Guiana's struggle for independence*. Chapel Hill: University of North Carolina Press.

Palmer, Ransford W. (2009). *The Caribbean economy in the age of globalization*. London: Palgrave Macmillan.

Panitch, Leo, and Sam Gindin. (2013). *The making of global capitalism: The political economy of American empire*. London: Verso.

Parker, Jason. (2002, June). Remapping the cold war in the tropics: Race, communism and security in the British West Indies. *International History Review, xxiv*(2), 318–347.

Parreñas, Rhacel Salazar. (2005). *Children of global migration: Transnational families and gendered woes.* Stanford, CA: Stanford University Press.

Patterson, Orlando. (1982). *Slavery and social death: A comparative study.* Cambridge, MA: Harvard University Press.

Patterson, Rubin. (2013). Transnational capitalist class: What's race got to do with it? everything! *Globalizations, 10*(5), 673–690.

Pattullo, Polly. (2005). *Last resorts: The cost of tourism in the Caribbean.* New York: Monthly Review Press.

Payne, Jonathan L., Andrew M. Bush, Noel A. Heim, Matthew L. Knope, and Douglas J. McCauley. (2016). Ecological selectivity of the emerging mass extinction in the oceans. *Science, 353*(6305), 1284–1286.

Peetz, David, and Georgina Murray. (2012). The financialization of global corporate ownership. In G. Murray and J. Scott (Eds.), *Financial elites and transnational business: Who rules the world?* (pp. 26–53). London: Edward Elgar.

Pellerano, Luis R. (2012). The Dominican Republic as investment jewel of the Caribbean. *International Financial Law Review.* Retrieved from http://www.iflr.com/Article /3099458/The-Dominican-Republic-as-investment-jewel-of-the-Caribbean.html.

Perelman, Michael. (2011). *The invisible handcuffs of capitalism: How market tyranny stifles the economy by stunting workers.* New York: Monthly Review Press.

Pérez, Louis A., Jr. (2003). *Cuba and the United States: Ties of singular intimacy.* Athens: University of Georgia Press.

Pérez, Louis, Jr. (2016). The cost of covert operations in Cuba. Retrieved from https://nacla .org/news/2016/12/16/cost-covert-operations-cuba.

Pertierra, Anna Cristina, and Heather A. Horst. (2009). Introduction: Thinking about Caribbean media worlds. *International Journal of Cultural Studies, 12*, 99–111.

Phillips, Peter. (2018). *Giants: The global power elite.* New York: Seven Stories Press.

Pierce, Justin R., and Peter K. Schott. (2012). The surprisingly swift decline of U.S. manufacturing Employment. *National Bureau of Economic Research.* Working Paper No. 18655.

Piketty, Thomas. (2014). *Capital in the twenty-first century.* New Haven, CT: Belknap Press/Harvard University Press.

Pilger, John, and Alan Lowery. (2000). *Paying the price: Killing the children of Iraq.* London: Carlton Television.

Pinto Pereira, Lexley M., Henry Fraser, and Francis Burnett. (1998). Assessment of generic drugs in the Caribbean. *Therapeutic Innovation and Regulatory Science, 32*(1), 145–150.

Podur, Justin. (2012). *Haiti's new dictatorship: The coup, the earthquake and the UN occupation.* London: Pluto Press.

Podur, Justin. (2017). Why won't American media tell the truth about what's happening in Venezuela? *AlterNet.* Retrieved from https://www.alternet.org/news-amp-politics /why-wont-american-media-tell-truth-about-whats-happening-venezuela.

Pollard, Velma. (2005). The short story and me. In M. Angus Lee (Ed.), *The writers on writing: The art of the short story* (pp. 23–26).

Portella, Eli. (2017). The Tricontinental. Talk at third biennial conference of the Network for Critical Studies of Global Capitalism. La Habana, Cuba.

Porter, Catherine. (2014). Haitian garment workers' low pay has them still going hungry. The Star. Retrieved from http://www.thestar.com/news/world/2014/02/11/haitian _garment_workers_low_pay_has_them_still_going_hungry.html.

Portes, Alejandro. (1997). Globalization from below: The rise of transnational communities. Princeton University Working Paper. Retrieved from http://www.transcomm.ox.ac.uk/working%20papers/portes.pdf.

Portes, Alejandro. (2013). Migration and development: Reconciling opposite views. In S. E. Eckstein and A. Najam (Eds.), *How immigrants impact their homelands* (pp. 31–50). North Carolina: Duke University Press.

Post, Ken. (1978). *Arise ye starvelings: The Jamaican labour rebellion of 1938 and its aftermath*. New York: Springer.

Potter, Robert B. (1989). Rural-urban interaction in Barbados and the Southern Caribbean: Patterns and processes of dependent development in small countries. In R. B. Potter and T. Unwin (Eds.), *The geography of urban-rural interaction in developing countries* (pp. 257–293). London: Routledge.

Potts, Lydia. (1990). *The world labor market: A history of migration*. Zed Books.

Poulantzas, Nicos. (1978). *State, power, socialism*. London: New Left Review.

Prashad, Vijay. (2008). The darker nations: A people's history of the third world. New York: New Press.

Prepetit, Claude. (2000). *Memento pour l'histoire: chronologie de secteur minier haitien, de 1492 à 2000*. Règublique d'Haïti: *Buerea des mines et de l'energie*.

Presecon. (2012). Quienes somos? Retrieved from http://presecon.blogspot.com /p/que-espresecon-vision-convertirnos-en.html.

Preston, Andrew. (2012). Evangelical internationalism: A conservative worldview for the age of globalization. In Laura Jane Gifford and Daniel K. Williams (Eds.), *The Right Side of the Sixties: Reexamining Conservatism's Decade of Transformation* (pp. 221–240). New York: Palgrave Macmillan.

Price, Richard. (1996). *Maroon societies: Rebel slave communities in the Americas*. Baltimore: John Hopkins University Press.

Pringle, Heather. (2014). The origins of inequality: Ancient roots of the 1%. Occupy.com. Retrieved from http://www.occupy.com/article/origins-inequality-ancient-roots-1.

Pyles, Loretta, Suran Ahn, and Juliana Svistova. (2017). Securitization, racial cleansing, and disaster capitalism: Neoliberal disaster governance in the US Gulf Coast and Haiti. *Critical Social Policy, 37*(4), 1–22.

Rabe, Stephen G. (2005). *U.S. intervention in British Guiana: A cold war story*. Chapel Hill: University of North Carolina Press.

Ramírez, S. (2012). Accumulation by dispossession: Barrick and Goldcorp's Pueblo Viejo Gold Mine in the Dominican Republic. MiMundo.org. Retrieved May 15, 2013, from http://www.mimundo.org/2012/07/30/accumulation-by-dispossession-barrick-goldcorp's-pueblo-viejo-gold-mine-in-the-dominican-republic/.

Ramos, Valeriano, Jr. (1982). The concepts of ideology, hegemony, and organic intellectuals in Gramsci's Marxism. Retrieved from https://www.marxists.org/history/erol/ncm-7/tr-gramsci.htm.

Rangel, Salvador, and Jeb Sprague-Silgado. (2017). The U.S. political scene: Whiteness and the legitimacy crisis of global capitalism. *Counterpunch*. Retrieved from http://www.counterpunch.org/2017/05/02/the-u-s-political-scene-whiteness-and-the-legitimacy-crisis-of-global-capitalism/.

Reed, Adolph, Jr. (2000). Race and class in the work of Oliver Cromwell Cox. *Monthly Review*. Retrieved from http://monthlyreview.org/2001/02/01/race-and-class-in-the-work-of-oliver-cromwell-cox/.

Regalado, Roberto. (2007). *Latin America at the crossroads: Domination, crisis, popular movements, and political alternatives*. Melbourne, Australia: Ocean Press.

Regan, Jane. (2004). Labour-Haiti: Workers fight for rights in free trade zone. *Inter Press Service*. Retrieved from http://www.ipsnews.net/2004/07/labour-haiti- workers-fight -for-rights-in-free-trade-zone/.

Regan, Jane. (2013). "Haiti is open for business!" Government complicity in wage theft by foreign factories. *Haiti Liberté*. Global Research, December 05.

Resch, Robert Paul. (1992). *Althusser and the renewal of Marxist social theory*. Berkeley: University of California Press.

Reyes-Santos, Alaí. (2015). *Our Caribbean kin: Race and nation in the neoliberal Antilles*. New Brunswick, NJ: Rutgers University Press.

Ribbe, Claude. (2005). *Le crime de Napoléon*. Paris, France: Editions Privé.

Richardson, Bonham C. (1993). *The Caribbean in the wider world, 1492–1992: A regional geography*. Cambridge: Cambridge University Press.

Ridgeway, James. (1994). *The Haiti files: Decoding the crisis*. Washington, DC: Azul Editions.

Robinson, William I. (1996). *Promoting polyarchy: Globalization, U.S. intervention, and hegemony*. Cambridge: Cambridge University Press.

Robinson, William I. (2001). Social theory and globalization: The rise of a transnational state. *Theory and Society, 30*(2), 157–197.

Robinson, William I. (2003). *Transnational conflicts: Central America, social change, and globalization*. London: Verso.

Robinson, William I. (2004). *A theory of global capitalism: Production, class, and state in a transnational world*. Baltimore, MD: John Hopkins University Press.

Robinson, William I. (2005). Gramsci and globalisation: From nation-state to transnational hegemony. *Critical Review of International Social and Political Philosophy, 8*(4), 1–16.

Robinson, William I. (2008). *Latin America and global capitalism: A critical globalization perspective*. Baltimore, MD: John Hopkins University Press.

Robinson, William I. (2009). Beyond the theory of imperialism: Global capitalism and the transnational state. In Alexander Anievas (Ed.), *Marxism and world politics* (pp. 61–76). London: Routledge.

Robinson, William I. (2010a). Giovanni Arrighi: Systemic cycles of accumulation, hegemonic transitions, and the rise of china. *New Political Economy, 16*(2), 267–280.

Robinson, William I. (2010b). Global capitalism theory and the emergence of transnational elites. WIDER Working Paper 2010/002. Helsinki: UNU-WIDER.

Robinson, William I. (2011). Globalization and the sociology of Immanuel Wallerstein: A critical appraisal. *International Sociology, 26*(6), 723–745.

Robinson, William I. (2012). Global capitalism theory and the emergence of transnational states. *Critical Sociology, 38*(3), 349–363.

Robinson, William I. (2014a). *Global capitalism and the crisis of humanity*. Cambridge: Cambridge University Press.

Robinson, William I. (2014b). The Story of Salsa: Panel discussion with Angel Lebron, Marisol Berrios Miranda, and Raul Fernandez. Retrieved from https://www.youtube .com/watch?v=PkC6BLprVkE.

Robinson, William I. (2016). Global capitalism, the BRICS, and the transnational state. In Jeb Sprague (Ed.), *Globalization and transnational capitalism in Asia and Oceania*. London: Routledge.

Robinson, William I. (2017). What is behind the renegotiation of NAFTA? Trumpism and the new global economy. *Truthout*. Retrieved from http://www.truth-out.org/news /item/41365-what-is-behind-the-renegotiation-of-nafta-trumpism-and-the-new -global-economy.

Robinson, William I. (2018). Capitalist development in Nicaragua and the mirage of the Left. *Truthout*. Retrieved from http://www.truth-out.org/news/item/44490-capitalist -development-in-nicaragua-and-the-mirage-of-the-left.

Robinson, William I., and Kent Norsworthy. (1987). *David and goliath: The U.S. war against Nicaragua*. New York: Monthly Review Press.

Robinson, William I., and Xuan Santos. (2014). Global capitalism, immigrant labor, and the struggle for justice. *Class, Race and Corporate Power, 2*(3), 1–16.

Robinson, William I., and Jeb Sprague. (2018). The transnational capitalist class: Origin and evolution of a concept. In Mark Juergensmeyer, Manfred Steger, Saskia Sassen, and Victor Faesse (Eds.), *The oxford handbook of global studies*. Oxford: Oxford University Press.

Rodney, Walter. (1981). *How Europe underdeveloped Africa*. Washington, DC: Howard University Press.

Rodrigue, Jean Paul, Claud Motois, and Brian Slack. (2013). *The geography of transport systems*. New York: Routledge.

Rodriguez, Robyn Magalit. (2010). *Migrants for export: How the Philippine state brokers labor to the world*. Minneapolis: University of Minnesota Press.

Rodriguez-Garavito, C. (2008). Sewing resistance: Transnational organizing, anti-sweatshop activism, and labor rights in the US-Caribbean basin apparel industry (1990–2005). Woodrow Wilson School of Public and International Affairs, Center for Migration and Development, Working Papers 01/2008. Princeton, NJ: Princeton University.

Rohde, David. (2012). The swelling middle. *Reuters*. Retrieved from http://www.reuters .com/middle-class-infographic.

Roland, L. Kaifa. (2010). *Cuban Color in tourism and la lucha: An ethnography of racial meanings*. Oxford: Oxford University Press.

Roorda, Eric Paul., Lauren H. Derby, and Raymundo Gonzalez. (Eds.). (2014). *The Dominican reader: History, culture, politics*. Durham, NC: Duke University Press.

Rothkopf, David. (2009). *Superclass: The global power elite and the world they are making*. Farrar, New York. Straus and Giroux.

Rowling, Nick. (1987) *Commodities: How the world was taken to market*. London: Free Association Books.

Roy, Arundhati. (2014). The NGO-ization of resistance. *Pambazuka News*. Retrieved from https://www.pambazuka.org/governance/ngo-ization-resistance.

Royal Caribbean. (2009). Oasis of the seas. Retrieved from http://www.oasisoftheseas.com /presskit/Oasis_of_the_Seas.pdf.

Royal Caribbean. (2013). Royal Caribbean to base explorer of the seas out of Port Canaveral. Retrieved from http://www.royalcaribbeanblog.com/2013/05/24/royal-ca ribbean-base-explorer-seas-out-port-canaveral.

Safa, Helen I. (2002). Questioning globalization: Gender and export processing in the Dominican Republic. *Journal of Developing Societies, 18*(2–3), 11–31.

Sakwa, Richard. (2013). The soviet collapse: Contradictions and neo-moderniasation. *Journal of Eurasian Studies, 4*(1), 65–77.

Salas Porras, Alejandra. (2017) Las élites transnacionales mexicanas. Talk at the 2017 Havana, Cuba conference of the Network for Critical Studies of Global Capitalism. Retrieved from https://www.youtube.com/watch?v=7VvuLG3Dy6w.

Sanatan, Amílcar. (2017). Building political power in the Caribbean youth. *teleSUR*. Retrieved from http://www.telesurtv.net/english/opinion/Building-Political-Power -in-the-Caribbean-Youth-20170113-0017.html.

Sansavior, Eva, and Richard Scholar. (Eds.). (2015). *Caribbean globalizations, 1492 to the present day*. Liverpool, U.K.: Liverpool University Press.

Sargent, John, and Linda Matthews. (2009). China vs. Mexico in the global EPZ industry: Maquiladoras, FDI quality and plant mortality. Edinburg: University of Texas Pan America Center for Border Economic Studies.

Sassen, Saskia. (1988). *The mobility of labor and capital: A study in international investment and labor flow*. Cambridge: Cambridge University Press.

Sassen, Saskia. (1991). *The global city: New York, London, Tokyo*. Princeton, NJ: Princeton University Press.

Sassen, Saskia. (2014). *Expulsions: Brutality and complexity in the global economy*. Cambridge, MA: Harvard University Press.

Schavelzon, Salvador, and Jeffery R. Webber. (2017). Podemos and Latin America. In Óscar García Agustín and Marco Briziarelli (Eds.), *Podemos and the new political cycle: Leftwing populism and anti-establishment politics*. Basingstoke, U.K.: Palgrave Macmillan.

Schlesinger, Stephen, and Stephen Kinzer. (2005). *Bitter fruit: The story of the American coup in Guatemala*. Cambridge, MA: David Rockefeller Center for Latin American Studies.

Schmidt, Hans. (1995). *The United States occupation of Haiti, 1915–1934*. New Brunswick, NJ: Rutgers University Press.

Schopfle, Gregory, and Jorge F Perez-Lopez. (1992). Export-oriented assembly operations in the Caribbean. In Irma Tirado de Alonso (Ed.), *Trade issues in the Caribbean*. Philadelphia: Gordon and Breach.

Schrank, Andrew. (2001). Export processing zones: Free market islands or bridges to structural transformation? *Development Policy Review, 19*(2), 223–242.

Schuller, Mark. (2007). Haiti's CCI: The tail wagging the dog? *HaitiAnalysis*. Retrieved from http://haitianalysis.blogspot.com/2007/10/haitis-cci-tail-wagging-dog.html.

Schulman, Jeremy. (2015). How 19 big-name corporations plan to make money off the climate crisis. *Mother Jones*. Retrieved from http://www.motherjones.com/environment/2015/12/climate-change-business-opportunities.

Schwartz, Mattathias. (2011). Massacre in Jamaica. *New Yorker*. Retrieved from https://www.newyorker.com/magazine/2011/12/12/a-massacre-in-jamaica.

Scipes, Kim. (2011). *AFL-CIO's secret war against developing country workers: Solidarity or sabotage?* Lanham, MD: Lexington Books.

Scott, Julius S. (2018). *The common wind: Afro-American currents in the age of the Haitian Revolution*. London: Verso.

Scully, Pamela, and Diana Paton. (Eds.). (2005). *Gender and slave emancipation in the Atlantic world*. Durham, NC: Duke University Press.

Seed, Patricia. (2015). How globalization invented Indians in the Caribbean. In Eva Sansavior and Richard Scholar. *Caribbean globalizations: 1492 to the present day*. Liverpool, U.K.: Liverpool University Press.

Segovia, Alexander. (2002). *Transformación estructural y reforma económica en El Salvador: El funcionamiento económico de los noventa y sus efectos sobre el crecimiento, la pobreza, y la distribución del ingreso*. Guatemala City, Guatemala: F y G Editores.

Sender, John. (1987). *The development of capitalism in Africa*. London: Routledge.

Senior, Olive. (2014). *Dying to better themselves: West Indians and the building of the Panama Canal*. Mona, Jamaica: University of the West Indies Press.

Shamsie, Yasmine. (2009). Export processing zones: The purported glimmer in Haiti's development murk. *Review of International Political Economy, 16*(4), 649–672.

Sheller, Mimi. (2003). *Consuming the Caribbean: From Arawaks to Zombies*. London: Routledge.

Sheller, Mimi. (2015). Aluminum: Globalizing Caribbean mobilities, Caribbeanizing global mobilities. In Eva Sansavior and Richard Scholar (Eds.), *Caribbean Globalizations, 1492 to the Present Day*. Liverpool, U.K.: Liverpool University Press.

Shenk, Tim. (2009). La Barrick Gold y Organización Cisneros: 2 empresas que amenazan al pueblo dominicano. *Justicia Global: Organización política y social*. Retrieved from https://enjusticiaglobal.wordpress.com/2009/12/14/la-barrick-gold-y-organizacion -cisneros-2-empresas-que-amenazan-al-pueblo-dominicano/.

Shenk, Tim. (2015). Dominican movement to halt mining faces repression, suspected arson. *CUSLAR*. Retrieved from https://cuslar.org/2015/05/13/dominican-movement -to-halt-mining-faces-repression-suspected-arson/.

Shepherd, Verne, and Hilary Beckles. (1999). *Caribbean slavery in the Atlantic world: A student reader*. Kingston, Jamaica: Ian Randle.

Silvera, Makeda. (1992). Man-royals and sodomites: Some thoughts on the invisibility of Afro-Caribbean lesbians. *Feminist Studies, 18*(3), 521–532.

Singh, Supriya. (2013). Transnational family money: Remittances, gifts and inheritance. *Journal of Intercultural Studies, 33*(5), 475–492.

Sirkeci, Ibrahim, Jeffrey H. Cohen, and Dilip Ratha. (Eds.). (2012). *Migration and remittances during the global financial crisis and beyond*. Washington, DC: World Bank.

Sklair, Leslie. (1989). *Assembling for development: The maquila industry in Mexico and the United States*. Boston: Unwin Hyman.

Sklair, Leslie. (2001). *The transnational capitalist class*. Hoboken, NJ: Wiley-Blackwell.

Sklair, Leslie. (2002). *Globalization: Capitalism and its alternatives*. Oxford: Oxford University Press.

Sklair, Leslie. (2009). The emancipatory potential of generic globalization. *Globalizations, 6*(4), 525–539.

Sklair, Leslie. (2012). Culture-Ideology of consumerism. In George Ritzer (Ed.), *The Wiley-Blackwell encyclopedia of globalization*. Malden, MA: Blackwell.

Smith, Adam. (2003). *The wealth of nations*. New York: Bantam Classics.

Smith, John. (2016). *Imperialism in the twenty-first century: Globalization, super-exploitation, and capitalism's final crisis*. New York: Monthly Review Press.

Smith, Mathew J. (2009). *Red and black in Haiti: Radicalism, conflict, and political change, 1934–1957*. Chapel Hill: University of North Carolina Press.

Smith, Michael Garfield. (1965). *The plural society in the British West Indies*. Berkeley: University of California Press.

Snowden, Frank M. (1983). *Before color prejudice: The ancient view of blacks*. Cambridge, MA: Harvard University Press.

Solomos, John. (1986). Varieties of Marxist conceptions of "race," class and the state: A critical analysis. In J. Rex and D. Mason (Eds.), *Theories of race and ethnic relations* (pp. 84–109). Cambridge: Cambridge University Press.

Spencer, Herbert. ([1863] 2018). *The principles of biology*. CreateSpace Independent.

Spivak, Gayatri. (1995). *The Spivak reader: Selected works of Gayati Chakravorty Spivak*. London: Routledge.

Sprague, Jeb. (2006a). Invisible violence: Ignoring murder in post-coup Haiti. *Extra. The Newsletter of FAIR*. Retrieved from https://fair.org/extra/invisible-violence/.

Sprague, Jeb. (2006b). A Lavalas mayor in hiding: An interview with Jean Charles Moise. *Left turn: Notes from the global intifada*. Retrieved from http://jebsprague.blogspot .com/2006/07/interview-with-moise-jean-charles.html.

Sprague, Jeb. (2008). Labor, neoliberalism, and the 2004 coup in Haiti. *HaitiAnalysis.* Retrieved from http://haitianalysis.blogspot.com/search?q=neoliberalism+labor.

Sprague, Jeb. (2009). Transnational capitalist class in the global financial crisis: A discussion with Leslie Sklair. *Globalizations, 6*(4), 499–507.

Sprague, Jeb. (2010). Statecraft in the global financial crisis: An interview with Kanishka Jayasuriya. *Journal of Critical Globalisation Studies, 6*(4), 499–507.

Sprague, Jeb. (2011a). Empire, global capitalism, and theory: Reconsidering Hardt and Negri. *Current Perspectives in Social Theory, 29,* 187–207.

Sprague, Jeb. (2011b). Review of Peter Dicken, global shift: Mapping the changing contours of the world economy. *Journal of Sociology, 47*(2), 219–221.

Sprague, Jeb. (2011c). Review of Robyn Magalit Rodrigeuz, *Migrants for export: How the Philippine state brokers Labor to the world.* Minneapolis: University of Minnesota Press. *Science and Society, 75*(3), 442–444.

Sprague, Jeb. (2012a). *Paramilitarism and the assault on democracy in Haiti.* New York: Monthly Review Press.

Sprague, Jeb. (2012b). Transnational state. In G. Ritzer (Ed.), *The Wiley-Blackwell Encyclopedia of Globalization* (pp. 2031–2037). Malden, MA: Blackwell.

Sprague, Jeb. (2012c). Reviving Haiti's army would harm democracy. *Miami Herald.* Retrieved from http://www.miamiherald.com/news/local/community/article 1942504.html.

Sprague, Jeb. (2013). Island of Hispaniola: Coalitions and cross-border solidarity. *Pambazuka News, Pan-African Voices for Freedom and Justice.* Retrieved from http://www.pambazuka.net/en/category.php/features/88549.

Sprague, Jeb. (2014a). Transnational corporations in twenty-first century capitalism: An interview with Grazia Ietto-Gillies. *Critical Perspectives on International Business, 10*(1), 35–50.

Sprague, Jeb. (2014b). Review of Leo Panitch and Sam Gindin, The making of global capitalism: The political economy of American empire. *Critical Sociology, 40*(5), 803–807.

Sprague, Jeb. (2014c). Jamaica and the politics of debt trap. *TeleSUR.* Retrieved from http://www.telesurtv.net/english/opinion/Jamaica-and-the-Politics-of-Debt-Trap-20141218-0034.html.

Sprague, Jeb. (2015). From international to transnational mining: The industry's shifting political economy and the Caribbean. *Caribbean Studies, 43*(1), 71–110.

Sprague, Jeb. (Ed.). (2016). *Globalization and transnational capitalism in Asia and Oceania.* London: Routledge.

Sprague, Jeb. (2018). US-backed Haitian government agents accused of conducting massacre. *The Canary.* Retrieved from https://www.thecanary.co/global/world-analysis/2018/12/19/us-backed-haitian-government-agents-accused-of-conducting-massacre/.

Sprague, Jeb. (2019). The Caribbean and global capitalism: Five strategic traits. In Ino Rossi (Ed.), *Frontiers of globalization research: Theoretical and methodological approaches* (2nd ed.). New York: Springer.

Sprague, Jeb, and Grazia Ietto-Gillies. (2014). Transnational corporations in twenty-first century capitalism: An interview with Grazia Ietto-Gillies. *Critical Perspectives on International Business, 10*(1/2), 35–50.

Sprague, Jeb, and Wadner Pierre. (2007). Haiti: Poor residents of capital describe a state of siege. IPS. Retrieved from http://www.ipsnews.net/2007/02/haiti-poor-residents-of-capital-describe-a-state-of-siege/.

Sprague-Silgado, Jeb. (2016). Polyarchy in the Dominican Republic: Elite versus the elite. *NACLA website.* Retrieved from https://nacla.org/news/2016/05/06/polyarchy-dominican-republic-elite-versus-elite.

Sprague-Silgado, Jeb. (2017a). The Caribbean cruise ship business and the emergence of a transnational capitalist class. *Journal of World Systems Research, 23*(1), 93–125.

Sprague-Silgado, Jeb. (2017b). The transnational capitalist class and relations of production in Asia and Oceania. *Research in Political Economy, 32*, 133–158.

Sprague-Silgado, Jeb. (2017c). Toward an understanding of transnational capitalism in the Caribbean: A review of Hilbourne Watson, globalization, sovereignty and citizenship in the Caribbean. *Latin American Perspectives, 44*(4), 209–216.

Sprague-Silgado, Jeb. (2018a). Global capitalism, Haiti, and the flexibilization of paramilitarism. *Third World Quarterly, 39*(1).

Sprague-Silgado, Jeb. (2018b). Global capitalism in the Caribbean. *NACLA, 50*(2).

Stabroek News. (2009). Exploited, undocumented Guyanese would rather stay in Barbados. Retrieved from https://www.stabroeknews.com/2009/news/stories/06/07/exploited-undocumented-guyanese-would-rather-stay-in-barbados/.

Standing, Guy. (2013). *The precariat: The new dangerous class.* Bloomsbury Academic.

Stark, Oded. (1978). *Economic-Demographic interactions in agricultural development: The case of rural-to-urban migration.* Food and agriculture organization of the United Nations, Rome.

Statista. (2017). Total revenue of the top mining companies worldwide from 2002 to 2016 (in billion U.S. dollars). Retrieved from https://www.statista.com/statistics/208715/total-revenue-of-the-top-mining-companies/.

Stavrianos, Leften. (1998). *A global history: From prehistory to the 21st century.* London: Pearson.

Stephens, Evelyne Huber, and John D. Stephens. (1986). *Democratic socialism in Jamaica: Transformation in dependent capitalism.* London: Palgrave Macmillan.

Struna, Jason. (2009). Toward a theory of global proletarian fractions. *Perspectives on Global Development and Technology, 8*, 230–260.

Suki, Lenora. (2004). Financial institutions and the remittances market in the Dominican Republic. Center on Globalization and Sustainable Development Working Paper Series. New York: Earth Institute at Columbia University.

Sweezy, Paul M. (1942). *The theory of capitalist development: Principles of Marxian political economy.* New York: Monthly Review Press.

SZ Jug. (2013). The history of free trade zones worldwide. Retrieved from https://web.archive.org/web/20130423022843/http://www.szjug.rs/the-history-of-free-trade-zones-worldwide.html.

Szymanski, Albert. (1983). *Class structure: A critical perspective.* New York: Praeger.

Tablada, Carlos. (1998). *Che Guevara: Economics and politics in the transition to socialism.* New York: Pathfinder Press.

Taylor, Michael A., Tannecia S. Stephenson, A. Anthony Chen, and Kimberly A. Stephenson. (2012). Climate change and the Caribbean: Review and response. *Caribbean Studies, 40*(2), 169–202.

Telecompaper. (2003). Digicel to launch mobile service. Retrieved from http://www.telecompaper.com/news/digicel-to-launch-mobile-service--379368.

Terry, William C. (2013). The perfect worker: Discursive makings of Filipinos in the workplace hierarchy of the globalized cruise industry. *Social and Cultural Geography, 15*(1), 73–93.

Thai, Hung Cam. (2014). *Insufficient funds: The culture of money in low-wage transnational families.* Stanford, CA: Stanford University Press.

Theobald, William F. (2004). *Global tourism.* New York: Routledge.

Thomas, Clive Y. (1968). A model of pure plantation economy: Comment. *Social and Economic Studies, 17*(3), 339–348.

Thomas, Clive Y. (1984). *The rise of the authoritarian state in peripheral societies.* New York: New York University Press.

Thompson, Alvin O. (1997). *The haunting past: Politics, economics and race in Caribbean life.* London: Routledge.

Thompson, Alvin. (2006). *Fight to freedom: African runaways and maroons in the Americas.* Mona, Jamaica: University of the West Indies Press.

Thompson, Derek. (2013). Bash brothers: How globalization and technology teamed up to crush middle-class workers. *The Atlantic.* Retrieved from http://www.theatlantic.com/business/archive/2013/08/bash-brothers-how-globalization-and-technology-teamed-up-to-crush-middle-class-workers/278571/.

Thompson, E. P. ([1963] 2002) *The making of the English working class.* London: Penguin.

Thorin, Maria. (2001). The gender dimension of globalization: A survey of the literature with a focus on Latin America and the Caribbean. *International Commerce, 17.* United Nations.

Todoroki, Emiko, Matteo Vaccani, and Wameek Noor. (2009). *The Canada-Caribbean remittance corridor: Fostering formal remittances to Haiti and Jamaica through effective regulation.* Washington, DC: World Bank Working Papers.

Tornhill, Sofie. (2010). Capital visions: Scripting progress and work in Nicaragua free-trade zones. *Latin American Perspectives, 38*(5), 74–92.

Tortello, Rebecca. (2006). Somewhere beyond the sea: Jamaica's role in the history of the cruise line industry. *Jamaica Gleaner.* Retrieved from http://jamaica-gleaner.com/pages/history/story0076.html.

Trade Winds. (2014). Carnival synergies hunt could extend to new buildings. Retrieved from http://www.tradewindsnews.com/weekly/333994/carnival-synergies-hunt-could-extend-to-newbuildings.

Travel Weekly. (2003). Carnival, P&O princess tackle synergies. Retrieved from http://www.travelweekly.com/Cruise-Travel/Carnival-P-O-Princess-tackle-synergies.

Trotz, D. Alissa, and Beverly Mullings. (2013). Transnational migration, the state, and development: Reflecting on the 'diaspora option'. *Small Axe, 41.*

Trouillot, Michel-Rolph. (1997). *Silencing the past: Power and the production of history.* Boston: Beacon Press.

Trouillot, Michel-Rolph. (2000). *Haiti: State against nation.* New York: Monthly Review Press.

Uebersax, Mary B. (1996). Indecent proposal: Cruise ship pollution in the Caribbean. *Planeta.com.* Retrieved from http://www.planeta.com/planeta/96/0896cruise.html.

UNCTAD. (2017). UNCTAD Statistics. Retrieved from http://unctad.org/en/Pages/statistics.aspx.

UNCTC. (1991). *Transnational business information: A manual of needs and sources.* New York: United Nations.

UNEP. (2012). Growing greenhouse gas emissions due to meat production. Retrieved from http://www.unep.org/pdf/unep-geas_oct_2012.pdf.

UNICEF. (2017). The UN inter-agency group for child mortality estimation. Retrieved from http://www.childmortality.org/index.php?r=site/compare.

United States Environmental Protection Agency. (2017). Climate change indicators: Sea level. Retrieved from https://www.epa.gov/climate-indicators/climate-change-indicators-sea-level.

UNWTO. (2011). Tourism towards 2030 global overview. United Nations World Tourism Organization. Retrieved from http://www.e-unwto.org/content/w45127/?p=189899a5998f428f99f66ca0e17d2218.

UNWTO. (2012). International tourism hits one billion. United Nations World Tourism Organization. Retrieved from http://media.unwto.org/press-release/2012-12-12/international-tourism-hits-one-billion.

Urry, John. (1990). *The tourist gaze: Leisure and travel in contemporary societies*. Thousand Oaks, CA: Sage.

U.S. Department of State. (2014). Investment climate statements. Bureau of Economic and Business Affairs.

U.S. Tariff Commission. (1949). Mining and manufacturing industries in Haiti, Washington, DC: U.S. Government Publishing Office.

USAID. (2019). Foreign aid explorer. Retrieved from https://explorer.usaid.gov/data.html.

Valdez, Gilberto, and Humberto Miranda. (1999). *Las trampas de la globalizacion*. La Habana, Cuba: Galfisa—Editorial Jose Marti.

van Apeldoorn, Bastiaan. (2003). *Transnational capitalism and the struggle over European integration*. London: Routledge.

van der Pijl, K. (1998). *Transnational classes and international relations*. London: Routledge.

van Dijk, Teun Adrianus. (2009). *Racism and discourse in Latin America*. Lanham, MD: Rowman and Littlefield.

van Fossen, Anthony. (2012). *Tax havens and sovereignty in the pacific islands*. Brisbane, Australia: University of Queensland Press.

van Fossen, Anthony. (2016). Flags of convenience and global capitalism. *International Critical Thought, 6*(3), 359–377.

Velayutham, Sivakumar. (2016). National champions in a global arena: Rhetoric and inequality in global capitalism. In Jeb Sprague (Ed.), *Globalization and transnational capitalism in Asia and Oceania*. London: Routledge.

Vieira, Constanza. (2013). Open pit miners strike in Colombia. Retrieved from http://www.ipsnews.net/2013/02/open-pit-miners-strike-in-colombia/.

Villegas, Harry. (2017). *Cuba and Angola: The war for freedom*. Pathfinder Press.

Virgill, Nicola A.V. (2009). *Export processing zones: Tools of development or reform delay?* (Doctoral dissertation). George Mason University, Baltimore, Maryland. Retrieved from http://digilib.gmu.edu/xmlui/bitstream/handle/1920/4509/Virgill_Nicola.pdf?sequence=1.

Wacaster, Susan. (2010). The mineral industries of the Dominican Republic and Haiti. In *2009 Mineral Yearbook*. Washington, DC: USGS.

Wacaster, Susan. (2011). The mineral industries of the Dominican Republic and Haiti. In *2010 Mineral Yearbook*. Washington, DC: USGS.

Wacaster, Susan. (2012). 2011 minerals yearbook: Islands of the Caribbean [Advance release]. Washington, DC: USGS. Retrieved from http://minerals.usgs.gov/minerals/pubs/country/2011/myb3-2011-aa-bf-bb-uc-cu-jm-td.pdf.

Wacaster, Susan. (2013). 2012 minerals yearbook: Islands of the Caribbean [Advance release]. Washington, DC: USGS. Retrieved from http://minerals.er.usgs.gov/minerals/pubs/country/2012/myb3-2012-aa-cu-dr-jm-td-ac-bf-bb-do-st-sc-vc.pdf.

Wacaster, Susan. (2014). 2013 minerals yearbook: Islands of the Caribbean [Advance release]. Washington, DC: USGS. Retrieved from https://minerals.usgs.gov/minerals/pubs/country/2014/myb3-2014-aa-bf-bb-dr-jm-td.pdf.

Wah, Tatiana, and François Pierre-Louis. (2004). Evolution of Haitian immigrant organizations and community development in New York City. *Journal of Haitian Studies*, 10(1), 146–164.

Walker, J. (2010). Reason No. 9 not to cruise: Bunker fuel-nasty tar sludge! Retrieved from http://www.cruiselawnews.com/2010/05/articles/pollution-1/reason-no-9-not-to-cruise-bunker-fuel-nasty-tar-sludge/.

Wallerstein, Immanuel. (1979). *The capitalist world-economy*. Cambridge: Cambridge University Press.

War on Want and ITF. (2002). Sweatships. Retrieved from http://www.waronwant.org/attachments/Sweatships.pdf.

Warren, Bill. (1980). *Imperialism: Pioneer of capitalism*. London: Verso.

Waters, Colin N., Jan Zalasiewicz, Colin Summerhayes, Anthony D. Barnosky, Clément Poirier, Agnieszka Gałuszka, Alejandro Cearreta, Matt Edgeworth, and Erle C. Ellis. (2016). The anthropocene is functionally and stratigraphically distinct from the Holocene. *Science*. 351.

Watson, Bruce. (2015). Murky waters: The hidden environmental impacts of your cruise. *The Guardian*. Retrieved from https://www.theguardian.com/sustainable-business/2015/jan/05/cruise-ship-holidays-environmental-impact.

Watson, Hilbourne. (1985). Transnational banks and financial crisis in the Caribbean. In G. Irvin and X. Gorostiaga (Eds.), *Toward an alternative for Central America and the Caribbean*. London: George Allen and Unwin.

Watson, Hilbourne. (1990). The changing structure of world capital and development options in the Caribbean. In Judith Wedderburn (Ed.), *The future of the Caribbean in the world system*. Kingston, Jamaica: Friedrich Ebert Stiftung.

Watson, Hilbourne. (1991). Coalition security development: Military industrial restructuring in the United States and defense electronics production in the Caribbean. *Caribbean Studies*, 24(1–2).

Watson, Hilbourne. (1992). The United States-Canada Free Trade Agreement and the Caribbean with a case study of semiconductors in Barbados." *Social and Economic Studies*, 41(3).

Watson, Hilbourne. (Ed.). (1994a). *The Caribbean in the global political economy*. Boulder, CO: Lynne Rienner.

Watson, Hilbourne. (1994b). Beyond Nationalism: Caribbean options under global capitalism. In Hilbourne Watson (Ed.), *The Caribbean in the global political economy* (pp. 225–230). Boulder, CO: Lynne Rienner.

Watson, Hilbourne. (2013). Transnational capitalist globalization and the limits of sovereignty: State, security, order, violence and the Caribbean. In Lindin Lewis (Ed.), *Caribbean sovereignty, development and democracy in an age of globalization* (pp. 35–67). London: Routledge.

Watson, Hilbourne. (Ed.) (2015). *Globalization, sovereignty and citizenship in the Caribbean*. Mona, Jamaica: University of the West Indies Press.

Watson, Hilbourne. (2018). Crisis of global capitalism, global white supremacy, and the new nationalism. Global Studies Association-North America. Retrieved from https://www.youtube.com/watch?v=W8CjnRWPXsY.

Watson, Hilbourne. (2019). *Errol Walton Barrow and the postwar transformation of Barbados. Volume one*. Mona, Jamaica: University of the West Indies Press.

Weaver, David. (2001). Mass tourism and alternative tourism in the Caribbean. In David Harrison (Ed.), *Tourism and the less developed world*. Wallingford, U.K.: CABI.

Weber, Max. (1958). *From Max Weber: Essays in sociology*. Oxford: Oxford University Press.

Weiner, Tim. (2013). *Enemies: A history of the FBI*. New York: Random House.

Weisbrot, Mark. (2011). Haiti's election: A travesty of democracy. *The Guardian*. Retrieved from http://www.guardian.co.uk/commentisfree/cifamerica/2011/jan/10/haiti-oas-election-runoff.

Weisbrot, Mark. (2015). *Failed: What the "experts" got wrong about the global economy*. Oxford: Oxford University Press.

Weisbrot, Mark. (2017). Trump's tough new sanctions will harm the people of Venezuela. *The Hill*. Retrieved from http://thehill.com/blogs/pundits-blog/foreign-policy/348276-trumps-tough-venezuela-sanctions-do-more-harm-than-good.

Werner, Marion. (2016). *Global displacements: The making of uneven development in the Caribbean*. Chichester, U.K.: Wiley-Blackwell.

Werner, Marion, and Jennifer Bair. (2009). After sweatshops? Apparel politics in the circum-Caribbean. *NACLA Report on the Americas, 42*, 6–10.

Western Union. (2001). Company history. Retrieved from http://www.payment-solutions.com/history.html.

Western Union. (2014). Our rich history. Retrieved from http://corporate.westernunion.com/History.html.

Williams, Eric. (1944). *Capitalism and slavery*. Chapel Hill: University of North Carolina Press.

Williams, Eric. (1959). *Economics of nationhood*. Port of Spain: Trinidad and Tobago Office of the Premier and by the Ministry of Finance.

Williams, Eric. (1984). *From Columbus to Castro: The history of the Caribbean, 1492–1969*. New York: Vintage.

Williams-Raynor, P. (2011). NEPA gets flak over Falmouth Port. *Jamaica Observer*. Retrieved from http://www.jamaicaobserver.com/environment/NEPA-gets-flak-over-Falmouth-Port_8318051.

Willmore, Larry. (1996). Export processing in the Caribbean: Lessons from four case studies. *United Nations Economic Commission for Latin America and the Caribbean*. Retrieved from http://repositorio.cepal.org/bitstream/handle/11362/17047/LCcarG407.pdf?sequence=1.

Willmore, Larry. (2000). Export processing zones in Cuba. *Economic and Social Affairs*. Discussion Paper No. 12. United Nations. Retrieved from http://www.un.org/esa/esa00dp12.pdf.

Willoughby, Jack. (2007). Western union: ATM to the world. *Barron's*. Retrieved from http://www.barrons.com/articles/SB119647392837610317.

Wilpert, Gregory. (2006). *Changing Venezuela by taking power: The history and policies of the Chavez government*. London: Verso.

Wolf, Eric. (1997). *Europe and the people without history*. Berkeley: University of California Press.

Wonders, Nancy A., and Raymond Michalowski. (2001). Bodies, borders, and sex tourism in a globalized world: A tale of two cities—Amsterdam and Havana. *Social Problems, 48*(4), 545–571.

Wood, Ellen Meiksins. (1998). The agrarian origins of capitalism. *Monthly Review, 50*(3). Retrieved from http://monthlyreview.org/1998/07/01/the-agrarian-origins-of-capitalism.

Wood, Ellen Meiksins. (2002). *The origin of capitalism: A longer view*. London: Verso.

Wood, Ellen Meiksins. (2005). *Empire of capital*. London: Verso.

World Bank. (1992). Export processing zones. Washington, DC: World Bank.

World Bank. (1996). *A mining strategy for Latin America and the Caribbean*. Washington, DC: World Bank.

World Bank. (2003). Dominican Republic country assistance evaluation. Operations Evaluation Department. Washington, DC: World Bank. Retrieved from http://docu ments.worldbank.org/curated/en/717581468746721319/pdf/264830DO.pdf.

World Bank. (2007). Close to home: The development impact of remittances in Latin America. Washington, DC: The World Bank. Retrieved from http://siteresources .worldbank.org/INTLACOFFICEOFCE/Resources/ClosetoHome_FINAL.pdf.

World Bank. (2012). World is locked into ~1.5°C warming and risks are rising, new climate report finds. Retrieved from http://www.worldbank.org/en/news/feature/2014/11 /23/climate-report-finds-temperature-rise-locked-in-risks-rising.

World Bank. (2013). Developing countries to receive over $410 billion in remittances in 2013, says World Bank. Retrieved from http://www.worldbank.org/en/news/press release/2013/10/02/ developing-countries-remittances-2013-world-bank.

World Bank. (2015a). Migration and development brief. Migration and remittances team, development prospects group, 24. Retrieved from http://siteresources.worldbank.org /INTPROSPECTS/Resources/334934-1288990760745/MigrationandDevelopment Brief24.pdf.

World Bank. (2015b). Remittances to developing countries edge up slightly in 2015. Retrieved from http://www.worldbank.org/en/news/press-release/2016/04/13/remittances-to -developing-countries-edge-up-slightly-in-2015.

World Bank. (2017). World Bank open data. Retrieved from https://data.worldbank.org.

World Bank's Development Prospects Group. (2012). The migration and development brief. Retrieved from http://siteresources.worldbank.org/INTPROSPECTS/Resources /334934-1288990760745/MigrationDevelopmentBrief19.pdf.

World Travel and Tourism Council. (2013). Economic impact 2012. Retrieved from http:// www.wttc.org/site_media/uploads/ downloads/world2012.pdf.

Worrell, DeLisle. (1994–1995). The Barbadian economy since the 1930s. *Journal of the Barbados Museum and Historical Society, XLII,* 80–81.

Wright, Eric Olin. (1980). Varieties of Marxist conceptions of class structure. *Politics and Society, 9*(3), 323–370.

Wright, Eric Olin. (1998). *Classes.* London: Verso.

Wu, Irene. (2010). Citizens' news vouchers: $200 for everyone? Retrieved from http:// reboot.fcc.gov/futureofmedia/blog?entryId=282115.

Wucker, Michele. (2000). *Why the cocks fight: Dominicans, Haitians, and the struggle for Hispaniola.* New York: Hill and Wang.

Xie, Boyi. (2012). Mining industry overview. Columbia University. Retrieved from http:// www.columbia.edu/cu/consultingclub/Resources/Mining_Boyi_Xie.pdf.

Yasha, Levine. (2018). *Surveillance Valley: The Secret Military History of the Internet.* New York: Public Affairs.

Yelvington, Kevin. (1995). *Producing power: Ethnicity, gender, and class in a Caribbean workplace.* Philadelphia: Temple University Press.

Žižek, Slavoj. (1997). Multiculturalism, or, the cultural logic of multinational capitalism. *New Left Review, 225,* 28–51.

Index

Jeb Sprague is a lecturer at the University of Virginia and formerly taught at the University of California, Santa Barbara. He is the author of *Paramilitarism and the Assault on Democracy in Haiti*, and the editor of *Globalization and Transnational Capitalism in Asia and Oceania*. He is a founding member of the Network for Critical Studies of Global Capitalism (NCSGC). Visit him online at: https://sites.google.com/site/jebsprague/.